The Savings and Loan Crisis:

Lessons from a Regulatory Failure

The Milken Institute Series On Financial Innovation And Economic Growth

Series Editors

James R. Barth
Auburn University
Senior Fellow at the Milken Institute
Glenn Yago
Director of Capital Studies at the
Milken Institute
Other books in the series:

Barth, James R., Brumbaugh Jr., R. Dan and Yago, Glenn, (eds.)
    Restructuring Regulation and Financial Institutions

Evans, David S., (ed.)
    Microsoft, Antitrust and the New Economy: Selected Essays

Trimbath, Susanne:
    Mergers and Efficiency: Changes Across Time

Mead, Walter Russell and Schwenninger, Sherle, (eds.)
    *The Bridge to a Global Middle Class: Development, Trade and
    International Finance*

The Savings and Loan Crisis:

Lessons from a Regulatory Failure

**James R. Barth, Susanne Trimbath,
and Glenn Yago
Editors**

MILKEN INSTITUTE
SANTA MONICA, CALIFORNIA

Distributors for North, Central and South America:
Kluwer Academic Publishers
101 Philip Drive
Assinippi Park
Norwell, Massachusetts 02061 USA
Telephone (781) 871-6600
Fax (781) 681-9045
E-Mail <kluwer@wkap.com>
Distributors for all other countries:
Kluwer Academic Publishers Group
Post Office Box 17
3300 AH Dordrecht, THE NETHERLANDS
Tel: +31 (0) 78 657 60 00
Fax: +31 (0) 78 657 64 74

E-Mail <services@wkap.nl>

    Electronic Services <http://www.wkap.nl>

Library of Congress Cataloging-in-Publication Data
The Savings and Loan Crisis: Lessons from a Regulatory Failure
        edited by James R. Barth, Susanne Trimbath and Glenn Yago
    ISBN HB: 1-4020-7871-4 (alk.paper)
    ISBN E-book: 1-4020-7898-6

TABLE OF CONTENTS

SUMMATION

NOTE FROM THE SERIES EDITORS

James R. Barth
Auburn University and Milken Institute;
Former Chief Economist, Office of Thrift Supervision and Federal Home Loan Bank Board

Glenn Yago
Milken Institute

Our nation's banking institutions were in a constant state of turmoil throughout the 1980s. During that period and into the early 1990s, 1,273 savings and loans with assets of $640 billion failed, 1,569 commercial and savings banks with $264 billion in assets failed, and 2,330 credit unions with $4 billion in assets failed. The cost of resolving this crisis in the banking industry eventually surpassed $190 billion, the majority of which was paid for by the taxpayers.

The savings and loan crisis that gave this book its title, though painfully real in its economic consequences, was largely a politically manufactured event. It was a classic case of financial institutions facing structural and macroeconomic changes that were exacerbated by politically motivated policy missteps resulting in a crisis produced by regulatory failure. The replication of this pattern of inappropriately restrictive regulations repeats itself around the world in massively costly bank runs and market collapses that burden governments and taxpayers and close capital markets to firms.

A remarkable consensus emerges from the data and analysis in this volume. Former regulators, scholars, and legal and financial practitioners converge in their conclusions now, despite the fact that they had often taken opposing positions in the troubled decade of the eighties. The U.S. savings and loan crisis was not a unique event but was rather a precursor of banking crises around the world. Two thirds of IMF members have suffered a banking or financial market crisis. Moreover, the causes of the crisis here were the same as those found in crises around the world: government-directed lending combined with inappropriate deposit insurance and poorly devised regulations that restricted a class of financial institutions to holding specific asset classes.

The resulting unnecessarily fragile financial sector is evidence of the importance of diversification.

Another conclusion reached in this volume is that one must consider the industry and its regulation as a whole. In order to fully understand the problems of the 1980s, one must examine the whole process of financial service provision – from how managers make decisions about products and investments to how regulators generate and enforce the rules governing the actions of those managers. In order to derive the important lessons for the future, one must understand the regulatory, political, sociological, legal and economic events, and how they react in confluence.

Typically, governments act only after the onset of a crisis and then overcompensate in their reaction, thereby exacerbating problems. During the savings and loan crisis, the government deregulated too late in response to the interest-rate crisis, inappropriately deregulating liabilities before assets. Such a regulatory flip-flop explains how the government entered into contracts that it subsequently breached, creating the final stage of the savings and loan crisis – the goodwill stage highlighted in this volume.

This crisis was, ironically, largely a creation of poorly designed deposit insurance, faulty supervision, and restrictions on investments that prevented savings and loans from using financial innovations to successfully hedge the interest rate and credit risks they faced in the late 1970s and early 1980s. The inability of savings and loans to diversify their portfolios beyond fixed-rate home loans lay at the root of this crisis. Despite any impressions to the contrary, it is made clear in this volume that the collapse of this financial industry sector was not caused by fraud. The savings and loan industry exploded when an unexpectedly sharp rise in interest rates in the late 1970s and early 1980s drove virtually all savings and loans into massive economic insolvency. Nobel Laureate economist Robert Mundell noted in private correspondence that the savings and loan crisis occurred in the context of the appreciation of the dollar against other currencies causing a twist in the term structure that created savings and loans losses from which, as this volume shows, they could not extricate themselves given the regulatory chokeholds imposed upon them. From 1979 to 1983, unanticipated double-digit inflation coupled with dollar depreciation led to negative real interest rates. When savings and loans extended their lending base and their capital ratios worsened, conditions weakened in the industry. When the Federal Reserve then belatedly tightened monetary policy, short term rates soared over 20 percent, savings and loans were squeezed, and the crisis was underway.

The sociology of the crisis is also examined in this volume and important conclusions are drawn. Once a crisis erupts, finger-pointing rather than problem-solving triggers "herd behavior" by the media, the government and the public. This makes it difficult to distill reality from perception, all too often resulting in the wrong parties being blamed. The complex web of events that comprise what we know now as the "savings and loan crisis" were distorted by media misrepresentations that bled into and out of the political and regulatory environment.

Following the crisis, litigation as a form of regulation became the policy of the Federal Deposit Insurance Corporation, the federal government and the Resolution Trust Company (RTC). By bringing great pressure to bear on the owners, officers and even employees of seized savings and loans, the government was able to coerce most defendants to settle. However, for those that sought their day in court, the result was more often than not exoneration. The government's record in cases that went to trial in 1994 was about two losses for every win. Some of the highest profile cases that the government was forced to make in court, including Charles Keating's Lincoln Savings and Loan, and Thomas Spiegel's Columbia Savings and Loan, resulted in acquittals or in the reversal of convictions on appeal. Indeed, most sanctions were reversed in the obscurity of the federal appellate courts, which concluded that the government had abused the judicial process (e.g., Crestmont, Delta Savings, Franklin Savings, Gibraltar, and National).

That regulatory witch-hunt contributed heavily to precipitating a collapse in the prices of the assets that it tainted. Profitable institutions were converted into government-owned "basket cases." Nowhere was this more apparent than in the high-yield market, which was singled out by regulators and politicians for especially harsh treatment, despite the fact that high-yield bonds only ever comprised a maximum of 1.2 percent of the industries' total assets. Indeed most of the ultimately "resolved" savings and loans that held high-yield bonds were already insolvent by 1985 before any of them had invested a penny in the high-yield market. Moreover, prior to the regulatory taint that induced a price collapse in 1989, high-yield securities were the industry's best performing long-term asset.

The savings and loan crisis resulted in the single largest nationalization of private property in U.S. history. The government seized solvent and insolvent institutions with some $640 billion in assets. Through the passing of the Financial Institutions Reform and Recovery Act and the creation of the RTC, the government pursued a retribution-centered response to America's depository institution crisis.

With the passage of time, data analysis replaces accusations and cooler heads prevail in drawing the lessons of regulatory failure that are so aptly described in this volume. Over a decade after the savings and loan crises, the

Milken Institute in conjunction with the Andersen School of Business at UCLA gathered data and scholars from varying perspectives to reflect upon the policy failures that resulted in the crisis.

As in medicine, the careful study of classic cases yields abundant information to students, scholars, and practitioners. Each can learn how to devise better policies to enable financial institutions to adjust to changes in their operating environment, rather than preventing them from engaging in the effective risk management that can ensure sustainable growth and profitability.

In sorting the fact from the fiction of the regulatory failures that made up the savings and loan crisis, this definitive volume teaches the lessons of how to avoid future financial-policy pratfalls. Most of the factors responsible for initiating and exacerbating the industry's problems were preventable as is documented in this volume.

What happened to the savings and loan industry during the 1980s was regrettable and costly both in financial and in human terms. However, this situation provided our nation with both a challenge and an opportunity. The challenge was to correct bad policies while simultaneously resolving the failed savings and loans. The opportunity was to learn from the mistakes that were made. The savings and loan crisis taught us the important lesson that one must design banking regulations in such a manner as to allow institutions to adapt to changing competitive market forces. This basic message applies not only to the U.S., but to every other country around the world. This volume seeks, not only to set the record straight about what caused the savings and loan crisis, but also to focus attention on the lessons that should have been learned from this difficult period in the history of U.S. banking and thereby help prevent future banking crises everywhere.

FOREWORD

Robert L. Bartley
Editor Emeritus, *The Wall Street Journal*

As this collection of essays is published, markets, regulators and society generally are sorting through the wreckage of the collapse in tech stocks at the turn of the millennium. All the more reason for an exhaustive look at our last "bubble," if that is what we choose to call them. We haven't had time to digest the lesson of the tech stocks and the recession that started in March 2001. After a decade, though, we're ready to understand the savings and loan "bubble" that popped in 1989, preceding the recession that started in July 1990.

For more than a half-century, we can now see clearly enough, the savings and loans were an accident waiting to happen. The best insurance for financial institutions is diversification, but the savings and loans were concentrated solely in residential financing. What's more, they were in the business of borrowing short and lending long, accepting deposits that could be withdrawn quickly and making 20-year loans. They were further protected by Regulation Q, allowing them to pay a bit more for savings deposits than commercial banks were allowed to. In normal times, they could ride the yield curve, booking profits because long-term interest rates are generally higher than short-term ones. This world was recorded in Jimmy Stewart's 1946 film, *It's a Wonderful Life*.

This world came apart in the inflation of the 1970s (I would say, though this is another book, with the collapse of the Bretton Woods monetary system culminating in Richard Nixon closing the gold window on August 15, 1971). There used to be an unlovely word, "disintermediation," meaning that savers were not satisfied with the paltry returns on savings accounts, and pulled out their money looking for more profitable alternatives. These withdrawals undermined the capital base regulators required savings and loans to hold against their outstanding loans. The loans, moreover, typically were at fixed rates of interest – fixed, that is, before inflation drove all interest rates higher. The savings and loans' profits turned to losses as inflation pushed short rates above long rates fixed in steadier times. And their deposit base collapsed with financial innovation, in particular the spread of money market funds allowing savers a market rate of interest.

Not so incidentally, the federal government insured thrift deposits, and was on the hook if savings and loans didn't have the cash flow to cover withdrawals. In its wisdom, or rather through a midnight coup by savings and loan champion Representative Fernand St Germain, Congress increased the limit on deposit insurance to $100,000 per account in 1980, in one swoop more than doubling the government's exposure.

Then came a double whammy, not only inflation, but double-dip recessions in 1980 and 1982. In mid-1981, Richard T. Pratt, the chief thrift regulator as chairman of the Federal Home Loan Bank Board, testified that 80 percent of the 4,600 institutions under his care were suffering operating losses, and that a third of them were not "viable under current conditions." The "most troubled" 263 savings and loans faced losses totaling $60 billion, against capital value of some $15 billion.

Mr. Pratt decided that the economy could ill afford a string of savings and loans failures in the midst of a recession, and in a series of highly controversial decisions offered "regulatory forbearance" to postpone the inevitable to a day when the general economy might better bear it. He explained what he was doing, and indeed another day arrived with the boom starting in 1983. Yet as the economy grew healthier little or nothing was done about the savings and loans, as various Congressmen intervened to stop regulators from closing their pets and contributors. In 1989, finally, Congress passed FIRREA, the Financial Institutions Reform, Recovery and Enforcement Act. I consider this the most destructive single piece of legislation since the Smoot-Hawley Tariff. In effect, it nationalized the thrift industry at a market peak, to liquidate its assets in the succeeding trough. Taxpayers are paying the price all over again as the Court of Claims rules in favor of certain savings and loans closed despite earlier governmental promises of forbearance and good will.

It's too early to say what we'll ultimately decide about the tech stocks; perhaps their "bubble" was indeed spontaneous. But it's now clear that the savings and loans bubble was not a market failure. It was one regulatory boondoggle stacked on another. The essays in this book elaborate in a more scholarly fashion.

Oh, readers may wonder how the whole debacle got started, why weren't savings and loans more diversified, why were they only in the business of borrowing short and lending long? The answer to this lies in the New Deal banking legislation, designed by Congress and the Roosevelt administration to splinter the financial industry and break the power of the House of Morgan and other evil bankers. A historic sideshow called the Pecora hearings focused on banking skullduggery in the midst of the stock market crash, fixing in the public mind that the problem was bankers, rather than, say, mistaken monetary policy, the tariff or the horrendously mistimed tax increase in 1932.[1]

---

[1] Editor's note: The Pecora hearings of 1933 focused on allegedly abusive commercial banking practices.

The savings and loans crisis, that is, was born in the efforts of politicians to scapegoat businessmen and financiers for the Great Depression.

In memoriam. Robert Bartley, editor emeritus of the *Wall Street Journal,* died December 10, 2003.

ABOUT THE AUTHORS
(In alphabetical order)

JAMES BARTH

Barth is a Senior Fellow at the Milken Institute and Lowder Eminent Scholar in Finance at Auburn University. His research focuses on financial institutions and capital markets, with special emphasis on regulatory issues. Barth was the Chief Economist of the Office of Thrift Supervision and previously served as the Chief Economist of the Federal Home Loan Bank Board. He was Professor of Economics at George Washington University, Associate Director of the Economics Program at the National Science Foundation, Shaw Foundation Professor of Banking and Finance at Nanyang Technological University, and visiting scholar at the U.S. Congressional Budget Office, Federal Reserve Bank of Atlanta, Office of the Comptroller of the Currency, and the World Bank. He has authored more than 100 articles in professional journals, has written and edited several books, serves on several editorial boards and is included in *Who's Who in Economics*. Barth received his Ph.D. in economics from Ohio State University.

R. DAN BRUMBAUGH, JR.

Brumbaugh is a Senior Fellow at the Milken Institute. He is an expert in banking and global financial markets and has consulted for a wide range of financial service firms. He was a senior research scholar at the Center for Economic Policy Research at Stanford University from 1989 to 1990. From 1986 to 1987, he was President and CEO of the California-based Independence Savings and Loan. He was Deputy Chief Economist at the Federal Home Loan Bank Board from 1983 to 1986. He has authored several books and numerous professional journal articles on subjects in which he has expertise, and has testified frequently before congressional committees. He received his Ph.D. in economics from George Washington University.

MICHAEL DARBY

Darby is the Warren C. Cordner Professor of Money and Financial Markets in the Anderson Graduate School of Management and in the Departments of Economics and Policy Studies at the University of California, Los Angeles, and Director of the John M. Olin Center for Policy in the Anderson School. He is Chairman of The Dumbarton Group, Research Associate with the National Bureau of Economic Research, as well as Associate Director for both the Center for International Science, Technology, and Cultural Policy in the School of Public Policy & Social Research and the Organizational Research Program of the Institute of Social Science Research at UCLA. From 1986 to 1992, Darby served in a number of senior positions in the Reagan and Bush administrations, including Assistant Secretary of the Treasury for

Economic Policy (1986-1989), Member of the National Commission on Superconductivity (1988-1989), Under Secretary of Commerce for Economic Affairs (1989-1992), and Administrator of the Economics and Statistics Administration (1990-1992). He has received many honors, including the Alexander Hamilton Award, the Treasury's highest honor. Darby received his Ph.D. from the University of Chicago.

CATHERINE ENGLAND

England is currently Chair of the Accounting, Economics, and Finance faculty at Marymount University in Arlington, Virginia. She joined the Marymount faculty in the fall of 1998. England was previously a member of the finance faculty at George Mason University. From 1984 to 1991, England was a regulatory analyst at the Cato Institute and Senior Editor of *Regulation* magazine where she edited *The Financial Services Revolution: Policy Directions for the Future* (with Thomas Huertas) and *Governing Banking's Future: Markets vs. Regulation.* Among other topics, England has written and spoken extensively about the role of deposit insurance in the savings and loan and banking crises of the 1980s. England's most recent publication (with Jay Cochran, III) is *Neither Fish nor Fowl: An Overview of the Big Three Government-Sponsored Enterprises in the U.S. Housing Finance Markets.*

CATHERINE GALLEY

Galley is Senior Vice President at Cornerstone Research, where she heads the firm's financial institutions practice. She consults on all aspects of financial institutions issues in a variety of legal disputes and works extensively on savings and loan and banking issues involving the analysis of the economics, structure and regulation of the industry, performance of institutions, directors' and officers' responsibilities, auditors' and attorneys' duties, and estimation of damages. She is currently assisting plaintiffs in a number of supervisory goodwill cases in the Court of Federal Claims. Her expertise also extends to the insurance industry, mutual funds, and securities and real estate issues that arise in financial institutions litigation. She has managed cases involving punitive damages and valuation issues as well as cases in industries such as high technology and retailing. Prior to joining Cornerstone Research, Galley was a consultant with McKinsey & Company, active in the financial institutions practice, and assistant director of research in the Stanford Graduate School of Business. Galley received her MBA from the Graduate School of Business, Stanford University.

EDWARD KANE

Kane is James F. Cleary Professor in Finance at Boston College. Kane was Everett D. Reese Chair of Banking and Monetary Economics at Ohio State University from 1972 to 1992. Kane has consulted for the World Bank, the Federal Deposit Insurance Corporation, the Office of the Comptroller of Currency, the Federal Home Loan Bank Board, the American Bankers' Association, three foreign central banks, the Department of Housing and Urban Development, various components of the Federal Reserve System, and the Congressional Budget Office, Joint Economic Committee, and Office of Technology Assessment of the U.S. Congress. Kane is a past president and fellow of the American Finance Association and a former Guggenheim fellow. Kane is a research associate of the National Bureau of Economic Research. He served as a charter member of the Shadow Financial Regulatory Committee for 11 years and as a trustee and member of the Finance Committee of Teachers Insurance for 12 years. Kane received his Ph.D. from the Massachusetts Institute of Technology.

GEORGE KAUFMAN

Kaufman is John F. Smith Professor of Finance and Economics and Director of the Center for Financial and Policy Studies at the School of Business Administration, Loyola University Chicago. Kaufman was a research fellow, economist and research officer at the Federal Reserve Bank of Chicago until 1970 and has been a consultant to the Bank since 1981. From 1970 to 1980, he was the John Rogers Professor of Banking and Finance and Director of the Center for Capital Market Research in the College of Business Administration at the University of Oregon. Kaufman also served as Deputy to the Assistant Secretary for Economic Policy of the U.S. Treasury in 1976. Kaufman has been a consultant to government and private firms, including the Federal Savings and Loan Insurance Corporation Task Force on Reappraising Deposit Insurance, the American Bankers Association Task Force on Bank Safety and Soundness, the American Enterprise Institute Project on Financial Regulation, and the Brookings Institution Task Force on Depository Institutions Reform. He was co-chair of the Shadow Financial Regulatory Committee and executive director of Financial Economists Roundtable. He received his Ph.D. in economics from the University of Iowa.

ARTHUR LEIBOLD

Leibold has been a lawyer in private practice since 1965 representing savings and loan associations, savings and loan holding companies, private mortgage insurers, mortgage bankers, savings and loan industry groups, and officers and directors of savings and loan associations. His government service experience includes the Federal Home Loan Bank Board, Federal Savings & Loan

Insurance Corporation where he was General Counsel, and the Federal Home Loan Mortgage Corporation. Leibold has also litigated on behalf of insurers and savings and loans associations. He received his J.D. from the University of Pennsylvania.

DONALD MCCARTHY

McCarthy is a Research Analyst at the Milken Institute and works primarily on developing metrics for measuring entrepreneurs' access to financial capital and financial innovations designed to democratize access to capital. Prior to joining the Milken Institute, McCarthy was an economist at a leading London-based public policy think tank where he focused on Eastern European emerging markets and a researcher in the Public Policy Group at the London School of Economics. He is a graduate of the London School of Economics and the University of Essex.

LAWRENCE NICHOLS

Nichols is associate professor of sociology, and chair of the Division of Sociology and Anthropology, at West Virginia University. He is also editor of *The American Sociologist*, a national quarterly. Nichols has long been interested in white collar crime and public policy, having concentrated in criminology and social change during his doctoral studies. He has taught on white collar crime, as well as the sociology of business, at West Virginia University since the late 1980s. In his published research, Nichols has examined the social processes by which crime and deviance are interpreted, with particular emphasis on official investigations and mass print media. His works have illumined the crucial role of narrative in defining "the crime problem," while also analyzing the larger dialogue about social problems and public policy. Nichols received his Ph.D. from Boston College.

JAMES NOLAN III

Nolan is an Assistant Professor in the Division of Sociology and Anthropology at West Virginia University. The current focus of his research is crime measurement, organizational deviance, and police procedures. Nolan is currently the primary investigator on three research projects funded through the Office of Juvenile Justice and Delinquency Prevention of the United States Department of Justice. Nolan's publications have appeared in *American Behavioral Scientist, Journal of Quantitative Criminology, Journal of Contemporary Criminal Justice, The Justice Professional*, and *The American Sociologist*. Nolan's professional career began as a police officer in Wilmington, Delaware. In 13 years with that department, he rose to the rank of lieutenant. He is a 1992 graduate of the Federal Bureau of Investigation National Academy prior to joining the faculty at West Virginia University,

Nolan worked for the FBI as a unit chief in the Criminal Justice Information Services Division. Nolan received his Ph.D. from Temple University.

KENNETH THYGERSON

Thygerson is President and Founder of Digital University, Inc., which provides training and information resources to employees of financial institutions and other professionals via the Internet. He is also Professor Emeritus of Accounting and Finance at California State University, San Bernardino. Thygerson spent more than 10 years as director of the Division of Research and Economics and Chief Economist of the United States League of Savings Institutions. He was also president and CEO of Freddie Mac, president, CEO and vice chairman of Imperial Corporation of America, and president of Western Capital Investment Corporation. Thygerson received his Ph.D. in finance from Northwestern University.

SUSANNE TRIMBATH

Trimbath is a Research Economist at the Milken Institute and an experienced business professional with nearly 20 years in financial services, including operations management. Her overlapping academic teaching experience includes economics courses at New York University. Her research focuses on mergers and acquisitions, and capital market development. Prior to joining the Milken Institute, Trimbath was Senior Advisor on the Capital Markets Project for the United States Agency for International Development, which laid the foundation for a capital market infrastructure in Russia. Prior to that, she was in operations management for national trade clearing and settlement organizations in San Francisco and New York. Trimbath holds an MBA in management from Golden Gate University and received her Ph.D. in economics from New York University.

KEVIN VILLANI

Villani is an international financial consultant. From initial public offering to the March 2000 merger, he was the Vice Chairman of Imperial Credit Commercial Mortgage Investment Corporation. Prior to that, he was executive vice president and chief financial officer of Imperial Credit Industries Inc. and president and CEO of Imperial Credit Asset Management. He served in similar capacities at Imperial Corporation of America in the mid-1980s, and from 1982 to 1985 he was chief economist and chief financial officer at the Federal Home Loan Mortgage Corporation. Villani began his public policy career with the Federal Reserve System in 1974 as a monetary and financial institution economist. He spent 15 years in Washington, D.C. as a senior government official in the Ford, Carter and Reagan administrations and advisor to the World Bank, IFC, USAID and various think tanks. Villani earned Ph.D. degrees in economics and finance from Purdue University.

LAWRENCE WHITE

White is Arthur E. Imperatore Professor of Economics at New York University's Stern School of Business. From 1986 to 1989 he was on leave to serve as Board Member, Federal Home Loan Bank Board, and from 1982 to 1983 he was on leave to serve as Director of the Economic Policy Office, Antitrust Division, U.S. Department of Justice. White served on the senior staff of the President's Council of Economic Advisers from 1978 to 1979, and he was chairman of the Stern School's Department of Economics from 1990 to 1995. He is the author and co-editor of numerous books and articles. White received his M.Sc. from the London School of Economics and his Ph.D. from Harvard University.

GLENN YAGO

Yago is Director of Capital Studies at the Milken Institute. He specializes in financial innovations, financial institutions, and capital markets, and has extensively analyzed public policy and its relation to high-yield markets, initial public offerings, industrial and transportation concerns and public and private sector employment. Two additional focus areas for Capital Studies are Emerging Domestic Markets and Israel Economic Development Projects. Yago previously held positions as an economics faculty member at the City University of New York Graduate Center and senior research associate at the Center for the Study of Business Government at Baruch College–City University of New York. He was also a Faculty Fellow at the Rockefeller Institute of Government, Director of the Economic Research Bureau at the State University of New York at Stony Brook and Chairman of the New York State Network for Economic Research. Yago received his Ph.D. from the University of Wisconsin, Madison.

INTRODUCTION

James R. Barth
Auburn University and Milken Institute; Former Chief Economist, Office of Thrift Supervision
and Federal Home Loan Bank Board

Susanne Trimbath
Milken Institute

Glenn Yago
Milken Institute

Journalism, it has been said, is history's first draft. Consequently, the passage of time permits more measured analysis and data to emerge and inform our understanding of events. The conventional wisdom about the causes and consequences of the "savings and loan crisis," as it came to be understood by contemporary writers, has been so seriously distorted by the legal, political and media battles in the 1980s, it is necessary to sheer away the hype and hysteria surrounding the industry's collapse and later recovery. This volume presents diverse perspectives unified by a dispassionate assessment of the empirical evidence about what actually occurred during this important period of U.S. financial history.

Depending on the analyst and the particular ax he or she chose to grind, the savings and loan crisis was caused by brokered deposits, high yield bonds, daisy chain real estate transactions, mortgage-backed securities, fixed-rate home mortgages or deposit insurance. The theme of these often lurid stories was usually the danger posed to society by high-tech gambling with financial instruments.[1] These popular intrigues, as we shall see, explained little of the reality behind the extraordinary costs of the savings and loan crisis.

Such stories did make for short, snappy headlines and animated cocktail party conversation. But the truth of the savings and loan crisis, as truth can often be, is more complicated than the stuff of deadline journalism and tabloid economics.[2] In this volume, as in previous work (Yago, 1991; Yago, 1993;

---

[1] Pilzer with Deitz (1989), pp. 123-124. For more examples of sensational accounts of the savings and loan crisis see Pizzo (1989) and O'Shea and Roseman (1990).

[2] Fraud accounted for no more than 10 percent of total savings and loan losses. "If there was so much fraud...why are we just hearing about it today," James Barth told *The Wall Street Journal* in an article that appeared July 20, 1990. "If it was there for all those years, who is committing the fraud, the government or the people at the institutions?" See also National Commission on Financial Institution Reform, Recovery and Enforcement, "Origins and Causes of the S&L Debacle: A Blueprint for Reform," July 1993. See also Barth (1991), Brumbaugh and Carron (1987), Brumbaugh and Litan (1991), Barth, Bartholomew and Labich (1990), Barth, Bartholomew and Bradley (1990), Barth and Brumbaugh (1994a), Barth and Brumbaugh (1994b), Barth and Wiest (1989), Barth, Brumbaugh, Sauerhaft and Wang (1989).

Yago and Siegel, 1994; Yago and Trimbath, 2003), we seek to separate myth from reality.

The implications of this specific episode of financial crisis go far beyond the events of the last quarter of the 20th century. The savings and loan crisis is a classic textbook case of financial institutions breaking down through a unique combination of macroeconomic conditions, interest rate and tax policy shifts, structural changes in capital markets and financial institutions, and, ultimately, regulatory chokeholds and policy missteps that created a perfect financial policy storm that temporarily, but devastatingly, constricted credit channels in the economy and destroyed asset values in what became the largest nationalization of private property (through the Resolution Trust Corporation) in U. S. history.

The disposition of assets by the Resolution Trust Corporation (RTC) suggests even greater consequences about the management of financial crises. This pattern of expedited sell-off by the RTC was documented by the Southern Finance Project, which found that from its inception through August 1, 1992, the agency sold off $220 billion in total deposits from 652 savings and loans. This enabled larger firms to consolidate their positions in markets throughout the country by buying valuable, low-yielding deposits. As a group, the RTC's top ten buyers obtained roughly half of all core deposits transferred in single-buyer transactions. The cost of these single-buyer resolutions, and the market concentration resulting from expedited asset sales, increased resolution costs to the taxpayers. This pattern was consistent also in the accelerated sell-off of the RTC's high yield inventory.[3] This led to bank runs that further amplified price declines in assets held by savings and loans. Later research revealed that auction sell-offs resulted in major transfers of wealth. During the last stage of the RTC, a shift towards aligned interest transactions maximized returns to taxpayers of 30 to 35 percent higher than auction sell-offs of real estate, corporate bonds, deposits and other savings and loan assets at the beginning of the resolution process.

FINANCING CAPITAL OWNERSHIP IN COMMUNITIES: HISTORICAL BACKGROUND

To understand the savings and loan crisis one must understand the history of the savings and loan industry. And, while we do not wish to rehash a subject that has been more than adequately handled by others, we want to

---

[3]Southern Finance Project, "Fortunate Sons: Three Years of Dealmaking at the Resolution Trust Corporation," September 9, 1992, p. 2.

provide an overview to establish context and terminology for the discussion that follows.[4]

The context within which we examine the history of savings and loans in this country is that of the role played by private access to capital in the country's economic growth. Periods in which private citizens and emerging businesses have been able to access the capital markets have been periods of exceptional economic growth. When the capital markets are closed to these borrowers, the economy stagnates. All of this is a lesson in how policy can destroy equity through restrictions in the credit channels. And, as we shall see, the growth of the savings and loan industry closely parallels the increasing access to capital necessary for the growth of the republic.

The founding of today's savings and loans began with the legacy of early British settlers. They used their familiarity with British building societies to establish similar lending operations in the U.S. The development of savings institutions in the U.S. grew along two paths: mutual savings banks and building and loan societies.

The first American mutual savings bank was the Provident Institution for Savings of Boston, founded in 1816; the first building and loan association was established in Frankford, Pennsylvania, in 1831.

Mutual savings banks were owned by their depositors rather than by stockholders.[5] Any profits belonged to the depositors. Most of the funds deposited in mutual savings banks had to be invested in municipal bonds, which financed the growth of our greatest municipalities. At the end of the Civil War, about one million people had deposited approximately $250 million in 317 U.S. savings banks. By 1900, more than six million depositors had deposited nearly $2.5 billion in 1,000 banks.

The building and loan associations, in contrast, were created to promote home ownership. But the building societies were corporations; the members were shareholders required to make systematic contributions of capital – regular deposits, in other words – which were then loaned back for home construction. The number of associations, shareholders and net assets grew dramatically through the end of the 1800s.

Eventually, the building societies took on some aspects of savings banks. They extended loans to building association members who did not have significant funds on deposit to borrow for a home, for example. Ultimately,

---

[4] See Friedman and Schwartz (1971) and Kendall (1962).
[5] For the following discussion the authors are deeply indebted to Pilzer and Deitz (1989), England (1992), and Fabritius and Borges (1990).

the societies accepted deposits from people who did not intend to take out a building loan.

This separation between depositors and borrowers is in retrospect a significant event that gave rise to the characteristics that we most associate with the savings and loans, as the building and loans came to be known: individuals deposited money in sums as small or large as they could afford and these funds were then loaned out in the same community for home loans.

Although mutual savings banks and building and loan societies retained individual characteristics, they were often lumped together. Some of the greatest differences could be observed during the Depression: 438 savings and loans failed between 1930 and 1933, compared to only one mutual savings bank during that same time period. Mutual savings banks actually had a net inflow of deposits every year during the Depression.

When Congress passed the Wilson Tariff Act in 1894 to tax the net income of corporations, building and loan associations, and other corporations that made loans only to their shareholders, were excluded from taxation. Thus began the special legal consideration for savings and loans based on their purpose of providing financing for home ownership. This freedom from taxation would remain in effect until 1963.

In 1913, Congress passed the Federal Reserve Act establishing a central banking system and, for the first time, distinguishing among deposit classes. Time deposits, which needed advance notice before they could be withdrawn, would require lower reserves than demand deposits. Between 1886 and 1933, 150 separate proposals were introduced in the Congress to establish deposit guarantees. Oklahoma established deposit insurance in 1908, followed by the Dakotas and Texas, among others.

The problem with deposit insurance then, as now, was that the insurance funds were undercapitalized and that excess risk was not reflected in additional premiums. Therefore, strong, well-managed institutions bore the risks of weaker institutions. The state insurance funds could not survive the agricultural depression of the 1920s, and none of the state insurance funds were operating by 1929. National deposit insurance was a controversial proposition, and it was one of the themes that dominated the 1932 presidential campaign.

Two of the most prominent players in the debate were Representative Henry Steagall of Alabama, chair of the House Banking and Currency Committee; and Senator Carter Glass of Virginia, former Secretary of the Treasury under Wilson, who had contributed profoundly to the 1913 legislation creating the Federal Reserve System. In January 1933, Glass proposed several reforms to the banking system: a separation of commercial and investment banking; increased Federal Reserve authority over national banks; permitting national banks to establish branches in states that permitted state-chartered banks to open branches; and limited deposit guarantees for national banks. The Glass bill passed the Senate 54-9. But before any further action could be taken, Roosevelt took office and introduced his emergency banking bill, which was quickly passed and overwhelmed earlier bank legislation.

Two months later, the Roosevelt administration introduced a bill to overhaul the banking system. The bill combined elements of Glass's Senate bill and a bill that Steagall had introduced into the House. The result, the Glass-Steagall Bill, dominated capital markets regulation in this country until the passage of the Garn-St Germain Bill and other pieces of deregulatory (and re-regulatory) legislation in the 1980s.

In the context of this intervention to shore up the country's financial institutions in the midst of the Depression, the Federal Home Loan Bank System (FHLBS) was established in 1932; the Home Owners Loan Corporation (HOLC) in 1933 (HOLC itself provided home loans); the Federal Deposit Insurance Corporation (FDIC) in 1933 began insuring deposits in commercial banks; and the Federal Savings and Loan Insurance Corporation (FSLIC) began insuring savings and loan accounts in 1934. The creation of this last organization gave us the first leg of the savings and loan crisis, for although FSLIC was called an insurance fund, it was not precisely that. While mutual savings banks were permitted to join the FDIC, savings and loans were not. The FDIC had been created as an independent agency; the FSLIC was created as a subsidiary of the Federal Home Loan Bank Board (FHLBB) – and the bank board was not only a regulatory agency but also the chief spokesman for the savings and loan industry. While the conflict of interest is clear to us today, it was not so obvious then. By legislation, deposits protected by the FDIC were backed by the "full faith and credit" of the United States government – but deposits protected by FSLIC were not similarly protected, although many people believed that they were. On the contrary, FSLIC insurance existed to the extent that the Congress could be convinced to appropriate funds to cover the deposits. This distinction would become painfully clear to depositor and taxpayer alike in the 1980s.[6]

Prior to 1933, only states granted charters to savings and loan associations, but the Home Owners Loan Act provided for federal savings and loans to be administered by the FHLBB. Thus, the system of dual charters and conflicting standards and regulation was born. A federal charter required mutual ownership until 1976. But FSLIC insurance was available whether a

---

[6] Pilzer (1989) pp. 52-53; White (1991) pp. 180-193

state or federal charter was held. So state charters came to be more desirable, and during the 1950s and 1960s the number of state-chartered savings and loans grew and came to outnumber federal institutions. And, in many states, state-chartered institutions were able to invest in a much wider range of loans and other instruments.

The post-World War II mission of the U.S. savings and loan industry was shaped by statutory changes that re-emphasized the importance of savings and loans to undertake the widespread financing of home mortgages and associated real estate development. Further funding and legislation extended savings and loan lending during the period of long-term stable interest rates that survived until the 1960s.

For most of the post-World War II period, the savings and loan business was relatively straightforward. Federal law and regulation allowed operators to exchange a stable business for government guarantees. Savings and loans were required to gather household savings in short-term deposits and invest those savings in 30-year, fixed-rate mortgages secured by property within a 50 mile radius of the institution's home office. Deposits were guaranteed through the FSLIC and state-sponsored deposit insurance funds.[7] The FHLBB financed Regional Federal Home Loan banks that were able to lend member institutions funds at subsidized rates. In an environment of stable, long-term interest rates, interest rate risk was relatively minor. Savings and loans borrowed money short (i.e., through time deposits) at lower rates than they lent in long-term fixed rate mortgage contracts and which were often refinanced as homes sold prior to the maturity of their mortgage. Since the risk of mortgage lending was well-subsidized by the federal government and deposits were also insured, the savings and loan industry for nearly three decades proved to be a stable, if not exciting, financial services business.

Yet another part of the foundation for the savings and loan crisis was laid in the 1950s when government regulations first constrained savings and loan liabilities to short-term obligations, and it was then that the tax laws first favored long-term assets. By the end of the 1950s, the mismatching of assets and liabilities was firmly rooted in the U.S. savings and loan industry.

In the mid-1960s the United States experienced a rapid and steep rise in short-term interest rates, and savings and loans had to pay higher rates in order to attract deposits. Also by the mid-1960s, commercial banks, which heretofore had not shown much interest in the deposits of individual savers – had begun to issue certificates of deposit and with these competed for consumer deposits.

---

[7] England (1992); Fabritius and Borges (1990).

Regulators responded with the Interest Rate Adjustment Act in 1966 (allowing savings and loans an interest rate differential compared to commercial banks) and the Financial Institutions Supervisory Act (which granted the FHLBB the ability to issue "cease and desist" orders to prevent savings and loans from tying up the Board in court). The Board then lowered liquidity requirements, from 7 percent to 6.5 percent of assets, and expanded the category of liquid assets to include federal funds, reverse purchase agreements, and municipal bonds, as well as cash and government securities.

Macroeconomic developments in the 1970s abruptly challenged the savings and loan industry. With the onset of inflationary expectations, interest rates rose with considerable volatility. The housing market stagnated. Savings and loan earnings stalled as well.

Not surprisingly, savings and loan regulators responded by changing the regulations. The President's Commission on Financial Structure and Regulation, appointed in 1970 by Richard Nixon (commonly known as the Hunt Commission for Chairman Reed O. Hunt) suggested many changes, as did the House-commissioned "Financial Institutions and the Nation's Economy" (FINE) study that actually would not be addressed until later in the decade. Those reforms included phasing out interest rate ceilings, allowing savings and loans to extend adjustable-rate mortgages, and allowing savings and loans to invest in other types of loans, as banks were permitted to do.

But the recommendations of both commissions were ignored, by both the Congress and the Executive Branch, and in the late 1970s and early 1980s what could have been a normal exercise in managing interest rate risk turned into a major disaster. As interest rates climbed, brokerage houses and banks established money market mutual funds, and money began to flow out of savings and loans at a dramatic rate. The Congress then lifted the ceilings on savings and loan interest rates in 1984. This did indeed work to prevent further disintermediation. But by deregulating the liability side of the balance sheet without concurrently deregulating the asset mix, the Congress pushed the savings and loan industry further into insolvency.

In contrast, the recommendations of the Hunt and FINE commissions had specified liberalized rules for both sides of the equation; alternatively, the Congress could have done nothing at all, leaving the equation in balance and letting the savings and loans shrink to nothing – at much less cost to the American taxpayer. But the Congress deregulated only the liability side of the equation, and, forced to pay higher rates to attract deposits while collecting the same income from their portfolios of fixed-rate mortgages, the savings and loan industry slid into insolvency.[8]

Many savings and loan operators had nothing to lose, and everything to gain, by betting the farm on the highest risk and transactions offering the highest possible rewards, especially in agriculture, energy, and real estate development. Granted, unscrupulous savings and loan operators counted on deposit insurance to bail them out if things didn't work out. But the owners and managers of hundreds of other savings and loans were simply caught in the bind created by the Congress and the regulators, and were simply doing their best to keep their heads above water.

DIMENSIONS OF THE SAVINGS AND LOAN CRISIS

The history of the savings and loan crisis reflects the failure of government policy and private management on four fronts. Savings and loans were unable to adapt to nonbank channels of capital flow, to shifting credit and interest rate risks, to costs of financial capitalization, and to relative deposit insurance costs.

It is critical, in the context of the rapid structural changes in capital markets, for financial institutions to measure, monitor and manage the flow of capital investments flexibly and quickly. In the savings and loan crisis, we can study a series of events, decisions and actions that conspired to undermine financial institutions, increase all categories of investment risk, and ultimately increase the cost to both the government and the savings and loan industry of resolving the problems.

At the end of the 1980s, concerns about the reregulation of financial institutions focused first on savings and loan institutions, and later shifted to banks, insurance companies, and pension and mutual funds. The savings and loan industry crisis is a model of the challenges financial institutions face as managements struggle to adapt to changing circumstances. How managements respond through business strategy, financial management, restructuring of operations, and capitalization informs the ongoing debate about the role of the government in deregulating, reregulating, and overregulating the savings and loan industry and financial institutions in general.

---

[8] Robert E. Litan noted in *The Wall Street Journal* (July 29, 1993) that the savings and loan industry was insolvent by more than $100 million by 1981.

It is axiomatic that strong financial institutions provide the institutional infrastructure for a growth economy. This volume will examine the industrial, organizational, economic, political, and managerial effects that undermined savings and loans as financial institutions.

REASSESSING THE SAVINGS AND LOAN CRISIS 20 YEARS LATER

The business and public policy issues – deregulation, capital structure and strategy, supervisory policies, regulatory and financial mismanagement and accounting transparency – in the history of savings and loans reappear with increasing frequency in every subsequent financial crisis we have observed. The Mexican banking crisis of the 1980s, the Latin American Tequila Crisis of the 1990s, the Asian Crisis and Russian Default of 1997-98, as well as subsequent financial institutions and capital market challenges in Argentina, Brazil, Turkey and elsewhere all echo the issues and problems confronting business, policy and regulatory practitioners involved in the savings and loan industry during the last quarter of the 20th century.

Several common themes emerge from the papers in this volume: the degree and pattern of regulation and returns for savings and loans are inversely related. As regulations increased and distorted the institutional evolution of savings and loans, savings and loans' asset base and rates of return deteriorated. Inappropriate regulations and supervision failures not only failed to inhibit the incidence of savings and loan failure, but amplified those rates of failure.

Each of the following chapters brings a unique viewpoint – indeed, former regulators and industry figures, as well as prominent academics and commentators are included – and highlights a particular aspect of the crisis or a specific lesson that can be learned from it.

George Kaufman considers two of the lessons that supposedly have been learned from the crisis and the problems of forbearance: prompt corrective action and least cost resolution. Using recent bank failures as his examples, Kaufman presents a picture of lessons only partly learned by the regulatory community. We have, he argues, some way to go before forbearance is no longer a feature of the regulation of depository institutions.

Lawrence White provides a 21st century perspective on the savings and loan crisis and its lessons. High amongst these is the need for an appropriate capital structure. White argues persuasively that one key to imposing market discipline on depositary institutions is the requirement that they issue subordinated debt. As was noted by at least one of the attendees of the Anderson School-Milken Institute research roundtable, federal and state prosecutors did not have the same view of subordinated debt as White, as a number of institutions' managers were later indicted over their issuance of junior debt.[9] Nevertheless, a consensus does seem to have emerged both domestically and internationally (in the form recommendations from the Bank for International Settlements in Basel) that greater variegation and flexibility in financial institutions' capital structures through subordinated debt issuance is valuable.

Arthur Leibold provides a timely update of a classic paper produced at the height of the savings and loan crisis. Reflecting on the crisis and the resulting legislation, he provides a review of the performance of the RTC and other government bodies and draws parallels between FIRREA and the reactive legislation enacted or proposed in the wake of the accounting scandals of 2002.

Catherine England provides insight into the historical background of the savings and loan industry and the origins of its crisis. Her conclusions include the lessons that regulatory systems should be designed for the worst economic conditions, not the best, and that politicians and regulators must be wary of attempts to bend market forces to serve the political will.

The paper by R. Dan Brumbaugh and Catherine Galley overviews the three phases of the savings and loan crisis and provides an alternative view of forbearance. While a number of participants at the Anderson School-Milken Institute research roundtable insisted that forbearance is the enemy of the taxpayer, Brumbaugh and Galley dispute this.[10] The maximum possible cost of regulators' forbearance in the 1980s was, they contend, $43 billion dollars and a case can be made that forbearance was not an inappropriate policy as it bought regulators time to close institutions and increased the ultimate cost of the crisis by a relatively small amount.

Michael Darby suggests that the root causes of the savings and loan crisis were monetary. At the Federal Reserve before Paul Volcker's tenure, there was a failure to fully understand that inflation is a monetary phenomenon. In thinking that money didn't matter and thus allowing the money supply to grow out of control, the Federal Reserve sowed the seeds for double-digit inflation and ultimately for the decimation of the savings and loan industry.

In his paper, Edward Kane asks what lessons Latin American and Asian countries should have learned from the U.S. savings and loan crisis. Crises in

---

[9] See "Proceedings of the Savings and Loan Roundtable" in this volume for more detail.
[10] Ibid.

these countries are not, Kane contends, a result of deregulation but rather of two features these countries' banking industries have in common with the 1980's U.S. savings and loan industry: a policy of desupervision of institutions and inadequate constraint on the pursuit of self-interest by government officials.

Kevin Villani continues the international comparison by presenting an international development perspective on the savings and loan crisis. Villani concludes that much of the advice frequently offered emerging market countries inappropriately emphasizes the value of the U.S. Government Sponsored Enterprises such as Freddie Mac and Fannie Mae.

A dispassionate treatment of the media hysteria that obfuscated the real issues of the savings and loan crisis is provided by Lawrence Nichols and James Nolan in their paper on Lincoln Savings. They argue that Lincoln Savings represented what is known as a "landmark narrative" in the financial history of the 1980s. Lincoln became a symbol of the savings and loan crisis, despite the fact that it was not the largest savings and loan to have failed or the most costly bailout. Additionally, Lincoln has become synonymous with alleged theft and fraud despite the fact that no officer of the institution was ever successfully prosecuted for either.

An empirical reassessment of the savings and loan crisis appears in James Barth, Susanne Trimbath and Glenn Yago's paper. This is the first comprehensive empirical analysis of the universe of Thrift Financial Reports required by government supervision spanning all aspects of this troubled period of the savings and loan industry (1977-1995) that systematically tests alternative propositions about the savings and loan crisis. Propositions about the causes, costs, and likelihood of failure are rigorously tested. We find that, contrary to conventional wisdom, many savings and loans did not fall, but were pushed by regulatory chokeholds that destroyed their capital structure and strategies for survival. Rather than finding that asset diversification was the death knell of the savings and loan industry, we find the evidence to be consistent with the view that not only would savings and loans have not failed without regulations on asset diversification, they would have survived profitably. Policy interventions were, in fact, policy failures that increased the public and social costs of the savings and loan crisis instead of mitigating them.

The savings and loan crisis is explored by Donald McCarthy through case studies of five institutions, each of which illustrates a specific aspect of the regulatory debacle. The cost of forbearance and the role of poor management in the crisis are highlighted by the case of Madison Guaranty. The damage caused by FIRREA is illustrated by the cases of CenTrust, which failed due to the regulatory flip-flop over supervisory goodwill; Columbia, a well capitalized and profitable institution destroyed by FIRREA's treatment of high yield bonds; and Imperial, a thinly capitalized savings and loan that was seized following the attack on the high yield bond market. The fifth case study details World Savings, a large savings and loan that escaped unscathed from the crisis by focusing on home loans, the only major asset class that was not subject to a major change in regulation.

As a preface to the full proceedings, Kenneth Thygerson provides an overview of the Anderson School-Milken Institute research roundtable on savings and loans and draws important lessons and conclusions from the views expressed at the conference.

The final chapter surveys the savings and loan literature and provides a complete bibliography on the topic. One can find more than one explanation here, and more than one lesson to be learned. We invite you to further explore the various aspects of this momentous event in financial history.

REFERENCES

Barth, James R. and Philip F. Bartholomew (1992). "The Thrift Industry Crisis: Revealed Weaknesses in the Federal Deposit Insurance System," in Barth, James R. and R. Dan Brumbaugh, Jr. (eds); *The Reform of Federal Deposit Insurance.* New York: HarperBusiness.

Barth, James R., Philip F. Bartholomew, and Carol J. Labich (1990). "Moral Hazard and the Thrift Crisis: An Empirical Analysis," *Consumer Finance Law Quarterly Report*, Winter.

Barth, James R., Philip F. Bartholomew, and Michael G. Bradley (1990). "The Determinants of Thrift Institution Resolution Costs," *Journal of Finance*, 45(3), July.

Barth, James R. and R. Dan Brumbaugh, Jr. (1994a). "Moral-Hazard and Agency Problems: Understanding Depository Institution Failure Costs," *Research in Financial Services*, January.

Barth, James R. and R. Dan Brumbaugh, Jr. (1994b). "Risk Based Capital: Information and Political Issues," *Global Risk Based Capital Regulations*, 1.

Barth, James R. and Philip R. Wiest (1989). *Consolidation and Restructuring of the U.S. Thrift Industry Under the Financial Institutions Reform, Recovery, and Enforcement Act.* Washington, D.C.: Office of Thrift Supervision.

Brumbaugh, R. Dan Jr. and Andrew S. Carron (1987). "Thrift Industry Crisis: Causes and Solutions," *Brookings Papers on Economic Activity*, 2.

Brumbaugh, R. Dan Jr. and Robert E. Litan (1991). "Ignoring Economics in Dealing with the Savings and Loan and Commercial Banking Crisis," *Contemporary Policy Issues*, January.

England, Catherine (1992). "Lessons from the Savings and Loan Debacle: The Case for Further Financial Deregulation," *Regulation*, Summer: 36-43.

Fabritius, Manfred and William Borges (1990). *Saving the Savings and Loan: The U.S. Thrift Industry and the Texas Experience, 1950-1988.* New York: Praeger.

Friedman, Milton and Anna J. Schwartz (1971). *A Monetary History of the United States, 1867 – 1960.* Princeton: Princeton University Press.

Kendall, Leon (1962). *The Savings and Loan Business.* Englewood Cliffs: Prentice Hall.

O'Shea, James and Jane Roseman (1990). *The Daisy Chain: How Borrowed Billions Sank a Texas S&L.* New York: Crown.

Pilzer, Paul Z. with Robert Deitz (1989). *Other People's Money: The Inside Story of the S&L Mess.* New York: Simon and Schuster.

Pizzo, Stephen (1989). *Inside Job: The Looting of America's Savings and Loans.* New York: McGraw-Hill.

Rose, Peter and Donald Fraser (1988). *Financial Institutions.* New York: Basic Publications.

White, Lawrence J. (1991). *The S&L Debacle: Public Policy Lessons for Bank and Thrift Regulation.* New York: Oxford University Press.

Yago, Glenn (1991). *Junk Bonds – How High Yield Securities Restructured Corporate America.* New York: Oxford University Press.

Yago, Glenn (1992). "Scapegoat Litigation: The Economic Costs of Criminalizing Business," prepared for Policy Forum on The Crisis in Professional Liability, Manhattan Institute, Harvard Club, New York City, June 11, 1992.

Yago, Glenn, (1993). "Ownership Change, Capital Access, and Economic Growth," *Critical Review*, 7(2).

Yago, Glenn and Donald Siegel. (1994). "Triggering High Yield Market Decline: Regulatory Barriers in Financial Markets." *Merrill Lynch Extra Credit* 21.

Yago, Glenn and Susanne Trimbath (2003). *Beyond Junk Bonds: Expanding High Yield Markets.* New York: Oxford University Press.

WHAT HAVE WE LEARNED FROM THE THRIFT AND BANKING CRISES OF THE 1980s?

George G. Kaufman
Loyola University Chicago

INTRODUCTION

Let me skip right to the bottom line conclusion. What have we learned from the thrift and banking crises of the 1980s?[1] The academics, I think, have learned a great deal.[2] The regulators have also learned a great deal, but primarily in theory. In practice, the jury is still out. But, as I will argue below, it does not look promising. Do the wide scale failures and resolutions of the savings and loan associations and commercial banks in the 1980s provide useful perspectives for today? The answer is definitely yes.

How have I come to this conclusion? Since 1995, which sort of represents the end of the cleanup of the savings and loan and commercial banking mess, few banks and thrifts have failed, that is, been placed into receivership or conservatorship by the regulators. As can be seen from Table 1, less than ten banks and thrifts failed per year, and even fewer institutions of any size failed. As of mid-2002, only three institutions with total assets of $1 billion or more have failed and none with assets of more than $2.5 billion at the date of failure (Table 2). I add a fourth bank to this list that is a lot

Table 1: Number and Cost of Bank and Thrift Failures, 1995 – 2002

Year	Number	Total Assets ($ bn)	Estimated Loss		
			Average**	Low	High
1995	6	0.8	14%	10%	28%
1996	6	0.2	26%	11%	40%
1997	1	***	14%	14%	14%
1998	3	0.4	48%	6%	54%
1999	8	1.5	56%	0%	74%
2000	7	0.4	10%	4%	17%
2001	4	2.4	24%	1%	24%
2002*	8	2.2	NA	NA	NA

* Through June
** Weighted by total assets
*** Less than $100 million
Source: Federal Deposit Insurance Corporation (various dates, see references) and press reports

---

[1] For reviews of the 1980s crises, see Barth (1991); Barth and Litan (1998); Kane (1989); and Kaufman (1995).
[2] The numerous published recommendations by academics on how to deal with the recent banking crises in Japan, East Asia and other countries clearly reflect the experiences of the United States with the crisis of the 1980s.

George C. Kaufman

Table 2: Selected Bank and Thrift Failures, 1995 – 2002*

Year	Institution	Total Assets ($bn)	Estimated Loss (share of assets)
1998	Best Bank	0.23	50%
1999	First National Bank of Keystone	1.12	75%
2001	Superior Federal Savings	1.77	20%-40%
2002	Hamilton National Bank	1.41	30%

* Through June

Source: Federal Deposit Insurance Corporation *Bank and Thrift Failure Reports* (various dates) and press reports

smaller, but of interest for purposes of this analysis. The Best Bank (Boulder, Colorado) with $230 million in assets failed in 1998.

So far, so good. But, although very few banks failed, things change dramatically if one looks at the cost of the failures to the Federal Deposit Insurance Corporation (FDIC) and uninsured depositors and creditors at the bank (Table 2). Estimates of this loss or the negative net worth of the institutions on the date of resolution are frequently made by the FDIC and reported in the press release announcing the failure. In cases where the FDIC does not report this estimate, estimates are often reported in the press based on information provided by bank analysts. The estimates are periodically updated until the resolution of the bank is completed. Relying on the most recently available credible estimates, the loss on Keystone is estimated at near $800 million or 75 percent of its assets; on Superior, $500 million to $800 million (before a payment to the FDIC by the Pritzker family, the primary owner) or 20 to 40 percent of its assets; on Hamilton $400 million (even though the Comptroller of the Currency proudly announced he had closed the bank before its risk-based capital ratio declined below 8 percent), or 30 percent of its assets; and on Best Bank, $170 million or more than 50 percent of assets[3]. These large losses focus attention on two areas of concern where the lessons of the 1980s do not appear to have been fully learned by the regulators: 1) effective regulatory intervention to minimize losses from failure through, among other powers, application of prompt corrective action and its

---

[3] What is in a name? Instead of being named First, Superior, Hamilton, and Best, these failed banks might more correctly have been named Last, Inferior, Burr and Worst.

corollary, least cost resolution[4], and 2) design of a government-sponsored deposit insurance structure that minimizes poor behavior by both banks and bank regulatory agencies. The remainder of this paper examines these two areas.

EFFECTIVE REGULATORY INTERVENTION

The large losses associated with a number of the bank and thrift institution failures in recent years do not seem to be what most people had in mind when Congress enacted prompt corrective action and least cost resolution in the Federal Deposit Insurance Corporation Improvement Act (FDICIA) of 1991. There appears to be no reduction in the average cost of bank failures after the enactment of FDICIA from before its passage and the costs of some of the individual failures are considerably greater. The recent costly failures are spread over all federal regulators. The Comptroller (OCC) had two, the FDIC had one, and the Office of Thrift Supervision (OTS) had one. But this does not clear the Federal Reserve, because the Hamilton's parent holding company was also in trouble, and the Federal Reserve has authority over bank holding companies. One could also go back to the problems at the Daiwa Bank in the mid-1990s, which was under Federal Reserve supervision.

What went wrong? Are these four banks outliers or mainstream? Are there many more such banks waiting in the wings to be discovered?

One could make a case that they are outliers. Each one of these involved massive fraud and legal maneuvers by the bank to delay responding to the enforcement actions of the regulators. In some cases, there was even physical interference with and intimidation of the supervisors and the examiners. These banks concentrated on very risky loans. Keystone and Superior securitized sub-prime loans, which are risky to begin with, and increased their risk exposure further by holding on to the first dollar loss tranche, which is widely referred to as the "toxic waste" tranche. Hamilton, a bank in Miami of less than $1.5 billion in assets, was heavily involved in loans to distant Ecuador.

But, on the other hand, these institutions had many of the same red flags flying high that were flying during the savings and loan crisis in the 1980s. There was rapid growth. Superior doubled in size in the three years from 1996

---

[4] Prompt corrective action and least cost resolution go hand-in-hand in minimizing resolution costs. Achieving least cost resolution, which requires that the FDIC resolve failures in a manner "least costly to the deposit insurance fund," requires effective prompt corrective action.

to 1999. Keystone grew even faster. There was a rapid runoff of uninsured deposits that were replaced by insured deposits. In addition to the risky lending, these institutions did very complex lending and some engaged significantly in derivatives activities. While these later activities might make sense and be appropriate for larger institutions, one can wonder whether a small institution has both the skill-set and the management capabilities required to engage in these activities successfully. Moreover, there were frequent misclassifications and misreporting of activities on the call reports that were provided to the regulators and the public, substantial underreserving for loan losses, and very high off-balance sheet recourse exposures relative to the size of the institution.

What happened? Were the regulators caught unawares with their pants down? I do not think so. They knew for many years that there were serious problems in each of these banks, and they filed enforcement actions and even cease and desist actions. But they were often stalled. And when the regulators were stalled, they did not follow through aggressively. There appears to have been no sense of urgency. While one may not necessarily be in favor of regulatory bullying of institutions and unwarranted intervention, as sometimes happened in the 1980s, in these four cases, there was effectively regulatory "chickening-out." The Inspector General of the Department of the Treasury's report on Keystone was highly critical of the lack of aggressiveness by the Comptroller and the failure to respond clearly to visible red flags and to harassment of his staff on site (Office of Inspector General, 2000).[5]

But, the lessons from this failure were not learned and it was "*deja vu* all over again."[6] Almost exactly the same things happened in both Superior and Hamilton. If anything, the Inspector Generals of the FDIC and the Treasury Department were even more scathing in the Superior Bank debacle. The new game of regulatory chickening-out leads to the same old-time forbearance practices that have been criticized widely and correctly so. What is the result? To some people, the moral is that prompt corrective action is not working and should be repealed. But, as I see it, it is not the fault of prompt corrective action or least cost resolution, but of the regulators. Prompt corrective action was neither applied in a timely fashion nor with enthusiasm and gusto in these cases and thus neither was least cost resolution.

The numerical values of the capital trip-wires for supervisory sanctions are set by the regulators, not by legislation. Only the value of the minimum

---

[5] FDICIA requires the Inspector General of the Federal regulatory agencies involved to prepare a public report whenever a bank resolution results in a material loss to the FDIC, subject to review and verification by the U.S. General Accounting Office.

[6] Yogi Berra is alive and well in Washington!

capital-ratio for resolution is specified in FDICIA. If the regulators believe that the trip wires are set too low – which I have argued for many years now – the regulators have it within their authority to raise the values of the capital ratios to where they could get at the banks even sooner and start corrective action more promptly. How capital is measured is also determined by the regulators. Book value capital is correctly criticized as being a lagging indicator of the condition of an institution. This is particularly true for troubled banks that tend to underreserve and delay recognizing other losses in order to prop up reported earnings and capital. FDICIA encourages the regulators to give serious thought to making greater use of market value accounting and reporting to supplement book value accounting and reporting. But, to date, the regulators have rejected this. In all four of the bank failures noted above, reported capital was vastly overstated and had to be revised sharply downward shortly before or at failure. But this did not imply that the regulators did not know better on a timely basis. They had additional information.

Moreover, the capital-asset ratios available to supervisors are not the only criterion for downgrading a bank in FDICIA. The regulators have a great deal of discretion. The specified capital-asset ratio is just the final trigger. The regulators can also downgrade banks on the basis of regular or special examinations and even put them in receivership when, in the regulators' opinion, the banks have insufficient assets to meet their obligations, are experiencing losses that will deplete their capital, or are engaging in unsafe and unsound practices (12 U.S.C. 1821 (c) (5)). If the regulators do not do anything else earlier, then the capital ratio forces them into action. The mandatory sanctions specified in FDICIA are the last line of defense for the regulators, not the first. Better late than never.

If one does not favor the use of prompt corrective action, what does one favor? Does one return to the bad old days of greater regulatory discretion? That is, a return to non-prompt, non-corrective, non-action, which was equivalent to excessive forbearance? That has not served the banking industry, or the country, well.

DEPOSIT INSURANCE DESIGN

In addition to failing to learn some of the important lessons of the 1980s with respect to prompt corrective action and least cost resolution, the regulators also appear to have failed to learn the lessons with respect to the potential adverse effects of a poorly designed and structured government-sponsored deposit insurance system on the number and cost of depository institution failures. As has been discussed in the academic and professional literature *ad infinitum*, poorly designed deposit insurance systems encourage both excessive moral hazard risk-taking by insured institutions and poor agency behavior by bank regulators (in the form of excessive forbearance) (Kane, 1989). The increased risk-taking by banks occurs because of the reduced incentives of *de jure* or perceived insured depositors to monitor and discipline their institutions for such behavior. The reduction in the incentive for these depositors to discipline their banks by withdrawing funds or running on troubled institutions, in turn, maintains their funding and reduces the likelihood of potential liquidity problems. This permits them to remain in operation and lessens the pressure on regulators to close the institutions on a timely basis when they are unable to meet their depositor claims in full and on time. Before the introduction of deposit insurance, regulators did not have this option. The inability to meet depositor claims forced immediate voluntary or regulatory suspension of operations. Evidence clearly shows that the longer insolvent institutions are permitted to continue in operation, the larger on average are the losses ultimately associated with failure likely to be.

Both bank moral hazard and regulator poor agency problems can be reduced, although probably not eliminated altogether, by properly structuring the deposit insurance system. FDICIA introduced a number of important improvements to reform deposit insurance and achieve such results. Among other changes, the FDIC is required to increase insurance premiums on insured institutions whenever its reserves decline below 1.25 percent of aggregate insured deposits to regain this minimum ratio value within one year (Kaufman, 2001a and 2002). If this is not achieved, the FDIC is required to impose an average high premium of 23 basis points on total domestic deposits at insured institutions until it is. Before 1989, the FDIC was effectively unable to raise premiums above a maximum of 8.33 basis points, regardless of its losses. Thus, losses greater than the ability to be financed by these premiums were shifted to and paid by the federal government.

Moreover, if the FDIC suffers a loss in protecting an insolvent large bank's *de jure* uninsured depositors or other creditors, whom it is otherwise explicitly prohibited from protecting, by invoking the systemic risk exemption, which permits it to do so and has replaced the previous "too big to fail" policy, it is required to recoup the loss expeditiously by imposing a special assessment on all the other banks. In addition, invoking this exemption was made considerably more difficult. It now requires a written recommendation by two-thirds of both the Board of Directors of the FDIC and the Board of Governors of the Federal Reserve System to the Secretary of the Treasury to make a determination, after consultation with the President, that not assisting these claimants "would have serious adverse effects on economic conditions or financial stability" and that "any action or assistance... would avoid or mitigate such adverse effects." Thus, since 1992, deposit insurance in the United States has effectively been a privately funded system. Contrary to popular belief, the government becomes liable for losses only if the capital of the banking system is depleted to the point where the remaining solvent banks cannot afford to pay the required increases in insurance premiums. This condition would not have occurred at the height of the 1980s bank and thrift crisis and not either even in the 1930s crisis. As a result, deposit insurance is now of considerably less public policy importance.

But some bank regulators are working to change this structure through legislation to increase the probability of returning to the "bad old days" that put the federal government at greater risk. All regulators are supporting legislation currently pending in Congress that would increase the flexibility of the FDIC to extend the maximum time period for it to recoup its losses without imposing the 23 basis point "cliff-rate" premium[7]. This increases the likelihood that the FDIC will delay the painful increases in rates and in the process run out of funds to pay the losses and need to tap the Treasury for what may turn out to be permanent funding. The primary reason provided for this proposed change is to avoid increasing insurance premiums on the banks when they are in weak financial shape and least likely to afford the increases. That is, to avoid "hitting the banks when they are down." But private insurance firms tend to price along these lines. Hurricane insurance premiums rise after major hurricanes and flood insurance premiums rise after widespread floods, when the insurers have to recoup some or all of their unexpected losses. There is little, if any, reason to treat banks differently.

The FDIC, although not the other agencies, is also supporting legislation to increase the account coverage ceiling above the basic $100,000 adopted in 1980. The public policy implications of such an increase in coverage depend on how confident one is that the insurance system is now effectively privately funded by the insured banks as described above. If confidence is high, then the issue of coverage is primarily a private policy concern for the paying banks rather than public policy concern for the taxpayers. But if confidence in the lasting nature of the current arrangement is low, then the issue is of important public policy concern. Many analysts have attributed a considerable part of both the cause and severity of the thrift crisis in the 1980s to the increase in insurance coverage from $40,000 to $100,000 that was enacted by Congress in 1980. This reduced depositor concerns about the financial health

---

[7] This legislation was adopted in 2002 as H.R. 3717 and S. 1945.

of their insured depositories and made it considerably easier for depositors to divide larger accounts into smaller accounts at multiple banks that could qualify for full insurance coverage. These analysts fear that another increase would produce similar adverse effects and may again prove costly to the taxpayer.

CONCLUSION

I ended my testimony in the U.S. Senate on Superior's failure[8] (with a call for greater commitment by the regulators to the concept of prompt corrective action and recommended sensitivity training to raise their awareness levels (Kaufman, 2001b). The basic problem is not with the quality of the regulators, but with their incentive structure. To date, there is little penalty to the regulators for permitting high-cost failures and little credit for achieving low-cost failures or permitting orderly exit through failures. Attempts to prevent or delay failures frequently result in higher-cost failures. While entry into banking has been pretty well deregulated, exit apparently has not. Top regulators continue to be rewarded by being recycled to other sectors that are related to banking through a revolving door after their term of office is completed.[9]

In addition to increased regulatory sensitivity to prompt corrective action, laws should be strengthened to give the regulators both greater authority and greater incentive to move faster and more strongly in obvious problem cases and thus insure least cost resolution. The recent tardy actions by the regulators send a message to these troubled institutions and their lawyers to stall and delay even longer. If the regulators cannot deal efficiently and effectively with the current few failures of reasonably small banks, what will they do and how will they act if we ever have a larger number of failures again and particularly of larger banks?

Bank regulators still, at times, appear to let parochial concerns over the short-run well-being of the banking industry color their recommendations on public policy. This will only lead to poorer performance and higher costs for both the industry and the economy at-large in the long-run. That is, regulators have failed to sufficiently take to heart two of the more important lessons of the 1970s – prompter intervention in troubled institutions and reduced

---

[8] Which started on September 11, 2001, was rudely interrupted, and was completed on October 16, the day they found anthrax in the adjoining Senate office building

[9] For example, Ellen Seidman, who was Chairperson of the OTS during the Superior Bank problem, now serves on the Democratic staff of the House Banking Committee.

government incentives for banks to increase risk-taking and for regulators to forbear.

The American philosopher George Santayana admonished us that "those who cannot remember the past are condemned to repeat it." To me, this is not as interesting a question to ask as "what happens to those who do remember the past?" Unfortunately, all too often it appears that they agonize first and then repeat it again. The behavior of the bank regulators in the last ten years with respect to prompt corrective action and deposit insurance structure suggests that my modification of Santayana's admonition holds true, at least in their case.

REFERENCES

Barth, James R. (1991). *The Great Savings and Loan Debacle*. Washington, D.C.: American Enterprise Institute.

Barth, James R. and Robert E. Litan (1998). "Lessons from Bank Failures in the United States" in Caprio, G. Jr., Hunter, W. C., Kaufman, G. G. and Leipziger, D. M. eds. *Preventing Bank Crises: Lessons from Recent Global Bank Failures*. Washington, D.C.: World Bank. pp. 133-171.

Federal Deposit Insurance Corporation. *Annual Report*. Washington, D.C.: Federal Deposit Insurance Corporation. Various years.

Federal Deposit Insurance Corporation. *News Release*. Washington, D.C.: Federal Deposit Insurance Corporation. Various dates.

Kane, Edward J. (1989). *The S&L Insurance Mess*. Washington, D.C.: Urban Institute Press.

Kane, Edward J. (2002). "What Can an Examination of S&Ls Reveal about Financial Institutions, Markets and Regulation." This volume.

Kaufman, George G. (1995). "The U.S. Banking Debacle of the 1980s: An Overview and Lessons," *The Financier*. May, pp. 9-26.

Kaufman, George G. (2001a). "Reforming Deposit Insurance - Once Again," *Chicago Fed Letter*. No. 171, November.

Kaufman, George G. (2001b). "The Failure of The Superior Federal Bank, FSB: Implications and Lessons," Testimony before Committee on Banking, Housing, and Urban Affairs, U.S. Senate Washington, D.C., September 11 and October 16.

Kaufman, George G. (2002). "FDIC Reform: Don't Put Taxpayers Back at Risk." *Policy Analysis*. No. 432 (Cato Institute), April 16.

Office of Inspector General (2002). *Issues Related to the Failure of Superior Bank, FSB, Hinsdale, Illinois (Audit Report No. 02-005)*, Washington, D.C.: Federal Deposit Insurance Corporation.

Office of Inspector General (2000). *Material Loss Review of the First National Bank of Keystone. (01G—00—067).* Washington, D.C.: U.S. Department of the Treasury.

Office of Inspector General (2002). *Material Loss Review of Superior Bank, FSB (01G-02-040).* Washington, D.C.: Department of the Treasury.

Rush, Jeffrey Jr. (2002). "Testimony before the Senate Committee on Banking, Housing and Urban Affairs," Washington, D.C. February 7.

Charticle 1
Impact of Interest Rate Reversals

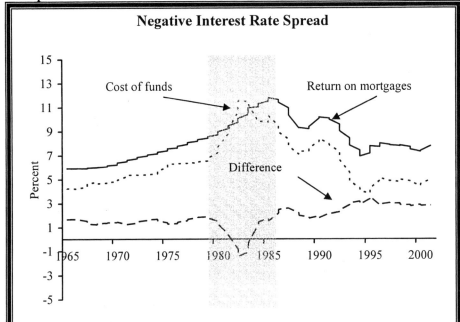

Semiannual data. Source: Office of Thrift Supervision, and Federal Home Loan
Board, Savings & Home Financing Source Book, various years.

Between 1980 and 1984, savings and loans experienced historically
unfavorable interest rates spreads – the difference between what they
could earn with mortgage lending and what they had to pay to attract
investable deposit funds. From June 1982 through December 1983, in
fact, their interest rates spread turned negative, so that savings and
loans were paying more interest than they were earning.

THE SAVINGS AND LOAN DEBACLE:

A PERSPECTIVE FROM THE EARLY TWENTY-FIRST CENTURY*

Lawrence J. White
Stern School of Business, New York University;
Former Board Member, Federal Home Loan Bank Board

* This essay draws heavily on White (1991, 1993, 2002)

INTRODUCTION

The savings and loan debacle of the 1980s was a costly but important learning event for depository regulation in the United States. The origins of the debacle lay in restrictive government regulation that eventually led to financial difficulties for savings and loan institutions in the late 1970s and early 1980s. The Congress and at least three presidential administrations delayed for far too long in undoing the restrictions. When the restrictions were loosened in 1980 and 1982, safety-and-soundness regulation also was weakened at just the time when it needed to be strengthened. The debacle followed, with an eventual cost of $160 billion.

This essay is about that experience, and about the learning that has followed from it, as well as the lessons that (unfortunately) have yet to be absorbed.

THE BACKGROUND

The roots of the debacle of the 1980s can be found in the earlier debacle of the stock market crash of 1929-1933 and the banking collapse that accompanied it. Thousands of commercial banks became insolvent and failed between 1929 and 1933, as did thousands of savings and loans. The latter were state-chartered depository institutions that largely made residential mortgage loans and financed them by taking in passbook savings deposit accounts.[1] Reform legislation in 1933–1935 greatly strengthened the federal role in bank regulation and included the institution of deposit insurance for banks, provided by the newly created Federal Deposit Insurance Corporation (FDIC), and the power (by the Federal Reserve) to set ceilings on the interest rates paid by banks to their depositors. This latter power was embodied in the Federal Reserve's Regulation Q.

Further, for the first time a strong federal regulatory presence was created for savings and loans. In 1932 the Federal Home Loan Bank Act created a system of 12 regional Federal Home Loan Banks (FHLBs) to provide liquidity and low-cost finance for savings and loans and established the Federal Home Loan Bank Board (FHLBB) in Washington to oversee the system. In 1933, the Home Owners' Loan Act (HOLA) created a federal

---

[1] Because savings and loans were so closely associated with household saving and thus with thrift, they were frequently described as "thrifts"; that term is still frequently used.

charter for savings and loans as an alternative to state charters,[2] along with a regulatory regime that embraced all savings and loans (federal and state-chartered) and that was embedded in the FHLBB. And in 1934 the National Housing Act established deposit insurance for all savings and loans,[3] on a par with that offered to commercial banks, offered by the newly created Federal Savings and Loan Insurance Corporation (FSLIC), which was an arm of the FHLBB. As was true for commercial banks, the deposit insurance premium paid by savings and loans was a flat rate and unrelated to any risks that might be undertaken by the savings and loans; those risks were expected to be contained by the safety-and-soundness regulations established and enforced by the FHLBB.

The last major change of the 1930s was the replacement of the standard residential mortgage of the time – the five-year-maturity balloon-payment mortgage – with the long-term (20 to 30 year) fixed-rate self-amortizing mortgage. This change came about largely at the urging of the Federal Housing Administration (which was also a creation of the HOLA of 1933).

Consequently, the savings and loan industry emerged from the 1930s as a heavily regulated set of depositories that were restricted to offering fixed-rate long-term residential mortgages, which in turn were financed by short- term passbook savings deposits (that were federally insured).[4] So long as interest rates stayed stable, declined, or rose only gradually, savings and loans could earn an income spread on the difference between the higher long-run interest rates that they charged on their mortgage loans and the lower short-term interest that they paid on their deposits.

Lurking in this structure, however, were the seeds of eventual disaster: If the general level of interest rates were to rise sharply,[5] savings and loans would be caught in a financial squeeze. They would have a portfolio of long-term fixed-rate assets that would decline in value as a consequence of the rise in interest rates, while the value of their deposit liabilities would remain relatively unchanged. Equivalently, their interest income from their portfolio of already-made fixed-rate mortgage loans would remain relatively unchanged, while their interest costs on their short-term deposits would have

---

[2] Federal charters as an alternative to state charters had been created for commercial banks by the National Currency Act of 1863 and the National Bank Act of 1864. With a federal savings and loan charter, came required membership in the FHLB system; state-chartered savings and loans could choose whether to join.

[3] Federally chartered savings and loans were required to carry deposit insurance; it was optional for state-chartered savings and loans.

[4] In general finance parlance, savings and loans were borrowing short and lending long.

[5] Or if, as occasionally happens, the yield curve were to invert, so that long-term interest rates were lower than short-term rates.

to rise with the rise in general interest rates.[6]

Fortunately for the savings and loan industry, the first two decades of the postwar era were a favorable climate. General government policy encouraged the expansion of housing of all kinds but especially encouraged single-family suburban residences – to be financed by the mortgages provided by savings and loans. The macroeconomic climate was benign; interest rates were stable or rose only gradually. Few savings and loans had difficulty earning adequate returns and staying solvent. The industry thus posed few safety-and-soundness problems to its federal and state regulators.

The first clouds appeared around 1964–1965. The U.S. escalated its involvement in the Vietnam War, which necessitated increased federal expenditures that were not matched by increased federal taxes. Inflationary pressures developed, and with them interest rates began to rise. Savings and loans began to experience the squeeze just described, and the industry asked the Congress to remedy the situation. The Congress replied in 1966 with the Interest Rate Control Act, which applied a "patch": the extension of Regulation Q's control over deposit interest rates (which previously had applied only to commercial banks) to savings and loans. The FHLBB (in coordination with the Federal Reserve) promptly began limiting the interest rates that savings and loans could pay to their depositors.

For the next decade or so, this patch worked, allowing savings and loans to pay interest rates that were below market rates and thus avoiding the financial squeeze that otherwise would have occurred. The patch worked largely because the inflationary pressures subsided and because savings and loan depositors had few good alternatives that offered comparable liquidity and safety but with market rates of interest – since all federally insured and regulated savings and loans were similarly affected by Regulation Q's restrictions,[7] and so were commercial banks.[8]

---

[6] If a savings and loan failed to pay higher interest rates to its depositors in the higher rate environment, the depositors would withdraw their funds and redeposit them with a competitive institution that was paying higher rates. And the former institution would have to liquidate its mortgages – at the lower sales prices that were appropriate to the higher rate environment, thus directly realizing the capital loss on the mortgages.

[7] There were a number of state-chartered and state-insured banks, notably in Ohio and Maryland, that were not part of the federal system and were not affected by Regulation Q. They were not numerous enough to undermine the Regulation Q restrictions. Also, there were questions as to whether state-based deposit insurance systems were as solid as federal deposit insurance – questions that became legitimate when both state systems experienced failures in 1985.

[8] In 1970, the Treasury moved to restrict alternatives yet further by raising the minimum denomination for Treasury bills from $1,000 to $10,000. At the time, the average deposit in a

During the 1970s at least three study groups or commissions highlighted the long-run fragility of the savings and loans' arrangements and recommended alternatives: permitting adjustable rate mortgages (ARMs) so that interest rate rises would not squeeze savings and loans; permitting the diversification of savings and loans' lending into other consumer and even commercial fields so as to allow them to diversify and reduce their interest-rate sensitivity; and ending Regulation Q. But an important ethos of Washington – "if it ain't broke, don't fix it" – prevailed and no significant changes were made.[9]

THE CRISIS, AND THE DEBACLE

The Crisis

In the late 1970s, inflationary pressures again gathered steam, and interest rates began increasing rapidly – this time into double digits. The immediate culprit was a sharp rise in the price of crude oil. But Regulation Q's patch no longer protected the savings and loan industry because better alternatives for depositors were present – primarily money market mutual funds (MMMFs). MMMFs had come into existence only in 1972 and had grown slowly for the next five years. At year-end 1977, total MMMF assets were only $3.3 billion. However, by year-end 1982 they had grown to $236.3 billion.

The savings and loan industry again went to Congress. This time the Congress responded with legislation, in 1980 (the Depository Institution Deregulation and Monetary Control Act) and again in 1982 (the Garn-St Germain Act), that belatedly undertook the deregulatory actions that had been urged in the previous decade. First, savings and loans were permitted to originate ARMs. Second, they were permitted to diversify (in limited percentages) into other forms of consumer lending and even into commercial real estate and other commercial lending and direct ownership. Importantly, many states (especially in the Sun Belt) at this time permitted their state-chartered (but federally insured) savings and loans to invest in a yet wider and riskier variety of loans and assets, with fewer restrictions. Third, Regulation Q was phased out within a few years for both savings and loans and commercial banks. And fourth, the deposit insurance amount (for both savings and loans

---

savings and loan was only $3,045, so the larger amount effectively precluded Treasury bills from becoming an alternative for most savings and loan depositors. See Kane (1970).

[9] The FHLBB considered changing its regulations at least twice, so as to permit federally chartered savings and loans to originate ARMs; but each time Congressional pressure caused the agency to withdraw the initiative.

and commercial banks), which had been at $40,000 per deposit, was raised to $100,000.

Though belated, these actions were sensible.[10] But they needed to be accompanied by stepped-up safety-and-soundness regulation because the financially stressed (low capital levels) state of the savings and loan industry at the time (as a consequence of the sharp increase in interest rates) provided strong incentives for risk-taking. Unfortunately, in the deregulatory climate of the era, safety-and-soundness regulation was instead *weakened* in three important ways. First, the capital (net worth) requirements for savings and loans were decreased, which reduced the number of savings and loans that would be in violation of the capital standards and thus subject to heightened regulatory scrutiny. Second, the accounting framework (which provided regulators with the crucial information about a savings and loan's financial position) was weakened, so as to allow more savings and loans to portray themselves as healthy. Third, the number of in-the-field examiners and supervisors was reduced.

The Debacle

Between 1983 and 1985 the savings and loan industry – with its expanded investment powers, improved deposit-gathering capabilities to finance those investments (paying market rates of interest on deposits that were insured up to $100,000), and relaxed safety-and-soundness regulation – expanded rapidly. By year-end 1985 the industry was 56 percent larger (as measured by assets) than it had been three years earlier. Not all savings and loans embarked on a path of rapid growth. However, hundreds did, with many of them doubling or tripling in size over these three years, and some expanding even faster.

Rapid expansion places stresses on and induces mistakes by most enterprises, even under the best of circumstances. But the fast growers within the savings and loan industry, initiating this expansion at a time when most savings and loans were financially stressed to begin with, would be even more prone to investment errors and exaggerated risk-taking. Also, aggressive entrants, who recognized the opportunities that the expanded investment powers and deposit-gathering capabilities offered, came into the industry for the first time.

---

[10] The expanded deposit insurance amount was the subject of substantial retrospective criticism. However, this author believes that extensive deposit insurance is a worthwhile back-up for depositors against failures of safety-and-soundness regulation and thus a worthwhile protection against depositors' runs on depositories.

This dangerous situation was then exacerbated by three external events that eventually caused the debacle to be even worse. First, in the early 1980s the price of crude oil (after having risen sharply in the late 1970s) was expected by many (especially in the Southwest) to rise even further. Many commercial real estate projects in the Southwest were undertaken – and financed by savings and loans – on the expectation that oil prices would remain high or go higher, thus creating high incomes and wealth for entrepreneurs and employees in oil-related businesses in the Southwest and fueling the demand for offices, hotels, and other facilities of these projects.

In contrast to these expectations, however, oil prices peaked in 1981, drifted gently downwards for the next few years, and then fell sharply in 1986. The lower price of oil undercut the profitability and value of many of the real estate projects, generating large losses for their owners – and for the savings and loans that had provided the financing.

Second, the Economic Recovery Tax Act of 1981 included provisions that made commercial real estate a tax-favored investment. Much commercial real estate in the following few years was planned and financed on the expectations that this tax favoritism would continue. But the Tax Reform Act of 1986 reversed course, reduced the tax-favored position of commercial real estate, and even applied some of its more stringent provisions retroactively to income earned on pre-1986 investments. The 1986 changes again undercut the profitability and value of many investments, with associated losses for owners and finance providers.

Third, a regional enforcement office of the FHLBB (covering the states of Arkansas, Louisiana, Mississippi, New Mexico, and Texas) was moved from Little Rock to Dallas in 1983. Though the reasons for the move were sensible, the timing turned out to be inadvertently abysmal. Too few personnel moved with the office, and enforcement of safety-and-soundness regulation was seriously impaired in that district for about two crucial years (when the industry was expanding rapidly).

Thus, all of the pieces were in place for a debacle to occur. And occur it did. Much of the commercial real estate lending and ownership that fueled the savings and loans' rapid growth of the 1983-1985 period fared badly, losing value and driving more than one thousand savings and loans eventually into insolvency. The insolvent savings and loans' assets were grossly inadequate to cover their deposit liabilities, since the FSLIC had insured virtually all of the savings and loans' deposits; and since the FSLIC's reserve funds were wholly inadequate for covering those insolvencies, taxpayer funds would eventually be required. [11]

THE CLEANUP

In late 1984 the leadership of the FHLBB began to realize that things were going wrong and that a substantial tightening in safety-and-soundness regulation was needed. Gradually, over the next two years, the agency's powers and capabilities were strengthened. The number of field-force examiners and supervisors were doubled, capital requirements were raised, accounting standards were improved, and restrictions on direct ownership of commercial ventures were tightened. By late 1986 the regulatory system was far improved, as compared with 1983. [12]

But the damage had been done. The bad loans and investments had been made during the 1983-1985 period of rapid growth. They were irrevocably on the books of many hundreds of savings and loans, waiting to be written down (whenever the savings and loans' accountants or the FHLBB's examiners got around to recognizing their impaired values).

Beginning in 1985, the FHLBB substantially expanded its activity in disposing of insolvent savings and loans. A few savings and loans that had little or no salvage value as going concerns were liquidated, with direct payouts to insured depositors. In most instances, however, the FHLBB could find acquirers, provided that the agency could promise an acquirer sufficient cash or other assets to bring the savings and loans back to break-even solvency. The acquirer would then be expected to provide fresh capital to the revived savings and loan (and, of course, to operate it in a safe-and-sound manner).

Because some favorable tax provisions that would reduce acquirers' costs (and thus reduce the FHLBB's costs) were scheduled to expire at the

---

[11] It is less well known that almost 1,500 commercial banks became insolvent in the 1980s and early 1990s; but the aggregate size of their insolvencies was substantially smaller, and the FDIC's insurance fund for covering banks was substantially larger than the FSLIC's fund had been, so that the banks' insolvencies never required the use of taxpayer funds. See FDIC (1997).

[12] Also, prior to 1986, enforcement personnel may have been lulled into a false sense of security by the fact that the industry had not caused significant problems (except for the interest-rate squeeze, which was beyond its control) during the 50 years between 1933 and 1983. Industry lobbying reinforced the idea that savings and loan owners and managers were basically "good guys" who just needed more time to regain solvency. By 1986, any such notions that the "good guy" characterization applied to all savings and loans had been dispelled, at least at the agency.

end of 1988, calendar year 1988 was an especially active year in which 205 insolvent savings and loans were disposed of, many of them in Texas (which had an especially large number of insolvent savings and loans). But the extent of the problem – hundreds more insolvent savings and loans required disposal – far exceeded the FSLIC's available funds and its ability to issue FSLIC notes (against future deposit insurance premiums and the expectation that the Treasury would make good on the FSLIC's deposit insurance obligations).[13]

In early 1989 the incoming Bush administration faced up to the reality that taxpayer funds would be required, and drafted legislation – eventually passed in August as the Financial Institutions Reform, Recovery, and Enforcement Act (FIRREA) – that authorized an initial tranche of funds (which proved not to be sufficient); that tightened savings and loans' lending restrictions, including a ban on the holding of below-investment-grade ("junk") bonds; and that raised capital requirements to make them commensurate with those applicable to commercial banks. The FHLBB (including the FSLIC) was abolished. In its place, the FDIC absorbed the deposit insurance function in a fund that was (and still is) separate from the commercial bank fund; the Office of Thrift Supervision (OTS), within the Treasury, was created to carry on the federal regulation of savings and loans; the Resolution Trust Corporation (RTC) was created, under the aegis of the FDIC, to continue the cleanup process of insolvent savings and loans; and the Federal Housing Finance Board (FHFB) was created to oversee the borrowing and lending activities of the twelve FHLBs.[14] Also, the remaining (healthy) savings and loans were directly taxed (through higher deposit insurance premiums) and indirectly taxed (through levies on the FHLBs, which reduced members' dividends) to help cover the costs of the cleanup.

Subsequent legislation in 1991 – the Federal Deposit Insurance Corporation Improvement Act (FDICIA) – provided more funds for the cleanup and also put into law the concept of prompt corrective action: that regulatory restrictions on banks and savings and loans should grow substantially tighter as a depository's capital fell farther below fully capitalized standards. By 1995, after yet more funds had been appropriated, the RTC was able to cease its operations and hand any remaining cleanup activities to the FDIC.

---

[13] In 1987, the Congress, in the Competitive Equality Banking Act, authorized the FSLIC to borrow $10.825 billion, but no more than $3.75 billion in any 12-month period. The Congress, responding to industry lobbying (especially from Texas), apparently was afraid that the FSLIC would use the funds to preemptively close savings and loans that deserved greater time and leniency.

[14] Also, membership in the FHLBs was expanded to include commercial banks that undertake a significant amount of residential mortgage lending.

The cost of the debacle has been estimated at about $160 billion, of which $132 billion has been borne by taxpayers.[15] .

LESSONS LEARNED, AND NOT YET LEARNED

The safety-and-soundness regulatory system for depositories that exists in 2002 is much improved over the one that existed in 1982. Much of this improvement and learning occurred as a consequence of the savings and loan debacle. Unfortunately, there are still some lessons that have not been learned. We will first discuss the lessons learned and then those that still need to be learned.

The Lessons Learned

1. *The importance of capital.* Today, far more clearly than was true in 1982, regulators understand the role of capital as a buffer to ensure solvency and protect the deposit insurer and as a disincentive for the owners of a depository to take risks (since they have more at stake). Further, regulators recognize that levels of capital should be commensurate with the risks undertaken by the depository.

2. *Prompt corrective action* (PCA). The PCA concept of gradually tightening the restrictions on a depository's actions as its capital became thinner had been in practice at the FHLBB and the bank regulatory agencies before its enactment into law in FDICIA. But its placement in law was opposed at the time by regulators because it reduced some regulatory discretion.

The PCA idea makes good sense, since less capital exposes the deposit insurer to greater risks of loss and also provides greater incentives for the owners and managers of depositories to engage in risk-taking (e.g., through investing in risky assets), since they have less to lose. Also, the removal of the depository's owners at or before insolvency is another important part of the PCA concept. If owners (because of limited liability) can escape liability to creditors (liability holders) and the deposit insurer must bear the costs of the insolvency, the owners' rights as to the future course of the depository should be extinguished.

PCA's placement into law both reflects and has reinforced its wider

---

[15] See FDIC (1997, p. 187).

acceptance.[16]

3. *Safety-and-soundness regulation as protection for the deposit insurer.* As of 1982 bank and savings and loan failures had been comparatively few since 1933, and the deposit insurance funds had been more than adequate to handle the occasional insolvency. As a consequence, the crucial role of safety-and-soundness regulation as the primary protection for the deposit insurance funds against excessive risk-taking by depositories was not well understood. It is today.

4. *The importance of adequate numbers of well-trained examiners and supervisors.* The importance of in-the-field personnel to check the competency of depositories' managements, as well as to verify procedures and verify asset and liability values, is now far more clearly understood than was true in 1982.[17]

The Lessons Not Yet Learned

1. *The importance of market value accounting.* Maintaining the true solvency of depositories, so that the values of their assets exceed the values of their liabilities, is the ultimate goal of safety-and-soundness regulation. But measurement of solvency – the measurement of capital (net worth) levels – is entirely an accounting concept. Unfortunately, the accounting system used for these regulatory purposes is the standard system that applies to all publicly traded companies in the United States: Generally Accepted Accounting Principles (GAAP). The problem with GAAP is that it is backward-looking in its orientation, focused on the historical (acquisition) values of assets and liabilities rather than on their current market values. But it is the latter – current market values – that represent (when netted) the actual available protection for the deposit insurer and thus the true effective level of capital.

By using GAAP, with its historical cost bias, regulators needlessly hamstring themselves.[18] It gives depositories a valuable and potentially dangerous option: to continue to value an asset at its historical value, even if its value has declined since its acquisition, while also being able to sell the asset if it rises above its historical value and thus recognize a gain. Allowing an institution to recognize gains (which may then be paid out to owners) while hiding losses is an invitation to invest in high-variance assets and a recipe for

---

[16] Important advocacy of PCA can be found in Benston and Kaufman (1988a, 1988b).

[17] See the discussion in FDIC (1997).

[18] A flavor of this can be found in FDIC (1997), where FDIC officials observe that they knew that some banks were really in trouble but the GAAP balance sheets indicated solvency.

a balance sheet that in the long run is only hiding losses.

2. *Forward-looking stress tests.* As a supplement to market value accounting, safety-and-soundness regulation should require stress tests of depositories: how well (and how long) does their (market value) capital hold up under various pessimistic economic scenarios? Some stress testing is implicit in the risk modeling that is likely to be a part of the capital standards that are currently being developed by the Bank for International Settlements.[19] However, it is currently unclear how much stress testing will be involved, how standardized it will be, or even how many depositories will avail themselves of these sophisticated approaches (as compared to just a modification of the current standards, with somewhat modified risk weights[20]).

3. *The importance of long-run subordinated debt.* Long-run subordinated debt brings to the institution a set of market-based, sophisticated stakeholders whose interests are similar to (although not identical to) those of the deposit insurer. The pricing of this debt is likely to provide bank regulators with signals as to the financial markets' assessment of a depository's prospects. Unlike uninsured deposits, however, long-term debt is not "runable" and thus cannot destabilize a depository (and its peers). Also, covenants may allow the debt holders to exert some influence over management.

Unfortunately, many bank regulators continue to see subordinated debt as "debt," with obligatory interest payments that are not as capable of being deferred as are the dividend payments on equity. Also, the flotation of subordinated debt may present a scale problem for very small depositories, of which there are still many thousands in the U.S.[21]

4. *The appropriate structure for a depository.* The American populist tradition of keeping banks small and limited in their powers continues to hamper the development of sensible thinking about the appropriate structure for a depository institution. Despite the passage of the Gramm-Leach-Bliley Act of 1999 and the development of large multi-function financial institutions, a safety-and-soundness based approach to depository structure – what banks should and should not be allowed to own and do – has yet to be widely accepted.

---

[19] These internal (to a depository) risk modeling approaches, which are part of the new capital proposals frequently referred to as "Basle II," are described by the Bank for International Settlements as the "advanced" and "foundation" approaches.

[20] This modification is described by the Bank for International Settlements as the "standardized approach to credit risk."

[21] As of December 31, 2001, there were over 5,000 commercial banks and savings institutions with less than $100 million in assets.

The logic of a safety-and-soundness approach would argue for the following: anything that is examinable and supervisable – i.e., activities and assets about which depository regulators can make judgments as to the competence of the depository in managing the activity or the asset, and for which the regulators can set informed capital requirements – should be permitted within the depository.[22] Anything else should not be permitted within the depository but should be permitted to be located in a holding company or a separately capitalized subsidiary of the depository.[23] And any transactions between the depository and its holding company or subsidiary must be on arms-length terms and subject to close regulatory scrutiny, so as to prevent the siphoning of assets out of the depository and ultimately to the owners.

CONCLUSION

The savings and loan debacle remains as an important event in U.S. financial history, and is likely to remain so for many decades to come. It was a costly experience, but an educational one as well. Depository regulation is substantially improved today as compared with two decades ago.

Unfortunately, even more should have been learned. One can only hope that the American polity will not need another such costly experience in order to learn the remaining important lessons.

---

[22] This logic is laid out in Shull and White (1998).

[23] If the subsidiary is separately capitalized, the depository cannot count as an asset the net worth of the subsidiary.

REFERENCES

Benston, George J. and George G. Kaufman (1988a). "Risk and Solvency Regulation of Depository Institutions: Past Policies and Current Options." *Monograph Series in Finance and Economics* No. 1988-1, Salomon Brothers Center for the Study of Financial Institutions, New York: New York University.

Benston, George J. and George G. Kaufman (1988b). "Regulating Bank Safety and Performance," in Haraf, W. F. and Kushmeider, R. M. eds., *Restructuring Banking and Financial Services in America.* Washington, D.C.: American Enterprise Institute. pp. 63-99.

Federal Deposit Insurance Corporation (1997). *History of the Eighties: Lessons for the Future.* Washington, D.C.: Federal Deposit Insurance Corporation.

Kane, Edward J. (1970). "Shortchanging the Small Saver: Federal Discrimination Against the Small Saver during the Vietnam War," *Journal of Money, Credit and Banking.* No. 2, November, pp. 513–522.

Shull, Bernard and Lawrence J. White (1998). "The Right Corporate Structure for Expanded Bank Activities," *Banking Law Journal.* No. 115, May, pp. 446-476.

White, Lawrence J. (1991). *The Savings and Loan Debacle: Public Policy Lessons for Bank and Thrift Regulation.* New York: Oxford University Press.

White, Lawrence J. (1993). "A Cautionary Tale of Deregulation Gone Awry: The Savings and Loan Debacle," *Southern Economic Journal.* No. 59, pp. 496-514.

White, Lawrence J. (2002). "Bank Regulation in the United States: Understanding the Lessons of the 1980s and 1990s," *Japan and the World Economy.* No. 14, April, pp. 137-154.

Charticle 2
Impact of Regulatory Chokeholds

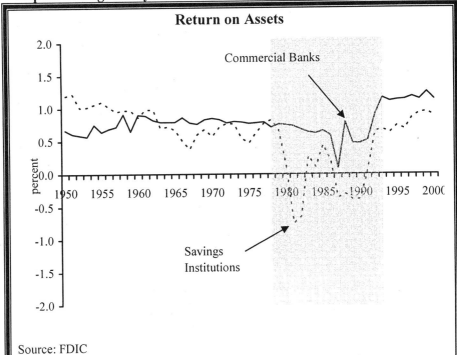

Source: FDIC

The dramatic economic events occurring throughout the 1980s had a cataclysmic effect on the savings and loans because of the regulatory chokehold they were under at the time. The devastating impact on profitability resulted in more than a thousand institutions being closed.

SOME HOPE FOR THE FUTURE, AFTER A FAILED NATIONAL POLICY FOR THRIFTS

Arthur W. Leibold, Jr.
Dechert Price & Rhoads;
Former General Counsel, Federal Home Loan Bank Board,
Federal Savings and Loan Insurance Corporation, and the
Federal Home Loan Mortgage Corporation

Editors' note: This paper was first written in 1989 during the savings and loan crisis. It was updated by the author in 2002 for this volume.

INTRODUCTION

The savings and loan legislation enacted into law on August 9, 1989[1] is a point of demarcation between the past and future for the financing of housing in the United States and the regulation of financial intermediaries which obtain deposits primarily for that purpose. This paper will discuss that legislation, after discussing some of the reasons for the current plight of the savings and loan industry in the United States.

Savings and loan associations in the United States came into being in the 1830s[2] to provide a means for persons of limited income to save money and to acquire home ownership by borrowing a substantial portion of the purchase price. In the 19th century and early 20th century in the United States, many commercial banks, especially those in large urban areas, were not structured to encourage customers of limited means either to deposit their funds or to obtain loans secured by mortgages or other collateral.[3] Thus, many small savings and loan associations were chartered throughout the United States to serve such customers.[4] A number of these associations initially served identifiable nationality groups, did not open every work day and were not, for most purposes, competitors of commercial banks.

At the time of the Great Depression[5] in the United States, what could be described as the current era of savings and loan association history began. Legislation was necessary because, like commercial banks, many savings and

---

[1] The Financial Institutions Reform, Recovery and Enforcement Act of 1989, P.L. 101-73, 103 Stat. 183 (1989) [hereinafter "FIRREA"].

[2] In 1831, the Oxford Provident Building Society was organized in Frankford, PA. It was the first savings and loan association in the United States. Committee on Savings and Loan Associations, Section of Corporation, Banking and Business Law. American Bar Association, *Handbook of Savings and Loan Law*. 8 (1973). Ironically, the Oxford's first borrower, Comly Rich, fell behind in his repayments and the association "confiscated" his land. Symons and White, *Banking Law*, 55 (2d ed. 1986). See also Williams, *Savings Institutions: Mergers, Acquisitions and Conversions*, 1.02[1] (1989) (describing the evolution of the savings institution industry).

[3] Adams and Peck, *The Federal Home Loan Banks and the Home Finance System*, 43 Business Law. 833, 835 (1988) (explaining that associations were formed to meet the need for housing loans, but commercial banks concentrated mostly on agricultural and commercial lending).

[4] By 1890, Oklahoma was the last of the then states to charter an association. An 1893 government census reported that 560 building and loan associations existed nationwide. Symons and White, *Banking Law*, 55 (2d ed. 1986); see *Handbook of Savings and Loan Law* at 8-14 (describing the growth of savings and loan institutions).

[5] The stock market crash occurred on October 29, 1929, precipitating the Depression of the 1930s. Some economists, although recognizing that the economy became stronger in the mid-1930s, believed another depression could have occurred in the late 1930s had it not been for the outbreak of World War II in Europe.

loan associations in the early 1930s could not pay their customers upon demand, in part because borrowers could not repay their mortgage loans,[6] and partly because collateral, particularly real estate, could not be liquidated for amounts approaching book value.[7]

The Congress of the United States passed the Federal Home Loan Bank Act in July 1932,[8] the Home Owners' Loan Act in June 1933,[9] and Title IV of the National Housing Act in June 1934.[10] These statutes created the Federal Home Loan Banks, the Home Loan Bank Board and the Federal Savings and Loan Insurance Corporation. This statutory framework, implemented by regulations, stayed in place, admittedly with numerous amendments, until August 9, 1989.

What went wrong during the 1980s, or before? Since history is ultimately what historians say it is, what went wrong depends upon the analysts and their frame of reference. Attached as an appendix is a list of "15 major causes for losses that hurt the savings and loan business in the 1980s," as compiled by Norman Strunk, former chief executive officer of the U.S. League, the largest savings and loan industry group in the United States, and Fred E. Case, Professor Emeritus at the Graduate School of Management of the University of California at Los Angeles.[11] This list[12] does not include a reference to the

---

[6] Most mortgage loans then in effect were not amortizing mortgages; the principal became payable on the due date. The borrower paid his monthly amount into a separate savings account and the association distributed dividends to the borrower's account. When the savings account balance plus dividends equaled the loan amount, the loan was cancelled and the borrower owned his home. A. B. Theobald, *Forty-Five Years on the Up Escalator*, 24-25 (1979). When an association failed, this had a tragic effect on the borrower, who still owed the entire amount of his mortgage, but might or might not recover the amounts paid into his savings account when the association was liquidated. *Id.*at 24. In addition, this system "padded" the balance sheet; its abandonment in favor of a system of applying all the payments by the borrower directly against the loan naturally caused a decrease in the assets of the association undergoing the change." *Id.*

[7] As a result, 1,700 savings institutions failed in the early years of the Depression. Adams and Peck, "The Federal Home Loan Banks and the Home Finance System," 43 *Business Law* 833, 835 (1988).

[8] 12 U.S.C. 1421, *et seq.* amended by Section 702 of FIRREA P.L. 101-73, 103 Stat. 183 (1989).

[9] 12 U.S.C. 1461, *et seq.* (1933) amended by Section 301 of FIRREA, P.L. 101-73, 103 Stat. 183 (1989).

[10] Formerly, 12 U.S.C. 1724, *et seq.* Repealed by § 407 of FIRREA, P.L. 101-73, 103 Stat. 183 (1989) effective August 9, 1989. See also § 401(a) (1) that abolished the Federal Savings and Loan Insurance Corporation, effective on the day of enactment of FIRREA.

[11] Editors' note: see appendix at the end of this chapter.

[12] Strunk and Case, *Where Deregulation Went Wrong: A Look at the Causes Behind Savings and Loan Failures in the 1980s*, 14-16 (U.S. League of Savings Institutions, 1988). Some of the causes stated in the list could be considered consequences, rather than primary causes. See, as examples, numbers 7, 8 and 9.

form of charter, mutual or stock, nor does it discuss the U.S. federal budget deficits and their consequences in the 1980s, two possible, additional causes that will be discussed in this paper.

This paper will indicate the perceptions of this "historian," who did not become familiar with the savings and loan industry until 1969, when he became General Counsel of the Federal Home Loan Bank Board and the Federal Savings and Loan Insurance Corporation in Washington, D.C., the federal regulator of and the federal insurer for most of the savings and loan industry in the United States.[13]

By 1969, the savings and loan associations were subject to some federal income taxation.[14] During many prior years, they were not, for the associations, particularly those in the majority which were mutual (no stockholder) form, were considered by many legislators as being "quasi-philanthropic" institutions, useful in implementing the twin social goals of savings and loan and home ownership spelled out in § 5(a) of the Home Owners' Loan Act of 1933.[15] Some of those same legislators appeared to believe that all savings and loan associations should make 25- and 30-year amortizing mortgage loans for low, fixed rates of interest (while permitting payoffs without penalties at the discretion of the borrowers), while paying even lower rates on passbook accounts to customers who, by custom and usage, could withdraw their funds at will and within days of depositing them.

This gave rise to the recognized weakness of savings and loan associations which borrowed short and loaned long. When interest rates were reasonably stable, when inflation was low and under control and when the depositors wittingly or unwittingly were agreeable to subsidizing housing finance by receiving low rates of interest (mandated in large part by federal statutes and regulations), this concept remained workable.

But when, in the late 1970s and early 1980s, the U.S. suffered double

---

[13] The Chairman of the Federal Home Loan Bank Board from 1969 until 1972 was Preston Martin, who also served as Vice Chairman of the Board of Governors of the Federal Reserve System from March 31, 1982, to April 30, 1986.

[14] Savings and loan associations first became subject to federal corporate income tax in 1951. Tax revisions in 1962 and 1969 further eroded the associations' heretofore exempt status. *Handbook of Savings and Loan Law* at 72-74. See also, Adams and Peck, "The Federal Home Loan Banks and the Home Finance System," 43 *Business Law* 833, 845 (1988) (describing how the "quasi-governmental nature" of the Federal Home Loan Banks renders them exempt from most state and local taxation (except surtaxes, estate, inheritance and gift taxes).

[15] 12 U.S.C. 1464(a), as amended by § 301 of FIRREA, P.L. 101-73, 103 Stat. 183 (1989).

digit inflation,[16] when interest rates rose and fell unpredictably[17] and by large percentages, when older savers, including people who expected to and, in fact, did live longer, had more money to save and were interested in maximizing return rather than subsidizing housing and when many savers desired higher rates of interest, regardless of whether the accounts were federally insured,[18] the savings and loan structure was no longer stable. In large part, the system became unworkable, despite attempted piecemeal legislative and regulatory "fixes."

Meanwhile, commercial banks were becoming more interested in acquiring the savings accounts and checking accounts of individuals, and were paying competitive rates to get them.[19] When non-federally insured money market or mutual funds paid even higher rates than savings and loans or commercial banks,[20] the savings and loan associations, to remain competitive, were forced to pay higher rates to their own depositors. In turn, they sought to make investments that provided higher (albeit somewhat riskier) rates of return. The legislative and regulatory framework, particularly in the 1980s, could not and did not accept this stress.

The mutual form of many savings and loan associations, as noted earlier in this paper,[21] was not a source of strength for long-term survival.[22] The

---

[16] In 1979 (11.3 percent), 1980 (13.5 percent) and 1981 (10.4 percent). Strunk and Case, *Where Deregulation Went Wrong: A Look at the Causes Behind Savings and Loan Failures in the 1980's*, 3 (U.S. League of Savings Institutions, 1988).

[17] The 90 day T-bill rate was 6.995 percent in June 1980 and was 16.295 percent in May 1981. The prime rate averaged 18.87 percent in 1981 with a high of 21.5 percent. *Id.*

[18] Mutual fund investment at the end of 1979 stood at $94.2 billion. Ten years later [1989], the industry is ten times as large, with total assets of $936.6 billion at the end of July, 1989. *Chicago Tribune* (September 11, 1989) at C3. There has been a "dramatic expansion in the number and types of funds available," *Id.* At the beginning of the decade, there were 524 funds with just under 10 million shareholder accounts. By contrast, in 1988, there were 2,718 funds with close to 55 million accounts. *Id.* It is believed that the 1980s mutual fund boom has gone "too far for too long" and represents only a temporary growth spurt. *Id.*

[19] Regulation Q limited the interest rate on commercial bank time and savings deposits to 3 percent from 1933-1962. Regulation Q became applicable to savings and loan associations and savings banks in 1966 but permitted them to pay 25-50 basis points more than commercial banks.

[20] See Footnote 17, *supra.*

[21] In the stock form of a savings association, shareholders contribute permanent capital in exchange for shares of stock which represent ownership interests in the association. In a mutual association, the customers lend capital to the association by placing funds in withdrawable savings accounts evidenced by a passbook or certificate. *Handbook of Savings and Loan Law*, at 12-14.

[22] When the Home Owners' Loan Act of 1933 (12 U.S.C. 1464, *et seq.* (1933) was enacted, virtually all savings institutions were organized in the mutual form, Williams, *Savings Institutions*, at § 7.01[1]. By 1973, approximately 88 percent of all savings and loan

mutual institution, which by definition could not sell stock or other equity securities, could increase its reserves (capital or net worth) only through net earnings.[23] As all savings and loan associations suffered through interest rate cycles that sometimes resulted in the payment of interest to depositors at rates higher than the average rate of return on mortgage loans, some of which had been made at low coupon rates years before, net earnings were not enough, and in some years did not exist.

After a number of false starts, the Federal Home Loan Bank Board in the mid-1970s permitted mutual associations to convert to the stock form, and approximately 727 associations of the total of 3,462[24] mutual federally-insured associations in the United States in 1975 did convert (see Table 1).[25] This paper is not the appropriate place to chronicle the history of such conversions, but conversions, when finally permitted, became time-consuming and expensive procedures, which benefited lawyers, accountants, investment bankers and others. The end result, for a time, was even beneficial to the savings and loan industry, but overall the benefits of conversion were too little, and came too late.[26]

---

associations in existence were mutuals. *Handbook of Savings and Loan Law* at 12. Currently, however, 68 percent of savings and loan assets are in the stock form. (This figure includes *de novo* stock associations.) Figures provided by L. Fleck, Deputy General Counsel, U.S. Office of Thrift Supervision, Washington, D.C.

Until the 1970's, only state-chartered savings associations were allowed to operate under the stock form of organization. Today [1989], however, existing federal associations may freely convert to stock form, and new federals may begin operations under a stock charter. United States League of Savings Institutions, *Savings Institutions Sourcebook* 6 (1988).

[23] In some instances, directors of mutual institutions were asked by regulatory authorities to pledge savings accounts. Except for newly-chartered institutions, in which the directors were the moving parties, directors typically were not willing to pledge their own savings accounts. If the capital of the institution increased, the accounts would be released to the directors, but if it did not, pledged deposits were lost.

[24] This figure includes 2,048 federally-chartered savings and loans plus 1,414 state-chartered associations. *Combined Financial Statements*, Office of Economic Research, Federal Home Loan Bank Board (1976) at 7-8. In addition, there were 616 state associations in the stock form. *Id.* at 9.

[25] See Leibold and Wilfand, *The Conversion Process; Mutual to Stock Savings and Loan Associations*, 30 *Business Law* 129, 130 (November 1974) (discussing test case conversions of the early 1970s).

[26] It may be necessary to convert many of the remaining mutual associations to the stock form in order to raise the capital required by FIRREA.

Table 1: Stock Conversions for Years 1975 to 1989

Year	Stock Conversions
1975	1
1976	14
1977	14
1978	5
1979	15
1980	16
1981	37
1982	31
1983	83
1984	96
1985	78
1986	86
1987	130
1988	98
1989	23

Source: L. Fleck, Deputy General Counsel, U.S. Office of Thrift Supervision, Washington, D.C.

The mutual form, with its absence of evaluation by equity owners based on earnings per share, its absence of required public disclosure and its lack of broad scale incentives to those who did not hold the accountholders' and borrowers' proxies, was not a business format for all seasons.[27] The mutual form did not encourage innovation nor did it attract innovators into the business. These characteristics, combined with the inability of mutual savings and loans to raise additional capital except through conversion to the stock form and retained earnings, handicapped many members of this segment of the industry during the 1970s and the 1980s.

This paper is not intended to be critical of all managers who used the mutual form; many had no alternative. Furthermore, as analysts survey the savings and loan failures of the l980s, they will find as many or more failures in number, and certainly in absolute size, in stock institutions. The stock format provided entry to a number of new investors and innovative managers, including some buccaneers, who will be referenced later in this paper.

Prior to the 1980s, when a savings and loan association got into financial difficulty, the federal regulators typically merged it into a healthy institution,

---

[27] Choice of format was not available in many states, even in the 1970s. In 1974, only 23 states in the United States permitted the chartering of new, stockholder-owned associations. That number increased substantially, however, in the mid- and late 1970s.

often with financial assistance from the Federal Savings and Loan Insurance Corporation (FSLIC).[28] In this type of transaction, the mutual form of charter was a benefit to the regulators, for there were no stockholders to complain about the lost value of their stock or to institute lawsuits against the regulators. Often there was no necessity for the appointment of a receiver, since the claims of all creditors were satisfied by the resulting institutions in the mergers.[29] When the FSLIC provided financial assistance for stock institutions, and this was virtually never done for the benefit of stockholders, the likelihood of a receiver was much higher. The overall policy purpose of these assisted mergers was the creation of a resulting, surviving institution which was viable and would not become another supervisory case within a short period of time.

President Reagan was sworn in January 1981, having campaigned against high federal budget deficits. These very large budget deficits would continue (see Table 2), and would, in fact, be exacerbated by federal income tax reforms that would decrease the maximum percentages[30] and the operation of "trickle down" or supply-side economics. Prior to FIRREA, FHLBB-FSLIC funds did not come from the U.S. Treasury but rather from: (1) examination fees from regulated institutions; (2) income from FSLIC invested funds; (3) yearly federal insurance premiums paid by insured associations;[31] and (4) assessments from the 12 Federal Home Loan Banks. Nonetheless, the expenditures of those non-Treasury funds were so-called "on line" budget items and, thus, increased the federal deficits when expended by the FSLIC in supervisory cases.

---

[28] 12 U.S.C. 1729 (now repealed by § 407 of FIRREA). Section 401(a) (1) of FIRREA abolished the Federal Savings and Loan Insurance Corporation.

[29] See, e.g., 12 C.F.R. 546.3 (stating that all the assets and property of the merging associations, as well as their liabilities, became the property of the resulting association).

[30] Tax reform in the 1980s began with the Economic Recovery Tax Act of 1981, P.L. 97-34, 95 Stat. 172 (1981), and the Tax Equity and Fiscal Responsibility Act of 1982, P.L. 97-248, 96 Stat. 324 (1982). There was further reform in 1984 with the Tax Reform Act of 1984, P.L. 98-369, 98 Stat. 494 §§ 5-1082 (1984), and again two years later with the Tax Reform Act of 1986, P.L. 99-514, 100 Stat. 2085 (1986).

[31] 12 U.S.C. 1727, now repealed by § 407 of FIRREA.

Table 2: Budget Deficit Figures for Years 1979 to 1988

Year	Deficit ($ billions)
1979	41
1980	74
1981	79
1982	128
1983	208
1984	185
1985	212
1986	221
1987	150
1988	155

Source: Congressional Budget Office

The Administration chose not to expend sufficient FSLIC funds to resolve the early 1980s supervisory cases. These cases in great part resulted from associations paying high interest rates to current depositors, while collecting lower interest rates on long-term mortgages in portfolios (and surviving or not surviving the consequences of 8.5 percent usury statutes in states such as Illinois and New York). Instead, the Administration, through the FHLBB and FSLIC: (1) urged greater investment powers for savings and loan associations which, arguably, would increase their net income (such authorities were provided by the Garn-St Germain legislation of 1982);[32] (2) provided, by regulation, accounting procedures or practices, called RAP accounting,[33] which differed from generally accepted accounting principles and which tended to hide or mask the true accounting and financial status, as well as the limited reserves, of institutions; (3) invited new investors in

---

[32] Garn-St Germain Depository Institutions Act of 1982, P.L. 97-320, 96 Stat. 1469 (1982).

[33] One example of such accounting practices was the permission to associations to defer losses, upon the sale of mortgages and other assets, over a period of time such as the expected life of the mortgages. 12 C.F.R. 563c.14 (1981) amended by 54 F.R. 34148 (August 18, 1989). The theory upon which this deferral was based was that the sale proceeds would be reinvested in higher earning assets. A substantial amount of the proceeds was invested in commercial real estate loans in areas such as Texas which later had a severe real estate depression or in high coupon mortgage-backed securities which, contrary to the expectations of the investors, paid off quickly when interest rates dropped and the holders of the high interest rate collateral mortgages paid them off. The associations which did this, mostly mutual (GAAP did not allow the deferral), were inhibited from converting thereafter to the stock form because of the necessity for using GAAP accounting during and after the conversion.
This program, actively pushed by the Federal Home Loan Bank Board, was a disaster. When the Congress passed FIRREA, it ignored deferred loan losses which are intangible assets. A number of institutions are or will be insolvent as a consequence of their inability to count these RAP "assets."

savings and loans to provide funds, in limited amounts, to add capital to supervisory cases on the theory that a savings and loan institution charter was as valuable or more so than a commercial bank charter; (4) used optimistic FSLIC financial scenarios to indicate that the structured acquisitions and mergers of supervisory cases would be less expensive to FSLIC than liquidation with the resulting payment of insurance to accountholders, or alternatives requiring more financial assistance;[34] and (5) merged multiple supervisory cases into one institution on a phoenix concept,[35] which seldom resulted in anything of substance rising from the ashes, and which on its face violated the axiom that the whole is no larger than the sum of its parts.

Unfortunately, as the 1980s passed, the prospective cost of resolving the problem of supervisory cases (phoenix associations and many others) became larger and larger, in the context of a policy of benign neglect referred to in part as "deregulation" of the savings and loan industry. The situation became worse, but neither national political party appeared willing to do much, if anything, about it.

The Republican Party controlled the White House and the Federal Home Loan Bank Board; the Democrats, after 1986, controlled both houses of Congress. But even in the 1988 Presidential election, neither party wanted to throw stones at the other on the subject of the savings and loan industry for fear, one could suggest, that the opposing party would direct an accusatory

---

[34] FHLBB selected June 1, 1981 as the dividing point between expensive FSLIC contribution agreements and much less costly agreements under new theories and procedures. Statement of Richard T. Pratt on H.R. 5568 before the Subcommittee on Housing and Community Development of the Senate Committee on Banking, Finance and Urban Affairs, March 24, 1982; The FSLIC – Yesterday, Today and Tomorrow; Remarks by H. Brent Beesley at the 49th Annual Stockholders Meeting of the Federal Home Loan Bank of Chicago, April 12, 1982. See *infra*, note 36 (noting that the use of the phoenix institution helped the regulators buy time to find other solutions rather than liquidating failed institutions and subsequently paying out insurance to accountholders).

[35] The phoenix concept was utilized by FSLIC to combine one or more distressed savings and loans into a single operating unit which could then be rehabilitated or merged, (41 *Savings and Loans*, 261 (BNA) (August 22, 1983)) with FSLIC then infusing capital into the phoenix institution. 40 *Savings and Loans*, 85 (BNA) (January 17, 1983). The phoenixes were established as a last priority, "when no other institution could be found to merge with or acquire a failing savings and loan and the only alternative would have been liquidation." *Id.* This policy demonstrated the Administration's policy of avoiding the political and financial costs of paying out insurance to accountholders. It cost FSLIC 60 percent to 80 percent less in dealing with failing institutions between March, 1981 and January, 1983. *Id.* There was a middle ground, however, between paying insurance of accounts and creating a phoenix association, that is, contributing sufficient capital to create one or more viable institutions. Critics of the phoenix concept argued that, at best, the regulators were buying time. According to Kenneth A. Randall, former FDIC Chairman, "[t]he bird the regulators are creating is not a phoenix; it's a turkey." *American Banker*, 2 (April 16, 1982).

finger.

In 1984, Congressman St Germain scheduled hearings on the savings and loan industry. Its problems were already quite apparent, although not of the magnitude they would later achieve, but after testimony was prepared by various witnesses, including this writer, the Congressman called off the hearings. He didn't say why.

Referring back to the methodology of the Administration and the Federal Home Loan Bank Board in the early 1980s, it included inviting entrepreneurs, both individual and corporate, to invest in savings and loan supervisory cases. A number of such investors – potential pillagers – accepted the invitation and turned small, local savings and loan institutions into huge, multi-million, even billion dollar associations that ostensibly made profits, *inter alia*, by making commercial loans on real estate developments and taking the front end points into income. Some associations also invested, primarily under state law, in activities of questionable propriety for savings and loan institutions. In part because of recessions in oil and gas producing areas of the country, in part because of depressions in real estate values, and in part because of mismanagement, conflicts of interest and unparalleled avarice, a number of these savings and loan institutions, swollen in size, ultimately became hopelessly insolvent.[36]

When these occurrences were superimposed on an industry that was barely competitive with other financial intermediaries because of the lending long characteristic, which in part was in a business form unsuited to the times, and which had suffered from inadequate supervision, the lack of adequate federal financial support, and unsuitable alternatives for eight years, it was not surprising that there were serious savings and loan problems in 1989, that not only should have been recognized years before but about which something should have and could have been done.

So, in 1989, the Bush Administration and the Congress have come to the rescue of the savings and loan industry – after the election – in a form that has been termed a "bailout." What have they done?

The regulatory structure has been changed. The Federal Home Loan Bank Board no longer exists (it has been abolished, with an effective date no later than October 9, 1989), but its former Chairman, one of three former

---

[36] In addition, there have been recent allegations that organized crime looted savings associations and used savings and loans to launder money. *The Washington Post*, Sept. 7, 1989, F2, Col. 1. It has been estimate[d] that up to half of the S&L losses were the result of fraud." *Id.* This writer believes that such an estimate is much too high.

members, is now the Director of the new Office of Thrift Supervision.[37] That Office, with many of the same employees, will regulate and supervise both federally-chartered and state-chartered savings and loan associations.[38] The Office of Thrift Supervision (OTS) is not an independent agency but rather is an "office," subject to the "general oversight" of the Secretary of the Treasury.[39]

The federal insurance fund for savings and loans has been moved from the control of the FHLBB, and its successor agency, OTS, to the Federal Deposit Insurance Corp.[40] (FDIC), and that agency now will insure the accounts of both commercial banks and savings and loans, with a bifurcated fund that will have for some years a different premium structure, depending upon commercial bank or savings and loan charter.[41] The FDIC Board has been expanded from three to five members, one of whom is the Director of the OTS.[42]

The FSLIC has been abolished, as of August 9, 1989.[43] The functions of the FSLIC have been divided among and between the FDIC, the Resolution Trust Corp. (RTC) and the FSLIC Resolution Fund. The RTC,[44] subject to the regulation of an Oversight Board, is authorized to liquidate savings associations that were insured by the FSLIC and have been or will be placed into receivership or conservatorship on and after January 1, 1989, and ending three years after the enactment of FIRREA.[45] A corporation called the Resolution Funding Corporation will raise the funds to assist the RTC to liquidate those savings and loans.[46]

If the savings and loan receivership or conservatorship predates January 1, 1989, the FSLIC Resolution Fund apparently handles such entities.[47] The Fund is not a government agency. It is to be "managed" by the FDIC, but it is

---

[37] Section 301 of FIRREA; § 3 of the Home Owners' Loan Act of 1933, as amended.

[38] Section 301 of FIRREA; § 4 of the Home Owners' Loan Act of 1933, as amended.

[39] Section 301 of FIRREA; § 3 of the Home Owners' Loan Act of 1933, as amended.

[40] Section 205 of FIRREA; § 4 of the FDI Act, 12 U.S.C. 1814(a).

[41] Sections 208 and 211 of FIRREA; § 7 of the FDI Act, 12 U.S.C. 1817, and § 11(a) of the FDI Act, 12 U.S.C. 1821(a).

[42] Section 203 of FIRREA; § 2 of the FDI Act, 12 U.S.C. 1812.

[43] Section 401(a) of FIRREA.

[44] Section 501 of FIRREA; new § 21A of the Federal Home Loan Bank Act, 12 U.S.C. 1421, *et seq.*

[45] Ibid. [Eds: The RTC did not go out of business until December 31, 1995.]

[46] Section 511 of FIRREA; new § 21B of the Federal Home Loan Bank Act, 12 U.S.C. 1421, *et seq.*

[47] Section 215 of FIRREA; 12 U.S.C. 1821; new § 11A of the FDI Act. The RTC would not have jurisdiction under § 501 of FIRREA.

to be separately maintained and its assets are not to be commingled with those of the FDIC.[48]

This is one example of why the statutory language may have to be amended. The statute does not indicate whether the assets and liabilities of numerous receiverships in which the FSLIC has been receiver are transferred to the Fund and, even if they are, the recipient of the assets and liabilities, the Fund, is not a government corporation but rather a "fund." This is similar to contributing money to someone's trouser pocket, rather than to the individual, and indicating that the owner of the trousers may not commingle those funds with his funds. Who owns the fund and who may proceed in court based on this legislative construct is unclear.

Returning to agency structure, the 12 Federal Home Loan Banks no longer will be under the control of the three members of the FHLBB but rather under the control of a five-person agency called the Federal Housing Finance Board.[49]

Within six months of the enactment of FIRREA, the Federal Home Loan Mortgage Corporation (Freddie Mac), formerly under the direction of the Federal Home Loan Bank Board, will be under the direction of a Board of Directors of 18 members, five of whom are appointed by the President of the United States and 13 of whom will be elected by the stockholders of Freddie Mac.[50] The Secretary of the Department of Housing and Urban Development will have general regulatory authority over Freddie Mac, including the aggregate amount of cash dividends on its common stock.[51]

In the FIRREA competition between the various arms of the Federal Government, the winners were the Department of the Treasury, the Department of Housing and Urban Affairs and the FDIC. The successor to the FHLBB, that is, the OTS, has much less total authority than its predecessor within the U.S. Government, but it retains and has received even more power over individual savings and loan associations.[52] Whereas there had been

---

[48] FIRREA specifically indicates in new § 11A(2)(A) of the FDI Act:
"(A) In General - Except as provided in Section 21A of the Federal Home Loan Bank Act [applicable to RTC and its Oversight Board], all assets and liabilities of the Federal Savings and Loan Insurance Corporation on the day before the date of enactment of the [FIRREA] shall be transferred to the FSLIC Resolution Fund." (§ 215 of FIRREA)

[49] Section 702 of FIRREA; new § 2A of the Federal Home Loan Bank Act, 12 U.S.C. 1421.

[50] Section 731 of FIRREA; § 301 of the Federal Home Loan Mortgage Corporation Act, 12 U.S.C. 1451.

[51] Section 731 of FIRREA; § 303 of the Federal Home Loan Mortgage Corporation Act, 12 U.S.C. 1451, *et seq.*

[52] Section 301 of FIRREA; 12 U.S.C. 1461, *et seq.*

questions about the FHLBB's power over some aspects of the operations and particularly the investments of state-chartered but federally-insured savings and loan associations (the authority over which came through the FHLBB's direction of the FSLIC, the deposits insurer), FIRREA provided very substantial power, directly and indirectly, over the operations, investments and supervision of state-chartered associations.[53]

What are some of the practical consequences of this legislation over what remains of the savings and loan industry?[54]

(1) The funding requirements of the legislation will be a substantial burden on the earnings of the 12 Federal Home Loan Banks.[55] Thus, savings and loan associations, all of which are members of the System, will receive smaller dividends on their stock investments in the Federal Home Loan Banks, thereby decreasing their net income.

(2) The FDIC and the RTC (including its Oversight Board) may find that there are not a huge number of potential acquirers willing to invest substantial funds to obtain savings and loan franchises. Because of the number of institutions already in receivership and conservatorship[56] and the number of institutions that do not and cannot obtain adequate capital to satisfy the minimum FIRREA statutory capital requirements,[57] the supply of franchises may exceed the acquirers in the short run.

(3) There will be numerous real estate transactions with RTC and other agencies, if the price is right. However, in certain areas of the country such as Texas, Arizona, Louisiana and Oklahoma,

---

[53] See the supervisory authority provided to the Office of Thrift Supervision by Title IX of FIRREA. See also the definition of "savings association" as contained in § 2(4) of the Home Owners' Loan Act of 1933, as amended by § 301 of FIRREA.

[54] Less than 3,000 associations, including those in receivership and conservatorship, remain. There were over 4,000 federally insured savings and loans in 1975 and approximately the same number at year end 1980.

[55] Section 721 of FIRREA. Income from the Banks will be used for the Affordable Housing Program and the Resolution Funding Corporation.

[56] As of September 15, 1989, there were 257 associations in conservatorship.

[57] As of September 15, 1989, the amount of such capital requirements was uncertain. Because the statute (§ 301 of FIRREA; § 5(f) of the Home Owners' Loan Act of 1933, as amended) requires three different types of capital, that is, core, tangible and risk-based, and all of the measurements are related to requirements of the Comptroller of the Currency for commercial banks, requirements formulated for different business entities, translating commercial bank requirements into a construct for savings and loan associations is not easy. The risk-based requirements present the most problems, for the banking regulators have not determined a minimum level, as of September 15, 1989.

the amount of real estate available and the severely depressed state of the market may encourage some purchasers to wait out the agencies, hoping for even lower prices.

(4) The incorporation of commercial banking capital standards (risk-based capital) may result in an even higher level of capital for savings and loans than expected by the Congress.[58] As noted above, Congress may have to revisit this legislation soon, and it should necessitate more than mere "technical corrections."

(5) The Congressional attack on the intangible asset of goodwill has had and will have unforeseen consequences. The Congressional debates over goodwill clearly indicated that goodwill would not be counted[59] in the tangible capital requirement of 1.5 percent of assets. Even for the three percent core (or leverage) capital requirement, only part of it (50 percent) could be satisfied by supervisory goodwill.[60]

But what had not been trumpeted was the fact that when Congress borrowed from the commercial banks and its regulator (the Comptroller of the Currency), the limitations on loans to one borrower, that is, 15 percent of "unimpaired capital and

---

[58] See Footnote 56, *supra*.

[59] Section 301 of FIRREA; § 5(t) of the Home Owners' Loan Act, as amended.

[60] Goodwill became a "whipping boy" for the Congress during the debates and discussions about FIRREA. Up to that time, goodwill was an appropriate asset under GAAP. For example, if association X acquired the stock of association Y and paid 1.50 times book, the .50 was treated as an asset of the acquirer, that is, goodwill.

In the early 1980's when the FSLIC did not have sufficient funds or chose as a government policy not to spend them because of federal deficits, persons, companies and other savings and loans acquired supervisory cases and received no financial assistance or financial assistance in an amount less than the difference between the then market value and historical book value of assets (liabilities also were valued but often were not a significant factor). This goodwill could be written off over 25 years (under GAAP) and sometimes longer under RAP. It was not an earning asset, it was not a tangible asset, but it was a valid asset under GAAP. (When interest rates were very high—much higher than coupon rates on mortgages, mortgage-backed bonds and U.S. Treasury bonds—the difference between historical book and market became a quite substantial figure, some of which could not have been satisfied with financial assistance. For example, to finance "underwater" treasuries with financial assistance probably would have been inappropriate.)

Under FIRREA, this goodwill, supervisory and non-supervisory, has been labeled a very bad asset not includable for tangible and only partly for risk-based and core capital. Time reaction of the members of Congress and the press was of great interest and was a 1989 example of the potential of propaganda.

There probably will be a number of lawsuits, in addition to the one referred to in footnote 62 of this paper, by institutions which believe strongly, and in this writer's opinion, properly, that the U.S. Government abrogated contracts with them and took their property without due process of law, contrary to provisions in the U.S. Constitution.

unimpaired surplus," goodwill probably could not be counted in these touchstone terms;[61] thus a number of associations, already being punished by Congress for doing the Federal Government a favor in the 1980s by taking over supervisory cases and receiving supervisory goodwill, were further being punished by limiting their loans to one borrower in many instances to no more than $500,000.[62] Some associations which had very substantial regulatory (and GAAP) capital prior to August 9, 1989, and had made safe and appropriate commercial loans and real estate development loans, in effect now were out of those markets.

(6) Many associations, which used service corporation subsidiaries to engage in profitable activities while protecting the parent association from potential liability, find they now have substantial impediments to continuing those activities.[63] Whereas, prior to August 9, 1989, loans by the parent to the service corporations were not limited by the loans to one borrower regulation (§563.9-3(a)(2)(ii) of the Insurance Regulations), no such exception was included in § 5(u) of the Home Owners' Loan Act, as amended by FIRREA.[64]

Subject to special FDIC dispensations, after January 1, 1990 the service corporations of state-chartered associations may not engage in any activities in which the service corporations of federally-chartered associations may not engage.[65] Thus, state-

---

[61] This rubric already was applicable to commercial loans made by savings and loans, pursuant to the Garn-St Germain legislation, but the Federal Home Loan Bank Board adopted a broad definition of "unimpaired capital and unimpaired surplus," in § 563.9-3(a)(4) of the FSLIC regulations. Stricter conformity to the Comptroller of the Currency's regulations almost certainly will be required under FIRREA, particularly on the goodwill component. The Bank Board's definition, which still remains in effect until modification, reads as follows: "(4) *Unimpaired capital and unimpaired surplus.* The term "unimpaired capital and unimpaired surplus" means regulatory capital plus specific reserves for loan losses, less appraised equity capital."

[62] The Long Island Savings Bank has sued the appropriate agencies of the U.S. Government contending that the FIRREA legislation on the issue of goodwill is an abrogation of its contract and is a taking, contrary to the due process clause of the U.S. Constitution. Long Island Savings Bank F.S.B. v. Federal Savings and Loan Insurance Corp., CV-89-2699 (E.D.N.Y. August 25, 1989). See, 53 *Banking Rpt.* 274 (BNA) (1989). [See the discussion of the supervisory goodwill cases in the 2002 Epilogue to this paper.]

[63] See 12 C.F.R. 545.75 for a list of approved activities for service corporations of federally-chartered associations.

[64] Section 301 of FIRREA.

[65] Section 222 of FIRREA; § 28(g) (1) and § 28(a) of the FDI Act. See also § 28(b) of the FDI Act.

chartered associations which owned certain types of insurance companies, as well as many other companies with activities not on the federal permitted activity "list," probably will have to divest those service corporation subsidiaries. The end result of divestiture was contemplated by the Congress, but the procedures for and possible losses as a consequence of divestiture probably were not foreseen.

(7) The Congress must have foreseen the primary consequence of requiring savings and loan associations to divest all "junk bond" holdings, i.e., savings and loans no longer could own junk bonds.[66] Whether this was a good approach, and whether the associations' replacement investments (theoretically at a lower rate of return to maintain or increase their capital with less risk) can bring in a sufficient net return is highly debatable.

When one analyzes the required and higher (70 percent) qualified savings and loan lender test, lower returns from investment in Federal Home Loan Bank stock, the inability to invest in junk bonds, the lower loans to one borrower limitation (in some cases, no more than $500,000), the more limited investment authority in service corporations, and the limitations on investments in non-residential real estate loans (4 times capital for federal associations—if capital consisted of goodwill, 4 times 0 is 0), one can only conclude that Congress was picturing the idyllic savings and loan of the 1950s making single family dwelling loans and being the subject matter of more Jimmy Stewart movies.

That dream, if it existed, is a bad dream. If the industry wasn't competitive in the 1970s, it is not going to be more competitive in the 1990s by removing all of the aforementioned mechanisms for earning greater income. That does not mean a substantial number of institutions won't survive —many will, if they enter the 1990s with a high percentage of capital.

But the good fortune of some (and some of those associations may be fortunate because they simply ignored the changes in the industry in the 1970s and 1980s) will not resolve the problems of the hundreds of associations that don't have sufficient capital.

Under FIRREA, commercial banks and commercial bank holding companies will be able to acquire healthy savings and loans and either hold them separately or, under some circumstances, merge them into the commercial banks. This had been permitted prior to FIRREA only with reference to savings and loan supervisory cases. This authority, as well as

---

[66] Section 301 of FIRREA; § 5(d) of the Home Owners' Loan Act.

savings and loan demand deposit authority identical to that of commercial banks, were two of the few additions provided by FIRREA that some commentators would consider benefits or potential benefits to savings and loans.

There is no ability, however, to control a mutual institution until it converts to the stock form. Such control of a converted association typically is not permitted without OTS prior approval for three years after conversion unless the mutual association was a supervisory case and is converted pursuant to a voluntary supervisory conversion or modified conversion. In such conversions, the acquirer agrees with the federal regulators to invest a pre-determined amount of capital, and those levels have not yet been published in the post-FIRREA atmosphere.

What will be the short-term and long-term effect of FIRREA on the financing of housing in the United States? In the short run, the legislation may make more funding available for housing because of the limitations on the size and types of other loans described in this paper. Many savings and loans, desirous of making other types of loans, may not be permitted to do so by loans-to-one-borrower limitations, their capital posture and the qualified savings and loan lender test. Even acquiring mortgage-backed securities may not be an alternative because of accounting regulations already adopted by the OTS whose effective date has been postponed until January 1990. Such regulations could require "mark to market" of such securities, but would not be applicable to mortgage loans.

The longer term effect on housing finance, however, should be analyzed in depth, and there is a question whether the Congress did that in passing FIRREA. The Congress was most interested in protecting depositors and the federal insurance fund—they were interested in savings. But home loans are also an objective of savings and loans in the United States. Whether home ownership was a long-term beneficiary of the new legislation remains to be seen as more savings and loan associations are sold or go into conservatorship or receivership.

EPILOGUE

This country and the savings and loan industry now are 13 years into the "future," past the passage and effective date of FIRREA – August 9, 1989 – and after the preparation and delivery on September 9, 1989 of this paper in Strasbourg at a meeting of the International Bar Association, Business Law Section. Some of the consequences of FIRREA now are readily perceived.

(1)   The Resolution Trust Corporation (RTC) handled hundreds of savings and loan receiverships (approximately 747 during 1989-1995). Billions of dollars of assets of those savings and loans were sold (approximately $455 billion of a total of $465 billion), and hundreds of lawsuits were instituted against former officers and directors of savings and loans, as well as against law firms and accounting firms. The RTC went out of business on December 31, 1995, and most of its responsibilities as well as its assets were taken over by the FDIC.[67]

This writer has not yet seen an objective analysis of what the RTC accomplished and what it did not. Its press releases and semi-annual reports, if believed, indicated that overall it did a wonderful job, including an efficient costs/benefits ratio. The true picture very likely is less rosy, but space prevents this author from additional analyses at this time.

(2)   Lawsuits against the Federal Government, as a result of the FIRREA change in the treatment of supervisory goodwill as capital, continue on. Approximately 120 such suits have been instituted; approximately 100 remain pending. After the early decisions of the Court of Federal Claims, the U.S. Court of Appeals for the Federal Circuit, and the U.S. Supreme Court[68] held that FIRREA resulted in breaches of contract and, as a consequence, Federal Government liability, optimism ran high about many millions, even billion dollar recoveries. The potential recovery by plaintiffs has been estimated to be a maximum of $20 billion. Today, as decisions of the Court of Federal Claims and the Federal Court of Appeals on damages have been handed down, some of the early victories may have been pyrrhic. One settled case has resulted in a plaintiff receiving money; ten cases have been tried and are on appeal. Thus, most of the cases are not over. Possibly 13 years from now, the final chapter on the goodwill cases, resulting from FIRREA, can be written.

---

[67] See FDIC, Managing the Crisis: The FDIC and RTC Experience, Chapter Eighteen - Epilogue, p. 207.

[68] See the important case of Winstar Corp. v. U.S., 994 F.2d 797 (Fed. Cir. 1993), decision vacated by court *en bamic*, 64 F, 3d 1531 (1995), affirmed and remanded, 518 U.S. 839, 135 L. Ed. 2d, 964, 116 S. Ct. 2432 (1996).

(3)   The Office of Thrift Supervision (OTS) remains with us, but rumors continue to circulate that it will be merged into – absorbed by – the Office of the Comptroller of the Currency (OCC). Since the OCC also is an Office within the Department of the Treasury, such an absorption very likely could be handled fairly easily. The number of employees at OTS has decreased, and reductions in forces (RIFs) continue.

OTS had no permanent Director for five years, from December 4, 1992, until October 28, 1997. For almost four of those years, one of the Office of Supervision staffers, Jonathan Fiechter, was an "Acting Director," based on delegations of authority issued by OTS Director Ryan. Thereafter, from October 10, 1996 until October 1997, Nicolas Retsinas from HUD acted as the non-permanent Director. Finally, on October 28, 1997, Ellen Seidman was sworn in as the Director of OTS, after having been confirmed by the Senate. On November 28, 2001, post the 2000 election, James F. Gilleran was confirmed as the new Director of OTS and currently holds that position.

Why was there no permanent Director of OTS for years? Very likely because neither political party wanted a confirmation fight, just a few years after the savings and loan crisis surfaced. Having no Director, however, did not enhance the prestige of the Office of Thrift Supervision.

It also created legal issues about some of the quasi-judicial actions of the "Acting Director."[69]

(4)   The drive by the FHLBB/FSLIC staff in the late 1980s for mark-to-market accounting for certain savings and loan assets – but not real estate loans – has never resulted in a comprehensive final agency regulation. If such a regulation were adopted for all savings and loan assets – or even for certain categories of assets – many or most savings and loans

---

[69] See Doolin Savings Bank v. OTS, 139 F. 3d 203 (D.C. Cir., 1998); petitioner Recall of the Mandate, 156 F. 3d 190 (D.C. Cir. 1998). See also United Savings Association of Texas, OTS Order No, AP 95-40 (Dec. 26, 1995) presently before the OTS Director on Exceptions to the Recommended Decision (in favor of respondents on all claims) of Arthur Shipe, dated September 12, 2001. Both cases involve the authority of Jonathan Fiechter to institute cease and desist actions.

would be insolvent during periods of rising interest rates. Even rules applicable to savings and loans that act as "dealers" in certain securities have interpretive problems, as well as financial consequences.

(5)   The participation of the Reagan Administration in the savings and loan crisis, with its emphasis on budgetary consequences of potential FSLIC actions, has been recognized but not discussed in any detail.[70]

(6)   The junk bond market has had its ups and its downs since 1989 and FIRREA, but by no means can be classified as the great danger portrayed by Congress in FIRREA. As a consequence of FIRREA, however, and its requirement that high yield bonds no longer be held by savings and loans, purchasers of the bonds from savings and loans – sold off at fire sale prices – made multiple fortunes in the early 1990s.

(7)   The number of savings and loan associations has decreased dramatically since 1989. As of December 31, 2001, there were 1,019 savings and loan associations in the United States, down from over 3,000 in 1989. Receiverships, resulting in part from the higher capital requirements of FIRREA, as well as substantial modifications about what could be counted as capital (e.g., supervisory goodwill), brought about a large diminution in the absolute number of savings and loans. The "black spot" of being called a "savings and loan association" brought about conversions of savings and loan charters to commercial bank charters. Charter characteristics also were relevant to such conversions from savings and loan to commercial bank charters. There also were a substantial number of mergers of savings and loans between 1989 and 2002.

(8)   Mutual savings and loan associations have continued to convert from the mutual to stock form, although the timing of such conversions usually is keyed to the vitality of the stock market. From 1989 through 2001, 640 more mutual

---

[70] See Lawrence J. White, *The S&L Debacle: Public Policy Lessons for Bank and Thrift Regulation,* pp. 136-137, and unpublished speech of Thomas Vartanian, former FHLBB/FSLIC General Counsel, given on September 21, 1990, at the meeting of Committee U, Business Law Section, International Bar Association in New York, New York.

associations were converted to stock form (1,344 such conversions since 1975). As of December 31, 2001, of a total of 1,019 associations, 397 remained mutually chartered. As of the same date, of total assets of $978 billion, only $64.6 billion were assets of mutually-chartered associations.

(9)   The share of the home mortgage origination by savings and loans dropped dramatically in the 1990s. Whereas savings and loan associations originated 50 percent of home loans in 1980, its share was 42 percent in 1988, and by 1991 it had dropped to 25 percent. By 1997, that percentage had dropped again to 18 percent.

The remaining percent of home mortgages, as of 1997, were made as follows:

Mortgage Companies:	56 percent
Commercial Banks:	25 percent
Others, including Credit Unions:	1 percent

Based on information supplied by the National Association of Mortgage Bankers, approved applications to the various types of financial institutions support the above data. The statistics for loan approvals for the years 1993 and 1999 were as follows (Table 3):

Table 3: Approved Mortgage Applications by Financial Institution Type

Year	Type of Business	Amount of Loans ($billions)
1993	Savings and Loans	503
1999		583
1993	Mortgage Companies	1,252
1999		2,407
1993	Commercial Banks	613
1999		927
1993	Credit Unions	25
1999		68

Source: National Association of Mortgage Bankers

(10)   The mutual fund industry has continued to grow. As of December 31, 2001, its assets approximated $7 trillion dollars, seven times the assets of the savings and loan industry.[71] Money Market Funds, arguably more comparable to savings and loan deposits, totaled $2.3 trillion as of December 31, 2001.

(11)   FIRREA has not been revisited in detail post-August 9, 1989. There have been some amendments, including "clarifying" the status of the FSLIC Resolution Fund, but a detailed overhaul may have remained during the 1990s a potato too hot to handle.

---

[71] Investment Company Institute, *2002 Mutual Fund Book* (May 2002).

CONCLUSION

The savings and loan industry has decreased in numbers substantially since 1989. As of June 30, 2002, the number of savings and loans in the U.S. fell below 1,000. The number, including savings and loans which were not federally insured, totaled almost 4,800 to 4,994 in 1969 and exceeded 3,000 in 1989. The mutual segment of the industry now is only 39 percent of all associations, and only 6.6 percent of total assets.

The housing market, however, has not been appreciably injured by the decrease in the number of savings and loan associations. Other lenders have filled the gap as indicated by Table 3 above.

Many potential savings and loan depositors have selected money market and mutual funds, and that industry, not directly related to the financing of housing, has grown to $7 trillion, seven times its size in 1989. Federal insurance of accounts no longer appears to be a substantial factor for many potential depositors who want to "invest" their finds.

What was the cost to the taxpayers of the savings and loan crisis or debacle? I don't know, and I question if anyone does. Figures such as $150 billion are used, but they are not broken down. Until the supervisory goodwill cases discussed above are settled or come to final judgments, no total figure properly can be determined. As noted above, approximately $20 billion may be involved in those cases.

I don't believe there is any doubt that the taxpayer direct cost would have been – could have been – much lower if federal action had been taken earlier, that is, in the 1980's, rather than waiting until August of 1989, when the FIRREA legislation took effect.

Attempting to obtain hard figures on the ultimate cost of an individual savings and loan receivership is very frustrating. Whether proceeding under the federal Freedom of Information Act or under a specific provision of FIRREA (e.g., 12 U.S.L § 182l(d)(15)), the figures obtained from the agencies, particularly the FDIC, are close to useless. This writer has been advised also that the agency receivers are not required to issue financial statements about savings and loan receiverships and if they are prepared, they need not follow GAAP.

Misinformation continues to be supplied to the press by the agencies. *The Wall Street Journal* of April 10, 2002, in an article headed "Deals That Took Enron Under Had Many Supporters," indicated that the "amount of the federal [savings and loan] bailout" was $2 billion for CenTrust Federal Savings Bank of Miami. Considering the amounts of settlements and judgments, including those from Drexel Burnham Lambert, law firms, accounting firms and officers and directors, as well as the liquidation of that association's assets, the correct figure is nowhere close to $2 billion and might properly be a positive figure.

Prior to the February 1990 appointment of the RTC as receiver of CenTrust, Great Western offered an amount of money for approximately one-half of CenTrust's branches, an amount which was very close to what Great Western paid post-receivership for all of CenTrust's offices and other assets as well as its deposit liabilities. OTS would not approve the proposed pre-receivership transaction, for reasons best known to it, and that decision ultimately was very costly to the U.S. taxpayers.[72]

When one compares, however, the potential total taxpayer cost of the savings and loan crisis to the losses to all entities resulting from the Enron, WorldCom, accounting firms, and other similar debacles in 2002, the cost of resolving the savings and loan crisis pales by comparison.

Reactive legislation, arguably somewhat comparable to provisions in FIRREA, was enacted into law on July 30, 2002 (Sarbanes-Oxley Act of 2002; P.L. 107-204). Many of the provisions are directed at punishing those who have caused or participated in accounting fraud and other "book cooking" conduct. This legislation, prepared and enacted in a hurry and directed in part at political favor, may be no more effective than various punitive provisions of FIRREA. Legislation, post-animal departure, does relatively little for the barn door.

The current voluminous media coverage of the Enron, WorldCom, Arthur Anderson and similar matters also would remind survivors of the savings and loan debacle of media coverage during the late 1980s and 1990s. Based on historical precedent, the media very likely will lose interest rather soon and will go on to the next "hot" issue.

The savings and loan debacle was not as large as some members of the media, in the post-1989 period, would have us believe. It was, however, by no means insignificant. Theft and insider dealings were not nearly as large a component of the loss as some reporters and book authors suggested in contemporaneous publications.

Federal budget deficits, which were very relevant in the mid-1980s to the federal administration's policy on the treatment of savings and loans, as well as to federal tax cuts, have resurfaced as issues. An expected federal budget

---

[72] Editors' Note: CenTrust is included in the case studies in this volume.

surplus of $150 billion for fiscal year 2002 now is expected to be a deficit of $165 billion. Although the OMB contends that only 15 percent of the deterioration in the expected 10-year surplus is attributable to the 2001 federal tax cut, the Center on Budget and Policy Priorities estimated that 40 percent is the proper figure.[73] The advocates of "trickle down" economics and tax cuts at any cost do not appear to learn very much from prior experience, including the experience of the alleged "tax reforms" of the 1980s.

Do we learn by experience, from the experiences of the savings and loan crisis or other crises? One cannot answer a resounding yes.

---

[73] Paul Krugman, *New York Times* op-ed, p. A23 (July 30, 2002). See also Paul Krugman, *New York Times* op-ed, p. A10 (August 6, 2002). OMB apparently retracted its July 12, 2002, press release and its 15 percent assessment.

APPENDIX: 15 MAJOR CAUSES FOR LOSSES THAT HURT THE SAVINGS AND LOAN BUSINESS IN THE 1980S

Source: Strunk and Case, *Where Deregulation Went Wrong: A Look at the Causes Behind Savings and Loan Failures* in the 1980s, 14-16 (U.S. League of Savings Institutions, 1988).

1. Lack of net worth for many institutions as they entered the 1980s, and a wholly inadequate net worth regulation.

2. Decline in the effectiveness of Regulation Q in preserving the spread between the cost of money and the rate of return on assets, basically stemming from inflation and the accompanying increase in market interest rates.

3. Absence of an ability to vary the return on assets with increases in the rate of interest required to be paid for deposits.

4. Increased competition on the deposit gathering and mortgage origination sides of the business, with a sudden burst of new technology making possible a whole new way of conducting financial institutions generally and the mortgage business specifically.

5. A rapid increase in investment powers of associations with passage of the Depository Institutions Deregulation and Monetary Control Act (and the Garn-St Germain Act, and, more important, through state legislative enactments in a number of important and rapidly growing states. These introduced new risks and speculative opportunities which were difficult to administer. In many instances, management lacked the ability or experience to evaluate them, or to administer large volumes of nonresidential construction loans.

6. Elimination of regulations initially designed to prevent lending excesses and minimize failures. Regulatory relaxation permitted lending, directly and through participations, in distant loan markets on the promise of high returns. Lenders, however, were not familiar with these distant markets. It also permitted associations to participate extensively in speculative construction activities with builders and developers who had little or no financial stake in the projects.

7. Fraud and insider transaction abuses were the principal cause of some 20 percent of savings and loan failures the last three years and a greater percentage of the dollar losses borne by the FSLIC.

8. A new type of and generation of opportunistic savings and loan

executives and owners – some of whom operated in a fraudulent manner – whose takeover of many institutions was facilitated by a change in FSLIC rules reducing the minimum number of stockholders of an insured association from 400 to one.

9. Dereliction of duty on the part of the board of directors of some savings associations. This permitted management to make uncontrolled use of some new operating authority, while directors failed to control expenses and prohibit obvious conflict of interest situations.

10. A virtual end of inflation in the American economy, together with overbuilding in multi-family, condominium type residences and in commercial real estate in many cities. In addition, real estate values collapsed in the energy states – Texas, Louisiana and Oklahoma particularly – and weakness occurred in the mining and agricultural sectors of the economy.

11. Pressures felt by the management of many associations to restore net worth ratios. Anxious to improve earnings, they departed from their traditional lending practices into credits and markets involving higher risks, but with which they had little experience.

12. The lack of appropriate, accurate and effective evaluations of the savings and loan business by public accounting firms, security analysts and the financial community.

13. Organizational structure and supervisory laws, adequate for policing and controlling the business in the protected environment of the 1960s and 1970s, resulted in fatal delays and indecision in the examination/supervision process in the 1980s.

14. Federal and state examination and supervisory staffs insufficient in number, experience or ability to deal with the new world of savings and loan operations.

15. The inability or unwillingness of the Bank Board and its legal and supervisory staff to deal with problem institutions in a timely manner. Many institutions, which ultimately closed with big losses, were known problem cases for a year or more. Often, it appeared, political considerations delayed necessary supervisory action.

Charticle 3
Large Portion of the Savings and Loan Industry Affected
Adversely

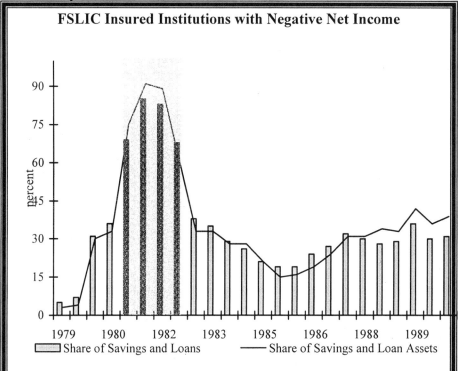

Semiannual data. Source: FHLBB Thrift Financial Reports

An extremely high percentage of savings and loans suffered net losses
during 1981 and 1982. Even more disconcerting, the share of total
savings and loan assets in institutions suffering losses was also
extremely high, so that neither small nor large savings and loans
avoided problems in the period.

REGULATORY REGIMES AND MARKETS:

THE CASE OF SAVINGS AND LOANS

Catherine England
Marymount University

> *"The art of economics consists in looking not merely at the immediate but at the longer effects of any act or policy; it consists in tracing the consequences of that policy not merely for one group but for all groups."* (Hazlitt, 1996, p. 5)

Ask today about the lessons learned from the savings and loan debacle of the 1980s, and you are likely to get a wide variety of answers. More than a decade after the savings and loan bailout, many people respond with a blank stare, unsure of what a savings and loan is (or was) or what the crisis was all about. Those who are a bit better informed talk about greedy and unethical behavior among savings and loan executives and (sometimes) politicians. A few persons place the blame on unwise investments, including risky loans, stocks, and junk bonds. It is a rare individual, indeed, who is aware, even on a general level, of the problems caused by government policies, including inflexible regulations, high inflation, and the existence of federal deposit insurance.[1]

For most economists, however, the roots of the savings and loan fiasco lie firmly embedded in policies pursued by federal and state governments beginning in the 1930s. Policies aimed at achieving high levels of homeownership, an end widely viewed as desirable, had long-term consequences that ultimately cost taxpayers $150 billion. When problems developed, policymakers responded with policy patches aimed at protecting the primary goal of expanded homeownership. By 1980, the savings and loan industry had sunk into insolvency. A major restructuring was necessary, although it would be postponed until 1989.

Interestingly, as Figure 1 shows, while policymakers put off reforms during the 1980s for fear of the impact on housing markets, homeownership rates declined – from 65.4 percent of households at the end of 1979 to 63.8 percent at the end of 1989. Since 1989, however, homeownership rates have increased dramatically to 68 percent at the end of 2001. Lower interest rates and a strong economy have, of course, contributed to the current vibrant housing market, but the restructuring and evolution of the mortgage industry clearly has not hurt.

---

[1] Shortly before attending the Anderson School of Management-Milken Institute conference on this topic in January 2002, I actually surveyed students and acquaintances to discover what they viewed as the cause of the savings and loan crisis.

Figure 1. Homeownership Rates

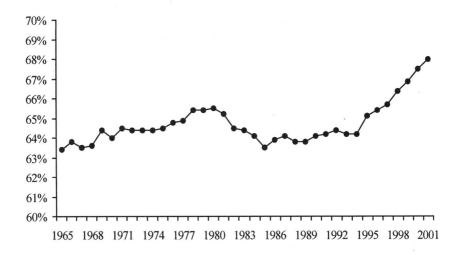

Note: Homeownership rates are for the fourth quarter of each year indicated.
Source: U.S. Census Bureau, Housing Vacancy Survey, First Quarter 2002, Table 5:
Homeownership Rates for the United States.

The failure to understand – and remember – the lessons of the savings and loan crisis places this country – and others – in danger of committing similar missteps in the future. Policies that supported subsidized, directed lending by financial institutions forced to specialize in residential mortgages left the system vulnerable to financial calamity. At least two government-sponsored studies in the early 1970s warned of the dangers associated with the existing financial structure and urged reform.[2] It would take a nationwide financial scandal and the bankruptcy of the Federal Savings and Loan Insurance Corporation before the federal government would act, however. The goal of this paper, then, is to provide a cautionary tale by reviewing how government policies over a half century led step by step to the savings and loan crisis of the 1980s.

---

[2] The Commission on Financial Structure and Regulation, better known as the Hunt Commission after Chairman Reed Hunt, was appointed by President Richard Nixon and issued its report in 1971. The House of Representatives Committee on Banking, Currency and Housing, Subcommittee on Financial Institutions Supervision, Regulation and Insurance also commissioned a study entitled Financial Institutions in the Nation's Economy (known as the FINE study), which was completed in 1975. See Davison (1997, pp. 91-92).

IN PURSUIT OF HOMEOWNERSHIP – THE 1930s

The seeds of the 1980s crisis were planted during the 1930s. Home mortgages of the period bore little resemblance to the loans with which we are now familiar. Bosworth, et al. (1987, pp. 48-50) describes a mortgage market in which down payments of 40 percent or more were common, loans generally matured in six years or less, and principal was not amortized, but was due in a lump sum on the loan's due date.[3] As long as the economy and the financial markets were functioning smoothly, borrowers were typically able to refinance their mortgages as they matured.

Not surprisingly, the arrival of the Great Depression had a devastating effect on this market. Increasing unemployment led to rising defaults, causing many institutions to curtail lending. Homeowners who had expected to refinance their mortgages were often unable to raise the funds needed to repay the balances due on their loans as they matured. Defaults increased further, making lenders even more cautious, and mortgage lending collapsed in a downward spiral.

By the waning days of the Hoover administration, Congress had determined that problems in the mortgage market required special attention. Not only would a reenergized housing market provide a powerful economic stimulus to other sectors of the economy, but expanded homeownership would also bolster political stability during a period of economic turmoil. Three pieces of Depression-era legislation were aimed particularly at revitalizing the mortgage market: the Federal Home Loan Bank Act of July 1932, the Home Owners' Loan Act of June 1933, and the National Housing Act of June 1934.[4] With these three new laws, federal policymakers accomplished two things. The first was to make mortgages more affordable for and attractive to households. The second was to make the more affordable mortgages palatable to the savings and loan lenders.[5]

As Bosworth, et al. (1987, pp. 49-50) note, provisions of the Home Owners' Loan Act and the National Housing Act jump-started the trend toward the long-term fixed-rate amortizing loans with which we are familiar today. The

---

[3] Borrowers with amortized loans repay principal along with interest in (generally) equal payments over the life of the loan.

[4] Barth and Regalia (1988, pp. 153-59) provide a table identifying and describing major pieces of legislation affecting depository institutions.

[5] Note that savings and loan associations, with their roots in cooperative neighborhood lending associations, were clearly preferred as the conduits through which expanded mortgage lending would take place. The received wisdom of the day held that prudent bankers held only short-term loans backed by self-liquidating collateral, i.e., "real bills." Longer-term loans backed by real estate were viewed as encompassing too much liquidity and interest rate risk for banks.

Home Owners' Loan Act created the Home Owners' Loan Corporation to purchase delinquent mortgages from financial institutions and provide refinancing with longer term, amortized loans at lower interest rates. The Home Owners' Loan Corporation thus provided a laboratory in which a new type of mortgage was tested. The National Housing Act created the Federal Housing Agency (later renamed the Federal Housing Administration) to provide mortgage insurance for the new-style fixed-rate amortizing loans, thus protecting lenders from default. Insured mortgages could have maturities of 20 years or more, and they could represent as much as 80 percent of the purchase price of the property. Clearly, these new loans were more attractive to potential homeowners. By locking in interest rates over the life of the loan, the new loans increased certainty about future mortgage payments and removed concerns about the need to repay or refinance property loans every few years.

While attractive to borrowers, mortgages with longer terms and fixed rates shifted considerable risk to mortgage lenders, however. Two related risks were of particular concern to savings and loan managers – liquidity risk and interest rate risk.[6] Both risks appear when the average life of a financial institution's assets does not match the average life of the institution's liabilities. A larger mismatch between assets and liabilities creates more risk. As the federal government encouraged changes in mortgage lending, savings and loans were expected to use passbook savings accounts to fund these new long-term fixed rate mortgages.

Because the deposits of savings and loan associations could be withdrawn on short notice, savings and loans' funding costs would increase rapidly if interest rates began to rise. Meanwhile, the longer-term, fixed-rate nature of the new mortgages would prevent savings and loans from increasing returns on their portfolios of loans as quickly. This risk, where increases in income will lag rising costs in a changing interest rate environment, is known as interest rate risk.[7]

Outweighing concerns about interest rate risk during the 1930s, however, was anxiety over liquidity risk. Before President Franklin Roosevelt declared a national bank holiday in March 1933, more than 9,000 banks and other

---

[6] A third risk facing lenders is credit risk, i.e., the risk that the borrower will not repay his or her loan on time and in full. Credit risk is, naturally, an important consideration for lenders of all stripes, but default rates on home mortgages are among the lowest of any type of consumer loan.

[7] More specifically, savings and loans faced refinancing (as opposed to reinvestment) risk. That is, savings and loans would need to constantly raise new funds to continue to support their existing loan portfolio. Because income from existing loans was fixed, the need to refinance in a higher interest rate environment would cause costs to rise more quickly than income. By contrast, reinvestment risk occurs when a financial institution's liabilities have a longer maturity than its assets.

depository institutions failed. These failures were often precipitated by bank runs – the most visible symbol of liquidity risk. As with interest rate risk, liquidity risk arises from the mismatch between long-term assets and short-term liabilities. Even a bank or savings and loan with a portfolio of sound loans had to be concerned about the possibility of depositors losing confidence in the institution's management and demanding their money on short notice. Longer-term loans could not be easily turned into cash if a savings and loan's depositors all appeared at its door on the same day. Alleviating liquidity risk was, therefore, an important focus of Depression-era efforts to support mortgage lenders.

First, the Federal Home Loan Bank Act created the Federal Home Loan Bank System, patterned after the Federal Reserve System. Twelve regional Federal Home Loan Banks were established to advance funds to savings and loans, accepting mortgages as collateral. As noted earlier, the Home Owners' Loan Corporation purchased delinquent mortgages from existing savings and loans, providing another source of liquidity. Both the Federal Home Loan Banks and the Home Owners' Loan Corporation enabled savings and loans to write new mortgages even if their deposit base was not growing. The National Housing Act created the Federal Savings and Loan Insurance Corporation to provide deposit insurance for savings and loans so that savings and loans could compete effectively with banks for deposits. Policymakers expected that federally insured depositors would be less likely to run. Finally, in 1938, Congress created Fannie Mae to buy FHA-insured mortgages from savings and loans.

INTEREST RATE RISK APPEARS – THE 1960s

For the next 30 years, the mortgage markets seemed to operate smoothly with savings and loans at their core. After falling from 47.8 percent in 1930 to 43.6 percent in 1940, the percentage of American families living in homes they owned began to increase rapidly. By 1950, 55 percent of American households were in owner-occupied homes, and by 1960, the homeownership rate had increased to 61.9 percent.[8] This expansion of homeownership was accomplished during a period of relative economic tranquility. As the country emerged from World War II, the economy expanded, incomes increased, and interest rates remained fairly stable.

The life of a savings and loan manager during the 1950s and early 1960s has been summed up in the "3-6-3 rule." Pay three percent on deposits.

---

[8] U.S. Census Bureau, "Historical Census of Housing Tables: Homeownership."

Charge six percent on mortgages. Be at the golf course by 3:00 p.m. As White (1991, p. 59) explains, this comfortable existence was due to a number of federal and state laws and regulations limiting competition among depository institutions, including savings and loans and banks. To begin, financial institutions' roles were clearly defined. Banks offered checking accounts and made short-term commercial and consumer loans. Savings and loans offered savings accounts and wrote mortgages. There was very little direct competition between different types of financial institutions. Nor did savings and loan managers need to worry much about new competition from other savings and loan associations. The experience of the 1930s left both federal and state regulators reluctant to grant charters to new savings and loan associations if the new institution might threaten in any way the financial stability of an existing savings and loan. Interstate branching was virtually unknown, and intrastate branching was often restricted. Finally, a savings and loan was prohibited from writing loans secured by property more than 50 miles from its home or branch offices.[9] This comfortable existence was about to change, however.

By the mid-1960s, U.S. involvement in Vietnam was escalating, while on the domestic front, President Johnson was pursuing his war on poverty. As federal budget deficits ballooned, inflation and interest rates began to rise, as Figure 2 shows. By late 1966, 3-month Treasury bills were yielding over 5 percent, and the savings and loans' depositors were becoming dissatisfied with their 3 percent returns. Savings and loan institutions found themselves competing for deposits, leading to higher costs and reduced profits.

Congressmen began hearing from unhappy savings and loan managers back home.[10] As White (1991, p. 62) reports, policymakers responded by subjecting savings and loans to Regulation Q beginning in September 1966. Regulation Q limited the interest that could be paid on passbook savings deposits to 4.75 percent, and ended price-based competition between savings and loans for funds.[11] Banks had been subject to similar interest rate ceilings since 1933, but as a result of the importance attached to housing finance, savings and loans were granted a 75 basis point (or 0.75 percent) rate

---

[9] This limit was expanded to 100 miles in 1971 and dropped altogether during the 1980s.

[10] Local bank and savings and loan owner/managers have long been a potent political force, often wielding more power than representatives of the larger, nationally known banks. The local finance committee of every elected official in Washington almost certainly included, if it was not chaired by, the owner or manager of area banks and savings and loans. When these individuals called their elected representatives, the politicians listened.

[11] Higher ceilings were imposed on deposits with longer maturities. See, for example, White (1991, pp. 63-64).

differential to enable them to compete effectively for funds necessary to support the housing market.

Figure 2. Selected Interest Rates

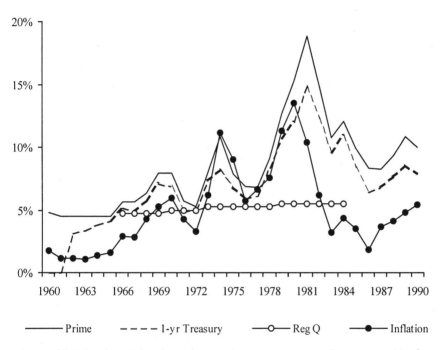

Source: Historic prime rates and average annual returns on one-year Treasury securities from the Federal Reserve at www.federalreserve.gov/releases/h15/data/a/prime.txt and www.federalreserve.gov/releases/h15/data/a/tcm1y.txt, respectively. Regulation Q ceilings on interest rates paid on passbook savings deposits from White (1991, p.63). Inflation rates from www.eh.net/ehresources/howmuch/inflationq.php.

The savings and loan industry heaved a sigh of relief as competitive pressures eased and funding costs became more predictable. By late 1969, however, interest rates were rising again, well above the rate allowed on passbook savings accounts. This time, depositors did not shift their savings among savings and loans. They left the industry altogether. Throughout 1969 and 1970, small savers began to invest in short-term Treasury securities. Three-month Treasury bills were yielding around 6.5 percent in 1969 and 1970, while one-year securities offered a return of close to 7 percent. Savings and loan executives complained again about the loss of funds, and the federal government again responded. In 1970, the Treasury increased the minimum size of a Treasury bill from $1,000 to $10,000. According to White (1991, p. 64) the average balance in a passbook savings account at the time was $3,045.

Small savers had few other alternatives. They were now captive financiers for the savings and loan industry – at least for the time being.

ENTER THE MONEY MARKET MUTUAL FUNDS – THE 1980s BEGIN

Returning to Figure 2, it is now apparent that the surges in interest rates during the 1960s and mid-1970s were only mild tremors compared to the much greater convulsion that was about to break over financial markets. One-year Treasury securities were yielding 4.95 percent in 1972. It was not until 1992 that the average yield on one-year securities fell below 5 percent again.[12] By 1981, investors holding one-year Treasury securities received returns of 14.8 percent, the prime rate quoted by banks averaged 18.9 percent, and new mortgages were being written with interest rates of over 16.6 percent.[13] Clearly, the old 3-6-3 days were gone, and despite efforts of the government and the industry to contain costs through Regulation Q, the savings and loan industry was about to be caught between rapidly increasing costs and stagnant returns.

Between 1970 and 1981, the financial world changed dramatically as inflation rates increased, interest rates became more volatile, and money began to flow more freely across regional and national boundaries. New types of less regulated financial instruments and institutions began to appear, among them money market mutual funds (MMMFs). MMMFs were created around 1972. Mutual funds that invested in stocks and bonds had been around for some time, but MMMFs invested in money market instruments – Treasury bills, commercial paper, bankers' acceptances, and large negotiable certificates of deposit (CDs) from banks and savings and loans.[14] The development of MMMFs was aided considerably by the advent of more powerful computers that could keep track of larger numbers of smaller accounts. As interest rates rose through the 1970s and into the 1980s, the minimum investment required to participate in MMMFs fell to $1,000 or less,[15] and MMMFs eventually allowed clients to write a limited number of checks on their accounts each month. Money began to flow out of traditional depository institutions – banks and

---

[12] See the Federal Reserve web site, www.federalreserve.gov/releases/h15/data/a/tcm1y.txt.
[13] See the Federal Reserve web site, www.federalreserve.gov/releases/h15/data/a/tcm1y.txt, www.federalreserve.gov/releases/h15/data/a/prime.txt, and www.federalreserve.gov/releases/h15/data/a/cm.txt.
[14] "Large negotiable CDs" are issued in denominations of $100,000 or more. They were not subject to Regulation Q ceilings during the 1980s.
[15] The increase in the minimum size of short-term Treasury bills clearly added impetus for the creation of MMMFs.

savings and loans – at ever increasing rates. Figure 3 shows the rapid expansion in assets held by MMMFs through the 1970s and 1980s.[16]

Figure 3. Assets of Money Market Mutual Funds

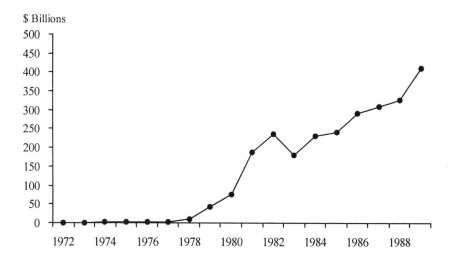

Source: White (1991)

Although MMMFs were good news for savers, they were bad news for savings and loans. Savings and loans had portfolios of outstanding mortgages that needed to be funded. Furthermore, the only way to increase returns was to make new mortgages at higher interest rates, and that required additional funds. As their passbook savings deposits evaporated, savings and loan managers were forced to turn to the money markets. One way to obtain funds was to issue large negotiable CDs not subject to Regulation Q ceilings. Thus, as money flowed out of savings and loans' passbook accounts into MMMFs, the mutual funds then purchased large CDs with double-digit returns from the savings and loan associations.[17]

---

[16] See White (1991, p. 69).

[17] Interestingly, there was resistance among many savings and loan managers to removing Regulation Q limits on interest they could pay. There were, after all, some passbook savings accounts remaining. Apparently the fear was that average funding costs would increase even more quickly if savings and loans were forced to pay market rates on all deposits and compete directly with one another for accounts.

Naturally, mortgage interest rates were rising, too. But the average returns on savings and loans' portfolios of mortgages increased much more slowly than the rates charged on new loans. Long-term fixed rate mortgages represent the other half of the interest rate risk pincer. Figure 4 presents graphically data collected by Kane (1985, p. 92) comparing interest rates on new mortgage loans with the average return on savings and loans' mortgage portfolios for the period 1965 through 1983. In 1981, when six-month CDs were yielding 15.8 percent and new mortgages were being written at over 16 percent, the average yield on savings and loan portfolios was 9.6 percent. Further, as market interest rates rose, the margin between current rates and mortgage portfolio yields widened.

Figure 4. Lagging Portfolio Returns

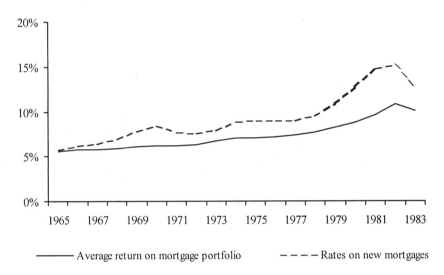

Source: Kane (1985).

During the 3-6-3 era, it was not uncommon for a family to purchase several houses during the lifetimes of the parents as family size changed and/or the family moved with new jobs. As interest rates on new mortgages began to increase, however, moving into a new house became significantly more expensive when it meant giving up an existing low-interest mortgage. Not surprisingly, housing turnover slowed. Nor could lenders be certain they would rid themselves of the old, low-rate mortgages when houses did change.

As a further protection for consumers, most states had laws and regulations favoring "assumable" mortgages. That is, the buyer could "assume" (or take over) the seller's existing fixed-rate mortgage. In such cases, the buyer only needed to obtain new, higher interest rate financing for the difference between the purchase price and the principal remaining on the old mortgage.

Consider, then, the plight of a savings and loan manager as the 1980s dawned. Caught between rising costs and stagnant returns, the institution, probably passed down from father to son, was rapidly approaching insolvency, if it was not already there. Kane (1985, p. 102) estimates that for the industry as a whole, liabilities exceeded the market value of assets by $150.5 billion by 1980.[18] Most importantly to the savings and loan executive, his difficulties were entirely the result of government policies. As required by law and regulation, almost 80 percent of savings and loans' assets were long-term fixed-rate mortgages in 1980, while their liabilities were primarily passbook savings deposits.[19] As inflation rose and interest rates became more volatile, this combination became untenable. Having done just what the government asked, the industry was about to collapse. Savings and loan executives called on their elected representatives again, asking what would become of the housing market if something was not done.[20]

DEREGULATION – 1980 AND 1982

By 1980, Congress was well aware that savings and loans around the country were struggling. White (1991, p. 72) reports that in 1979, Congress had finally allowed federally chartered savings and loans to begin offering adjustable rate mortgages, thus shifting some of the interest rate risk back to borrowers.[21] But the turnover in savings and loans' mortgage portfolios was too slow for the shift to ARMs to help noticeably, at least immediately.

The next efforts to provide relief appeared in the Depository Institutions Deregulation and Monetary Control Act (DIDMCA) passed in 1980. Barth and Regalia (1988, pp. 158-59) summarize both the 1980 legislation and the 1982 Garn-St Germain Depository Institutions Act. On the funding side, the 1980 DIDMCA began the six-year phase out of Regulation Q ceilings and authorized federally insured savings and loans to offer NOW accounts to

---

[18] Indeed, according to Kane's calculations, the industry as a whole had negative net worth on a market value basis as early as 1971. See Kane (1985, p. 102).

[19] *Ibid.*

[20] What would become of the congressman's finance committee?

[21] The Federal Home Loan Bank Board had tried in the early 1970s to introduce adjustable rate mortgages, but had been stymied by congressional objections. See White (1991, p. 65).

customers.[22] Policymakers hoped that the new checkable deposits would provide savings and loans with a lower-cost source of funds. The DIDMCA also increased federal deposit insurance limits from $40,000 per account to $100,000 per account.

Congress and savings and loan managers had to face the fact, however, that funding costs were going to be higher, at least for the foreseeable future. The next step, then, was to provide savings and loans with other investment opportunities, allowing savings and loan managers to better diversify their portfolios and, hopefully, to increase returns more quickly. Barth and Regalia (1988, p. 158) note that the DIDMCA widened savings and loans' investment opportunities by authorizing federally chartered savings and loans to issue credit cards, act as trustees, operate trust departments, and write mortgages backed by commercial real estate. Further, savings and loans could now invest up to 20 percent of their assets in a combination of short-term consumer loans, commercial paper, and/or corporate debt securities.

Unfortunately, the 1980 legislation did not stop the slide of savings and loans into insolvency, so Congress acted again in 1982 with the Garn-St Germain bill. To address savings and loans' funding problems, Garn-St Germain accelerated the elimination of Regulation Q ceilings, and authorized banks and savings and loans to offer money market deposit accounts (MMDAs), designed to mimic money market mutual funds in terms of returns and check-writing ability. Savings and loans were also allowed to offer standard individual and corporate checking accounts for the first time.

But the greater impact of the Garn-St Germain bill was on the asset side of savings and loans' balance sheets. The 1982 legislation largely freed savings and loans from the requirement that they focus exclusively on the residential mortgage market. They were now authorized to invest in commercial, corporate, small business, and/or agricultural loans. They could offer non-mortgage consumer loans, including educational loans. Mortgages on non-residential real estate could make up as much as 40 percent of a savings and loan's portfolio, and savings and loans could invest up to 10 percent of their assets in property they intended to lease. Finally, the Garn-St Germain bill removed all limits on savings and loans' investments in state and local government obligations. It was now possible for a savings and loan to exit the mortgage market entirely.

---

[22] "NOW" accounts (negotiable orders of withdrawal) were the first checkable accounts offered by savings and loans. They were first offered by state-chartered savings and loan institutions. Savings and loans paid interest on NOW accounts from the beginning while banks were still prohibited from paying interest on demand deposits.

It is important to remember that Congress was addressing very real problems facing the industry in 1980 and 1982. Although deregulation was generally a hot political topic, savings and loans were losing large amounts of money because they had been forced to adopt a model meant to encourage homeownership. It was only too apparent that 30-year fixed-rate mortgages could not be funded by short-term deposits during periods of high inflation and volatile interest rates. Policymakers set out to provide relief to the industry by granting them a broader range of investment opportunities. Unfortunately, in the short term, broader powers made matters worse.

POLICY MISTAKES COMPOUNDED

Had the industry been deregulated a decade earlier, this might have been a very different story. In 1970, owners of savings and loans still had an investment stake to protect, and while problems existed, conditions were not yet desperate. By 1980, the situation had changed.

When Congress acted in 1980 and 1982, it ignored the importance of equity capital in constraining the behavior of financial institution managers. As noted, by 1980, a significant portion of the industry was insolvent or rapidly approaching insolvency on a market-value basis. In other words, if the loan portfolios of savings and loans had been valued at current interest rates, the present value of the liabilities of the institutions (the money owed to depositors and other creditors) would have been greater than the present value of their assets.[23] Once their equity was gone, savings and loan owners had nothing more to lose. The worst that regulators could do was close the institution. Owners would lose the same amount of money whether the closed savings and loan's liabilities exceeded its assets by $1 or by $50 million. Consequently, the owner/managers of an insolvent or nearly insolvent savings and loan had little reason to act to minimize losses and every reason to gamble for the firm's recovery.

That raises the second problem with the timing of the deregulation. Savings and loan managers were familiar with one line of business – writing

---

[23] Loans are carried on the books of depository institutions at their "face value," which is measured by the remaining principal associated with the loan. This is a reasonable valuation for loans on which payments are being regularly made as long as interest rates are relatively stable. When interest rates rise, however, the value of the future stream of payments from a fixed interest rate loan is reduced. That is, if the lender could "call" the loan, forcing its immediate repayment, the recovered principal could be reinvested at a higher rate. Thus, higher interest rates reduce the "market value" of fixed return assets. Conversely, when interest rates fall, the value of fixed-rate loans in a portfolio increases.

residential mortgages. The sudden freedom to pursue new lines of business in 1980 and again in 1982 was clearly welcome, particularly since existing lines of business were proving unprofitable. But mounting losses in their mortgage business made it imperative that savings and loans add more profitable lines of business quickly. Playing it safe by adding new activities slowly as managers learned about pitfalls and opportunities or by investing in less risky federal, state, and local government securities (with their lower returns) would not generate the returns necessary to recoup past losses and rebuild capital. Savings and loan managers were desperate for investments that provided quick and relatively large returns on the funds available for investment. A desperate search for quick, large returns is a recipe for disaster.

Note finally that to this point there really are not any "bad guys" in the story. For 50 years, federal and state policymakers had regulated savings and loans with the goal of expanded homeownership ever in mind. Savings and loan owners and managers had lived by the regulations – and suffered the consequences as economic conditions became increasingly unsettled. By the early 1980s, existing laws and regulations had painted the savings and loan industry and policymakers into a corner with few options remaining. Congress could either authorize the liquidation of much of the industry or attempt to revamp the regulatory design to enable savings and loans to work their way out of their problems. Because policymakers feared the impact of liquidation both on the housing market and on their reelection chances, they chose the course of deregulation. The more sound policy of coupling deregulation with mandatory recapitalization, to the extent it was considered at all, was discarded as essentially equivalent to the liquidation option. So Congress took steps and encouraged regulatory responses designed to mask the increasing insolvency within the industry. Policymakers hoped that somehow these decapitalized institutions could grow their way back to health.

ENTER THE BLACK (AND GRAY) HATS

Despite falling interest rates and new regulatory freedom, conditions did not improve significantly for most savings and loans. Traditional owners and managers had become increasingly frustrated by the mid-1980s. Like Jimmy Stewart in *It's a Wonderful Life*, the long-time savings and loan owner understood mortgages and the local residential real estate market. He knew little about how to assess credit card debt or commercial real estate loans. Meanwhile, his deposit customers had deserted him at the same time the market for new mortgages collapsed. Losses continued to mount. When traditional savings and loan owners were approached by investors wanting to buy their institutions, the offer was tempting. Indeed, the savings and loan owner appeared to have few choices. Either he must invest aggressively in new financial products promising higher returns, or he must sell out.

But who were these new investors? Why would anyone invest in a savings and loan in the mid-1980s? To understand, consider the regulatory regime that now existed. First, the phase out of Regulation Q ceilings coupled with the increase in federal deposit insurance to $100,000 per account positioned savings and loans to engage in a nationwide bidding war for funds. Bennet (1990, pp. 42-43) explains how advertisements placed in respected national publications such as *Money* magazine, the *New York Times*, and *The Wall Street Journal* directed depositors to the highest rates available. Federal insurance meant that depositors need not ask about the uses to which their funds were being put.

Meanwhile, new savings and loan owners were willing to pursue much more imaginative investments than their predecessors had. The development of shopping malls, apartment and office buildings, and resorts, to name a few examples, could now be financed through savings and loans. Adding the final touch to the picture, resources available to the federal savings and loan regulators were cut during the 1980s, so that during this period of turmoil, government oversight was reduced. Indeed, had Congress devised a scheme to attract all the crooks in the country to a single industry, they could not have done much better than the regulatory regime to which savings and loan associations were subject during the mid-1980s. It is surprising, then, that estimates indicate that only between 3 and 10 percent of the losses suffered by the industry were a result of illegal or fraudulent activities.

EPILOGUE

The crisis was not over in the mid-1980s, of course. In many ways, things were just heating up, especially in terms of some of the industry's more exotic investments. Tax law changes introduced in 1982 that had affected commercial real estate investments were reversed in 1986. Suddenly, thousands of real estate loans were backed by uneconomic projects. In 1987, Congress made a half-hearted attempt to address the savings and loan crisis with the Competitive Equality Banking Act. In a classic case of too little, too late, the new law provided the FSLIC with $10.875 billion over three years with which to close insolvent savings and loans.[24] Unfortunately,

---

[24] See Davison (1997, p. 97).

policymakers were still unwilling to admit the extent of the problem, and a number of restrictions on the FSLIC's ability to actually close savings and loan institutions were written into the legislation. Finally, in 1989, Congress passed the Financial Institutions Reform, Recovery and Enforcement Act (FIRREA), putting in place the mechanism necessary to close insolvent institutions. Although there was plenty to criticize in FIRREA and the way it was enforced, at least federal policymakers had finally resolved to address the problem.

CONCLUSIONS

I draw three lessons from this historical overview. First, regulatory systems should be designed for the worst economic conditions, not the best. Second, because there is never a good time for regulatory reform, regulatory systems should be designed with care. Finally, policymakers should beware of attempts to bend market forces to serve the political will.

With respect to regulatory system design, policymakers during the 1930s were well aware of the risks they were building into their new system of mortgage finance. Having addressed immediate concerns, policymakers hoped that economic conditions would make the structure they designed sustainable. In fact, the system worked for decades until burgeoning inflation and volatile interest rates brought the whole structure crashing down. It is dangerous in the extreme to create a regulatory structure that relies for its success on a particular set of economic conditions. Perhaps the practice of monetary policy has advanced to the point that the United States will never again experience 13 percent inflation, but do we want to bet the financial health of an entire industry on that possibility?

That raises the second point. Policymakers and economists clearly understood the economic conditions that would cause distress among savings and loans. Government-sponsored studies during the 1970s identified weaknesses and proposed reforms. These warnings were ignored, however, in part because the system seemed to be working well at the time. Why fix something that is not broken? By the time it became obvious that regulatory reform was needed, the industry was in financial distress. Now it was difficult to institute meaningful reforms because of the hardship change would impose on already troubled institutions. In short, there is never a good time for reform. However often policymakers assure themselves that they can fine-tune regulatory structures down the road, inertia remains a powerful force in Washington.

Figure 5. Federally Insured Savings Institutions

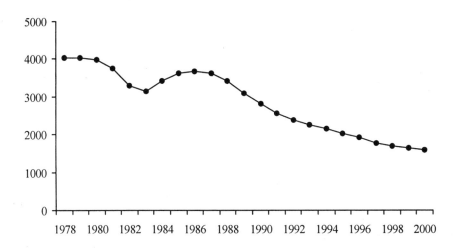

Source: FDIC and White (1991).

In the end, the question should be how much of the specialized structure was actually necessary. Once Congress gave into the need for reform and restructuring, the industry and the mortgage market changed radically. The number of federally insured savings and loans has fallen dramatically over the past decade, as Figure 5 shows. According to the FDIC's web site, in 1989, there were 3,087 federally insured savings and loans. By 2000, that number had dropped to 1,590.[25]

Even more telling, the role played by savings and loans in the mortgage markets has changed drastically. The left axis in Figure 6 shows the dollar value of home mortgages outstanding. The size of the market has obviously increased substantially over the past 35 years, while the home mortgages held by savings institutions has remained relatively flat by comparison. The right axis shows the portion of the market served by savings and loans. In 1970, savings and loans held almost 57 percent of residential mortgages, and in 1980, the industry still accounted for more than half of the market. By 1994, savings and loans held less than 15 percent of the residential mortgages. Congressional fears that homeownership rates would decline and the mortgage market would collapse if

---

[25] The number of commercial banks has also declined as limits on interstate branching have been eased.

the industry was restructured were clearly unfounded. The mortgage market has blossomed since 1989, so that Barta (2002, p. A1) recently asked whether there are some markets in which homeownership rates are as high as they can go. Earlier resistance to reform now seems to have been a mistake.

Figure 6. Savings Institutions Declining Role

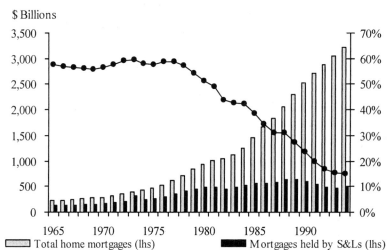

Source: Federal Reserve's Flow of Funds Accounts of the United States, "Table L.218 Home Mortgages."

In an article entitled, "How the Cleaver Family Destroyed Our S&Ls," James Bennet (1990, pp. 38-46) explains that the congressional dream of widespread homeownership worked well – if you were born at the right time. Families buying houses in the 1950s, 1960s, and even the early 1970s clearly benefited from the subsidized mortgage lending. When these same families moved their savings to money market mutual funds, and then back to savings and loans participating in the bidding war of the late 1980s, they gained even more. It was to these families that most of the $150 billion lost in the savings and loan fiasco went. Meanwhile, younger families hoping to purchase homes during the 1980s suffered, and taxpayers generally picked up the bill.

The question is: are there similar land mines in the regulatory structure that exist today? In a recent front page article in *The Wall Street Journal*, Barta (2002, pp. A1, A8) alludes to the savings and loan industry crisis and asks about the possible risk to the economy should either Fannie Mae or

Freddie Mac fail. According to Barta (2002, p. A8), Fannie Mae and Freddie Mac together either own or guarantee 44 percent of the residential mortgage market. Have government policies served to disperse risk from the savings and loan industry only to reconcentrate it in Fannie Mae and Freddie Mac?

There is also the recent proposal by the FDIC to increase the limits on federal deposit insurance. Admittedly, inflation over the past two decades has eroded the real value of $100,000, but at the same time, a wide variety of alternative investment products have been created. Would an increase in the deposit insurance limit reignite a bidding war among depository institutions?

Finally, we are being bombarded almost daily with stories of greed and corruption among corporate CEOs in the recent spate of accounting scandals. Policymakers seeking solutions to these and other problems would be well advised to tread carefully, keeping in mind that regulatory regimes in the past have caused more problems than they have solved when all was said and done.

REFERENCES

Barth, James R. and Martin A. Regalia (1988). "The Evolving Role of Regulation in the Savings and Loan Industry," in Catherine England and Thomas Huertas, eds.: *The Financial Services Revolution,* Boston, Mass.: Kluwer Academic Publishers.

Bennet, James, September (1990). "How the Cleaver Family Destroyed Our S&Ls," *Washington Monthly*, pp. 38-46.

Bosworth, Barry P., Andrew S. Carron, and Elisabeth H. Rhyne (1987). *The Economics of Federal Credit Programs*, Washington, DC: The Brookings Institution.

Davison, Lee (1997). "Chapter 2: Banking Legislation and Regulation," in *History of the Eighties–Lessons for the Future*. Washington, DC: Federal Deposit Insurance Corporation.

Hazlitt, Henry (1996). *Economics in One Lesson*, San Francisco, Calif.: Laissez Faire Books.

Kane, Edward J. (1985). *The Gathering Crisis in Federal Deposit Insurance*, Cambridge, Mass.: MIT Press.

U.S. Census Bureau (2002). Table 5: Homeownership Rates for the United States: 1965 to 2002, Housing Vacancy Survey, First Quarter 2002. www.census.gov/hhes/www/housing/hvs/q102tab5.htm.

U.S. Census Bureau, Historical Census of Housing Tables: Homeownership. www.census.gov/hhes/www/housing/census/historic/owner.html.

White, Lawrence J (1991). *The S&L Debacle: Public Policy Lessons for Bank and Thrift Regulation,* New York: Oxford University Press.

THE SAVINGS AND LOAN CRISIS:

UNRESOLVED POLICY ISSUES

R. Dan Brumbaugh, Jr.
Milken Institute;
Former Deputy Chief Economist,
Federal Home Loan Bank Board

Catherine J. Galley
Cornerstone Research

INTRODUCTION

The savings and loan crisis began in the early 1980s, when interest rates rose unexpectedly and both asset values and income plunged for savings and loans. The crisis then evolved in many ways over the entire decade, ultimately abating in the early 1990s. This paper provides an overview of the evolution of the crisis.[1] This overview is designed to provide a backdrop for the subsequent discussion of some of the as-yet-unresolved policy issues that the crisis raised.

The one major unresolved policy issue that the paper particularly addresses is whether regulatory forbearance is appropriate. For the purpose of the paper, forbearance is defined as leaving federally insured depositories known to regulators to be insolvent, open and operating. Forbearance tends to develop when an unexpected, dramatic decline in earnings and asset values occurs among depositories, and the relevant federal deposit-insurance fund has inadequate reserves to resolve the resulting insolvencies. The most frequently discussed criterion for whether forbearance is appropriate is whether it tends to increase or decrease the ultimate cost of resolution.[2]

THE FIRST PHASE OF THE SAVINGS AND LOAN CRISIS

Structural Vulnerability to Interest-Rate Changes

Due to the structure of the industry, when interest rates rose unexpectedly in 1980, short-term deposits repriced more quickly than long-term assets, and income plunged. As Figure 1 shows, over 30 percent of all insured thrifts reported negative net income by year-end 1980, and over 90 percent did so by year-end 1981. As the figure also shows, the percentage of total assets in thrifts earning negative net income rose by similar magnitudes.

---

[1] Several books provide analyses of the crisis and provide further references. See Barth (1991), Barth and Brumbaugh (1988, 1992), Benston, Brumbaugh (1986), Brumbaugh (1988, 1993), Carron (1982, 1984), England and Huertas (1987), Kane (1985, 1989), Kaufman and Kormendi (1986), Litan (1987), White Wilcox (1987).

[2] Although this paper does not address these issues in the context of commercial banks, many of the same issue evolved as commercial banks experienced difficulties in the 1980s and early 1990s. For an analysis, see Barth, Brumbaugh, and Litan (1992).

Figure 1: Percent of U.S. FSLIC- Institutions with Negative Net Income

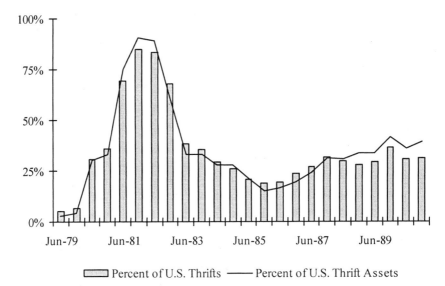

☐ Percent of U.S. Thrifts ——— Percent of U.S. Thrift Assets

Source: Federal Home Loan Bank Board Thrift Financial Reports, Cornerstone Research.

The structure of the industry that made it so vulnerable to significant fluctuation in interest rates was the requirement, established by law and regulation, that savings and loans could make only fixed-rate, long-term mortgages, even though they simultaneously funded those mortgages by shorter-term, more variable-rate deposits.

This structure led to a dramatic decline in the market value of the fixed-rate, long-term mortgages. By year-end 1980 the market value of the industry's fixed-rate mortgage portfolio was approximately negative 12 percent, growing to negative 18 percent by year-end 1981. At that time, based on the market value of their mortgage portfolios, almost every savings and loan in the U.S. was insolvent.

Though less widely understood, savings and loans were also vulnerable to falling interest rates. At least initially, when interest rates fell, shorter-term deposits repriced more quickly than longer-term fixed-rate mortgages, and spread income would rise. Falling interest rates, however, increased the incentive for homeowners to refinance. As they did so, spread income was affected.

Immediate Forbearance Abetted by Regulatory Accounting

Forbearance arose almost immediately because the unexpected increase in interest rates led so quickly to negative net income and market-value insolvency for so many thrifts. Throughout the savings and loan crisis, regulatory accounting was a central aspect of forbearance.

Savings and loans reported to regulators on the basis of Regulatory Accounting Principles (RAP) and Generally Accepted Accounting Principles (GAAP). Until 1989, the chief regulatory agency for all federally insured savings and loans was the Federal Home Loan Bank Board (Bank Board), which set regulatory accounting standards for the industry. Institutions reported to the Bank Board on the basis of RAP in semi-annual Thrift Financial Reports through 1983 and quarterly thereafter. The TFRs, as they are known, were publicly available shortly after institutions filed them.

Figure 2 indicates how accounting techniques were used to understate the extent of the problem and thereby abet forbearance. For the industry as a whole, Figure 2 presents net worth as a percentage of total assets based on RAP, GAAP and tangible net worth. Based on the reported accounting numbers, tangible net worth could easily be determined by subtracting intangible assets from GAAP net worth. As one can see, at the beginning of the crisis in 1980, RAP, GAAP, and tangible net-worth ratios were essentially the same at approximately 5 percent.

Market-value net worth was also relatively easy for the Bank Board to estimate in the early portion of the crisis because the decline in net worth was caused by the fact that as interest rates rose, the value of the industry's fixed-rate mortgage portfolio declined.[3] In the later stages of the crisis, calculating the industry's market value became more difficult, as the declining value of each institution's commercial real estate and commercial real estate loans became more important.

---

[3] For the method of calculation, see Brumbaugh (1988), p.50.

Figure 2: Capital-to-Asset Ratio for Savings and Loans: 1940-1988

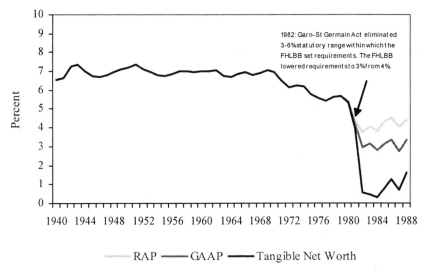

Source: Barth, James, R. (1991) *The Great Savings and Loan Debacle*. Washington, D.C.: The
AEI Press.

From the very beginning, however, negative market-values were not
publicly reported. Given the structure of the industry's assets, it was clear that
the reported net-worth of the industry bore no resemblance to the actual
negative market-value net worth of the industry. The Bank Board and the
entire regulatory apparatus, however, were well aware of the actual condition
of the industry. As the chairman of the Bank Board testified in the early
1980s, "By 1982, the real capital positions of all thrift institutions had been
completely eroded, and virtually all thrift institutions had large negative net
worth when their assets and liabilities were valued at actual market rates"
(Pratt, 1988).

Savings and loans were required to meet specified minimum net worth
requirements. For the purpose of calculating minimum net worth
requirements, RAP was used. If the requirements were not met, an institution
was subject to severe restrictions and intense regulatory scrutiny. Likewise,
the decision of whether to close an institution on the basis of insolvency was
made on the basis of RAP. As reflected in Figure 2, on the whole, the industry
met its minimum net-worth requirement in 1980, despite the fact that the
entire industry was substantially insolvent based on market values.

The Role of Book-Value Versus Market-Value Accounting

The discrepancy between the book-value accounting based on RAP and GAAP and the estimated market-value net worth of the industry raised the issue of whether the crisis would have been handled differently were institutions required to report and be regulated on the basis of market-value accounting versus book-value accounting.[4] On the one hand, some argue that had institutions been forced to report on the basis of market-value accounting, Congress and regulators would have been unable or less able, to engage in forbearance and prolong the crisis. Reporting on the basis of market-value accounting might also have helped avert the crisis, because institutions would have had an additional incentive to lobby to change the rigid structure that led to the crisis in the first place.

On the other hand, others argue that despite reporting on the basis of book values, all of the major participants—the industry, Congress, the Executive branch, and the regulators—were aware of the relative depth of the crisis. They, for example, ask a provocative question. As discussed immediately below, the Federal Savings and Loan Insurance Corporation (FSLIC) was insolvent no later than 1982 based on the cost of closure of book value tangibly insolvent institutions, and forbearance was the policy nonetheless. Why would reporting insolvency based on market-value accounting have made any difference? Why would Congress or regulators have significantly altered their approach? Likewise, the industry while reporting on the basis of book values, had certainly long been aware of the structural vulnerabilities of the industry nonetheless. Why would reporting on market values have changed either the perception or the outcome?

Another approach to the issue focuses on the fact that the crisis developed unexpectedly with the unanticipated rise in interest rates, and rapidly produced insolvencies that exceeded the federal deposit-insurance agency's reserves. The Bank Board apprised Congress on the market value of the industry, as it developed. Congress was in the position of either providing taxpayer dollars to augment the deposit-insurance funds, or adopting a forbearance policy – as it in fact did. This situation raises another provocative question. Why would the existence of market-value accounting have made any difference, if on the basis of existing information Congress knew it was

---

[4] White (1991) strongly favors market-value accounting, for example, while Barth(1991), Beaver, et al. (1992) disagree.

avoiding providing taxpayer dollars and adopting a policy of forbearance nonetheless?[5]

The Role of FSLIC and Congress in the Crisis and the Forbearance Policy

The FSLIC was the federal deposit-insurance agency for savings and loans, and was a division of the Bank Board. The FSLIC's reserves are presented in Figure 3. As the figure shows, reported FSLIC reserves were positive from 1980 through 1985. During that period, the reported level of reserves fluctuated at approximately $6 billion from 1980 through 1983. Thus, for example, at a time when the negative market-value net worth of the industry exceeded negative $100 billion in 1981, reported FSLIC reserves were $ 6.2 billion.[6]

By 1982 the FSLIC was insolvent even when its contingent liability for all book-value tangibly insolvent savings and loans was calculated. Reported FSLIC reserves were $6.3 billion. There were $220 billion in assets of tangibly insolvent savings and loans in 1982, when the estimated cost of resolution was 4.5 percent of those assets. Hence, the cost to close all tangibly insolvent savings and loans would have been approximately $10 billion. Based on its contingent liability, therefore, the FSLIC was insolvent by approximately $3.7 billion.

---

[5] Another provocative issue is what would happen if the flat-rate deposit-insurance premium, were replaced with a risk-based premium. For a discussion, see Horvitz (1983).

[6] Data on FSLIC resources and cost of closure from Barth (1991), p. 70.

Figure 3: FSLIC's Reserves 1980-1989

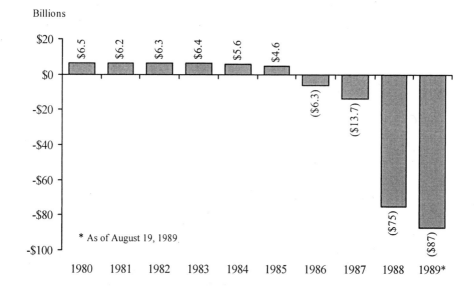

Source: 1980–1987: U.S. League of Savings Institutions Sourcebook, Table 88;
1988–1989: GAO Report to the Congress, Financial Audit: Federal Savings & Loan Insurance
Corporation's 1989 and 1988 Financial Statements; Cornerstone Research.

Legislative Responses to the First Phase of the Crisis

With its existing reserves at the time the FSLIC could not bear the cost that would have arisen had the FSLIC attempted to close more insolvent institutions. The Bank Board faced the choice of either attempting to increase the FSLIC's reserves in order to close more insolvent savings and loans, or to husband its existing reserves by selectively closing institutions.

Additional resources were potentially available from two sources, the industry itself and Congress. Traditionally, the industry provided the FSLIC with funds by paying a percentage of insured deposits to the FSLIC. The industry, however, could not provide additional funds without worsening its own condition. Congress essentially refused to provide taxpayer dollars to increase the FSLIC's reserves.

Instead, Congress passed two major pieces of legislation, first the Depository Institutions Deregulation and Monetary Control Act (DIDMCA) in 1980 and the Garn-St Germain Depository Institutions Act in 1982.[7] There were two central characteristics in both pieces of legislation. In each, statutory authority was granted to the Bank Board to lower minimum net-worth requirements, and broader authority was given to savings and loans to engage in wider – more commercial-bank like – assets and liabilities.

With the 1980 and 1982 legislation, Congress formally adopted a forbearance policy to be carried out by the Bank Board. The legislation provided the two key components of the forbearance policy that would exist until the end of the decade. Reduced capital requirements would allow troubled and insolvent savings and loans to continue to operate. Not only would they continue to operate, but many would also have the opportunity to grow, as the lower capital requirements allowed them to lever into additional assets. At the same time, additional asset and liability powers would allow the savings and loans to diversify away from their fixed-rate mortgage portfolios.

Throughout the 1980s, the FSLIC was itself audited by the General Accounting Office (GAO), an agency that reports to Congress. Despite the market-value insolvency of the industry and the cost to resolve tangibly-insolvent institutions, the GAO did not require the FSLIC to take into consideration its contingent liability for insolvent but open institutions until 1985 (Barth, 1991, p. 71). Thus, the GAO as independent auditor of the FSLIC, allowed the FSLIC to report solvency, when in fact it was insolvent and the GAO was aware of it. In 1985, for example, the estimated cost to close tangibly insolvent institutions exceeded $50 billion and the required contingent liability was $1.6 billion. Thus, the GAO was a participant in the general forbearance policy.

In 1986, the FSLIC reported insolvency for the first time. This was a turning point in the crisis because, after reporting insolvency, pressure began to grow on the Bank Board to estimate publicly the true extent of its contingent liability. In addition, Congress began to feel pressure to provide additional taxpayer funds to FSLIC. The GAO's role adds another layer to the issue of whether reporting on market-value accounting would have made any difference, as again book-value accounting provided ample data on the FSLIC's true condition.

Given the focus on accounting issues in 2002 and the establishment of a Congressionally mandated accounting oversight body, the Congressional and

---

[7] For a description of the major legislative and regulatory provisions throughout the 1980s and early 1990s, see Barth (1991), pp. 119-147.

GAO role in the savings and loan crisis may be instructive. It is clear that circumstances can arise when both a well-informed Congress and GAO will willingly and knowingly abide inaccurate or misleading accounting practices.

The Potential Perils and Promise of the Forbearance Policy

Moral Hazard or Hidden Action and Adverse Selection or Hidden Information

As the savings and loan industry deteriorated and the FSLIC reserves became inadequate, two forms of moral hazard or hidden action arose. In the first instance, once they became insolvent and yet remained open, the institutions themselves had an incentive to take greater risks. If they took greater risk and the risk succeeded, the institutions benefited. If they took greater risk, and failed, the FSLIC bore the cost.

Although insolvency created a clear incentive to take risks, whether that incentive led to excessive risk-taking is difficult to determine. A number of factors acted as a check on excessive risk-taking. One was the examination and supervisory process. During the crisis, examinations were remarkably well done, although at the peak of the crisis, examination and supervisory staffs were extraordinarily taxed and the frequency of examinations declined. Enforcement actions, which increased, were also a check on risk-taking.

The second form of moral hazard involved the government itself. Congress and the Bank Board (as head of the FSLIC) were essentially agents for taxpayers. Taxpayers ultimately bore the burden of deposit-insurance losses, if they ultimately exceeded the FSLIC's capabilities to absorb them through payments from the industry. Once the FSLIC became insolvent and Congress did not provide taxpayer dollars, both Congress and the Bank Board took significant risks that had never before been taken. Never, for example, had thousands of insolvent depository institutions been left open and operating. While open and operating, the prospect of significantly increasing losses existed.

Negative and Positive Unexpected Changes

Completely independent of the thrift industry, its regulators, and Congress, as long as the insolvent institutions were left open they were subject to both negative and positive unexpected changes in their operating environment. It could not be known whether the net effect of those future changes was going to be positive or negative.

Presumably, the passage of DIDMCA and Garn-St Germain in 1980 and 1982 were attempts to create the greatest likelihood that whatever changes did occur, the thrift industry was in the best position to improve. Yet, even this was highly uncertain. In principle, allowing the industry to diversify away from the fixed-rate mortgage, was appropriate. Whether under the circumstances the industry was capable of successfully making the transition, however, was uncertain. In addition, there was an implicitly greater reliance primarily on the future performance of commercial real estate and commercial real estate loans.

The first significant unexpected change was positive. In the fall of 1982, the savings and loans' cost of funds unexpectedly fell while the return on mortgages continued to rise. These changes began a period when the interest-rate spread and mortgage asset value difficulties of the industry abated. At the same time, however, other unexpected changes were exceedingly negative.

THE SECOND PHASE OF THE CRISIS

Improvement in Interest Rates, Decline in Commercial Real Estate Values

Due to the improvement in interest rates, the overall income of the industry became positive and remained positive from 1983 through 1986. During the same period, however, significant deterioration occurred among the worst performing institutions. For those institutions with GAAP net worth less than zero and net income less than zero, GAAP net worth and net income both declined in all but one quarter in 1984, 1985 and 1986 (see Brumbaugh, 1988, p.61). By the end of 1986, these institutions were reporting negative GAAP net worth of approximately $10 billion.

Unlike the interest-rate risk problems of the early 1980s, which affected literally every thrift institution, the difficulties that developed later in the decade largely revolved around falling asset values and increasing loan losses involving commercial real estate. The difficulties were highly concentrated in certain areas of the country. After 1984, for example, FSLIC losses were increasingly concentrated in Texas, where falling energy prices dramatically affected asset quality in thrift portfolios.

The passage of the Tax Reform Act of 1986, however, exacerbated the commercial real estate difficulties. The act reduced depreciation benefits on commercial real estate, and eliminated favorable capital gains treatment. More importantly, the act significantly limited the extent to which limited partnership syndications could offset losses on passive investment. These provisions were inserted into the legislation unexpectedly just before passage. The net effect was an immediate and significant decline in the value of commercial real estate – just at the time when real economic developments were also harming commercial real estate.

It is ironic, of course, that Congress should have passed these provisions of the 1986 tax act, which had predictable negative consequences to thrifts that had used the additional powers provided by Congress in the 1980 and 1982 acts, to diversify into commercial real estate. While Congress essentially "bought time" for many institutions to diversify their portfolios in 1980 and 1982, Congress itself became the source of a devastating blow to the same institutions in 1986.

Rising Cost of Resolution Accompanied by Inadequate Funding of the FSLIC

Thus, the second phase of the thrift crisis developed as the unexpected positive effects based on the behavior of thrift cost of funds and return on mortgages were replaced by the unexpected negative effects of declining commercial real estate asset values. Whereas the potential FSLIC losses associated with the interest-spread difficulties were relatively easy to calculate, the losses associated with commercial real estate asset quality problems were more difficult to calculate directly.

A very reliable indirect method to calculate the losses, however, was to multiply the losses incurred per dollar of assets of closed institutions in the most recent year, by the assets in insolvent institutions in the current year (Barth, 1991, p. 67-75). Based on this method, estimates of the cost of closure per dollar of assets in insolvent institutions soared in 1984 and more than doubled from that level by 1988. At the same time the assets in insolvent savings and loans also rose during that time period.

Losses estimated by this method were systematically and substantially higher than the estimates provided publicly by the Bank Board and the GAO. By year-end 1987, based on publicly available numbers on the cost of closure and the assets in tangibly insolvent institutions, closure of all insolvent institutions exceeded $60 billion. These estimates were available to the Bank Board, the GAO, and Congress.

In the same year, the Competitive Equality Banking Act (CEBA) was passed by Congress. The act provided a complicated funding mechanism by which the FSLIC could receive up to $3.75 billion per year up to an overall limit of $10.825 billion. These funds were borrowed by a financing corporation established by Congress, and did not involve taxpayer dollars.

Taxpayer Dollars for the Closure of Insolvent Institutions: The Financial Institutions Reform, Recovery and Enforcement Act (FIRREA) of 1989

Ultimately, the funds provided by CEBA proved to be inadequate and the final piece of legislation of the decade was passed in 1989. FIRREA was comprised of essentially five parts:

1. For the first time, FIRREA provided taxpayer dollars for the closure of insolvent savings and loans;

2. The regulatory and deposit-insurance structure for savings and loans was completely revised;

3. New minimum capital levels were established;

4. New allowable asset restrictions were imposed; and

5. Additional enforcement authority was provided to combat fraud in savings and loans.

The centerpiece of FIRREA was the provision of $50 billion, of which $40 billion was to go to the new Resolution Trust Corporation (RTC) to resolve insolvent institutions. FIRREA provided these funds through another complicated set of borrowing so that they would not affect the then imposed Gramm-Rudman-Hollings deficit constraint.

The new restrictions on allowable assets essentially reversed the trend since the late 1970s whereby federal and state laws allowed savings and loans to diversify away from their residential mortgage portfolio. Nonresidential and commercial real estate loans were restricted, and a new Qualified Thrift Lender test required thrifts to hold at least 70 percent of their assets in primarily housing-related assets.

As part of the asset restrictions, FIRREA essentially required the divestiture of corporate debt securities that were not rated in one of the four highest rating categories, securities commonly known as high yield or junk bonds, by July 1, 1994.[8] In 1988, the total percentage of high yield bonds in savings and loans was 1.1 percent, and represented 0.8 percent of assets in institutions closed that year. Of the total amount of high yield bonds in the industry at their peak, 31 percent were held by one institution. Due primarily to accounting interpretations, high yield bonds were required to be "held for sale" and marked-to-market – the only type of asset ever to be uniformly

---

[8] For an analysis of high yield bonds in savings and loan portfolios, see Barth, Bartholomew, and Labich (1990).

marked-to-market in the savings and loan crisis. In addition, establishing a date by which high yield bonds had to be sold lowered their value, exacerbating the problems caused by their mark-to-market.

As part of the new minimum capital requirements, one particular provision – that received little public attention at the time – provided the basis for the third phase of the savings and loan crisis. It did so by setting the stage for protracted litigation that added a new contingent liability for the government. As discussed above, in the early 1980s creative regulatory accounting techniques allowed the government to avoid costly expenditures due to insolvent savings and loans. One of these techniques was the use of what came to be known as "supervisory goodwill," which was used in some mergers to postpone or escape cash expenditures that would have otherwise depleted the FSLIC's resources.[9]

THE THIRD PHASE OF THE CRISIS: POST-FIRREA GOODWILL SUITS

The Use of "Supervisory Goodwill"

In the supervisory mergers utilizing supervisory goodwill, a healthy institution would work with the appropriate regulators to acquire an institution that was market value insolvent. The government, represented by the Bank Board, caused the acquiring institution to put on its books an asset, the supervisory goodwill, roughly equal to the amount by which the insolvent institution's liabilities exceeded it assets. The amount was often referred to as the "negative net-worth hole," because it was the amount by which the institution was insolvent.

Following the merger, the new institution would write off, or depreciate, the asset over a long period of time, up to 40 years. Over that period both the government and the acquirer hoped that the new institution would operate profitably, and generate from its operations net assets more than sufficient to replace the goodwill asset, which gradually was becoming smaller.

Between 1980 and 1988, there were 333 supervisory mergers and 411 assisted mergers. As Figure 4 demonstrates, over that period of time the supervisory goodwill represented a significant part of total regulatory capital for savings and loans – and a similar amount of savings to the FSLIC. At its peak, the amount of supervisory goodwill was approximately $10 billion.

---

[9] For a summary of the issues involved, see Barth, Brumbaugh, and Dykema (2001).

Figure 4: Savings and Loan Industry Goodwill as a Portion of Regulatory Net Worth

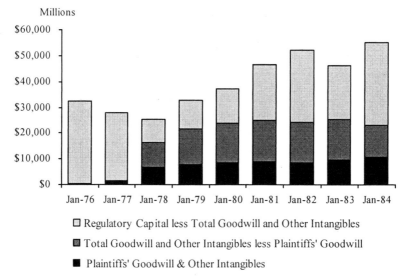

Source: FHLBB/OTS Thrift Financial Reports

The Government's Breach of Contract

FIRREA phased out supervisory goodwill from regulatory capital by January 1, 1995. In essence, Congress forced the very institutions that helped FSLIC, and by extension Congress itself, avoid billions in cost, to substantially accelerate the write-off of the goodwill in calculating regulatory capital.

The requirement set off a series of regulatory actions that often had devastating effects on the institutions. Many failed their minimum capital requirements, and some were seized as a result. Once they failed their capital requirement, they were subject to often brutal regulatory restrictions that significantly hampered their operations. Many had to shrink in size, forcing the sale of assets – most often some of their most valuable assets. Others were forced to raise capital under regulatory deadlines that resulted in smaller, and more costly, capital acquisition.

Damages: The Next Round of Government Costs

As a result, well over 100 institutions began filing claims against the government at the beginning of the 1990s, alleging that the government had breached contracts it had made with the institutions. In 1996, the U.S. Supreme Court found that FIRREA's changing of the accounting treatment of supervisory goodwill constituted a breach of contract by the federal government in Winstar et al. v. United States.

Having found in these cases that the government breached its contracts and was liable for damages, all the plaintiffs are now engaged in a lengthy battle to recover damages. As of early 2002, only a handful of the cases had been settled and most either were yet to be tried or had damage awards that were on appeal or reconsideration. Based on damages claimed, the total damages could amount to tens of billions of dollars, though it is likely that the amount eventually awarded will be substantially less.

The damage cases are being heard in the U.S. Court of Federal Claims, and appeals are heard by the U.S. Court of Appeals for the Federal Circuit. The Court of Claims has divided the cases into four groups known as the "priority," "first thirty," "second thirty" and "third thirty" cases. There are ten priority cases that have gone to trial on damages, and damage decisions have been rendered in nine, with one settling during trial. Another priority case settled prior to trial and a small number of the priority cases are awaiting trial. Of the remaining nonpriority cases only a handful have gone to trial, the rest await trial in 2003 or later.

Of the nine priority cases that received damage decisions from the Court of Claims, most, if not all, are in various stages of appeal and awaiting final resolution.

It is instructive, that although the initial claims were filed against the government in the early 1990s, as of year-end 2002 very few priority cases had gone to trial to determine damages, and very few have been completely resolved. The entire process, including some of the damage trials, has proven lengthy. The first damage trial did not begin until January 1997 and lasted fifteen months; another trial lasted more than 12 months. The remaining cases that have gone to trial have taken from a few weeks to several months to complete.

As of year-end 2002, no one can predict how long it will take for the priority cases that have been tried to go through the entire appeals process. As mentioned above, only a few of the first thirty cases have been through the trial stage, and only a few trials are scheduled for the second or third thirty cases. At the same time, no one can predict very precisely what the magnitude of the total damages may be.

As of year-end 2002, in the nine priority cases that are either in some stage of appeal or reconsideration, the initial damages awarded have been exceedingly small relative to the damages claimed. In the cases, damages claimed ranged from the low hundred million dollars to over two billion dollars, and the initial damages awarded have ranged from a low of zero to a high of almost $1 billion. In both the cases representing the low and high end of this range judgment was vacated by the Court of Appeals, subsequent reconsideration resulted in damages in the $150 million to $350 million range respectively, but appeals continue.

Given the total length of time that the cases have taken since the early 1990s, the expense of bringing the cases, and the relatively small size of the damage awards, it is possible that plaintiffs in some of the smaller remaining cases may choose not to pursue their claims. As for the remaining cases as of year-end 2002, the future is uncertain.

SUMMARY AND CONCLUSIONS

Leaving aside the ongoing contingent liability of the supervisory goodwill cases, the present value cost to resolve all of the savings and loan failures is approximately $153 billion. At the peak of the first phase of the crisis, the negative market value of the thrift industry portfolio of mortgages was approximately $110 billion. The difference of approximately $43 billion is one measure of the cost of forbearance. Among other things, that number assumes that nearly all of the savings and loan industry could have been closed in the early 1980s, and closed at a cost no greater than the negative value of their mortgage portfolio. It is unlikely that the cost would have been contained at that level.

Realistically, it was not feasible to close so many institutions under any circumstances at the time, and the cost of forbearance is thus less – probably substantially less – than $43 billion. Regardless, that amount is all but miniscule compared to U.S. GDP or even the federal budget in one year.

Thus, based on the criterion of cost to the government in the savings and loan crisis, a case can be made that forbearance was the appropriate policy because it bought time to deal with the crisis, and had minimal effect on the ultimate cost of closure. Yet, to conclude on that basis that forbearance is the appropriate policy to deal with unexpectedly large numbers of depository insolvencies is dangerous, because some combination of unexpected events could have led to an entirely different outcome.

REFERENCES

Barth, James R. (1991). *The Great Savings and Loan Debacle*. Washington: American Enterprise Institute.

Barth, James R., Philip R. Bartholomew and Carol Labich (1990). "The Determinants of Thrift-Institution Resolution Costs," *Journal of Finance*, 45, pp. 731-754.

Barth, James R. and R. Dan Brumbaugh, Jr. eds. (1992). *The Reform of Federal Deposit Insurance*. New York: HarperCollins Publishers Inc.

Barth, James R., R. Dan Brumbaugh, Jr., and Peter Dykema (2001). "Estimating Damages Associated with Federally Insured Banks," in Weil, Roman L., Michael J. Wagner, and Peter B. Frank, eds. *Litigation Services Handbook: The Role of the Financial Expert*. New York: John Wiley & Sons, Inc.

Barth, James R., R. Dan Brumbaugh, Jr., and Robert E. Litan (1992). *The Future of American Banking*. Armonk, N.Y.: M.E. Sharpe, Inc.

Beaver, William H., Srikant Datar, and Mark A. Wolfson (1992). "The Role of Market Value Accounting in the Regulation of Insured Depository Institutions," in James R. Barth and R. Dan Brumbaugh, Jr. eds., *The Reform of Federal Deposit Insurance*, New York: HarperCollins Publishers Inc.

Brumbaugh, R. Dan (1988). *Thrifts Under Siege: Restoring Order to American Banking*. Cambridge, Mass.: Ballinger Publishing Co.

Brumbaugh, R. Dan (1993). *The Collapse of Federally Insured Depositories: The Savings and Loans as Precursor*. New York: Garland Publishing, Inc.

Carron, Andrew S. (1982). *The Plight of the Thrift Institutions*. Washington, D.C.: The Brookings Institution.

Carron, Andrew S. (1984). *Reforming the Bank Regulatory Structure*. Washington, D.C.: The Brookings Institution.

England, Catherine, and Thomas Huertas, eds. (1987). *The Financial Services Revolution*. Norwell, Mass.: Kluwer Academic Publishers.

Horvitz, Paul M. (1983). "The Case Against Risk-Related Deposit Insurance Premiums," *Housing Policy Review* 2, pp. 253-263.

Kane, Edward J. (1985). *The Gathering Crisis in Deposit Insurance.* Cambridge, Mass.: MIT Press.

Kane, Edward J. (1989). *The S&L Insurance Mess: How Did It Happen?* Washington, D.C.: Urban Institute Press.

Kaufman, George G. and Roger C. Kormendi, eds. (1986). *Deregulating Financial Services, Public Policy in Flux.* Cambridge, Mass.: Ballinger Publishing Co..

Litan, Robert E. (1987). *What Should Banks Do?* Washington, D.C.: The Brookings Institution.

Pratt, Richard T. (1988). Statement before the Committee on Banking, Housing, and Urban Affairs. 100th Congress, 2nd session. August 3.

White, Lawrence J. (1991). "The Value of Market Value Accounting for the Deposit Insurance System," *Journal of Accounting, Auditing, and Finance*, 6.

Wilcox, James A. ed. (1987). *Current Readings on Money, Banking, and Financial Markets.* Boston: Little Brown & Co.

MACROECONOMIC SOURCES OF THE U.S. SAVINGS AND LOAN CRISIS

Michael R. Darby
The Anderson School
University of California, Los Angeles

The sources of financial institution crises differ for advanced market economies and economies in transition. Crises in developed market economies have their roots either in a sharp increase in the rate of inflation that wipes out equity in institutions that borrow short and lend long or in a prolonged and deep recession or depression that destroys equity through restrictions in the credit channel. In transition countries, on the other hand, crises are the product of government-directed lending. In non-market economies banks function very differently than in market economies. In the formerly communist countries, banks served the government authorities as alternative budgetary channels – as means of channeling money to appropriate state programs. This type of system was mirrored in emerging Asia and in Japan where industrial policy called for a system of banks to serve as conduits channeling resources to favored sectors, industries, firms (and indeed even relatives and cronies). The presence of these politically directed credits on banks' balance sheets causes problems for countries if they are not cleared from institutions' books before the transition to a market-based system.

U.S. savings and loans actually had some of the same features that non-market financial institutions typically possess. Prior to liberalization, the savings and loan industry quite closely resembled a system of government-directed credits targeted to politically favored borrowers. This system – which served to subsidize homeowner borrowers – was funded by government insured savings accounts. Accounts at savings and loans paid one-quarter of appoint above the interest paid on bank savings accounts under a *de facto* buyer's cartel administered by the Federal Reserve System, ensuring that the savings and loans would have adequate funding to lend on 30-year mortgages with low and fixed interest rates. Funding long-term loans with short-term variable rate deposits implied that the industry was characterized by a massive mismatch of asset and liability maturities. This system of lending long and borrowing short worked reasonably well during the low and stable interest rate period before the 1970s (see Figure 1) but broke under pressure from changing macroeconomic conditions beginning in the late 1970s.

The savings and loan industry was still solvent as a whole in 1970, but rising market interest rates were making it increasingly difficult to keep savings in savings and loan institutions. As shown in Figure 2, the 1970s saw a dramatic increase in interest rates that caused savings and loans' assets to collapse in value while their liabilities maintained their values. As rates soared, the cost of savings and loan deposits outpaced the interest earned on savings and loan mortgage portfolios. This asset-liability mismatch was a feature of the industry as a whole no matter whether one looks at it from an income statement or a balance sheet perspective.

Figure 1: The Prelude: 30-Year Conventional Mortgage versus 3-month Treasury Bill Yields

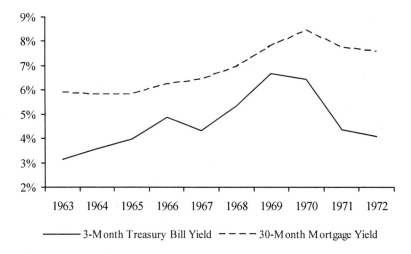

Sources: Federal Reserve and the Economic Report of the President.

Figure 2: The Crisis: 30-Year Conventional Mortgage versus 3-month Treasury Bill Yields

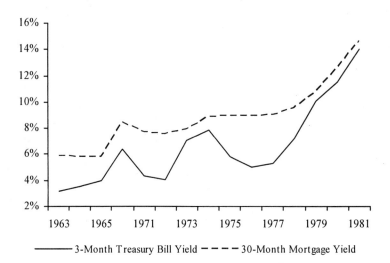

Sources: Federal Reserve and the Economic Report of the President.

In terms of regulation, forbearance was the great hope of those policy makers who sought to cover up the disaster that had occurred in the industry. The idea behind forbearance was that a sound monetary policy would permit interest rates to fall as inflation was brought under control. As rates fell, the problems that had beset the savings and loan industry would disappear and the savings and loans would return to profitability and the industry to its pre-crisis state. The macroeconomic environment that had sparked the savings and loan crisis did, in fact, improve (see Figure 3), but its improvement came too late for the industry. The problem with a policy of forbearance as advocated by U.S. Congressman Jim Wright and others during the crisis was that it did not work. Forbearance encouraged honest savings and loan operators to take what were basically one-sided bets and attempt to gamble their institutions back to health. It also provided – in allowing zero-value savings and loans to stay open – plentiful low-cost opportunities for dishonest purchasers to engage in excessively risky or fraudulent activities.

Figure 3. Where We Are Now: 30-Year Conventional Mortgage versus 3-month Treasury Bill Yields

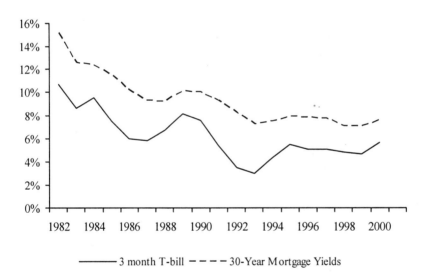

Source: Federal Reserve and the Economic Report of the President.

The question that presents itself is whether the macroeconomic origins of the savings and loan crisis arose accidentally or through bad luck or whether they were the result of bad policy. The answer is that the problems were caused by bad policy. As seen in Figure 4, the proximate cause of the increase in interest rates that ruined the savings and loan industry was inflation. A bivariate regression shows that interest rates are largely a function of inflation – measured here as the two year moving average trend change in the

Consumer Price Index. Indeed, the trend change in inflation explains 56 percent of the variance in yields on 3-month U.S. Treasury bills. The simple answer to the question of what caused the crisis was that, just as Irving Fisher showed (see Text Box below) interest rates rose with the increase in inflationary expectations. This increase in interest rates was exacerbated by the fact that interest was taxable to lenders but was tax-deductible to borrowers (Darby 1976). This asymmetry in the tax treatment of interest made for even greater volatility in interest rates.

Figure 4. The Proximate Cause: 3-month Treasury Bill Yields and 2-year Moving Average Trend CPI

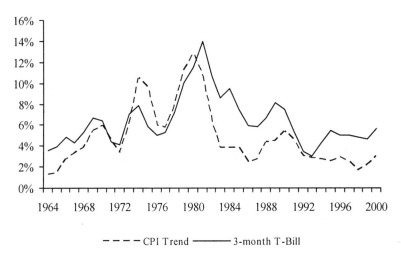

Sources: Federal Reserve and the Economic Report of the President.

However, inflationary expectations are merely the *proximate* cause of the increase in rates and thus not the *real*, underlying cause of the crisis. The actual cause of the difficulties experienced by the savings and loan industry was the Federal Reserve's belief that money didn't matter. At the pre-Volcker Federal Reserve, there was a failure to understand that, in the long run, inflation is a function of the money supply and thus money does matter. Figure 5 shows the relationship between the CPI and the two-year moving average trend change (lagged by 4 years) in M2.[1] Again, a simple bivariate regression shows that lagged M2 explains almost 45 percent of the variance in interest rates. Money matters, ultimately, because the price level – the change

---

[1] M2 consists of currency, traveler's checks, demand deposits, retail money market funds, savings and small time deposits.

in which is inflation – is the inverse of the price of money. The price level is the ratio of dollars to goods and the price of money is simply the ratio of goods to dollars. Thus inflation reflects the supply and demand of money. Such a simple relationship – supply and demand – one might expect central bankers to be aware of, but at the pre-Volcker Federal Reserve, they were not.

Figure 5. The Cause: Money and 2-year Moving Average Trend CPI

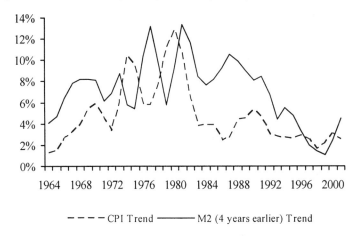

Source: Federal Reserve and the Economic Report of the President.

The question of whether there could be another crisis in the U.S. can be answered with an affirmative. While it will not likely affect the savings and loan industry, it is quite feasible that mismatched assets and liabilities elsewhere in the financial services industry could turn into a full-fledged crisis after a period of inflation caused by loose monetary policy. One need not worry however, if, as Greenspan tells us, recession, inflation and the importance of money are all old economy problems and thus things of the past.

The Fisher Equation

The nominal interest rate, according to Fisher's equation, is the sum of the real interest rate and expected inflation. At the time of making an investment decision, the lender expects to be compensated for, not only the intertemporal opportunity cost of using the money, but also its probable loss of purchasing power. Thus, the fluctuation of nominal interest rates also depends on the inflationary expectations which are fundamentally related to the demand and supply of money.

Holding money demand constant, an expansion in the money supply will decrease the value of money, which in turn will require more money to purchase the same amount of goods and services. In addition, the expected inflation will also cause money demand to decline as the opportunity cost of using money in the current time period increases. This process will increase expected inflation even further.

An understanding of this relationship is crucial for policy makers. In the 1970s, for example, U.S. monetary policy attempted to hold interest rates stable by increasing the money supply but actually induced interest rates to increase further due to inflationary expectations.

REFERENCE

Darby, Michael R. (1975). "The Financial and Tax Effects of Monetary Policy on Interest Rates," *Economic Inquiry,* June, 13, pp. 266-276.

Charticle 4
Excessive Growth of Savings and Loan Assets

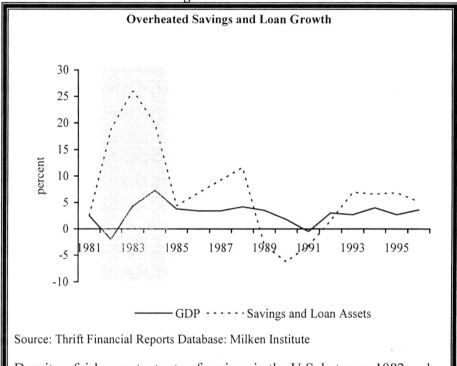

Overheated Savings and Loan Growth

——— GDP · · · · · · Savings and Loan Assets

Source: Thrift Financial Reports Database: Milken Institute

Despite a fairly constant rate of savings in the U.S. between 1982 and 1984, savings and loan asset growth peaked at over 25% (annual). Compared to overall growth in the economy, furthermore, savings and loans simply grew too fast, putting enormous pressure on themselves to find new and profitable investment vehicles.

WHAT LESSONS MIGHT CRISIS COUNTRIES IN ASIA AND LATIN AMERICA HAVE LEARNED FROM THE SAVINGS AND LOAN MESS?

Edward J. Kane
Boston College

Economic insolvency strikes a financial enterprise when it suffers losses that destroy its capacity to repay depositors and other creditors without outside assistance. Individual insolvencies are rooted in poor or dishonest management, bad luck, defective information systems, and superior competitors.

In the face of entry pressure from more-efficient and better-capitalized competitors, any governmental system of deposit insurance can easily degenerate into an expensive mechanism for retarding the exit of insolvent deposit-institution competitors. Although no two financial crises unfold in exactly the same way, such events are driven by the interaction of the risky lending and funding strategies that lead to the economic insolvency of individual institutions and the risky regulatory strategies that government supervisors and regulators use to handle institutional insolvencies when they develop.

The major lesson of the U.S. savings and loans mess is how egregiously regulatory and bank risk-taking can reinforce one another. For individual insolvencies to persist for years on end requires that—at some level of government—officials sell insolvent institutions protection against failure and conspire at least implicitly with internal and external auditors to conceal the holes in individual balance sheets. As long as the coverup succeeds, the lending policies of troubled institutions escape the ordinary weight of depositor discipline.

The explanation for accounting and regulatory dereliction is incentive conflict at a country's designated watchdog institutions. The solution conflict lies in reworking the watchdogs' incentives in the social contracts that are breaking down. The conflict at issue is the tradeoff between regulators' and accountants' social missions and the personal and bureaucratic costs of resisting client pressure for relief. Ironically, the accounting and regulatory strategies that ruined the Federal Savings and Loan Insurance Corporation (FSLIC) and the U.S. savings and loan industry were of the industry's own making. Even more ironically, these discredited strategies closely resemble the policies that multinational firms and the International Monetary Fund (IMF) have implicitly urged on crisis countries in Asia and Latin America (e.g., Fischer, 2001).

Guaranteeing the debt of insolvent institutions and covering up the loss exposures this creates for a country's taxpayers is costly in three ways. First, by allowing important institutions to operate in an insolvent condition, authorities leave poorly performing assets and franchises in the hands of managers whose lending and funding incentives are distorted by capital weaknesses. Because the downside of future returns belongs to the guarantor, insolvent firms are tempted to invest the savings entrusted to them in lottery-like projects that combine a negative present value with a small chance of a very large payoff. Second, until the cover-up begins to unravel, accounting disinformation insulates the guidance and forbearance decisions that government officials are making from financial and political review. Finally, any cover-up is likely to be accompanied by microeconomically inefficient pricing and entry restrictions intended to protect the markets of troubled firms from close competitors. However, because of their inefficiency, these restrictions are apt to boomerang against the industry in the long run.

Industry-welcomed restraints on stronger U.S. deposit-institution competitors ultimately helped less-regulated outside competitors such as foreign banks, money-market mutual funds, and brokerage firms offering cash management accounts to take market share from the industry they were supposed to help. While troubled savings and loans implored government officials to wall off intra-industry access to their customer base behind deposit-rate ceilings and geographic barriers, differently chartered institutions devised substitute instruments that used emerging electronic technologies to innovate through and around the industry's regulatory defenses.

Effective long-run regulatory performance requires improved accountability for policy mistakes and accountability begins with accurate information. Throughout the savings and loan mess, authorities showed a propensity for blocking flows of information that threatened to harm their individual and collective reputations.

Incentive reform must start with a serious effort to reduce the benefits of accounting cover-up. To increase the timeliness and accuracy of information that managers of insured institutions, managers of deposit insurance funds and incumbent politicians supply to taxpayers, improved economic and political incentives are needed in government service. The more a country's political and cultural environment tolerates *de facto* corruption, the more useful it would be to offer deferred compensation to the chief executives of banks and deposit insurance enterprises and to tie retiring officials' right to draw down this compensation either to the absence of crisis during the first five years after their departure or (if information systems permit) to a market-value measure of the change in the insurer's net loss exposure observed during their term in office (Kane, 2002).

ACCOUNTING COVER-UPS IN THE SAVINGS AND LOAN MESS

In the 1960s and 1970s, the core activity of U.S. savings and loan institutions was to make long-term mortgage loans financed with short-term deposits. These short-funded portfolios exposed these institutions' economic income and net worth to losses whenever interest rates rose. The secular rise in interest rates and interest-rate volatility experienced between 1965 and 1982 generated unbooked losses on savings and loan mortgages that devastated the economic value of industry income and net worth.

FSLIC furnished dividend-free risk capital and supplied enough of it to fill in the holes in troubled firms' balance sheets for over 30 years. During this interval, red ink flowing through savings and loan income and balance sheets seeped into the accounts of FSLIC and, through FSLIC, onto U.S. taxpayers.

Although savings and loan and government accountants refused to formally recognize these losses as they were accruing, the damage being done could not be hidden completely. Across an institution's portfolio, the impact of interest-rate movements could be estimated with a reasonable degree of accuracy by appraisal techniques. For example, estimates summarized by Kane (1989) and Brumbaugh (1988) clarify that, at least from 1971 on, the savings and loan industry could not expect to repay its deposit liabilities from its own resources. The survival of these institutions depended on the black magic of government guarantees rather than on the earning power of their assets. What kept insolvent savings and loans from being closed down by depositor runs was the willingness of the FSLIC to promise depositors credible protection against loss. Their perverse life-in-death existence may be likened instructively to that exhibited by the hordes of marauding zombies featured in George Romero horror movies.

When individual insolvencies spread and deepen in any country, the long-run problem for a deposit insurance enterprise lies in keeping its guarantees credible to deposit-institution customers. A private guarantor would do this by identifying and forcing the recapitalization of troubled institutions as soon as they weaken. Tolerating widespread insolvency plants and fertilizes the seeds of a deeper crisis. A government insurer can avoid a crisis as long as it keeps its loss exposure small enough that depositors can reasonably rely on the faith and credit of the national Treasury to explicitly or implicitly augment the insurer's resources. However, on average, risk-taking incentives at zombie firms tend to make the insurer's loss exposure grow over time. Crises develop when and as the market value of the implicit government debt embodied in the Treasury's support begins to swamp the incremental tax capacity a nation needs to service it.

Around the world, the valuation and itemization principles that deposit-institution accountants and regulators use to measure banking profits and net worth contain options that make it possible for large opportunity losses to be hidden from public view. Until and unless challenged by economic analysis, using these options can generate phantom and nonrecurring profits that overstate net worths for years on end. Cooked books and the earnings projections based upon them resemble the digital readouts from a scale rigged by a dishonest butcher. With a show of irrelevant precision, authorities can systematically and repeatedly mismeasure the obligations that deposit insurance is putting on taxpayers' bill.

A private guarantor would recognize and seek to counter an insolvent client's interest in fabricating profit and net worth. Part of the policy scandal embodied in the savings and loan mess was authorities' repeated willingness to creatively extend the accounting leeway that savings and loans and FSLIC could use to further slow down reportable deterioration in FSLIC's balance-sheet position. Table 1 shows that until 1986 *official* estimates of FSLIC's net reserves remained reassuringly positive. Table 2 illustrates the increasing magnitude of the economic losses that authorities were covering up. Using market-value estimates of the enterprise-contributed net worth of every FSLIC-insured institution existing or closed in fiscal years 1985-1989, the table displays the aggregate loss exposure that bureaucrats at FSLIC managed to keep off their books until the cover-up unraveled.

Table 1: Official Estimates of FSLIC Reserves, 1960-1986

Year end	Total reserves ($ million)	Percentage of value of accounts insured
1960	381	0.62%
1965	1537	1.35
1970	2903	2.05
1975	4120	1.48
1980	6462	1.28
1985	4600	0.54
1986	-6300	-0.71

Source: Kane (1989, p. 9).

Table 2: Estimates of Taxpayers' Unbooked Loss Exposure in FSLIC, 1985-1989

Date*	Exposure ($ billion)
September 30, 1985	86.4
September 30, 1986	122.5
September 30, 1987	106.8
September 30, 1988	161.3
August 9, 1989	161.1

* In these years FSLIC's fiscal year ran from September to September. August 9, 1989, was the last day on which FSLIC officially existed. Even these estimates understate the size of FSLIC's losses because they neglect the implicit financing cost of carrying these losses.

Source: Kane (1993).

If government guarantees had not been supplied on favorable terms, private creditors would have forced insolvent savings and loans to recapitalize themselves (perhaps by transferring ownership in whole or in part to large creditors) or else see themselves merged or liquidated out of existence. To keep accrued losses from registering on FSLIC's books, regulators had to help insolvent savings and loans hide losses and resist forms of exit that would have revealed the size of their capital shortage. Because a guarantor assumes the deep downside of private creditors' exposure to loss, economic theory dictates that a conscientious deposit insurer should exercise market-mimicking disciplines. In not staking for itself an explicit claim to the future profits of zombie firms, FSLIC encouraged private owners and managers to take poorly structured, long shot gambles. For zombie savings and loans, the beauty of these gambles was that FSLIC took the downside and permitted savings and loan owners and managers to lay claim to much of the upside potential.

Opportunities for borrowers to over-leverage themselves could not have burgeoned unless insolvent lenders believed that they could shift their own expanding loss exposure to FSLIC. Loss exposures could be expanded because neither insolvent lenders nor their government regulators had strong incentives to fully evaluate and disclose the risks being taken.

In medicine, the word "crisis" describes the point in the course of a disease at which a decisive change occurs. Often a crisis may be averted by seizing one or more "golden moments" during which improved medical care can cure the disease relatively simply.

In retrospect, one can see that FSLIC passed up two golden moments for capping its losses. First, if, instead of nullifying market pressures for exit and recapitalization during the late 1960s, FSLIC had forced insolvent savings and loans to recapitalize, merge, or liquidate themselves, the savings and loan industry could never have remained short-funded and undercapitalized enough to load such large losses onto FSLIC in later years. Second, even if this opportunity had been missed, subsequent losses could have been reduced if recapitalization had been sought when disinflation sharply lowered interest rates in 1982-1983. In fact, the Federal Deposit Insurance Corporation appropriately seized this second window of opportunity to discipline the roughly 500 short-funded savings banks that it insured.

Sadly, by the time that interest rates turned down in mid-1982, savings and loan trade associations had successfully lobbied Congress for new ways to take and hide risk. Supplementing their traditional concentration in long-term home mortgage assets, many savings and loans began to load up with riskier loans aimed at financing residential and commercial real estate development and holdings of raw land. If insolvent savings and loans had been forced to recapitalize in 1982-1983, loans made under this new regulatory regime would have been better structured and would have therefore generated fewer losses. Such a recapitalization would have spared the nation a costly spate of overbuilding. Insolvent savings and loans would not have spent so many years pouring funds into an overheated U.S. real estate market in an industry-approved and regulator-authorized effort to help insolvent savings and loans "grow out of their weakness."

UNBOOKED FISCAL DEFICITS AS A SOURCE OF FINANCIAL FRAGILITY[1]

Three strategic elements characterized pre-crisis policies toward savings and loans and these same three elements appear in the banking policies of almost every country in the world today:

1. *Politically directed subsidies to a politically favored class of bank borrowers.* The policy framework either requires or rewards banks for making credit available to designated classes of borrowers at a subsidized interest rate;
2. *Subsidies to bank risk-taking.* The policy framework commits government officials to providing on subsidized terms either explicit or conjectural guarantees to holders of bank liabilities;

---

[1] This section draws heavily on Kane (2000a).

3. *Defective monitoring and control of the subsidies.* The contracting and reporting framework for government officials fails to make them directly accountable for controlling the size of either subsidy.

Rent-seeking theory explains why short-horizoned authorities would allow banks to extract wealth from taxpayers and would require loan officers to transfer some or all of that wealth to politically favored borrowers. The third element in the strategy explains what prevents taxpayers from seeing the implicit expenditures generated by the first two elements and from disciplining inappropriate transfers in a timely fashion through political action or parliamentary review. Imposing civil and criminal penalties on officials who can be shown after the fact to have *willfully* provided less than their best estimate of their enterprise's economic value would reduce the benefits of forbearance. It would create an enforceable obligation for regulators to report truthfully to taxpayers and watchdog institutions the size of the dual subsidies. Passing this information through the government budget would make authorities accountable for explaining whether and how taxpayer benefits generated by the subsidies justify the costs that they impose on taxpayers.

Without side payments from the rent-seeking sectors, it would be unlikely that a growing flow of subsidies could prove incentive-compatible for top government officials even for short periods. To enlist high-ranking regulators permanently into the benefit-redistribution game, two further conditions must hold. First, taxpayers must be prevented from assessing by indirect means the magnitude of the costs they face in funding the subsidies. Second, regulators themselves must receive suitably laundered incentive compensation from banks and borrowers. The compensation offered must be sufficient to balance exposure to legal penalties and the risk of damage to the reputations of policymakers and the regulatory bureaus they head if, during their watch on the bridge, the system for covertly financing the subsidy were to break down.

A banking-policy regime that greatly subsidizes risk-taking may be portrayed as an accident waiting to happen. A banking crisis occurs when a sufficient amount of bad luck hits a banking system whose managers have made their institutions vulnerable to this amount and type of bad luck. The savings and loan mess teaches us that the odds of experiencing a bureaucratic breakdown in a country's intersectoral cost-shifting process may be modeled as an evolutionary process in which the odds of breakdown increase as the size of unbooked government guarantees grows.

The larger accumulated opportunity-cost losses become, the larger the off-balance-sheet debt with which fiscal authorities are being saddled. What we may call a "silent run" begins *not* when a bank becomes a zombie, but when the accumulated implicit fiscal deficit from the government's unbooked loss exposure in zombie banks begins to scare large-denomination depositors. As more and more depositors and investors rationally begin to doubt whether officials can or will continue to support the guarantees, the silent run on a country's banking system gathers steam.

Doubts about a government's willingness and capacity to make taxpayers absorb the unfunded cost of guaranteeing the country's zombie banks are a function of its tax capacity. The triggering condition is that the aggregate guarantees soar so far above dedicated reserves that taxpayer resistance is expected to develop. This political resistance threatens the incumbent government's survival and promises to undermine its ability to raise the funds needed to pay the bill in full. We describe runs by sophisticated large depositors as silent because pressure on a troubled bank from savvy depositors generates far less adverse publicity than a line of panicked small depositors does when a bank is experiencing a conventional run.

A silent run speeds the endgame because it generates an observable increase in each zombie bank's funding costs. In developing countries, a zombie bank's first line of defense against a silent run is usually to arrange loans from relatively well-informed foreign banks. Like the sophisticated depositors that zombie bankers manage to retain, foreign banks demand higher interest rates and appropriate collateralization for their claims. The net outflows of domestic deposits that zombie banks experience are financed by a combination of selected asset sales and high-rate new debt. In consciously deciding to finance a silent run, foreign banks may feel confident that (as in Mexico in 1994) they can successfully lobby the IMF, their host government, and their home governments to protect them against defaults by host country banks. (Table 3 reports the amounts and types of external assistance received by seven crisis countries in recent years.) Foreign banks may also find it advantageous to speculate against the currency in offshore derivatives markets.

Table 3: Assistance Offered Crisis Countries by the International Community

	Commitments [a] ($ billion)			
	IMF	Multilateral[b]	Bilateral	Total
Brazil	$18.10	$9.00	$14.50	$41.60
Indonesia	$11.20	$10.00	$21.10	$42.30
Korea	$21.10	$14.20	$23.10	$58.40
Mexico	$17.70	$0.00	$31.30[c]	$49.00
Philippines [d]	$1.60	$0.00	$0.00	$1.60
Russian Federation[e]	$15.10	$6.00	$1.50	$22.60
Thailand	$4.00	$2.70	$10.50	$17.20
Total	$88.80	$41.90	$102.00	$232.70

(a) The rescue packages for each country cover resources made available for time periods specific to each case; (b) World Bank and Regional Development Bank; (c) includes $10 billion credit line from BIS; (d) as of end of 1998; (e) through end of 1999.

Sources: Garcia (1998, p. 27) and Christiansen (2001, p. 134).

Unless and until bank regulators take steps to increase the credibility of their guarantee system (e.g., by establishing a substantial line of credit with the IMF), a silent run on a nation's banking system tends to escalate. This is because zombie banks' asset sales and funding-cost increases make the fragility of the zombies' condition visible to less-sophisticated observers by causing an inescapable deterioration in the accounting values of income and net worth. When a zombie bank sells assets at market value, its unbooked losses on subsidized loans become a larger proportion of its footings. Similarly, the more liabilities that a zombie bank rolls over at increased interest rates, the more severely its accounting and economic profit is going to be squeezed.

A silent run increases pressure on regulators to acknowledge that zombie banks are benefiting from government guarantees and that stronger banks and ordinary taxpayers will be asked to pay the bill. As the pressure builds, it progressively undermines the willingness of taxpayers and stronger banks to tolerate the regulatory *status quo*. The transfer of benefits to insolvent institutions from taxpayers and viable banks becomes progressively greater the longer a silent run proceeds. Regulatory efforts to retard the exit of inefficient and insolvent deposit institutions lower the profit margins that strong banks can earn on borrowed funds and push their prospective costs for funding the government's guarantee services above the value of the guarantees that they themselves receive.

This theory of crisis may be contrasted with that of authors such as Chang and Velasco (1998) who locate the trigger for financial crisis directly in a growing mismatch in the *maturity* of a country's international assets and liabilities. Our theory predicts that such an imbalance in maturity develops as an endogenous consequence of insolvency-driven silent runs. A shortening of the maturity of capital inflows is triggered by foreign lenders' increasing concern for being able to unwind the positions they establish in economically insolvent host-country banks. But for troubled banks to receive new funding, their government's guarantees must remain credible domestically.

In country after country, officials have actively encouraged loss-causing patterns of credit allocation and compounded the damage from credit losses by not resolving individual-bank insolvencies until their economic capital had deteriorated disastrously. When the cover-up dissolves, domestic (and sometimes foreign) taxpayers are billed to bail out banks, depositors, and deposit insurance funds. Caprio and Klingebiel (1999) report that taxpayers' bills for making good on implicit and explicit guarantees has typically run between 1 and 10 percent of GDP. The size of these bills underscores the real costs of allowing the corrupted risk-taking preferences of high government officials to shape the flow of aggregate investment.

GOVERNMENT EXIT RESISTANCE

Taxpayers (including strong financial institutions) are likely to be forced eventually to finance deposit insurance losses. Efficiency requires that taxpayers be able to observe and control politically the depth and breadth of deposit-institution insolvencies as they are developing. Regulatory tolerance of go-for-broke risk taking by insolvent institutions undermines the stability of a country's financial system and allows institutional losses to cumulate relentlessly. In the U.S. and abroad, regulators' tolerance for risk-taking is negotiated behind closed doors in an unacknowledged and corrupt market for political clout.

The ultimate cause of deep crises is the displacement of healthy market discipline by unaccountable systems of government supervision. Asian and Latin American taxpayers and public servants need to understand that bad luck, aggressive management, and looting are not exogenous "causes" of financial crises.

Improvements in financial technology and increasing price volatility for financial instruments have been transforming the equilibrium market structure of the financial-services industry in and across countries. Starting in the mid-

1960s, the U.S. deposit insurance system began to counteract natural market pressure on failing savings and loan institutions to voluntarily recapitalize themselves or exit through merger or liquidation. This exit resistance was the root of FSLIC's *aggregate* losses. Individual client losses were caused by bad economic luck, poor management, insider crime, structural weaknesses in risk-management controls, and the slower-acting effects of well-meaning regulatory interference. However, in trying to sustain the inefficient market structure they inherited, authorities transformed government deposit insurance in the U.S., which had enjoyed 30 years of initial success, into a system for nurturing inefficient and unsound firms and perversely rewarding socially imprudent investments. Not forcing insolvent institutions to promptly resolve their insolvencies rewarded unsound banking practices and effected an unintended, badly structured, but (happily) temporary nationalization of a large segment of the nation's financial assets and institutions.

After a long period of expansion, in the mid-1990s Asian and Latin American banking industries faced parallel pressure for domestic-bank exits. In many countries, foreign and nontraditional financial firms had to introduce themselves in circumventive ways. They did host country business by making creative use of substitute products, substitute organizational forms, or substitute offshore locations. As in the savings and loan mess, in most countries a new entrant's ability to use differently regulated substitute opportunities was facilitated by longstanding and burdensome restrictions on how local deposit institutions could compete domestically.

Again, as in the savings and loan mess, authorities in these countries were reluctant to encourage the prompt recapitalization of banks that were weakened by outside competition or to estimate the size and publish the opportunity cost of the risk capital that protecting these banks required their taxpayers to supply. Politically and administratively, it was much easier in the short run to use loopholes in bank and government accounting principles to conceal the extent of industry weakness from public view and to suppress information that might generate political pressure for a different and stricter course of action.

In public-policy discussions, lobbyists euphemistically describe as "regulatory forbearance" the insolvency-management policies that are more lenient than those that one would expect informed taxpayer "principals" to prefer. What makes forbearance strategies attractive are: (1) the campaign donations and other forms of monetary tribute that government officials can collect in exchange and (2) the long period of time during which government and trade-association spokespersons can credibly hide the extent of insolvency. Political deal making is further assisted by the understanding that the flawed accounting records they certify will make it difficult later to credibly pin the consequences of inappropriate forbearance decisions on the particular officials who conceived and executed them.

Side payments, the lack of reliable measures of an insurer's true condition, and the absence of audit trails for forbearance decisions or their consequences encourage officials to delay recapitalization pressure and to gamble on making a "clean getaway" either to a longer term in office or to a high-paying job in the private sector. By blaming officials disproportionately for whatever problems manage to surface while they are in office and by not nailing officials for the forecastable future damage they create when they adopt short-sighted supervisory strategies, the press and voting public reinforce authorities' propensity to gamble inefficiently with taxpayer money.

THE REGULATORY-GAMBLING THEORY OF FINANCIAL CRISIS

The seeds of the savings and loan mess lie in defective incentives for measuring and controlling the taxpayer loss exposures that politicians and top regulatory officials create (Kane, 1989; Barth, 1991; White, 1991). These incentive defects engender conflicts with bureaucratic and personal goals that, in tough times and in tough cases, tempt government officials around the world not to enforce the underwriting standards, coverage limitations, and takeover rights that constitute taxpayers' best theoretical defenses against cumulative deposit insurance losses.

Applying the theory of principal-agent conflict (Jensen and Meckling, 1976) to safety-net policies can explain allegedly inadvertent policy failures in the pricing and administration of government deposit insurance as calculated risk-taking behavior. Favoring the interests of a nation's decapitalized institutions can serve politicians' and regulators' interests at the expense of society in general. Forbearance may be expected to keep a politician's and regulator's watch on the bridge less turbulent, to preserve officials' reputations, to improve opportunities for reelection or post-government employment, and to generate a flow of implicit or explicit side payments. An acid test by which to distinguish an innocent mistake from a self-interested "calculated gamble" is the immediacy and sincerity of a perpetrator's regret. An error is regretted simply because it is wrong; a calculated gamble is regretted only if and because it fails.

Incumbent politicians and bureaucrats have short time horizons and narrow career and reputational interests that frequently diverge from those of taxpayers. What was and is missing from deposit insurance arrangements in most countries is timely *accountability* for the opportunity losses that tolerating insolvencies imposes on taxpayers. In a representative democracy, once the loss exposure of a government deposit insurance corporation outruns its budgeted resources, divergences in taxpayer and regulator interests make it rational for opportunistic authorities to abuse their discretion by covering up evidence of insolvencies at the institutions they supervise and by postponing painful loss-control activity to their successor's watch on the bridge.

Bankers want government guarantees as a competitive advantage. During their limited time on the bridge, politicians see government guarantees as a way to avoid being embarrassed by a wave of bank failures and in some cases as a way to directly or indirectly enrich themselves by corruptly selling options for delaying failure. Because taxpayers do not offer incentive payments and because officials' reputational and career interests leave them more directly answerable to politicians and bankers than to taxpayers, government regulators are pulled more strongly in practice toward subsidizing deposit-institution operations by avoiding failures than they are toward minimizing the long-run costs of taxpayer loss exposures. Although highly ethical individual regulators may routinely reject these temptations, the main lesson of the savings and loan mess is that it is fatuous for society to depend on a regulatory framework whose successful operation demands repeated acts of selflessness by its top managers. Although top government officials are explicitly screened for public spiritedness, temptations posed by defects in regulatory incentives become increasingly hard to resist once a deposit insurance enterprise develops a capital shortage.

In financial markets around the world, technological and political forces have forced decisions to deregulate *entry* on reluctant politicians and regulators. But markets have had a harder time forcing elected politicians and top regulatory officials to deregulate *exit*. Officials have a short-run reputational interest in retarding the exit of economically insolvent and inefficient firms when these happen to fall within their traditional client base. The principal-agent conflict this passes on to a country's taxpayers depends on the degree of accountability public servants feel.

Kane (2000a) shows that, in Asian crisis countries, Japanese banks (who have themselves been in continual crisis since the early 1990s) amassed the biggest pre-crisis positions and during crisis months beat the strongest retreat. The continued insolvency of major Japanese banks meant that banking policies and conditions in Japan created incentives for Japanese bankers to book extraordinarily high-risk loans at home and abroad (Kane, 2000a and

2000b). Even at year-end 1998, the exposure of Japanese banks in Indonesia, South Korea, and Thailand remained high.

The expansion of foreign lending by insolvent Japanese banks was bound to squeeze the profit margins of host-country banks. Host-country profit margins and economic net worth were also steadily undermined by domestic political pressure for banks to make subsidized loans to politically selected economic sectors. To restore industry profit margins to a sustainable level, exits had to occur. Crisis became a political mechanism for some insolvent institutions to finally be closed or absorbed into stronger enterprises.

SUMMARY IMPLICATIONS

Economic analysis supports the view that incentive incompatibilities inherent in representative democracy make opportunistic government officials a source of financial instability. They control their reporting frameworks and they can generate personal and bureaucratic benefits in exchange for adopting suboptimal strategies of cover-up and forbearance. Officials are perennially tempted to distort information flows about the quality of their performance in the short run and to repeatedly delay market-structure adjustments that would serve taxpayers' long-run interests.

It is dangerous for taxpayers not to contractually counterbalance officials' exposure to undisclosed side payments and lobbying pressure that might inappropriately persuade them to give government resources to crippled institutions. In crisis countries everywhere, longstanding systems for subsidizing inefficient loans to favored individuals imposed unbooked losses on their banking systems. Banking policies have been messy: marked by scandal, short-lived administrations, delays in making important decisions, and lack of transparency in decision-making processes.

Nevertheless, the messy policies have lasted for years. The messes turned into banking and currency crises only when doubts began to surface about authorities' willingness and ability to support the growing liabilities of their economically insolvent banking system. The savings and loan mess teaches us to view a regulation-induced banking crisis as the surfacing of tensions caused by the continuing efforts of zombie institutions to use the safety net to force the rest of society to pick up their unpaid bill for making bad loans. In the U.S., pressure to resolve the mess was triggered by silent runs that reflected a growing concern that taxpayers might resist paying the full value of conjectural government guarantees.

The wave of banking and currency crises splashing through Asia and Latin America is propelled by two trends. First, advances in information and communications technology are increasingly globalizing previously disconnected local banking markets and interconnected political markets for government subsidies. Second, the globalization of markets for banking and guarantee services is making it increasingly less costly for domestic corporations and wealthy investors to mount silent runs on a country's insolvent banks.

When banking markets are globalized, services that provide regulatory benefits to bank customers are available from foreign as well as domestic suppliers. The greater is customer access to foreign suppliers, the more easily the struggle for net regulatory benefits in one country can spill outside its national boundaries to involve foreign banks and their home-country suppliers of financial regulation.

Inadequate constraint on the pursuit of self-interest by government officials is the root cause of large taxpayer losses and continues to threaten countries with inappropriate supervision today. Financial deregulation did not cause the U.S. savings and loan mess. Nor has it caused recent Asian and Latin American crises. Financial deregulation may be defined as an unambiguous relaxation of the rules of financial services competition for all players. Modern crises are caused predominantly by corrupt de-supervision of the capital positions and risk exposures of insolvent and inefficient financial services firms.

Public-service incentives need to be reworked to make it less attractive for authorities to help troubled deposit institutions to resist healthy exit pressure. Using data covering 61 countries in the years 1980-1997, Demirgüç-Kunt and Detragiache (2000) show that deposit insurance perversely contributes to banking fragility in countries where institutional controls on incentive conflict are weak. Ideally, in every country managerial markets for the services of current and former government officials ought to reward rather than punish officials who protect taxpayer interests faithfully at the expense of having their reputations hammered by regulatory clients and their political allies. But to play this role, the press must be empowered to offer these labor markets much better information about the risks that banks and regulators take and when they take them.

REFERENCES

Barth, James R. (1991). *The Great Savings and Loan Debacle.* Washington: The AEI Press.

Brumbaugh, R. Dan Jr. (1988). *Thrifts Under Siege.* Cambridge, MA: Ballinger Publishing Co.

Caprio, Gerard and Daniela Klingebiel (1999). "Episodes of Systemic and Borderline Financial Crisis," Washington, D.C.: The World Bank, Financial Sector Strategy and Policy Development.

Chang, Roberto and Andres Velasco (1998). "The Asian Liquidity Crisis" Cambridge, MA: National Bureau of Economic Research, Working Paper No. 6796.

Christiansen, Hans (2001). "Moral Hazard and International Financial Crises in the 1990s," *Financial Market Trends.* 78, March, pp. 115-139.

Demirgüç-Kunt, Asli and Enrica Detragiache (2002). "Does Deposit Insurance Increase Banking System Stability?" An Empirical Investigation," *Journal of Monetary Economics.* 49(7), October, pp. 1373-1406.

Fischer, Stanley (2001). "Financial Sector Crisis Management," Seminar on Policy Challenges for the Financial Sector in the Context of Globalization, Sponsored by the World Bank, IMF, and Board of Governors of the Federal Reserve System. Washington D.C., June 14.

Garcia, Gillian (1998). "The East Asian Financial Crisis," in G. Kaufman (ed.) *Bank Crises: Causes, Analysis and Prevention, Research in Financial Services: Private and Public Policy*, 10. Stamford, CT: JAI Press, pp. 21-32.

Jensen, Michael and William Meckling (1976). "Theory of the Firm: Managerial Behavior, Agency Costs, and Ownership Structure," *Journal of Financial Economics.* 3, pp. 305-360.

Kane, Edward J. (1989). *The S&L Insurance Mess: How Did it Happen?* Washington: The Urban Institute Press

Kane, Edward J. (1993). "What Lessons Should Japan Learn from the U.S. Deposit Insurance Mess?" *Journal of the Japanese and International Economies.* 7, pp. 329-355.

Kane, Edward J. (2000a). "Capital Movements, Banking Insolvency, and Silent Runs in the Asian Financial Crisis," *Pacific-Basin Finance Journal.* 8, pp. 153-175.

Kane, Edward J. (2000b). "The Dialectical Role of Information and Disinformation in Regulation-Induced Banking Crises," *Pacific-Basin Finance Journal.* 8, pp. 285-308.

Kane, Edward J. (2002). "Using Deferred Compensation to Strengthen the Ethics of Financial Regulation," *Journal of Banking and Finance.*

White, Lawrence J. (1991). *The S&L Debacle: Public Policy Lessons for Bank and Thrift Regulation.* New York: Oxford University Press.

Charticle 5 Impact of Deregulation on Savings and Loans' Commitment to Housing

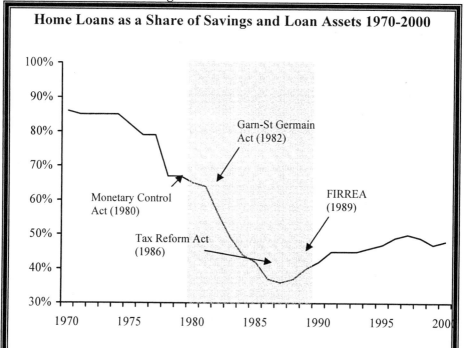

Home Loans as a Share of Savings and Loan Assets 1970-2000

Source: Board of Governors of the Federal Reserve, Flow of Funds

The deregulation of the early 1980s was followed by a period of aggressive diversification as savings and loans made full use of their new powers. Not until the Tax Reform Act and the return of restrictive lending regulations in the form of FIRREA did home loans as a share of assets rise again.

THE LESSONS OF U.S. SAVINGS AND LOAN INSTITUTIONS: AN INTERNATIONAL DEVELOPMENT PERSPECTIVE

Kevin Villani
Former Chief Economist, Freddie Mac; Former Chief
Financial Officer, Imperial Credit and
Imperial Corporation of America

INTRODUCTION

The Anderson School of Management and Milken Institute Research Roundtable has provided a forum for revisiting the causes of the savings and loan "debacle" in the 1980s. Many contributing factors were cited, and the myth that it was all caused by savings and loan crooks was generally debunked. There was a general consensus that politicians contributed to the crisis with numerous policies inappropriate for a liberalized competitive financial system. But this is not news to U.S. economists.

The distinguishing characteristic of the U.S. savings and loan experience is that the economic cost of this politicization eventually became quite large, and some of these costs were unavoidably transparently budgeted, giving rise to the subsequent political need for scapegoats. The distinguished economic commentators noted – but perhaps did not sufficiently emphasize – the irrelevance of this transparently budgeted cost – and hence political debacle – to the underlying economic debacle of the preceding politicization. This oversight leaves open the door to the charge that deregulation was the cause of the "debacle" rather than the cure.

The lessons from the U.S. experience in housing finance are perhaps most relevant to policymakers in developing and converting economies seeking better housing to improve living conditions and higher rates of homeownership to promote political stability. Effective housing finance policies are of keen interest in these countries. Therefore, it is this dimension of the savings and loan "debacle" that I will address.

BACKGROUND

Savings and loans in the U.S. were an offspring of the British building and loan societies (usually simply called building societies) common throughout the Commonwealth countries. This model worked for several centuries in many places through a variety of economic environments. The financial environment of the era was generally competitive and open, albeit less competitive than the U.S. financial system today. Moreover, the industry generally relied on government only for a system of mortgage laws regarding contract enforcement.

Unlike the Germanic mortgage bond system – the competing system of the era – this approach did not require highly developed capital markets, as savings were generated from within the building societies. Housing and homeownership generally flourished under this system, within the means of the economy in which it operated.

Building societies continued to flourish into the 21st century in Britain and Commonwealth countries. Today, they largely function as or have been merged into the commercial banking system. This is true of the U.S. savings and loan system survivors of the 1970s and 1980s "debacle" as well.

This raises two related questions. First, why was the U.S. savings and loan experience of the 1970s and 1980s different, and second, were U.S.-style *secondary mortgage markets* a fortuitous backstop to the U.S. housing finance system, or a contributing cause of their demise?

U.S. DIAGNOSIS: THE RISE AND FALL OF SAVINGS AND LOANS

Savings and loans began as closed-end mutual societies, with members entering into savings contracts. Eventually, when the contract was fulfilled, they were promised a mortgage. As closed societies, they could set both the asset and liability rates to safeguard solvency. (Similar contractual schemes still exist in the Nordic countries.) A historically viable industry was provided government "assistance" for the first time during the 1930s and in subsequent years, which gave rise to the subsequent politicization and eventual collapse.

The savings and loan (and building) societies proved to be effective risk managers prior to the Great Depression, which severely tested all components of the U.S. financial system. The absurdly high default and foreclosure rates were a major problem, bankrupting the entire mono-line private mortgage insurance industry. But, contrary to conventional wisdom, it did not bankrupt the savings and loan industry, which remained in significantly better shape than the commercial banking system on which it had relied for liquidity.

As remains the case today, politicians of the time significantly underestimated their role in causing the crisis with poor macroeconomic and financial market policies and significantly overestimated their potential role in solving the crisis with public market interventions. Two public insurance scheme "cures" fundamentally altered the future path of the savings and loan industry, government *sponsored* deposit and mortgage insurance. These eventually gave rise to public regulation and competition, respectively.

Savings and loans didn't need or want the deposit insurance and, believing that they would be forced to subsidize the premiums of much riskier commercial banks, they successfully opted out. Their victory was short lived, however, as their own independent federal deposit insurance scheme was soon forced upon them, albeit with a much lower premium than paid to the commercial bank insurance system. Once savings and loan liabilities were insured, they evolved in this environment to become increasingly money-like, indistinguishable from those of commercial banks. Their hard-won victory for "independence" may have been a source of their ultimate demise, as the banking system was later to reject their membership for the same reason the savings and loans had resisted membership in the bank insurance fund.

With deposit insurance came regulation, initially of the prudential variety but inevitably political. Knowingly *imprudent* politically motivated regulations on asset and liability design and pricing, branching, and other business activities were imposed. Commercial bankers were also subjected to imprudent regulations, but not nearly to the same extent, reflecting the politically tantalizing savings and loan specialization in home mortgage lending. The most striking regulatory difference relates to the prohibition on adjustable-rate mortgage lending imposed only on federally charted savings and loans, which forced them to borrow short and lend long. Congress "funded" this imprudence with tax subsidies and protective regulation. (Parenthetically, the tax subsidy made it virtually impossible to exit the savings and loan business.)

The introduction of federally sponsored mortgage insurance met with less industry resistance, perhaps because there were no private mortgage insurance survivors to oppose it. The federally sponsored Federal Housing Administration (FHA) was able to insure loans that potential new private entrants could not because it re-introduced the 30-year self-amortizing mortgage. This solved the household liquidity problem inherent in balloon payment mortgages, but ignored the fact that there were few potential investors for a 30-year credit instrument in this economic environment. Policymakers attempted to address this problem by proposing a federally sponsored investor.

The savings and loan industry recognized the early proposal to create a Federal National Mortgage Association (Fannie Mae) for what it really was, a government housing bank, and opposed the legislation on grounds that this represented unfair competition to private lenders. The political opposition of the time engendered charter restrictions that limited Fannie Mae activities to those of a pure broker-dealer, and promised subsequent privatization. This industry victory, like the previous deposit insurance victory, proved Pyrrhic.

FHA has for the most part stuck to its initial mortgage insurance mission, although federal "sponsorship" evolved into protection when the fund eventually became insolvent in the 1990s, and the revived competitive private mortgage insurance industry made FHA unnecessary and counter-productive. Rather than liquidate it, the federal government reorganized it. FHA insures diversifiable risks, so the subsidy tends to be contemporaneous and hence transparent, whereas the federally sponsored housing banks – euphemistically referred to as *secondary market agencies* – underwrite non-insurable systemic risk, the costs of which are more opaque. This subsidy and the other benefits of *agency status* confer significant advantages over private competitors. As a result, these government-sponsored intermediaries have developed a virtual monopoly on mortgage market intermediation within their legislatively prescribed market share.

Competing budget pressures in the 1960s produced deficits and increased oscillation of interest rate cycles in the 1970s and early 1980s and eventually inflation and the subsequent skyrocketing of interest rates. This significantly raised the cost of imprudent savings and loan regulations, particularly the forced maturity mismatch of federal savings and loans. At the same time, the prior tax benefits were being scaled back, and the relatively greater benefits granted to the federal housing banks squeezed the spreads available to mortgage market intermediation. These policies rendered much of the savings and loan industry technically bankrupt.

The same technical bankruptcy condition existed in the commercial banking industry, although the cause was more industry folly in Latin America than financially imprudent regulation. The Federal Reserve System has both the power and responsibility to protect the commercial banking system from bad macroeconomic policies leading to inflation and financial market instability, and it used these powers to protect large banks (and itself) from these risks, and their business follies as well.

While it had the power to protect the savings and loan industry from the combination of politically imprudent regulation and macroeconomic mismanagement, it was bureaucratically inclined in the opposite direction. The separately insured savings and loan industry remained outside the Fed's responsibility and regulatory reach, even though it issued money-like deposits, and the banks resisted their conversion and entry to the bank insurance system. Killing the industry was preferable to saving it from the Fed's policy and bureaucratic perspective, and the government sponsored enterprises (GSEs) – one of which was also deeply technically insolvent – could insulate the mortgage market from the savings and loan failure, mitigating political concerns.

The savings and loans were encouraged to "grow out of the problem" on their own by making primarily risky commercial real estate loans. This could work for a single institution, but not for an entire industry. Moreover, unlike mark-to-market losses due to interest rate risk (or the commercial bank losses on Latin American loans), credit losses on bad real estate had to be transparently booked, ultimately leaving regulators no alternative to closure. While the industry's prolonged agony and noisy death rattle was unfortunately not in the quiet opaque central banking tradition, the eventual outcome for the most part met the policy objective of merging the survivors into the publicly insured and regulated commercial banking system.

U.S. PROGNOSIS: GSE DOMINANCE

Mortgage capital markets in the U.S. predate the secondary mortgage market GSEs; in fact, mortgage bonds are said to have first appeared in Hungary about 300 years ago. The U.S. mortgage finance system remains a mix of deposit and capital market funding. It is difficult to say what the optimal mix would be without the GSE distortions. Given the large size of the U.S. capital markets today, it is likely that this market would have continued to grow along side the savings and loan industry. Indeed, there is a large U.S. mortgage capital market today for the segment not served by the GSEs. Hence the purported discrete policy choice between a retail savings and loan and wholesale capital mortgage market approach is artificial: each will develop in conjunction with the growth of financial markets generally, reflecting their relative competitive advantages.

During the conference, Robert Van Order of Freddie Mac (the other mortgage GSE) described the existing GSE approach as a "second best" system for the mortgage market.[1] This characterization is generally accurate *on average*. It is perhaps the *best* of all possible systems for GSE management and shareholders and for politicians, who take credit for the availability of mortgage credit without the risk and accountability, and perhaps among the *worst* of all possible systems for the general public, which bears the risk without the control or compensation.

What have we learned? The current GSE policy structure has proven politically durable. Legal charter restrictions are easily (and universally) ignored by national and international GSEs pursuing politically popular agendas. Partial privatization reduces the transparency of the costs, increasing political popularity.

---

[1] Editors' note: Details of the discussion of GSEs that occurred at the Anderson School of Management and Milken Institute Research Roundtable can be found in the Conference Proceedings in this volume.

PRESCRIPTION FOR OTHER COUNTRIES

The early experience of the U.S. deposit funded mortgage finance system suggests that a legal system of mortgage contract enforcement (and the associated property titling infrastructure) is both a necessary and sufficient condition for a viable, competitive mortgage finance industry. The caveat is that sufficiently bad and unpredicted macroeconomic and financial market policies can threaten the viability of any pre-existing financial system.

The situation in most developing and converting economies is a demand for mortgage credit that far exceeds the potential for surplus capital market savings. Hence housing finance schemes tied to retail savings deposits offer the only alternative. The uninsured contractual savings schemes (like the early savings and loans) that do not create a "moral hazard" for the government may be appropriate in some economies where savings are scarce and financial intermediation is underdeveloped.

The introduction of deposit insurance and prudential regulation subjects a retail savings-based system of housing finance to the potential for politically motivated populist regulation and protection. Subsequent deregulation and removal of these protections—motivated by the increasingly high economic costs—may leave the mortgage lending industry exposed and unprotected if it remains outside the central bank's purview. Moreover, politicians will likely oppose liberalization if the deregulation process makes the economic cost of the previous regulated regime transparent. Hence it is preferable to develop deposit funded mortgage finance within the commercial banking sector, and any pre-existing specialized deposit funded mortgage finance industry should be merged into the commercial banking system prior to deregulation.

For countries with a sufficiently well-developed commercial banking system, bank deposits are an acceptable source of housing finance within certain limits. First, prudential regulations need to appropriately reflect the liquidity, credit and interest rate risks of mortgage lending. Second, the liquidity risk cannot be transferred to households by excessively shortening the maturity with balloon payments.

One way to address the potential systemic liquidity risk of commercial bank long-term adjustable-rate mortgage lending is for the central bank to discount mortgages directly and proactively. This policy runs the risk of using the central bank's pricing advantage as a tool of credit allocation. But unlike the directed credit national housing bank approach, the costs remain in public control and do not undermine private competition. When implemented along the lines of the Cagamas in Malaysia modeled after the Federal Home Loan

Banks in the U.S., (i.e., with strict haircuts and full recourse to the lending bank), this approach appears to be the least distorting to private market competition.

U.S.-style secondary markets are not a model to emulate for several reasons. First, few developing or transitioning countries — South Africa is a notable exception — have significant capital market surpluses available for housing finance. While public policy in these countries should not inhibit the introduction of mortgage capital market instruments to attract these funds, the public sponsorship of mortgage credit intermediaries is unnecessary and likely counterproductive. Public sponsorship of intermediaries is not an appropriate mechanism to compensate for a weak legal infrastructure and/or a financial environment not conducive to long-term mortgage finance.

Moreover, public sponsorship of credit intermediaries is a one-way street to directed credit. No matter how well such institutions are initially designed and legally restricted to assisting and promoting competitive private sector development, their political appeal will likely insure their survival at the expense of potential private competitors. If a government-directed credit scheme is introduced as a long-run solution in a financial system intending to remain repressed, it should function as an arm of the Treasury and be budgeted and controlled accordingly.

CONCLUSIONS

The appropriate government role in providing housing depends on country-specific circumstances, and there is no one-size-fits-all policy prescription. The extent to which homeownership contributes to social stability will also vary among countries, and its priority should be an open policy issue. Within these caveats, there are appropriate public policies to foster a competitive housing finance system.

What lessons should policymakers in other countries draw from the U.S. savings and loan experience?

Often, the advice of U.S. and international consultants is to avoid the U.S. experience with the savings and loan industry, which attracts crooks as owners and managers and/or requires regulation and protection. The alternative is to emulate the U.S. style *secondary mortgage markets*, which are credited with the success of U.S. homeownership rates. This advice misses the mark in several ways.

First, the system of deposit funded mortgage finance worked well for centuries, until it was excessively politicized. Subsequent financial market liberalization and deregulation – while producing net economic benefits – makes the costs of this politicization transparent in potentially uncontrollable and politically embarrassing ways.

Second, the U.S. system is not a secondary market, but a primary market *directed credit* scheme. The publicly sponsored housing bank approach has significant economic costs, and also runs the risk of subsequent transparent failure and political embarrassment. In addition, this approach is a one-way street, as subsequent "privatization" will prove to be superficial and counterproductive to financial market liberalization.

Fundamentally sound macroeconomic, tax, legal and regulatory policies that promote a private competitive housing finance system may offer the greatest *long run* political as well as economic benefit. Competition from foreign banks will stimulate domestic banks to enter this market, as Citibank has demonstrated in Malaysia and elsewhere. Public policy short cuts and detours will likely prove counterproductive to a competitive mortgage finance system in the longer run.

THE LESSON OF LINCOLN:

REGULATION AS NARRATIVE IN THE SAVINGS AND LOAN CRISIS

Lawrence T. Nichols
West Virginia University

James J. Nolan, III
West Virginia University

INTRODUCTION

Social problems such as the crisis in the savings and loan industry involve an infinity of detail that is virtually incomprehensible to average persons. Indeed, even those technical experts most familiar with developments can hardly keep track of the extensive roster of problem savings and loans and their owners and staffers, as well as the innumerable accounting decisions and issues under litigation. The sheer scale of events and their intricate interrelationships can cause confusion and bewilderment.

Because human beings have a deep need for a sense of meaningful order, however, they have devised ways of making even the most complex problems comprehensible. One fundamental strategy is to convert selected details of perceived problems into stories involving central characters, plots and subplots, and concluding morals that affirm societal values and provide guidance for future conduct. Such stories are analogous to statistical "numbers crunching" procedures that reduce vast data sets to comprehensible statements of significant findings. Many types of stories are possible and the same social-problem data can be converted into numerous tales, some complementary and some irreconcilable. Those stories intended to represent and epitomize perceived widespread problems will be referred to here as "landmark narratives" (Nichols, 1997). Such narratives have a complex temporal orientation: they make sense of present problems; provide guidance for future behavior; and serve as vehicles for history or "collective memory" (Schudson, 1993).

A few examples will help clarify the concept and highlight some of the nuances involved in the construction and maintenance of landmark narratives. For instance, many defective products were manufactured and marketed during the last half of the twentieth century, but the Ford Pinto subcompact automobile has attained a special prominence in collective memory, largely as a result of the tale of "Pinto madness" (Dowie, 1977). In the same way, there has been a multitude of recent political scandals, but the Watergate affair towers above them all in collective consciousness, largely as a consequence of the story of "all the President's men" (Woodward and Bernstein, 1974). At present, the country is troubled by revelations of accounting abuses that have plunged major corporations into bankruptcy and have cost thousands of employees their jobs, while causing serious losses for investors. Because of our shared need to make sense of this problem, it is likely that one of the cases involved (e.g., Enron or WorldCom) will become the object of a new landmark narrative. In other words, the maintenance and modification of social orders involves the continual creation of special tales of good and evil that serve as guideposts, especially in times of intensive conflict and rapid change.

The social process by which landmark narratives emerge, gain credibility and attain special status, however, is not yet well understood. One major prerequisite seems to be extensive coverage of certain cases in mass media (Herman and Chomsky, 1988; Bagdikian, 1990; Barak, 1995) and in popular culture (Nichols, 1999), as well as in other outlets (e.g., professional and disciplinary media). For instance, the story of nuclear power whistleblower Karen Silkwood received wide coverage in newspapers and on television, and subsequently became the object of a popular biography and a movie, eventually emerging also as a frequently cited case in such professional and disciplinary media as textbooks in criminology, criminal justice and business ethics (e.g., Rashke and Bronfenbrenner, 2000). Yet publicity by itself does not guarantee landmark status. Indeed, the vast majority of highly publicized cases do not become landmarks. In order for a particular case to acquire special status, it must first be distinguished from other candidates and become the object of claimsmaking that imbues it with characteristics suitable for an exemplar (Surrette, 1992; Potter and Kappelev, 1998).

Some cases seem to attain landmark status largely on the strength of two basic elements of effective narrative: colorful characterization and engrossing plot. With regard to characterization, narratives may become especially memorable because of the presence of inspirational heroes and despicable villains that dramatize the social values involved. Thus, New York City detective Frank Serpico became the heroic figure in a tale of personal resistance to organizational corruption that was communicated through both a bestselling biography (Maas, 1973) and a successful Hollywood film. Interestingly, the distinctive stature of the Serpico narrative was reaffirmed quite recently, when Serpico himself accepted an invitation to return to New York and speak to police recruits. In parallel fashion, cases may ascend to landmark status via the appeal of fascinating villains, such as Ted Bundy who became the most recognizable image of the serial killer (Rule, 1981). Bundy exhibited a dual persona: he was an articulate, soft-spoken, seemingly trustworthy lawyer involved in conservative political causes; and yet he kidnapped and viciously killed young women and even a twelve-year-old girl.

With regard to plot, some tales have a powerful appeal because of complex twists and turns of events that make for suspenseful reading and viewing. In the case of Watergate, public interest suddenly increased following a letter from a defendant to a federal judge alleging perjury and an official cover-up. This revelation led to a highly publicized inquiry by a special committee in the U.S. Senate that uncovered the existence of a secret taping system in the White House. As testimony about abuses proliferated, a special prosecutor was appointed, only to be fired by President Nixon in an event nicknamed "the Saturday Night Massacre." Eventually, an incident that had been dismissed as a "third-rate burglary" led to a full-scale impeachment inquiry and the resignation of a president.

In some narratives, colorful characters and engrossing plots have a powerful combined effect. Thus, the Watergate story features not only an intricate plot but also the fascinating character of Richard Nixon, a contradictory figure at once the champion of law and order and a cynical evader of legal rules. Nixon was a political rationalist who masterfully engineered a landslide electoral victory and improved relations with the major adversaries of the U.S., but also simultaneously an irrational paranoid schemer whose hatred of perceived enemies led to his own destruction. Aligned against Nixon were several appealing figures: Senator Sam Ervin who combined a folksy style with a Harvard law degree; John Dean, a co-conspirator endowed with a photographic memory; and junior reporters Bob Woodward and Carl Bernstein who pursued the story when no one else would.

Even engaging characters and engrossing plots, however, do not ensure that a case will become a special symbol and guide for the future, for claims about cases may fail to persuade audiences. For instance, in the late 1980s some critics asserted that the Iran-Contra affair was actually a far more serious abuse of power than Watergate. The Iran-Contra case offered an array of memorable characters, especially the enormously popular President Ronald Reagan and the ardent patriot and chief witness Lt. Colonel Oliver North. At the same time, the case provided a plot even more intricate than that of Watergate. Nevertheless, for reasons that are not entirely clear, the American public has chosen to believe the morality play about Nixon's political arrogance while rejecting a similar tale about Reagan (Walsh, 1998).

Explaining the emergence and durability of landmark narratives therefore requires a sociology of credibility. One key element enhancing credibility is the activity of official bodies that conduct investigations of problems and make authoritative pronouncements about them, especially in such forms as the final reports of committees and special commissions (Nichols, 1991). Thus, the Senate Watergate Committee told the tale of abuses by the Nixon administration, which in turn became material for the impeachment investigation by the House Judiciary Committee. The Knapp Commission on police corruption placed on record an official story of Serpico. In earlier decades, the U.S. Department of Justice authored the tale of "atomic spies" Julius and Ethel Rosenberg. The McClellan Committee of the U.S. Senate assembled an influential narrative about the menace of "La Cosa Nostra" crime families. All these official tellings became orthodox accounts of contemporary problems.

Such orthodoxy, however, is always vulnerable, because credibility fluctuates over time in ways that cannot be predicted. Perhaps the best example is the Warren Commission's narrative about the assassination of President John F. Kennedy by a lone gunman with strong pro-Communist sympathies. For a time this explanation was widely accepted, but today the Warren Commission's version of events fails to persuade many Americans. Indeed, the story of the lone assassin is often ridiculed in such phrases as "the magic bullet" (Lane, 1966). Two competing narratives have emerged: (1) conspirators within the federal government killed the president; and (2) organized crime groups carried out the assassination.

The remainder of this paper will apply the concepts described above to the events of the savings and loan industry crisis of the late 1980s. Data will be presented to support the assertion that the case of Lincoln Savings and Loan has become a landmark narrative epitomizing alleged abuses and criminal violations, and that Charles H. Keating has emerged as the archetypal villain of the Savings and Loan Affair. The analysis will focus on two processes that set the Lincoln case apart: coverage in mass print media, and an official investigation by the Committee on Banking, Finance and Urban Affairs of the U.S. House of Representatives. The claims making activities of both the media and the congressional committee are in fact closely linked. Publicity about Lincoln was an important reason for its scrutiny in the House, and the public hearings became occasions of further negative publicity about both Lincoln and Keating.

Both the media organizations and the congressional investigators were compelled to make choices that shaped their final portraits of events. These included decisions about headlines, placement of articles, and amount of space to expend on coverage (Molotch and Lester, 1974; Tuchman, 1978; Gans, 1980). There were likewise crucial choices about how to organize public hearings (Dash, 1976; Cohen and Mitchell, 1989), which witnesses to call, and in what order. In both published articles and public hearings, moreover, it was necessary to credit certain versions of reality while rejecting other plausible narratives. Simultaneously, however, the media organizations and congressional inquisitors worked to protect their credibility by reaffirming their commitments to fairness and rules of evidence. The analysis below will examine the selectivity and artfulness of these practical accomplishments that set the Lincoln case apart from hundreds of others in the savings and loan industry.

MASS MEDIA COVERAGE OF LINCOLN SAVINGS AND LOAN

By far, the story of Lincoln Savings received more attention in major U.S. newspapers than any of the other failed savings and loans. One could surmise that this was because of the size of the savings and loan or the excessive cost to taxpayers to resolve. A Lexis-Nexis search[1] of the top fifty newspapers in the U.S. revealed that the size and cost may only be part of the story. For example, between 1986 and 1989 (when congressional hearings began), there were 205 news stories printed about Lincoln Savings. This is more than four times higher than the second most reported savings and loan, American Savings and Loan of Stockton, California. American Savings and Loan was both the largest failed savings and loan (in terms of its total assets) and the most costly (in terms of the total resolution costs). American's assets were more than six times larger than Lincoln's, and the resolution of American's failure cost taxpayers more than twice the amount of Lincoln's resolution.

Table 1 provides a more detailed picture of the relationships among failed savings and loans, by listing the ten most costly cases. For each, there is also a tabulation of newspaper articles in the periods 1986-1989 and 1990-1995.

As the table indicates, although Lincoln was only the fourth most costly resolution, it received coverage in 601 news articles, or nearly nine times as many as the 68 articles devoted to the most costly case, American Savings and Loan. Indeed, the other nine cases taken together were the subject of only 230 articles. For the entire period of 1986 to 1995, Lincoln was featured in seventy-two percent of stories about the ten largest failed savings and loans. In the earlier phase, 1986 to 1989, Lincoln was the focus of 205 out of 312 news stories, that is, sixty-five percent. In the later phase, 1990 to 1995, this proportion increased to 396 out of 519 articles, or seventy-six percent.

---

[1] We searched the Lexis-Nexis General Database of Major Newspapers (the top 50 in the United States) during two time periods. The first was 1986 to 1989, up to the start of the congressional hearings. The second period was 1990 to 1995, that is, during and after congressional hearings on the savings and loan crisis. Search terms included the name of the savings and loan, along with location within three words "AND S&L" with any of the following words in the same sentence: crisis, scandal, debacle "OR" failure. Searching with additional conditions eliminated articles about the savings and loan that did not pertain to the savings and loan scandal.

Table 1: Newspaper Coverage of the Ten Most Costly Savings and Loan Failures

Institution	Location	Resolution Costs (millions)	Assets* (millions)	Newspaper Articles 1986-1989	Newspaper Articles 1990-1995
American Savings & Loan	Stockton, CA	$5,751	$33,841	48	20
Sunbelt Savings & Loan	Dallas, TX	$3,788	$2,214	18	24
Gibraltar Savings Association	Houston, TX	$2,875	$6,398	12	2
Lincoln Savings	Irvine, CA	$2,661	$5,374	205	396
First Texas Savings Association	Dallas, TX	$2,545	$2,920	10	2
University Federal Savings Association	Houston, TX	$2,545	$3,762	8	5
Western Savings & Loan Association	Phoenix, AZ	$2,273	$6,467	1	41
Guaranty Federal Savings & Loan	Dallas, TX	$2,131	$1,961	3	11
Lamar Savings Association	Austin, TX	$2,018	$$1,919	5	5
San Jacinto Savings Association	Houston, TX	$1,795	$2,228	2	13

* Assets at time of takeover for RTC resolutions and at time of resolution for FSLIC transactions.

Sources: FDIC, *Managing the Crisis: The FDIC and RTC Experience 1980-1994* and Lexis-Nexis

Table 2 identifies the top ten failed savings and loans according to total assets. Lincoln Savings and Loan had assets approximately $1.1 billion below the tenth largest institution and is therefore not included in this listing.

Table 2: Newspaper Coverage of the Ten Largest Savings and Loan Failures

Institution	Location	Resolution Costs (millions)	Assets* (millions)	Newspaper Articles 1986-1989	Newspaper Articles 1990-1995
American Savings & Loan	Stockton, CA	$5,751	$33,841	48	20
HomeFed Bank	San Diego, CA	$1,256	$12,886	1	56
Gibraltar Savings Association	Simi Valley, CA	$777	$12,313	2	21
Franklin Federal Savings Association	Ottawa, KS	$118	$10,543	0	1
City Savings Bank	Somerset, NJ	$1,759	$10,228	0	8
Imperial Federal Savings Association	San Diego, CA	$696	$9,395	0	5
Great American Federal Savings Association	San Diego, CA	$1,231	$9,214	17	9
Empire Federal Savings Bank	Buffalo, NY	$1,567	$8,050	2	4
CenTrust Bank	Miami, FL	$1,281	$7,765	21	161
Western Savings & Loan Association	Phoenix, AZ	$2,273	$6,467	1	41

* Assets at time of takeover for RTC resolutions and at time of resolution for FSLIC transactions

Sources: FDIC, *Managing the Crisis: The FDIC and RTC Experience 1980-1994* and Lexis-Nexis

Even in this ranking there is a significant disparity between the amount of assets and the amount of news coverage. The ninth largest savings and loan, CenTrust Bank, was the focus of 182 stories, or more than twice the number devoted to the largest failed institution, American Savings and Loan.

Interestingly, many news stories about failed savings and loans presented these cases *as part of* a story about Lincoln Savings. For example, the following report from the *Los Angeles Times* was uncovered during a search for Imperial Federal Savings Association (the sixth largest failed savings and loan):

> Lincoln Savings & Loan, the Irvine-based thrift that has become a symbol of the nation's savings and loan debacle, was put up for sale Friday by federal authorities. ... Once owned by Charles H. Keating, Jr., Lincoln was one of 18 failed savings and loans put on the block by federal Resolution Trust Corp., the agency formed last year to clean up the S&L mess. Also put up for sale was Imperial Federal Savings Assn ... the largest failed thrift in the state. (Los Angeles Times, November 3, 1990).

A spin-off story about high-level political improprieties may have served to propel Lincoln further toward landmark status. In 1987, five U.S. Senators allegedly put pressure on federal regulators to "go easy" on Charles Keating, who had been a major contributor to their election campaigns.[2] In the press, the Senators became known as "the Keating Five," and they were mentioned as such in 432 news articles in major U.S. papers between 1988 and 1990.

The congressional investigation of the savings and loan scandal was a major press event in itself. Between October 1989 and March 1990, the six public hearings generated 38 news stories in major U.S. papers. Twenty-one of these mentioned Charles Keating, while 27 mentioned Lincoln Savings.

THE CONGRESSIONAL INVESTIGATION OF LINCOLN SAVINGS AND LOAN

One of the crucial events that set the Lincoln case apart was an investigation conducted by the Committee on Banking, Finance and Urban Affairs of the U.S. House of Representatives (hereinafter House Banking Committee). This inquiry extended from October 1989 to March 1990 and involved six public hearings at which witnesses testified. Published transcripts and related documents from these hearings totaled more than four thousand pages. No comparable official record has been produced by Congress for any other savings and loan case.

---

[2] The five Senators were Dennis DeConcini and John McCain of Arizona, Alan Cranston of California, John Glenn of Ohio, and Donald Riegle of Michigan. Charles Keating allegedly donated nearly $1.5 million to these officials.

From the perspective of interpretive sociology, congressional investigations may be understood as sense-making practices that generate official versions of events (Bogen and Lynch, 1989; Nichols, 1990, 1991). The inquisitors on such committees possess the legal power (via subpoena) to compel witnesses to appear and to obtain a wide variety of documents (e.g., correspondence, financial records). In preparation for public hearings, members of the staff of investigating committees undertake extensive research and organizational work, including the examination of potentially relevant documents and interviews with possible witnesses. A process of screening and filtering that is not visible to the general public takes place. On the basis of these preparatory activities, a series of hearings may be scheduled on a set of related topics. Such schedules may reflect an underlying strategy on the part of a committee, which may desire to establish particular facts in a particular sequence. Inquiries thus have dramatic, even choreographed features, and investigating committees may give the appearance of discovering during hearings certain versions of events which they already believe to be true before the first witness is called. As will be seen, by the time that witnesses favorable to Lincoln and Keating appeared, the House Banking Committee had committed itself to a condemnation of both the savings and loan and its owner.

At public hearings, members of congressional committees have opportunities to advance particular definitions of events (Nichols, 1990). They may do so, first, through opening statements that articulate what has been, or will be, established in testimony. Committee chairs sometimes restrict the number of statements read aloud, but committee members have the right to submit written statements that are incorporated into the record of hearings. A second important technique that promotes favored definitions is the direct questioning of witnesses. A third device is the submission of materials by inquisitors for the published record of hearings. Persons who testify likewise make opening statements and offer materials for the record, but they cannot interrogate the congressional investigators.

Under the rules of Congress, each committee has representation that is proportioned among members of political parties according to the results of the most recent national elections. The chair of each committee is from the majority party in the respective House of Congress. The minority party's major representative is its "ranking member," that is, the member with the longest continuous service on the committee. Ranking members sometimes function as virtual co-chairs, which may promote unanimity in final reports. The chair of an investigating committee, its majority faction (i.e., either the majority party members or an inter-party alliance), and the ranking minority member enjoy the greatest power to shape official definitions. Chairs also have such privileges as recognizing questioners, granting additional time for interrogation, and even ruling members out of order.

A crucial aspect of public hearings is the transformation of information into officially credited evidence. A letter, for example, is changed from a bit of routine business correspondence into an official exhibit that has significance for a particular reading of events. In some cases, such items are designated as "smoking guns" that prove culpability. The conversion of mundane data into evidence has a dramatic and ritualized aspect that is reflected in oaths sworn by witnesses, as well as the insignia of office on final reports. Hearings are thus organized as "certification ceremonies" that authoritatively establish evidence-based interpretations of events (Nichols, 1991).

Narrative Element One: "Regulatory Failure" and "Looting"

The above considerations are helpful for understanding how the Lincoln case emerged as a landmark narrative. An initial hearing (October 12, 1989) involved only a vote authorizing the issuance of subpoenas to prospective witnesses. Analysis of the second hearing (October 17, 1989), however, reveals an evident alliance among three key participants: committee chair, Rep. Henry Gonzalez (D – Texas), ranking minority member Chalmers Wylie (R – Ohio), and witness William Seidman, chairman of the Federal Deposit Insurance Corporation (FDIC). Each of these participants leveled serious accusations against Lincoln Savings and Loan, and characterized Lincoln as the most egregious offender in the savings and loan industry.

In an opening statement, Chairman Gonzalez entered into the official record a summary narrative of the case that emphasized regulatory failure as well as the cost of the Lincoln case to U.S. taxpayers. Gonzalez also accused the chief federal savings and loan regulator, Danny Wall, of favoritism toward Lincoln because of Wall's earlier decision to set aside the results of a 1986 examination of Lincoln by the San Francisco regional office of the Federal Home Loan Bank Board (FHLBB). As a warrant for the committee's focus on Lincoln, Gonzalez asserted that, "A $2 billion mistake surely requires a full explanation … about why the 'cops on the beat' were pulled off" (House Banking Committee, 2nd Hearing, p. 10).

Ranking member Wylie echoed these concerns, characterizing Lincoln as an unsound savings and loan that had strayed from its original mission of making home loans. To Wylie, Lincoln was "a rogue elephant run amok" and "the ultimate in high flyers." He asserted that the purpose of the committee's inquiry was to

> ... find out why Lincoln was able to stay in business so long. And
> why so many unusual regulatory moves were made to treat Lincoln
> differently than other institutions. It now appears that the problems
> at Lincoln were known for years (House Banking Committee, 2nd
> Hearing, p. 12).

Wylie concluded that the committee had "a responsibility to see that another Lincoln is never allowed to happen again."

Witness William Seidman next read an opening statement that portrayed Lincoln as a failed business in which an inner circle of executives had engaged in numerous abuses, some of them criminal. By Seidman's estimate, Lincoln had been insolvent in the amount of $800 million at the time it was placed in conservatorship (April 1989). As head of the FDIC, Seidman also oversaw the Resolution Trust Corporation (RTC), which was handling the savings and loan cleanup. Importantly, at the time of the hearing the RTC was involved in litigation against Lincoln. As Seidman noted:

> On September 15th, the RTC, acting as conservator for Lincoln,
> filed a lawsuit against Charles H. Keating, Jr. and other corporate
> officers and insiders charging that they devised a number of
> complex and interrelated schemes to divert assets of Lincoln to their
> personal benefit, ultimately contributing to Lincoln's insolvency
> (House Banking Committee, 2nd Hearing, p. 16).

In this way, a party to a lawsuit against Lincoln was allowed to enter its version of events into the official record without rebuttal by other litigants. In fact, a copy of the RTC's full legal brief was placed in an appendix.

The Banking Committee treated Seidman's testimony as an accurate factual summary of the Lincoln case. Gonzalez remarked at one point, "What I am trying to bring out is how the looting was done" (House Banking Committee, 2nd Hearing, p. 25). In the same vein, Rep. Jim Leach (R-Iowa) commented: "If the projection of the Government losses of this institution are valid, we are looking at the biggest bank heist in history" (House Banking Committee, 2nd Hearing, p. 31).

Several times, members of the Banking Committee asked Seidman and three of his staffers whether they knew of any cases comparable to Lincoln. Thus, Rep. Leach inquired whether there were other instances where a savings and loan dissatisfied with a regional regulator successfully requested a different regulator. In response, both Seidman and his associate Paul Fritts said they could not cite a comparable case. Rep. Doug Barnard (D-Georgia) asked whether any of the 251 institutions then in conservatorship displayed a pattern of insider abuse and fraud similar to that at Lincoln. William Roelle replied: "we have not found any that had quite the impact that Lincoln had" (House Banking Committee, 2nd Hearing, pp. 34-35). These exchanges had the effect of isolating Lincoln as the most egregious offender.

One committee member, Rep. David Dreier (D-California) raised the possibility of an alternative explanation: perhaps a downturn in the real estate market, rather than fraud and insider abuse, had caused Lincoln to fail. The FDIC's Seidman, however, quickly rejected this competing narrative:

> The basic problem was that the institution was being mismanaged in a fraudulent way and taking risks that were inappropriate .... Those risks came home when the real estate values plunged (House Banking Committee, 2nd Hearing, p. 58).

Narrative Element Two: Preferential Treatment of Lincoln by Regulators

The third hearing (October 31, 1989) continued the process of stigmatizing Lincoln Savings and Loan and defining it as representative of the worst abuses. Crucial to this outcome was an apparent alliance between congressional inquisitors and nine technical experts who had been involved in the examination of savings and loans at either the federal or state level. Testimony focused on examinations of Lincoln by the Federal Home Loan Bank Board (FHLBB) in 1986 and 1988, the former by the San Francisco regional office and the latter by Bank Board headquarters in Washington, D.C. Banking Committee members sought to establish two factual conclusions: (1) that the 1986 examination had revealed Lincoln's violations and shown sufficient cause for regulators to take control of Lincoln; and (2) that the 1988 examination was an exercise in political favoritism and a fatally flawed effort to keep Lincoln in business.

Chairman Gonzalez used his opening statement to assail the former head of the FHLBB, Danny Wall, for rejecting the San Francisco results. Gonzalez supported his accusations by referring to the official record of earlier testimony: "The record is clear that Chairman Wall and his key regulatory personnel not only ignored the critical warnings, but chose time and again to link arms with Charles Keating and Lincoln" (House Banking Committee, 3rd Hearing, p. 2). Ranking minority member Wylie expressed similar indignation, also citing the emerging record. After describing Lincoln as a "ticking time bomb," he declared: "Today we need to find out if the second exam was looking to get the facts or was it intended to be a whitewash" (House Banking Committee, 3rd Hearing, p. 3).

In subsequent testimony, witnesses asserted that the 1988 examination had been handled improperly and had given Lincoln preferential treatment. According to David Riley, an examiner for the Office of Thrift Supervision (OTS):

> My first concern stemmed from a speech that Steve Scott, the examiner-in-charge gave to the examiners that first day. Steve Scott said that any examiners who had harbored any prejudicial attitude toward Lincoln should go home ... I found that very odd, as I had never gotten a request like that from an examiner-in-charge before (House Banking Committee, 3rd Hearing, p. 33).

Riley also alleged that the second team of examiners had not been permitted to see the results of the 1986 exam by San Francisco regulators, which "was unusual because our routine procedures require us to follow up on items that have been criticized in preceding examinations" (House Banking Committee, 3rd Hearing, p. 33).

Another OTS examiner, Alex Barabolak, returned to a theme from the previous hearing, namely, the alleged abuse of Lincoln Savings and Loan by American Continental Corporation (ACC), its parent company. He asserted that, "ACC siphoned $94 million of improper tax payments from Lincoln, payments based on fictitious income" (House Banking Committee, 3rd Hearing, p. 39).

John Meek, also from OTS, linked the alleged regulatory whitewash to the personal greed of Charles Keating:

> Several times ... Mr. Keating stated to me ... that if Lincoln was taken over by the Government, the FSLIC [i.e., the federal fund that insured thrifts] would lose $2 to $3 billion. At the same time we were documenting that Mr. Keating and his family had taken at least $34 million in salaries, bonuses, and stock sales, from Lincoln and ACC" (House Banking Committee, 3rd Hearing, p. 42).

As the hearing drew to a close, congressional inquisitors summarized what had been established. Rep. Toby Roth (R-Wisconsin) put the following question to the panel of regulatory experts:

> ... basically ... Keating used a federally insured S&L to operate a carefully planned looting and he had the umbrella of political protection to keep you at bay. Does that pretty well summarize it? (House Banking Committee, 3rd Hearing, p. 70)

Following an affirmative answer, Roth posed a second question that portrayed the Lincoln case as unique: "How many S&L's in your experience have been given the favorable treatment that Keating has received? I mean, is there another S&L that you can point to and say, 'This is just like Keating?'" (House Banking Committee, 3rd Hearing, p. 70). The witnesses, predictably, answered in the negative.

Rep. Charles Schumer (D-New York) portrayed Lincoln as the exemplar of the savings and loan crisis: "if you want to take all of the problems of the S&L crisis and distill them into their worst essence, you would find it here in Lincoln" (House Banking Committee, 3rd Hearing, p. 82). Chairman Gonzalez echoed Schumer's characterization: "The reason that Lincoln has been selected is what Mr. Schumer just encapsulated as the prototype case" (House Banking Committee, 3rd Hearing, p. 82).

Narrative Element Three: Lone Hero (Gray) versus Villains ("Keating Five")

> The fourth hearing (November 7, 1989) featured the testimony of Edwin Gray, former chairman of the FHLBB, who was generally considered the chief adversary of Lincoln. Hearing transcripts indicate clearly that most congressional inquisitors formed an alliance with Gray and credited his statements as accurate. Indeed, the Banking Committee treated Gray as an heroic figure who had faithfully discharged his official duties at great personal cost.

> In accordance with established congressional procedures, Gray had submitted a written statement of his testimony prior to the hearing. This statement contained direct accusations against five current Senators, as well as against the chief savings and loan regulator, Danny Wall. After reading these allegations, Rep. Carroll Hubbard (D-Kentucky), a friend of Wall's, protested against the selection of some witnesses, the exclusion of others, and the sequencing of testimony:

>> But you haven't heard from Danny Wall or his assistants. Yet you seem to criticize him in every public statement. ... He has had to call in reporters ... to try to get his message out to the public, rather than be the victim of these continuing hearings which chastise him (House Banking Committee, 4th Hearing, p. 93).

Chairman Gonzalez responded: "The gentleman ought to know that witnesses have been requested by the committee after interviews by staff and an opportunity for each one of the witnesses to discuss with staff whatever testimony they feel is pertinent to the hearings" (House Banking Committee, 4th Hearing, p. 94). Gonzalez also reassured Hubbard that Wall and his staff would appear to testify.

During their interrogation of Gray, committee members made reference to an incident described in his written statement that became an important element of the landmark narrative of Lincoln Savings and Loan. This was a meeting on April 2, 1987 that included Gray and four U.S. Senators (Alan Cranston, Dennis DeConcini, John McCain, John Glenn) and was arranged by a fifth Senator, Donald Riegle. The Senators involved in this gathering had gained the nickname "the Keating Five" and had become the object of extensive media coverage. Gray accused the Senators of asking him to withdraw an official regulation (the direct investment rule) in order to assist their "friend" and generous contributor, Charles Keating (House Banking Committee, 4th Hearing, pp. 595-601).

Rep. Hubbard broke ranks with his colleagues by praising each of the accused Senators and attacking Gray's credibility and self-righteousness. After Hubbard charged Gray with violations of federal travel regulations, the following exchange occurred:

> Mr. Hubbard: It is just to tell a lot of people that you sit here and impugn the reputations of four long-time Senators who are not here to defend themselves, that you are not without some fault yourself ....
>
> Mr. Gray: ... then am I not supposed to tell the truth of what happened in that meeting?
>
> Mr. Hubbard: How do we know you are telling the truth? Your version of that meeting is entirely different from the four Senators who were there. (House Banking Committee, 4th Hearing, p. 118)

Shortly thereafter, Chairman Gonzalez intervened to defend Gray by ruling Hubbard out of order and interpreting his interrogation of Gray as a violation of House rules. The following exchange occurred:

> Mr. Hubbard: Your testimony may be flawed too, Mr. Gray.
>
> The Chairman: The Chair must rule that out of order as an improper contention in view of the fact that the witness is under oath, and if the gentleman has any evidence to impeach the testimony ... he must then advance it. ...

> Mr. Hubbard: What was it I said that you objected to? ... There is nothing improper in what I said, but that is your opinion.

> The Chairman: ... At no time has this Chair permitted the badgering, the abuse, or the maltreatment of any witness. ... I consider that last remark improper and in violation of that rule of courtesy. (House Banking Committee, 4th Hearing, p. 119)

Late in the hearing, Rep. Schumer reaffirmed the laudatory definition of Gray that was favored by a majority of the committee:

> ... I find it a little unfair for you to be blamed or excoriated today because you were the guy standing on the railroad track waving the red flag, and what basically happened is the locomotive came in and ran you over.

> And so I think the job you did is one that deserves praise, not blame. (House Banking Committee, 4th Hearing, p. 143)

Following Gray's departure, the committee interrogated Lawrence Taggart who had been the Savings and Loan Commissioner for California at the time when Lincoln was purchased by Keating's American Continental Corporation. In sharp contrast to their amicable treatment of Gray, committee members grilled Taggart intensively and expressed skepticism at his assertions. The sharpest exchange occurred after Taggart proposed an explanation at odds with the committee's reading of events, namely, that the entire savings and loan crisis was largely an illusion created by overzealous regulators. Taggart went so far as to assert that savings and loan regulators had engaged in a "witch hunt" at Lincoln Savings and Loan that caused its collapse. In response, Rep. Jim McDermott (D-Washington) asked whether Taggart had ever taken a course in accounting, thereby implying that Taggart's views must be the result of ignorance (House Banking Committee, 4th Hearing, p. 230). Chairman Gonzalez suggested that Taggart must have been an incompetent commissioner, because he had failed to notice a 1979 consent decree involving Keating and the Securities and Exchange Commission (SEC). Rep. Paul Kanjorski (D-Pennsylvania) ridiculed the witness by remarking that he intended to create a "Taggart award" for pro-business Pollyannas (House Banking Committee, 4th Hearing, p. 234). Neither Gonzalez nor any committee member, however, cited the rule of courtesy used to protect Gray.

Narrative Element Four: Lincoln Victimizes Small and Elderly Investors

The fifth hearing (November 14, 1989) added an important dimension to the emerging landmark narrative by eliciting testimony from alleged victims of Charles Keating and Lincoln. Testimony focused on allegations that ACC had deliberately misled investors by giving the impression that corporate bonds (subordinated debentures) sold at branches of Lincoln were federally insured. There were also charges that ACC had targeted an especially vulnerable group of investors, namely, senior citizens, who had lost large sums of money when ACC declared bankruptcy and the uninsured bonds became worthless.

Chairman Gonzalez asserted in an opening statement that victims of the scheme "were steered away from insured certificates of deposit and toward the ACC debentures" (House Banking Committee, 5th Hearing, p. 4). Ranking minority member Wylie expressed outrage that the "designs of just one man in the industry can result in thousands of people losing their life savings" (House Banking Committee, 5th Hearing, p. 5). Rep. Schumer charged that, "This is the most sordid episode in a long history of sordid episodes that Charlie Keating has written" (House Banking Committee, 5th Hearing, p. 6).

A panel of witnesses next described severe hardships allegedly caused by the uninsured bond scheme. Thus, Frances Rose spoke of her elderly parents:

> ... their standard of living has been radically reduced. They can no longer enjoy an occasional meal out in a restaurant or the pleasure of taking in an afternoon movie .... They have very carefully trimmed down all shopping for food and clothing to only the barest of essentials (House Banking Committee, 5th Hearing, p. 11).

Shirley Lampel, a widow with serious vision problems, attributed her investment losses to Keating's alleged political influence: "Up against the likes of Charles Keating and the influence he was able to buy from elected officials ... we didn't stand a chance. We had been targeted by Keating with the help of the Keating Five" (House Banking Committee, 5th Hearing, p. 16). Ramona Jacobs spoke of her frustrated desire to purchase a specially equipped van to transport her disabled daughter: "Mr. Keating and his co-conspirators had other plans for our money and many other victims' life savings" (House Banking Committee, 5th Hearing, p. 19).

Narrative Element Five: Regional Regulators Vindicated

At the sixth hearing (November 21, 1989), the committee engaged in a tense, sometimes acrimonious exchange with federal savings and loan regulators, especially Danny Wall and members of Wall's staff. In his opening statement, chairman Gonzalez returned to a theme established during the second hearing, namely, that regulatory failure had enabled Lincoln Savings and Loan to operate in a reckless and illegal manner. Gonzalez complained that the FHLBB, after rejecting the recommendations of its San Francisco regulators to place Lincoln in conservatorship, had settled for a weak and ineffective memorandum of understanding. Citing the official record generated by the investigation, Gonzalez defended the San Francisco regulators and characterized them as irreproachable:

> Some of the testimony to be presented here today suggests that San Francisco operates an incompetent shop ... and that its personnel are ... promoters of a secret agenda of bias against Lincoln ... this seems to stretch credibility pretty far. It goes contrary to findings of the Peer Review of the San Francisco Bank and the sworn testimony before this committee of examination and supervisory personnel from Dallas, Atlanta, Pittsburgh, Chicago, Seattle, and Sacramento. It seems to run contrary to basic points made by the Chairman of the Securities and Exchange Commission and the Chairman of the Federal Deposit Insurance Corporation (House Banking Committee, 6th Hearing, pp. 5-6).

Rep. Leach followed with a statement that characterized Charles Keating as totally indefensible while accusing Wall of moral cowardice:

> While leader of a moralizing campaign ... against pornography, Mr. Keating appears by the record to be an economic pornographer, defiling the value of the savings of the elderly ... given license to steal by a Bank Board headed by the Neville Chamberlain[3] of financial regulation (House Banking Committee, 6th Hearing, pp. 6-7).

Like Gonzalez, Leach appealed to the official record of the hearings for validation, glossing over the committee's control of the content of that record.

---

[3] Neville Chamberlain, a former Prime Minister of the United Kingdom, became notorious for sacrificing Czechoslovakia in an attempt to appease Adolf Hitler.

Rep. Schumer likewise cast Keating as the central villain of the emerging landmark narrative, suggesting in his opening statement that the only appropriate attitude toward Keating was moral outrage:

> ... I would like to ask Mr. Keating ... how can he continue to live his fancy life, take his expensive trips and look himself in the mirror? I sit through these hearings ... and I get angrier and angrier and angrier. ... As Americans begin to understand the magnitude of what happened, I think there is going to be real outrage from coast to coast. There's a good chance that Keating's name is going to go down with Jay Gould, Teapot Dome, Robert Vesco, associated with one of the great financial scandals of our time (House Banking Committee, 6th Hearing, p. 12).

Opening statements were next presented by a panel that included chief savings and loan regulator Danny Wall, as well as Rosemary Stewart, Director of Enforcement, and Darryl Dochow, Senior Deputy Director for Supervision Operations. Each of these witnesses argued that there had been a sincere effort to ascertain the facts about Lincoln Savings and to take appropriate regulatory action. Each also conceded, however, that Lincoln had engaged in deceptive and illegal practices. The witnesses, confronted with the committee's hostility toward Lincoln, defended their earlier regulatory stance by asserting that they had also been deceived.

Rosemary Stewart adopted a tone that would be construed as defiance, alleging that her office had been the victim of a series of misrepresentations. Stewart explicitly criticized the San Francisco regulators and questioned their motives:

> The second area of serious misrepresentation relates to that May 1, 1987 recommendation for conservatorship or receivership from the San Francisco district to the Washington Headquarters ....
>
> The fact that ... there was not an immediate action to appoint a conservator or a receivership has been portrayed by the San Francisco witnesses and many members of the press ... as evidence that there must have been an improper politically motivated deal here. That is absolutely untrue.
>
> The truth is that the May 1, 1987 memorandum, and the 1986 exam which had just been delivered a month before, did not contain sufficient evidence to support a conservatorship or receivership. (House Banking Committee, 6th Hearing, p. 16)

Stewart also complained that a letter she signed in connection with the Lincoln memorandum of understanding "has probably been more seriously misrepresented than anything else ... so distorted that someone should be investigated for perjury before this committee" (House Banking Committee, 6th Hearing, p. 22).

Darryl Dochow defended his decisions by echoing Stewart's contention that the 1986 exam by San Francisco had not provided sufficient grounds for action against Lincoln. Dochow, however, also affirmed the views expressed by congressional inquisitors, confessing that he had been wrong about the case:

> About a month after the [1988] examination started, we ... started getting indications about insider transactions ... improper tax payments ... were being made from Lincoln to ACC for the ultimate benefit of insiders. ... that ... was a turning point for me personally. Up to that time, I had believed ... that Mr. Keating was not doing illegal things for his own personal benefit. I was proved wrong (House Banking Committee, 6th Hearing, pp. 35-36).

Wall reaffirmed the major themes in the statements of both Stewart and Dochow, asserting that until 1988 there had not been sufficient information to justify a federal takeover of Lincoln. Wall also aligned himself with Banking Committee investigators by expressing moral outrage over the deceptive sales of ACC bonds in Lincoln Savings and Loan branches: "The subordinated debt ... was a human tragedy .... I sympathize with the people, the ladies who were at this table last week. It is a heart-rending situation ... the worst kind of viciousness" (House Banking Committee, 6th Hearing, p. 52). In conclusion, Wall appealed to the exceptional complexity of the Lincoln case and suggested that many parties shared responsibility for the regulatory failure and the insurance costs borne by taxpayers:

> Why did this problem occur? ... I offer the following reasons: The riskiness of Lincoln's business activities; duplicity of its management in hiding its violations; failure of San Francisco to obtain more accurate and timely information about Lincoln and its holding company American Continental Corporation; ineptitude at best of their outside auditors ...; and finally, the inability of San Francisco and the Bank Board staff to work cooperatively on this case (House Banking Committee, 6th Hearing, pp. 53-54).

Predictably, Banking Committee interrogators rejected the views of the witnesses and sought to discredit them. Chairman Gonzalez rebutted Wall by citing a 1987 memo from one of Wall's own staffers that recommended placing Lincoln in conservatorship. Gonzalez then dismissed Dochow's testimony as "a sort of mishmash of obfuscations" (House Banking Committee, 6th Hearing, p. 62). Rep. Leach scolded Wall: "You and your staff cannot shirk responsibility" (House Banking Committee, 6th Hearing, p. 71). Rep. Schumer scoffed at the regulators' claims of toughness: "And for you to say … that you went after Lincoln 'aggressively' is making a travesty of that word" (House Banking Committee, 6th Hearing, p. 101). Rep. Roth echoed Schumer's incredulity: "Mr. Wall, you tell us how tough you are, but when it comes to Mr. Keating, you seem to be rather wimpish" (House Banking Committee, 6th Hearing, p. 104). Rep. Bruce Vento apparently summed up the views of the majority of inquisitors, telling the witnesses: "Well, you were all wrong, and we want to hear you say that you were wrong" (House Banking Committee, 6th Hearing, p. 153).

The Banking Committee's insistence on crediting a particular version of events was manifested in an unusual maneuver. Ranking minority member Wylie, in response to the testimony by Wall and his associates, raised the issue of perjury:

> Now, there has been some disparity in the testimony here this morning between the testimony that we heard last week from Mr. Black and Mr. Patriarca and Mr. Cirona [i.e., the San Francisco regulators] … the areas of disagreement and disparity are significant enough that someone has perjured themselves (House Banking Committee, 6th Hearing, p. 63).

Following Wylie's assertion, Chairman Gonzalez intervened and summoned William Black forward to be sworn as a witness. Two Republican members of the committee objected to this action, to no avail.

In subsequent interrogation, Rep. Roth asked chief savings and loan regulator Wall: "had you listened to your own regulators in San Francisco, rather than Mr. Keating, wouldn't you have saved the American taxpayers $1 billion and kept 22,000 people, mainly elderly, from being fleeced by Mr. Keating?" (House Banking Committee, 6th Hearing, p. 104). Roth then elicited Black's views (already well known from his earlier testimony) as confirmation. The following exchange ensued:

> Mr. Roth: … Mr. Black … I want to ask you point-blank: As of August 1987, did you give your superiors enough information, enough evidence … to close down Lincoln?

Mr. Black: Yes … it was not simply a review of our examination findings; it was the review also of Lincoln's 768-page response … Mr. Smuzynski and Mr. O'Connell … concluded that Lincoln was in an unsafe and unsound condition …..They also told their boss, Mr. Dochow, that Lincoln's management had no credibility … an express legal ground for appointing a conservator or a receiver. …

Mr. Roth: Mr. Wall … the facts support what this man tells us.

Mr. Wall: I do not believe the facts are quite that supportive at that point in the process. We had unanimous position in Washington that said we did not have sufficient basis to take the action …

Mr. Roth: I am sorry. I do not buy that, nor does anyone else on this committee (House Banking Committee, 6th Hearing, p. 65).

In this way, the majority alliance on the House Banking Committee certified the version of reality favored by the San Francisco regulators and declared it to be officially true. The congressional inquisitors simultaneously rejected alternative narratives about insufficient information or bias by regional regulators.

CONCLUSION

The foregoing analysis has argued that Lincoln Savings and Loan became a special symbol of the savings and loan crisis, despite the facts that it was not the largest savings and loan to have failed nor the most costly bailout. Mass media organizations, as well as official inquisitors in the U.S. House of Representatives, played important roles in creating a landmark narrative about Lincoln and Charles H. Keating, the CEO of American Continental Corporation. According to this narrative, the enormous greed and unscrupulousness of Keating, combined with his political protection, resulted in the "looting" of a federally insured savings and loan that cost taxpayers more than $2 billion. In the process, Keating and his underlings deceived and injured thousands of innocent small investors, many of them senior citizens who had been deliberately "targeted." Adding to the pathos was the heroic effort of chief savings and loan regulator Edwin Gray and his colleagues at the San Francisco regional office of the Federal Home Loan Bank Board to bring Keating under control – an effort doomed because of political contributions by Keating. These contributions, according to the narrative, motivated five U.S. Senators to intimidate Gray into withdrawing an important regulation. Keating's alleged political influence was also said to have resulted in shameful appeasement by Gray's successor, Danny Wall.

The landmark narrative of Lincoln is a combination of a scandal story and high tragedy. This tale has considerable appeal, as narrative, because it contains elements of engrossing stories generally, especially striking personifications of good and evil. On the side of the angels are Edwin Gray, an almost Biblical "suffering servant" who subordinated his own conservative Republican views to a higher truth, and also the incorruptible savings and loan regulators in San Francisco. On the other side are Charles Keating, portrayed as arrogant, cunning, deceitful, greedy and insensitive to the pain of small investors. Allied with this prince of darkness are public officials corrupted by political donations (the "Keating Five" Senators) and morally weak regulators (especially Danny Wall).

Interestingly, in the process of generating this landmark narrative, the House Banking Committee also composed a self-portrait. The main image in this picture is that of fearless champions of the public interest who set aside petty partisanship to reveal the truth and prevent the recurrence of evil. Like the prophets of the Judeo-Christian scriptures, the congressional inquisitors proclaimed justice for the oppressed and called for judgment against the rich and powerful. The Banking Committee implicitly depicted itself as a worthy successor to such earlier counterparts as the Senate Watergate Committee or the Knapp Commission.

Like all landmark narratives, the tale of Lincoln as the "prototype" of abuses in the savings and loan industry remains vulnerable. Perhaps it will continue to have a widespread appeal because of its absorbing plot and colorful characters that trigger powerful emotions. Or perhaps it will become a target of revisionist analysis, as has happened recently with landmark narratives about "Pinto madness" and the shuttle *Challenger* disaster. Lee and Ermann (2002, p.282), for instance, have argued that, "The defining characteristic of the Pinto narrative is its misplaced emphasis on individual amoral calculation within a focal organization." This critique is further supported by the soul-searching account of Dennis Gioia (1996), who reports that his product safety office twice considered recalling the Pinto, but twice concluded that there was insufficient evidence to do so. In the same way, Vaughan (1996, 2002) has presented a revisionist account of the *Challenger* disaster, asserting that the accepted story of "amorally calculating managers" simply does not square with the available evidence.

When passions have subsided and major participants have passed from the scene, future observers may redefine the Lincoln narrative as a rush to judgment by congressional representatives eager to displace blame from themselves. For as some Banking Committee members themselves acknowledged, there would never have been a Lincoln owned by a swashbuckling Charles Keating except for the statutory deregulation enacted by Congress itself. Herein lies another tale that awaits the telling.

REFERENCES

Bagdikian, Ben (1990). *The Media Monopoly*, Boston: Beacon Press.

Barak, G., ed. (1995). *Media, Process and the Social Construction of Crime*, New York: Garland.

Bogen, David and Michael Lynch (1989). "Taking Account of the Hostile Native: Plausible Deniability and the Production of Conventional History in the Iran-Contra Hearings," *Social Problems* 36(2).

Cohen, William S. and George J. Mitchell (1989). *Men of Zeal*, New York: Penguin.

Dash, Samuel (1976). *Chief Counsel: Inside the Ervin Committee*, New York: Random House.

Dowie, Mark (1977). "Pinto Madness," *Mother Jones* 2 (September/October).

Gans, Herbert (1980). *Deciding What's News*, New York: Vintage.

Gioia, Dennis A. (1996). Why I Didn't Recognize Pinto Fire Hazards: How Organizational Scripts Channel Managers' Thoughts and Actions, in M. David Ermann and Richard J. Lundman, eds.: *Corporate and Governmental Deviance*, 5th ed., New York: Oxford University Press.

Herman, Edward S., and Noam Chomsky (1988). *Manufacturing Consent: The Political Economy of Mass Media*, New York: Pantheon Books.

Lane, Mark 1966. *Rush to Judgment, A Critique of the Warren Commission's Inquiry*, New York: Holt, Rinehart, Winston.

Lee, Matthew T., and M. David Ermann 2002, Pinto Madness: Flaws in the Generally Accepted Landmark Narrative, in M. David Ermann and Richard J. Lundman, eds.: *Corporate and Governmental Deviance*, 6th ed., New York: Oxford University Press.

Maas, Peter (1973). *Serpico*, New York: Harper.

Molotch, Harvey, and Marilyn Lester (1974). "News as Purposive Behavior: On the Strategic Use of Routine Events, Accidents and Scandals," *American Sociological Review*, 39 (1).

Nichols, Lawrence T. (1990). Discovering Hutton: Expression Gaming and Congressional Definitions of Deviance, in Norman K. Denzin, ed.: *Studies in Symbolic Interaction,* Stamford, Conn: JAI Press.

Nichols, Lawrence T. (1991). "'Whistleblower' or 'Renegade': Definitional Contests in an Official Inquiry," *Studies in Symbolic Interaction*, Stamford, Conn: JAI Press. 14(4).

Nichols, Lawrence T. (1997). "Social Problems as Landmark Narratives: Bank of Boston, Mass Media and 'Money Laundering,'" *Social Problems*, 44(3).

Nichols, Lawrence T. (1999). White-Collar Cinema: Changing Representations of Upper-World Deviance in Popular Films, in James Holstein and Gale Miller, eds.: *Perspectives on Social Problems.*

Potter, G. W., and V. E. Kappelev (1998). *Constructing Crime: Perspectives on Making News and Social Problems*, Prospect Heights, Ill: Waveland Press.

Rashke, Richard, and Kate Bronfenbrenner (2000). *The Killing of Karen Silkwood*, Ithaca, NY: Cornell University Press.

Rule, Ann (1981). *The Stranger Beside Me*, New York: Signet.

Schudson, Michael (1993). *Watergate in American Memory*, New York: Basic Books.

Surrette, Ray (1992). *Media, Crime and Criminal Justice*, Pacific Grove, Cal: Brooks/Cole.

Tuchman, Gaye (1978). *Making News: A Study in the Construction of Reality*, New York: Free Press.

U.S. House of Representatives (1989-1990). *Investigation of Lincoln Savings and Loan Association*, Washington, DC: Government Printing Office.

U.S. House of Representatives (1990). *Lincoln Savings and Loan Association*, Washington, DC: Government Printing Office.

Vaughan, Diane (1996). *The Challenger Launch Decision*, Chicago: University of Chicago Press.

Vaughan, Diane (2002). The *Challenger* Space Shuttle Disaster: Conventional Wisdom and a Revisionist Account, in M. David Ermann and Richard J. Lundman, eds.: *Corporate and Governmental Deviance*, New York: Oxford University Press.

Walsh, Lawrence E. (1998). *Firewall: The Iran-Contra Conspiracy and Cover-Up*, New York: Norton.

Woodward, Bob, and Bernstein, Carl (1974). *All The President's Men*, New York: Simon and Schuster.

LINCOLN SAVINGS:
A CODA

Donald McCarthy
Milken Institute

In June 1990, Charles Keating was indicted for violating the California Corporations Code §25401, a charge resulting from the issuance of subordinated debt securities by the parent company of Lincoln Savings, American Continental Corporation (ACC). The state of California alleged that Mr. Keating was guilty of defrauding the buyers of ACC bonds by masking the worsening financial health of the company. During the trial it became clear that, since Mr. Keating had no contact with ACC bond salesmen and sold no bonds himself, he could not be convicted under §25401. The judge presiding over the trial, Judge Lance Ito (who would later try the O.J. Simpson case) ruled that Keating could, however, be found guilty of aiding and abetting the violation of §25401.

After a six month trial, Charles Keating was convicted on seventeen of eighteen counts of securities fraud and sentenced to serve ten years in prison. That same month federal prosecutors indicted Mr. Keating on seventy-seven counts of racketeering and wire, mail, bankruptcy, securities and banking fraud. As with the California trial, the federal trial resulted in the conviction of Mr. Keating, this time on all seventy-seven charges. Sentenced to twelve years in prison (to run concurrently with his previous sentence), he was also ordered to pay $122 million in restitution.

Both of Mr. Keating's trials were found subsequently to have been fatally compromised by a series of errors and violations of due process. After having spent five years in prison, Mr. Keating was released after the Court of Appeals for the Ninth Circuit reversed his federal conviction and a federal district court granted his state petition of habeas corpus. The flaws to Keating's state trial were twofold. The first arose from Judge Ito's failure to properly instruct the jury to include a *mens rea* requirement in the charge of directly violating §25401. This was a breach of due process and a violation of Mr. Keating's legal rights. The second, and perhaps more shocking irregularity in the state trial was Judge Ito's decision to allow the jury to improperly convict Keating of aiding and abetting ACC salesmen in violating §25401 without finding that he had intended to swindle investors.

The federal trial was compromised by the jury learning of and, more importantly, discussing Mr. Keating's state conviction during the trial. The district court had ruled, before Keating's federal trial, that all evidence of his state conviction must be excluded from the federal trial. However, following Keating's conviction the defense learned that four of the jurors knew of Mr. Keating's state conviction before the federal trial began and, according to an alternate juror, "discussed the fact that Keating had been previously convicted by the State of California." The Ninth District Court and the Court of Appeals of the Ninth District found, in an opinion subsequently upheld by the U.S.

Supreme Court, that Mr. Keating's conviction was fatally poisoned by the jurors learning of Keating's state conviction and reversed his conviction. In its ruling on the case, the district court noted that:

> Once a juror learns of a defendant's prior conviction from any source, including pretrial publicity, because of the prejudicial nature of the information, the government cannot meet its burden of rebutting the presumption of prejudice. (U.S. Court of Appeals for the Ninth Circuit, 1998)

The overwhelming volume of pretrial publicity – all of an extremely prejudicial nature – suggests that it would have been difficult for any juror to not be aware of Keating's conviction and of the nature of his alleged offenses (Table 1).

Table 1: Prejudicial reporting on Charles Keating.

	Stories appearing during Keating's state trial (6/90–12/91)	Stories appearing after Keating's state conviction and before his federal trial (12/91–10/92)	Total appearing before Keating's federal trial
Including Charles Keating and "criminal"	1,401	534	1,935
Including Charles Keating and "guilty"	605	407	1,015
Including Charles Keating and "crook"	217	69	286
			3,233

Source: Lexis Nexis

In addition to presenting allegations of fraudulent business practices – practices which Keating was incidentally never convicted of – the media focused closely on Keating's lifestyle and possessions. Journalists made much of his personal airplanes and his houses in the Bahamas and invited their readers to conclude that these luxuries were purchased with money siphoned off from Lincoln Savings or ACC. These allegations were repeated at Keating's trial but were found to be baseless. In actuality, Keating had owned the luxury homes and the airplanes for more than 10 years before he even made a bid for Lincoln Savings. Furthermore, accounting experts in the employ of the government testified at Keating's trial that the earnings statements of Lincoln Savings did not contain a single misreported or misstated dollar.

Charticle 6
Impact of Forbearance

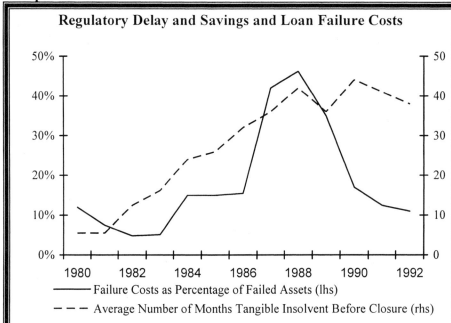

Regulatory Delay and Savings and Loan Failure Costs

—— Failure Costs as Percentage of Failed Assets (lhs)

– – – Average Number of Months Tangible Insolvent Before Closure (rhs)

Source: Barth, James R. and Robert E. Litan (1997).

Forbearance was the keystone of regulatory policy in the 1980s as insolvent savings and loans were allowed to remain open in the hopes that they might grow their way out of insolvency. It was, however, to be a disastrous policy as putting off prompt resolution caused the eventual clean-up to be far more costly than need be.

THE U.S. SAVINGS AND LOAN CRISIS IN HINDSIGHT:

20 YEARS LATER

James R. Barth
Auburn University and Milken Institute;
Former Chief Economist, Office of Thrift Supervision and
Federal Home Loan Bank Board

Susanne Trimbath
Milken Institute

Glenn Yago
Milken Institute

INTRODUCTION

In the early 1980s, almost every one of the approximately four thousand savings and loans in the United States was losing money and insolvent from an economic viewpoint. A decade later, nearly one-third of these institutions had been seized by the regulatory authorities and either closed or sold. Most of the $153 billion it cost to liquidate or induce others to take over these failed institutions came from taxpayers because the industry-supported federal insurance fund set up to protect depositors lacked the resources to manage the problem.

This dire situation was the first major breakdown of the federal regulatory and deposit-insurance system that was established a half century earlier during the Great Depression. Ironically, the regulatory system was designed to promote a safe and sound savings and loan industry but in fact it contributed to the collapse. The deposit-insurance system, moreover, was designed to ensure that any losses from failures would be borne by the industry-supported insurance fund, not taxpayers. Despite all assurances to the contrary, as the savings and loan crisis unfolded, that too did not happen. In early 1989 the President of the United States announced that taxpayer funds would be necessary to clean up the mess once and for all.[1]

To our knowledge, no industry in the U.S. has ever faced such a deep and widespread crisis as the savings and loan industry did in the 1980s. At least one savings and loan failed in every state of our nation during this period.[2] Nor have U.S. taxpayers ever been required to bear such a large sum as that eventually required to cover the losses flowing from the failure of so many firms in a single industry. Indeed, these losses were greater than those borne by depositors of savings and loans during the 1930s before the establishment of a federal deposit-insurance system (Barth and Litan, 1998).

Savings and loans were not alone in their financial turmoil. In the 1980s and early 1990s 1,273 savings and loans with assets of $2,437 billion failed, 1,569 commercial and savings banks with $2,683 billion of assets, and 2,330 credit unions with $92 billion of assets failed.[3] In the process, the Federal Deposit Insurance Corporation (FDIC) – the deposit-insurance fund for banks

---

[1] The use of taxpayer funds was provided for in the Financial Institutions Recovery, Reform and Enforcement Act (FIRREA) of 1989.
[2] Appendix 1 provides a broad overview of the changing structure and performance of the savings and loan industry from 1980 to 1996.
[3] Appendices 2 and 3 provide information on the commercial bank and credit unions comparable to that provided for savings and loans in Appendix 1.

– like its savings and loan counterpart, the Federal Savings and Loan Insurance Corporation (FSLIC), became insolvent. Fortunately for taxpayers, the FDIC's insolvency, unlike the case of the FSLIC, was short lived and remedied without direct taxpayer expenditures. Only the government bank insurance fund for credit unions, the National Credit Union Share Insurance Fund, remained solvent during this turbulent period.

Now that twenty years have elapsed since the beginning of the savings and loan crisis, it is important to reassess its causes and what lessons were learned from all these costly failures in such an advanced and mature country as the U.S. In view of the fact that two thirds of the member countries of the International Monetary Fund have also suffered a banking crisis, this assessment may contribute to the debate over what future course governments should follow to promote the development, efficiency and stability of financial systems in countries at all levels of income and in all parts of the world.

Regulatory restrictions on depository institutions can have both unintended and undesirable consequences. This was certainly the case for the savings and loan industry. For years the government effectively used it to further the goal of promoting home ownership. This strategy ultimately proved to be disastrous. Savings and loans were, in effect, forced to borrow (take deposits) short term and to lend (make mortgages) long term. A sudden shift in the term structure of interest rates, coupled with the impact of various laws and regulations, resulted in a dramatic reversal of performance at savings and loans. We trace the crisis through four distinct phases. During the first phase, from the late 1970s until about 1985, savings and loans were plagued by interest rate problems. The second phase was characterized by asset quality problems from 1985 through 1989. In 1990, the industry entered the third phase of the crisis, which entailed litigation over contractually agreed upon supervisory goodwill, which we will explain in detail below. The fourth and final phase continues even today as the U.S. financial industry re-invents itself in the context of global capital markets.

The remainder of the paper proceeds as follows. In the next section we discuss the interest rate problems that initially put pressure on industry profitability. Then we discuss the implosion of the industry that marked the first phase of the crisis. Next, we show how the second phase of the crisis, characterized by significant institutional failures, was induced by asset quality problems brought on by expanded investment options that were actually intended to save the industry. The third phase of savings and loan crises resulted from a breach of contract between the government and selected savings and loans that remains to be fully resolved. Then, we present empirical analyses which evidence the profit, asset quality, failure and cost of failure problems that define the savings and loan crisis. This is followed by a discussion of the lessons learned from the crisis, and a final forward-looking lesson that can be applied to all financial institutions that essentially embodies the fourth phase of the savings and loan industry.

REGULATING SAVINGS AND LOANS INTO DECLINE

Savings and loans were among the most highly regulated firms in the country at the beginning of the 1980s. They were forbidden by law to make adjustable-rate home mortgages because these were thought to expose home buyers to excessive mortgage payment risk. They could make no loan more than 50 miles from their home office because this protected local institutions from competition from other savings and loans outside their immediate geographic area. Nor could savings and loans originate most loans that commercial banks could make, such as commercial real estate loans or commercial loans to business, which limited competition between these two types of depository institutions. Savings and loans were not even allowed to offer their customers demand deposits until very recently largely due to opposition from commercial banks.

The range of the activities of savings and loans was almost entirely limited by law and regulation to fixed-interest-rate home mortgage loans. At the same time, the mortgages were funded by relatively short-term deposits whose interest rates were also fixed by law and regulation. At the beginning of the 1980s, for example, savings and loans earned an average of 9 percent on home mortgages and paid 7 percent on deposits. Thus, for every $100 of home loans they made, they received $2 in net interest income. This was virtually their only source of revenue, out of which they paid salaries and other expenses as well as taxes.

This traditional and apparently simple arrangement, however, was a ticking time bomb. Reacting to inflationary conditions in the late 1970s and early 1980s, the Federal Reserve changed its operating policy, focusing on monetary aggregates rather than interest rates. As a result of the subsequent monetary tightening, interest rates rose. The $2 in net interest income earned by savings and loans vanished as they raised the interest rate paid on deposits, which was facilitated by the elimination of the ceiling on deposit rates for savings and loans, in response to the new interest rate environment. If they didn't raise the rates they paid, depositors would have withdrawn their deposits and put them into unregulated financial intermediaries offering substantially higher interest rates. And, in fact, many depositors did just that. Almost every institution quickly lost money and, from an economic standpoint, became insolvent as the market value of its home mortgages fell below the value of the deposits funding them (Barth, 1991; Brumbaugh, 1988; Kane, 1989).

Nevertheless, the removal of the deposit rate ceiling prevented the far more serious and widespread deposit withdrawals that would have forced savings and loans to sell their home mortgages at a loss in order to obtain liquidity. The government considered it better to permit savings and loans to suffer reduced earnings by raising the interest rate they had to pay to retain deposits than to suffer even larger losses from the immediate sale of home mortgages. The latter course of action would have more rapidly depleted the minimum amount of regulatory capital that institutions were required to hold and thus more visibly exposed the depth of their problems. The overall governmental strategy being pursued at the time was designed to buy time for savings and loans until interest rates returned to more normal levels. The expectation, or perhaps more likely the hope, was that this reversal would occur sometime soon and restore profitability to the industry.

This example of the Federal Reserve reversing its policies typifies a common phenomenon in the heavily regulated and supervised banking industry. In general, government agencies must continually react to contain the disruptive impact on regulated industries from powerful market forces. In this particular case the Federal Reserve reacted to contain significant inflationary pressures. And, as the savings and loan crisis demonstrates, such reactions can come with disastrous side effects. In this case the adverse effects were confined to a fairly narrow segment of the entire financial system and thus less disruptive than otherwise could have been the case (Barth, Hall and Yago, 2000).

THE INDUSTRY IMPLODES

The first phase of the savings and loan crisis – roughly 1980-1985 – was entirely the result of laws and regulations that imposed too rigid a structure on institutions, permitting them to offer only fixed-rate, long-term home mortgages funded by deposits tied to short-term rates (Figure 1). Although there were many other less-risky ways to fund home mortgages in the late 1970s – from hedging interest-rate risk in the forward, futures, and options markets to offering adjustable-rate mortgages – savings and loans were largely forbidden to use these risk-reducing financial instruments. Only after the industry imploded did the government relent and allow their use.

Figure 1: The Savings and Loan Crisis: Interest Rate Risk Phase

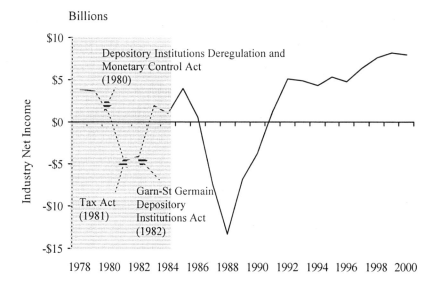

Source: Thrift Financial Reports, Milken Institute.

When the savings and loan industry plunged precipitously into economic insolvency, the regulatory procedures already in place were straightforward enough. The regulatory authorities were supposed to seize savings and loans known to be insolvent and either close or sell them, depending upon which alternative imposed the least cost on the deposit-insurance fund. One binding constraint, however, prevented them from resolving all the insolvencies in this manner. Compared to the breadth and depth of the insolvencies, the FSLIC's fund was totally insufficient to handle the problem. By the early 1980s, saving and loans throughout the country were insolvent by about $110 billion, while the fund was reporting only $6 billion in reserves (Barth, 1991; Brumbaugh, 1988; Kane, 1989). The FSLIC itself, in other words, was insolvent on the basis of its contingent liabilities. Yet, its auditor, the U.S. General Accounting

Office (GAO), did not require this significant liability to be recorded and reported to the public until 1986 (Barth, 1991).

As a result, the government – a major contributing culprit – was left to manage a huge bankruptcy proceeding in which it had a relatively simple, but terrifying choice. It could either require taxpayers to pay approximately $110 billion to resolve the insolvent savings and loans, or, with the hope that interest rates would fall and eliminate the immediate crisis, it could devise ways to postpone recognizing the embedded economic losses. Under the circumstances, it is not surprising that the Congress chose the latter course, without public opposition from the White House or the FSLIC's auditor, the GAO.

The Congress belatedly enacted two major laws to deal with the problem, the Depository Institutions Deregulation and Monetary Control Act in 1980 and the Garn-St Germain Depository Institutions Act in 1982. The new laws, however, provided no additional funds to allow the regulators to resolve insolvent institutions. Instead, by lowering the minimum level of capital that a savings and loan was required to hold to satisfy regulatory requirements, the laws enabled institutions to report artificially healthy financial conditions and thereby gave regulators more time to devise a more permanent solution. The laws also lowered enforcement standards for those institutions near insolvency, and gave the regulators authority to permit new forms of regulatory capital. As a result, many savings and loans known to be insolvent, even on the basis of accounting standards already in use, were allowed to report otherwise and some were even allowed to report a capital level that met the minimum requirement. Figure 2 shows the aggregate capital-to-asset ratio for savings and loans on the basis of several alternative accounting measures. The amount of capital that institutions reported on the basis of regulatory accounting practices (RAP) exceeded that reported on the basis of Generally Accepted Accounting Principles (GAAP) and even far more than that reported on the basis of tangible accounting principles (TAP). This fact, however, did not prevent the government from subsequently suing major accounting firms for "overstating" the financial condition of savings and loans that failed.

Figure 2: Capital-to-Asset Ratio for Savings and Loans: 1940-1988

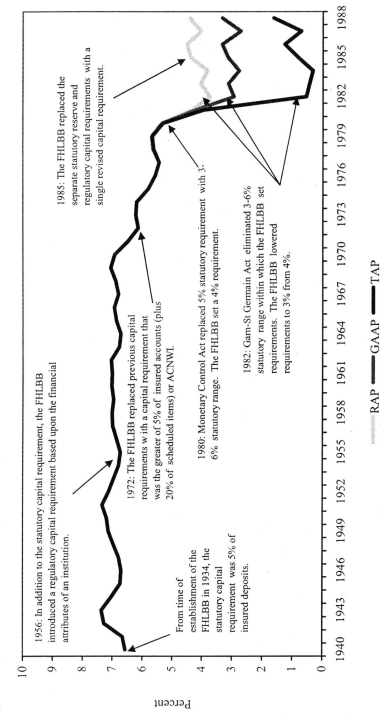

1956: In addition to the statutory capital requirement, the FHLBB introduced a regulatory capital requirement based upon the financial attributes of an institution.

1985: The FHLBB replaced the separate statutory reserve and regulatory capital requirements with a single revised capital requirement.

1972: The FHLBB replaced previous capital requirements with a capital requirement that was the greater of 5% of insured accounts (plus 20% of scheduled items) or ACNWI.

1980: Monetary Control Act replaced 5% statutory requirement with 3-6% statutory range. The FHLBB set a 4% requirement.

From time of establishment of the FHLBB in 1934, the statutory capital requirement was 5% of insured deposits.

1982: Garn-St Germain Act eliminated 3-6% statutory range within which the FHLBB set requirements. The FHLBB lowered requirements to 3% from 4%.

Percent

RAP   GAAP   TAP

Source: Barth, James, R. (1991) *The Great Savings and Loan Debacle.* Washington, D.C.: The AEI Press.

In other words, the Congress gave authority to the regulators to "paper" over the problem and to engage in regulatory forbearance. Since the Congress was unwilling to recapitalize the FSLIC with taxpayer dollars, it essentially forced regulators to buy time in the hope that insolvent savings and loans would return to profitability with an improved interest rate environment. It was hoped that when this happened institutions would have availed themselves of the opportunity to find ways to gain greater financial health through the new and expanded powers provided for in the laws enacted in the

early 1980s. The government strategy was to make savings and loans more like commercial banks, which were not anyway near as hard hit by the interest rate shock at that time.

PERVERSE INCENTIVES AND RISK MANAGEMENT

Lower capital requirements based largely on traditional accounting techniques, which can grossly overstate the health of a financial institution, were allowed in the 1980 and 1982 federal legislation. It also allowed savings and loans to begin to diversify into commercial real estate loans, direct equity investments, commercial loans, and other kinds of loans that commercial banks could already make. The savings and loans were also allowed to originate variable-rate home loans and to make loans nationwide. At roughly the same time, an increasing number of states granted broader lending and investment opportunities to their own state-chartered savings and loans, sometimes even broader than the opportunities authorized for federally chartered institutions. All these developments gave rise to the second phase of the savings and loan crisis.

All these changes, albeit belatedly, allowed savings and loans to reduce their interest-rate risk. At the same time, the changes exposed savings and loans to new risks. Whereas few borrowers default on their home mortgages, defaults and associated losses on other types of loans and investments are typically much higher. Furthermore, while home mortgages are secured by real property many of the loans that savings and loans began making were unsecured or backed by assets with difficult to determine market values. Nonetheless, combining interest-rate risk with credit risk spread over a wider geographical area can help provide greater opportunities for well-managed and well-capitalized institutions to choose an acceptable, overall balance of risk and return. Such a strategy provides potentially lower portfolio risk than with lending and investment powers restricted to a narrow range of activities.

Figure 3: The Savings and Loan Crisis: Non-Traditional Asset Quality Phase

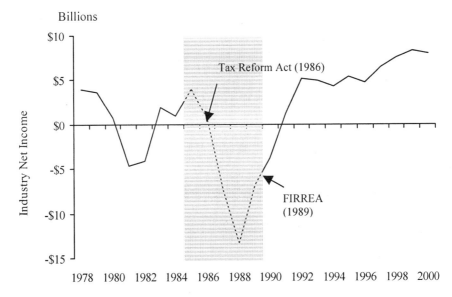

Source: Thrift Financial Reports, Milken Institute.

After being granted broader powers, many savings and loans began making commercial real estate loans and investments, new activities in which they were relatively inexperienced. The Economic Recovery Tax Act of 1981 spurred much of this activity.[4] As savings and loans moved into the commercial real estate market, commercial banks also increased their commercial real estate loan business, making the market still more competitive. This gave rise to the second phase of the crisis (Figure 3), earmarked by changes in the mix of assets held by savings and loans.

Perverse incentives were a by-product of the new, looser regulatory restrictions. Open but insolvent savings and loans had an incentive to take excessive risks, or "gamble for resurrection," in part because the insurance fund would bear the losses if everything went terribly wrong.[5] (See Table 1.)

---

[4] The Tax Act is indicated in Figure 1. Appendix 5 details how the 1981 tax law changes stimulated the demand for real estate.

[5] This is a result of limited liability laws in which owners are liable for losses only to the extent of the equity they contribute to an institution.

Yet, the owners would reap the rewards if everything went well. The strength of these perverse incentives varied, however, and attempts to act upon them could potentially be kept in check by appropriate regulation and supervision by the state and federal authorities.

Table 1: Bad Incentives: Open But Insolvent Savings and Loans

	Number of Resolutions	Months Insolvent Before Closure	Total Assets of Resolutions ($ mls)
1980	11	5	1,458
1981	28	5	15,908
1982	63	8	17,662
1983	36	16	4,631
1984	22	23	5,080
1985	31	26	6,366
1986	46	31	12,455
1987	47	35	10,660
1988	205	42	101,242
1989	37	40	9,774

The new, lower capital requirements and broader opportunities to lend and invest allowed some savings and loan executives to take excessive risks. With federally insured deposits and the ability to attract more deposits by offering higher rates of interest, even deeply troubled savings and loans always had ready access to additional funds. This enabled them to avoid the discipline of the marketplace and the need to rely on internally generated profits.

Greater competition, inexperience and perverse incentives – all of which were predictable and increasingly more obvious – led to problems. Even greater problems arose as the result of a series of unpredictable events in the mid- to late-1980s. After savings and loans began to make considerable real estate loans and investments, regional recessions struck the country, reducing commercial real estate revenues and values. For instance, an unexpected plunge in the price of oil in 1986 contributed to a regional recession in the Southwestern U.S.

Another unpredictable event came from Capitol Hill. In an attempt to increase tax revenues, Congress surprisingly passed legislation – the Tax Reform Act of 1986 – that more than eliminated the tax benefits to commercial real estate ownership it had conveyed only a few years earlier (Appendix 5). Commercial real estate values fell dramatically as a result. This is one of the great ironies of the savings and loan debacle. In 1981 and 1982 Congress provided savings and loans with a life line, largely through greater opportunities to lend and invest in commercial real estate. Then in 1986 Congress cut the life line, leaving the savings and loans floundering, trying to find a life preserver to hang onto.

BREACH OF CONTRACT UPS THE ANTE

The third phase of the savings and loans crisis began with the enactment of FIRREA in August of 1989 (Figure 4). In the process of imposing higher and more stringent capital requirements on savings and loans, the new law eliminated so-called supervisory goodwill as a component of regulatory capital. Although there was a phase-out period covering several years, more than 100 institutions were immediately and adversely affected. In response, these savings and loans sued the federal government for breach of contract. The basis for the suit was that this type of goodwill resulted from the supervisory approved merger and acquisition of insolvent institutions by stronger institutions during the early 1980s. Purchase accounting techniques were used during these transactions in which the assets and liabilities of the weaker institutions were marked-to-market. The resulting negative "net-worth hole" then become supervisory goodwill which was treated as an asset on the books of the surviving institution. The new and larger institution was then allowed to amortize this goodwill over a lengthy 40 years.

Figure 4: The Savings and Loan Crisis: Goodwill Litigation Phase

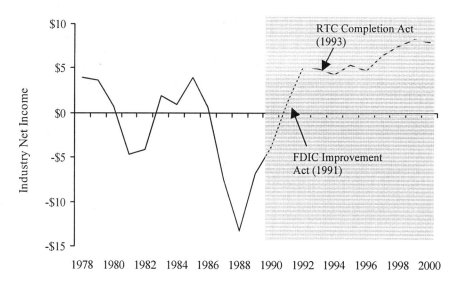

Source: Thrift Financial Reports, Milken Institute.

The government strategy at the time was to use these types of transactions as another means to buy time for the industry to recover. It also was a way to conserve on the very limited resources of the FSLIC relative to the magnitude of the problem it faced in the early 1980s. But things changed unexpectedly for those savings and loans that had entered into these transactions. When FIRREA became law, supervisory goodwill was eliminated and with it a significant portion of the regulatory capital of these institutions, even forcing some of them into insolvency. The third phase of the crisis began in 1996 when the U.S. Supreme Court agreed that the government had indeed breached its earlier contract with such savings and loans when the provisions of FIRREA were enforced.[6] The only issue remaining to be decided is the amount of the damages sustained by all the institutions when they could no longer count supervisory goodwill as regulatory capital (see Textbox: Supervisory Goodwill and Breach of Contract). Although this issue was still being litigated in 2003, some estimates put the ultimate cost to be borne by taxpayers at $20 billion. This is just one

---

[6] United States v. Winstar Corp. et al., 518 U.S. 839, Certiorari to the United States Court of Appeals for the Federal Circuit. No. 95-865. Argued April 24, 1996. Decided July 1, 1996.

example of the way in which regulatory "flip-flops" can produce undesired consequences.

SUPERVISORY GOODWILL AND BREACH OF CONTRACT

In 1990, Winstar Corporation, Glendale Federal and The Statesman Group filed claims against the federal government alleging that the regulations regarding supervisory goodwill enacted as part of FIRREA were a breach of contract. The three plaintiffs claimed that the federal government had entered into contracts allowing them to create "supervisory goodwill" in conjunction with their acquisitions of failed savings and loans. Yet the new capital standards adopted as part of FIRREA eliminated this goodwill and therefore breached the earlier contracts. Thus, the government was liable for the damages these institutions sustained.

In United States v. Winstar Corp., 116 S. Ct. 2432 (1996), the United States Supreme Court, by a ruling of seven to two, found in favor of the plaintiffs and ruled that the Federal government was liable for damages arising from its breach of contract. The case was then remanded to the U.S. Court of Federal Claims for the damages phase to be heard. The Winstar case was joined at this point by 125 other plaintiffs who had also entered into agreements with the Federal government regarding "supervisory goodwill" – agreements that were abrogated by FIRREA.

All of these cases – deemed Winstar related cases – were made subject to special case management procedures that also established a statute of limitations on claims against the government. Twenty four of the Winstar related cases were subsequently dismissed on grounds of having passed the statute of limitations. The remaining 104 cases, however, were allowed to be heard by the Court of Federal Claims. At this point, the FDIC joined more than forty of the cases involving savings and loans placed into receivership as Plaintiff-Intervener. In its capacity as receiver of the failed institutions, and supposedly to represent the interests of the failed savings and loans, the FDIC has sought to replace shareholders in these cases as plaintiff. This action has created the amusing spectacle of one branch of the federal government suing another. Indeed, the spectacle is even more curious because one part of the FDIC is plaintiff, while another part is defendant!

The damages claimed by the plaintiffs total more than $20 billion and represent an enormous potential liability for the government beyond the $155 billion already spent to resolve failed savings and loans during the 1980s. The amount of damages claimed by the plaintiffs represents the upper bound of the liability and, according to the Congressional Budget Office, the expected liability is substantially less at $9 billion. As of year end 2002, the Court of Federal Claims had ruled on just twenty one of the cases. Of these, thirteen cases were decided in favor of the U.S. Federal government and the remainder in favor of the plaintiffs. Typically, decisions have not awarded plaintiffs damages arising from allegedly forgone profits but instead have awarded restitution damages and damages equal to the transaction costs that an institution would have had to bear in order to raise sufficient capital to offset the loss of supervisory goodwill. To date, the Court of Federal Claims has awarded damages of $642 million, including $380 to Glendale Federal (now part of Washington Mutual). Although considerable, these awards fall far short of the damages claimed, which in the case of Glendale Federal alone amounted to over $2,000 million. The government has also settled two of the cases – those of Winstar and Statesmen – for approximately $100 million.

Savings and Loan	Case	Damages Claimed ($ mls)	Damages Awarded ($ mls)
Glendale Federal Bank	Winstar Corp. v. U.S	2,015	380
Windom Federal (Winstar Corporation)	Winstar Corp. v. U.S	NA	100
Federated Savings Bank (The Statesman Group)	Winstar Corp. v. U.S		
Western Empire Federal	Castle v. U.S.	NA	15
The Benjamin Franklin Federal Savings and Loan	Suess v. U.S.	1,168	35
California Federal	Cal Fed v. U.S.	1,500	23
Bank United of Texas	Bank United of Texas, USAT Holdings, Hyperion Holdings, Hyperion Partners v. U.S.	NA	$9
Oak Tree Savings Bank/Dixie Federal	Landmark Land Company, FDIC v. U.S.	Landmark Land: 22 / FDIC: 642	Landmark Land: 22 / FDIC: 0

Note: NA denotes information not available.
Source: United States Court of Federal Claims

The present-value cost to bail out failed savings and loans from 1980 through 1995, as noted earlier, is approximately $153 billion (Appendix 8). Two factors pushed this cost to these levels. First, the government regulated the savings and loan industry in a way that made it fundamentally unstable, prone to huge losses if the short-term interest rates they paid on deposits rose above the rates they earned on all the home mortgages they were required to hold. Second, the government-provided system of deposit insurance not only failed to be patterned after private insurer practices, but it also provided inadequate reserves to bail out serious widespread savings and loan insolvencies (Barth, Bartholomew and Bradley, 1991). This led the government to try to solve the savings and loan crisis while leaving known insolvent institutions open. This, in turn, gave the open insolvent institutions the opportunity, after being granted broader powers, to engage in excessively risky activities, which, without adequately protecting taxpayers, ultimately imposed higher resolution costs. These costs were incurred either as payments to depositors of institutions being closed less the value of their assets, or by paying the difference between insured deposits and the value of assets to institutions that purchased seized savings and loans.

EMPIRICALLY ASSESSING THE IMPACT OF REGULATORY RESTRICTIONS

In this section we conduct an examination of the impact of laws and government regulations on savings and loans. Our examination uses data obtained from the official thrift financial reports (TFRs) filed with the regulatory authorities by every federally insured savings and loan in the country. We specifically rely upon the TFRs for the years 1979 to 1995 and focus on four different dimensions of individual institution performance during this period. First, we examine the relationship between various regulatory-induced balance sheet items and the return on assets (ROA). Second, we examine the relationship between the size and capitalization of an institution and its portfolio composition. Third, given all the failures that occurred, we examine the relationship between several factors that some individuals have identified as responsible for an institution's failure and the actual determinants of failure events. Last, given the costliness of the failures, we examine the relationship between various balance sheet items and the cost of resolving a failure. Table 2 provides a description of the data variables used throughout this section.

Table 2: Data Description

Variable Name	Definition
Below Threshold Tangible Assets	Dummy: Tangible Assets if PTAP<3, 0 otherwise
Brokered Deposits	Fraction of brokered deposits to total assets
Commercial Mortgages	Fraction of commercial mortgages to total assets
Development Loan	Fraction of acquisition and development loan to total assets
Direct Investments	Fraction of direct investments to total assets
Federal Chartered	Dummy: federal chartered institution = 1, 0 otherwise
High Yield Time	High Yield Securities multiplied by failure time in Cox proportional hazard model
High Yield Securities	Fraction of high yield securities to total assets
Lenient States	Dummy: lenient states (CA, CT, FL, LA, OH, TX, UT) prior to resolution year = 1, 0 otherwise
Negative Tangible Assets	Dummy: Tangible Assets if PTAP<0, 0 otherwise
Residential Mortgages	Fraction of residential mortgages to total assets
Size of Institution	Natural log of total assets
Stock Ownership	Dummy: Stock ownership = 1, 0 otherwise
Tangible Assets	Fraction of tangible assets to total assets
Uninsured Deposits	Fraction of uninsured deposits to total assets

Profitability

Table 3 presents the empirical results for return on assets (ROA), which is a fairly widely used measure of an institution's overall financial performance. We find that on average institutions sustained losses over the entire time period. However, the losses were below average in the first half of the period and above average in the second half. Bigger institutions, moreover, performed better than smaller ones. Also, the more tangible capital an institution held the better its performance. Whether an institution's tangible capital-to-asset ratio was less than 3 percent or even negative, however, did not diminish this beneficial effect. Whether an institution operated with a federal or state charter matters for profitability only before portfolio composition is considered. Stock institutions clearly performed worse than mutual ones. Furthermore, the greater the extent to which uninsured deposits were used to fund loans and investments the higher the ROA. These results are virtually unchanged when various balance sheet items are added to the model.

Table 3: Return on Assets The Impact of Size, Capitalization, Charter and Ownership Types, and Portfolio Composition

Dependent Variable: ROA	Model 1	Model 2
Intercept	-0.0295***	-0.0323***
	(0.0022)	(0.0023)
Size of Institution	0.0023***	0.0025***
	(0.0001)	(0.0001)
Tangible Assets	0.1990***	0.1932***
	(0.0124)	(0.0125)
Negative Tangible Assets	0.0863	0.0796
	(0.0834)	(0.0816)
Below Threshold Tangible Assets	-0.0192	-0.0287
	(0.0318)	(0.0325)
Uninsured Deposits	0.0097***	0.0137***
	(0.0017)	(0.0016)
Federal Chartered	0.0004**	-0.0002
	(0.0002)	(0.0002)
Stock Ownership	-0.0047***	-0.0035***
	(0.0003)	(0.0003)
Asset Portfolio		
Direct Investments		-0.0635***
		(0.0141)
Residential Mortgages		-0.0118***
		(0.0009)
Commercial Mortgages		-0.0067***
		(0.0023)
High Yield Securities		-0.0370
		(0.0429)

Dependent Variable: ROA	Model 1	Model 2
Adjusted R2	0.38	0.39
F-Statistic	1356.02	1225.27
1st Wald Test, p-value, Chi-Square [ß3+ß4+ß5=0]	0.0003	0.0006
2nd Wald Test, p-value, Chi-Square [ß3+ß5=0]	0.0000	0.0010
No. of Observations	55,717	55,717

Note: ***, ** and * indicate significance at the 1, 5, and 10 percent levels, respectively. Standard errors are in parentheses.

The estimation method is OLS with Heteroskedastic Standard Errors and Covariance. The model specification can be written as follows:

$ROA_i = \beta_0 Intercept + \beta_1 Lnasset_i + \beta_2 Tassets_i + \beta_3 Tassets_i * D\_tasset1_i$

$+ \beta_4 Tassets_i * D\_tasset2_i + \beta_5 UninsuredDep_i + \beta_6 Federal_i + \beta_7 Stock_i + \phi' YearDummies_i + \varepsilon_i$

Year dummies from 1978 to 1995 are included in the regressions, but their results are not reported. The first Wald test shows that joint coefficients of overall tangible asset share of institution portfolio are positively and significantly related to return on equity in both specifications. The second Wald test shows that positive tangible asset share of institutional portfolio are positively and significantly related to return on equity in both specifications.

The primary interest here is in the relationship of the various balance sheet items to ROA. In particular, some have argued that savings and loans abused their powers by diversifying into such nontraditional assets as direct investments, commercial mortgages, and junk bonds. The results indicate that the greater the proportion of assets devoted to direct investments the lower the profitability. But somewhat surprisingly this also is the case for home mortgages. As regards junk bonds, contrary to what some have argued, there is no significant relationship between the fraction of assets devoted to these securities and profitability. They did not, in other words, adversely affect performance.

Asset Portfolio

Table 4 extends the analysis to an examination of the impact of capitalization, charter and ownership on the portfolio composition of institutions. As one would expect for savings and loans, the allocation to residential mortgages is positive in all years. Federally chartered institutions allocated more assets to commercial mortgages than on average. Stock institutions clearly allocated more to nontraditional assets. As noted previously, the amount of capital an institution has at risk may importantly affect its proclivity to engage in riskier activities. This does appear to be the case. The greater the tangible capital-to-asset ratio the lower the fraction of assets devoted to nontraditional loans and investments and the higher the fraction devoted to traditional home mortgages. There is some evidence, moreover, that this perverse incentive effect is even more pronounced for those institutions that are actually insolvent. A particularly interesting finding is that there is no relationship between the proportion of assets allocated to junk bonds and the tangible capital-to-asset ratio. There is, however, limited evidence that institutions with a ratio less than 3 percent held fewer junk bonds than those with higher ratios. It would appear that weakly capitalized institutions did not gamble for resurrection by investing in junk bonds. Rather, their nontraditional portfolio was more heavily weighted toward commercial mortgages.

Determinants of Failure Risk

Table 5 presents the empirical results from the estimation of a proportional hazard model, which enables one to assess the impact of various measures on the risk of failure to savings and loans. The findings indicate that bigger institutions were more likely to fail than smaller ones. Savings and loans in states granting the broadest powers, moreover, also faced a higher risk of failure than those located in other, more restrictive states. Whether an institution was federally or state-chartered does not appear to matter in a consistent manner. Stock institutions were more likely to be seized than mutual ones unless we include consideration of commercial mortgages as a share of assets, in which case stock institutions were no more likely to fail than mutual institutions. The greater the fraction of assets devoted to commercial mortgages the greater the risk of failure. On the other hand, the greater the fraction of assets devoted to home mortgages the lower the risk of failure. Interestingly enough, holdings of junk bonds actually reduced the risk of failure. However, this protection was eliminated when savings and loans were forced to divest their holdings as a result of FIRREA enacted in 1989, at which point the risk of failure actually increased with holdings.

Table 4: The Impact of Size, Charter and Ownership Type, and Capitalization on Portfolio Holdings

Dependent Variable:	Residential Mortgage	Commercial Mortgage	Direct Investments	Development Loan	High Yield Securities
Intercept	0.1406***	0.0388***	-0.0169***	-0.0025*	-0.0037***
	(0.0060)	(0.0026)	(0.0017)	(0.0015)	(0.0005)
Size of Institution	0.0002	0.0033***	0.0022***	0.0013***	0.0003***
	(0.0008)	(0.0002)	(0.0001)	(0.0001)	(0.0000)
Tangible Assets	0.0951***	-0.1364***	-0.0593***	-0.0676***	0.0004
	(0.0005)	(0.0082)	(0.0086)	(0.0055)	(0.0007)
Negative Tangible Assets	0.9787*	-0.3659	0.1530*	0.2302*	-0.0041
	(0.5230)	(0.2701)	(0.0863)	(0.1119)	(0.0203)
Below Threshold Tangible Assets	0.4875	0.6140**	-0.1492***	-0.1396	-0.0169**
	(0.4758)	(0.2542)	(0.0478)	(0.1002)	(0.0074)
Federal Chartered	-0.0083***	0.0060***	-0.0050***	-0.0050***	-0.0003***
	(0.0014)	(0.0005)	(0.0002)	(0.0003)	(0.0001)
Stock Ownership	-0.0618***	0.0270***	0.0082***	0.0168***	0.0005***
	(0.0016)	(0.0006)	(0.0002)	(0.0004)	(0.0001)

Table 4 (continued): The Impact of Size, Charter and Ownership Type, and Capitalization on Portfolio Holdings

Dependent Variable:	Residential Mortgage	Commercial Mortgage	Direct Investments	Development Loan	High Yield Securities
Adjusted R^2	0.61	0.10	0.14	0.11	0.01
F-Statistic	3729.28	259.50	392.20	291.69	31.53
1st Wald Test, P-value, Chi-Square [$\beta_3+\beta_4+\beta_5=0$]	0.0000	0.2110	0.4289	0.6354	0.2784
2nd Wald Test, P-value, Chi-Square [$\beta_3+\beta_5=0$]	0.2214	0.0607	0.0000	0.0394	0.0269
Number of Observation	55717	55717	55717	55717	55717

Note: ***, ** and * indicate significant level at 1, 5, and 10 percent respectively. Standard errors are in parentheses.
The estimation method is OLS with Heteroskedastic Standard Errors and Covariance. The model specification can be written as follow:

$PortfolioAssets_i = \beta_0 Intercept + \beta_1 Lnasset_i + \beta_2 Tassets_i + \beta_3 Tassets_i * D\_tasset_{1i}$
$+ \beta_4 Tassets_i * D\_tasset_{2i} + \beta_5 Federal_i + \beta_6 Stock_i + \phi YearDummies_i + \varepsilon_i$

Year dummies from 1978 to 1995 are included in the regressions, but their results are not reported. The first Wald test shows that joint coefficients of overall tangible asset share of institution portfolio are positively and significantly related to residential mortgage assets, but are not significantly related to other types of assets. The second Wald test shows that positive tangible asset share of institutional portfolio are positively and significantly related to every type of assets, except residential mortgage assets.

Table 5: The Impact of Size, Powers, Charter and Ownership Types, and Junk Bond Holdings on the Risk of Failure

	Model 1	Model 2	Model 3	Model 4	Model 5	Model 6
Size of Institution	0.1504***	0.1348***	0.1790***	0.1252***	0.0976***	0.0908***
	(0.0188)	(0.0191)	(0.0195)	(0.0196)	(0.0178)	(0.0182)
Lenient States	0.6261***			0.517***	0.4921***	0.4091***
	(0.0603)			(0.0646)	(0.0623)	(0.0617)
Federal Chartered			-0.1579***	0.0467		
			(0.0600)	(0.0602)		
Stock Ownership		2.6652***		0.4268***	0.199***	0.0404
		(0.0584)		(0.0604)	(0.0629)	(0.0636)
Residential Mortgage					-2.7382***	-2.7126***
					(0.1465)	(0.1542)
Commercial Mortgage						4.1025***
						(0.2712)
High Yield Securities	-34.9621***	-30.0838***	-26.8243***	-36.5876***	-49.3755***	-43.0667***
	(9.1426)	(8.8063)	(8.3773)	(9.3953)	(10.2609)	(10.6489)
High Yield Time	3.0415***	2.6652***	2.4373***	3.1421***	3.9605***	3.5499***
	(0.6621)	(0.6373)	(0.5991)	(0.6833)	(0.7518)	(0.7807)
Model χ^2	290.91***	267.59***	171.98***	360.08***	731.35***	. 1025.12***

Note: There are 4,887 firms; 1,142 failures; 55,717 observations. ***, **, and * indicate significant level at 1, 5, and 10 percent respectively. Standard errors are in parentheses. The estimation method is Cox Proportional Hazard model.

Cost of Failure

Table 6 presents the empirical results for the cost of resolving failed institutions. Not surprisingly, the lower the tangible capital-to-asset ratio the higher the resolution cost. Also, the cost of resolving failed institutions in those states granting the broadest powers was higher than the cost in more restrictive states. What is most interesting is that there is no significant relationship between the resolution cost and nontraditional loans and investments (i.e., direct investment, commercial mortgages and junk bonds). There is, however, a significant and negative relationship between resolution cost and the ratio of home mortgages to total assets. It should also be noted that asset size *per se* is not significantly related to resolution cost. But the year in which an institution was resolved does matter. Specifically, institutions resolved in 1988, 1989, and 1990 on average were more costly than those resolved in earlier years.

Table 6: The Impact of Size, Capitalization, Powers and Portfolio Composition on the Cost of Resolving Failed Institutions

Dependent Variable: Resolution Costs as a % of Assets	Model 1	Model 4	Model 2	Model 6	Model 5	Model 3	Model 7
Intercept	0.5914	0.5914	0.6146	0.9592	0.5674	0.5923	0.9388
	(0.4432)	(0.4434)	(0.4546)	(0.6108)	(0.4501)	(0.4568)	(0.6417)
Size of Institution	-0.0459	-0.0459	-0.0481	-0.0533	-0.0458	-0.046	-0.0527
	(0.0365)	(0.0363)	(0.0376)	(0.0396)	(0.0366)	(0.0378)	(0.0406)
Tangible Assets	-0.8909***	-0.8909***	-0.8765***	-0.8248***	-0.8863***	-0.8909***	-0.8185***
	(0.1566)	(0.1559)	(0.1623)	(0.1822)	(0.1555)	(0.1565)	(0.1826)
Lenient States	0.1453***	0.1453***	0.1395***	0.1354***	0.1435***	0.1452***	0.1332**
	(0.0461)	(0.0467)	(0.0478)	(0.0477)	(0.0463)	(0.0463)	(0.0492)
Uninsured Deposits		-0.002					-0.111
		(0.1868)					(0.205)

Table 6 (continued): The Impact of Size, Capitalization, Powers and Portfolio Composition on the Cost of Resolving Failed Institutions

Dependent Variable: Resolution Costs as a % of Assets	Model 1	Model 7	Model 3	Model 5	Model 6	Model 2	Model 4
Asset Portfolio:							
Direct Investments		0.1377				0.303	
		(0.1998)				(0.2462)	
Residential Mortgage		-0.4984*			-0.5118**		
		(0.2584)			(0.2516)		
Commercial Mortgage		0.1198		0.2408*			
		(0.1714)		(0.1237)			
High Yield Securities		-0.4851	0.0446				
		(0.5125)	(0.7568)				
Adjusted R^2	0.21	0.22	0.21	0.21	0.22	0.21	0.21
F-Statistic	29.88	20.87	27.14	27.23	28.51	27.24	27.14
No. of Institutions	1068	1068	1068	1068	1068	1068	1068

Note: ***, ** and * indicate significant level at 1, 5, and 10 percent respectively. Standard errors are in parentheses. The estimation method is OLS with Heteroskedastic Standard Errors and Covariance. The models are nested insofar as the number of institutions is restricted to be the same for comparison purposes.

WHAT ARE THE LESSONS FROM THESE PROBLEMS?

Despite the existence of an elaborate regulatory and supervisory structure in a mature economy, significant banking problems developed in the U.S. In trying to understand how to design appropriate bank regulations and supervisory practices to prevent future problems, it is helpful to derive some lessons from those problems. Some of the lessons discussed here are based upon U.S. depository institution problems and therefore may not be directly applicable to other countries at different stages of development and with different cultures and financial systems. Therefore, we are careful to note those lessons that could apply to both developed and developing country financial systems.

Lesson One: Do Not Limit The Financial Activities Of Financial Firms

The ongoing debate over the appropriate range of activities in which to allow banks to engage highlights the fact that federally insured depositories have been significantly limited by regulation in what they can do and where and when they can do it. This necessarily means that depository institutions have been unable to adapt freely to changing technological and competitive pressures in both domestic and global financial markets. The case of savings and loans represents the most extreme case in which institutions were unable to adapt in a timely manner to a changing financial environment. Despite repeated attempts to broaden their range of permissible activities (Appendix 4), savings and loans could essentially offer only long-term, fixed-rate home mortgages prior to the early 1980s. Only a threat to their very survival prompted the Congress to grant savings and loans, albeit too late for many of them, greater freedom to reduce their interest rate risk exposure.

The front and back endpapers of this volume present a broader perspective on bank regulation by providing information on the important developments affecting depository institutions in the U.S. over more than 200 years (Fromp, 1999). Based upon studies of this relatively long historical record, one learns that most bank regulation has not been proactive but rather reactive to actual or perceived banking problems. Furthermore, in the process of attempting to resolve problems, all too often new and potentially even more serious problems have been created. This was the case when savings and loans were first required to specialize in fixed-rate home mortgages and then encouraged to diversify into new activities, many of which they were allowed to do without either sufficient expertise or adequate owner-contributed equity capital. The result was disastrous. Changes in the regulatory structure not only change the opportunities for financial institutions to engage in what they consider to be the most profitable activities, but they also change the incentives with respect to the risk-taking behavior of the managers and owners.

The changes in the range of opportunities available to institutions to pursue various activities are viewed by their proponents as necessary to achieve a "safe and sound" banking industry. Viewed in a static context, such changes may appear to achieve their goal. But financial markets must be viewed in a dynamic context. Financial markets are subject to changes that cannot be controlled or even anticipated by the regulatory authorities.

In view of this situation, there is considerable merit to former Federal Reserve Bank of Cleveland President Jerry Jordan's view that, "Banking companies should not be required to get permission from regulators before doing something new. Rather, they should notify authorities of their intentions. If regulators want to prevent the action, the burden should be on them to intervene in a timely way to demonstrate that the costs exceed the benefits'' (Jordan, 1996). There is also considerable merit to Federal Reserve Bank of Kansas City President Thomas Hoenig's view that, "In light of the costs and difficulties of implementing prudential supervision for larger institutions who are increasingly involved in new activities and industries, the time may have come to sever the link between these institutions and the safety nets, making it feasible to significantly scale back regulatory oversight of their operations" (Hoenigs, 1996. p. II). Of course, if banks are permitted unrestricted access to new on- or off-balance sheet activities one would want to be sure such activities were conducted under appropriate conditions. In this regard, one could require that new activities (whether conducted in a subsidiary of a bank or a holding company) be capitalized by funds other than those used to meet the bank's required capital standards. Also, one could impose inter-affiliate lending restrictions on a bank and any new nonbank affiliate. In short, any expansion by banks into new activities should be accompanied by prudent limitations on the overall way in which such activities are conducted at home or abroad. This qualification applies as well to the design of an appropriate bank regulatory and supervisory structure for emerging market economies.

Lesson Two: Do Not Limit The Nonfinancial Activities Of Financial Firms

Many individuals believe banking institutions should be restricted to a fairly narrow range of activities because they have access to the federal safety net (i.e., access to deposit insurance, discount window borrowing and the Federal Reserve's guaranteed check clearing payment system). Indeed, much of the debate over whether or not to ease or eliminate the restrictions separating banks and nonbank firms relates to the safety net. A specific concern that has been expressed is that any subsidy associated with the safety net could flow from the bank to any affiliated nonbank firm. In this regard, one could prohibit nonbank affiliates which are creditors from reaching the assets of the bank by "piercing the corporate veil."

Yet, there is disagreement over whether any such subsidy even exists. Federal Reserve Chairman Alan Greenspan testified that there is a subsidy (1997). The former Comptroller of the Currency Eugene Ludwig testified that "no net subsidy exists [taking into account the cost of the regulatory burden imposed on banks]" (1997, p. 2). Former FDIC Chairman Ricki Helfer has testified that "if a net subsidy exists, it is very small" (1997, p. 2). Outside the bank regulatory agencies, the Shadow Financial Regulatory Committee concluded that the net subsidy is "probably not particularly large" (1997, p. 2). Obviously some effort should be made to measure the net subsidy, and if a net subsidy is found to exist, it should be eliminated in an efficient and timely manner. Once eliminated, the danger of the subsidy spreading to other affiliates is also eliminated.

The important point is that the mere existence of a subsidy should not be used to deny banks the opportunity to engage prudently in a wide range of activities, and correspondingly, for the mixing of banking and commerce. The U.S. is clearly out of step with almost all other countries around the world with respect to the extent to which banks are permitted to own nonfinancial firms, and vice versa (Barth, Caprio and Levine, 2003).

Lesson Three: Don't Sweep Problems Under The Rug; Let Market Discipline Work Without Interference

It is well known that various types of adverse selection, principal-agent, and moral hazard problems arise in banking. It is therefore incumbent upon the regulatory authorities to examine, supervise and regulate federally insured depositories to promote a stable, efficient and competitive banking industry. The authorities must also, of course, resolve troubled institutions in a timely and cost-effective manner so as to limit losses to the insurance funds and thereby better protect taxpayers. As the savings and loan situation in the U.S. so vividly demonstrates, and for that matter the current banking problems in Japan, regulatory forbearance can exacerbate an existing problem. The savings and loan institutions resolved in 1988, for example, had been reporting tangible insolvency on average three and a half years prior to resolution. The consequences of allowing insolvent institutions to remain open for lengthy periods of time are reflected in the enormous costs of failure resolution.

Many believe the enactment of the Federal Deposit Insurance Corporation Improvement Act in 1991 eliminated the possibility of any similar regulatory forbearance in the future. While there are certainly desirable features to this Act, one should not be overly optimistic that it will always work as intended. The reasons for some healthy skepticism are twofold. First, when savings and loans were devastated by the adverse movements in interest rates, existing statutory and regulatory capital standards were deemed to be too stringent and therefore simply eased with the effect of papering over the problem. Second, sufficient information was publicly available documenting the severity of the problems in the savings and loan industry throughout the 1980s and yet decisive action to resolve the situation once and for all was not taken until President Bush did so at the end of the decade. This suggests that even statutorily mandated regulatory discipline may be less than a perfect substitute for market discipline. Attempts should, therefore, be made to rely as much as possible on market discipline and less on regulatory discipline to prevent future banking problems (Barth, Caprio, and Levine, 2003; Calomiris, 1989, 1992 and 1997, and Kane, 1989 and 1992).

Lesson Four: Regulate Financial Functions, Not Financial Institutions

All too often it appears that policy decisions about bank regulation are made from a relatively narrow perspective. To demonstrate this point, it is well known that funds from savers do not flow to investors only through banks. Instead, funds may flow from savers to investors through money and capital markets and through a variety of financial intermediaries. Given the importance of investment for long-term economic growth and hence improved living standards, it is important that the flow of funds from savers to investors not be disrupted. Disruptions in the credit system and payment mechanism, or more generally the financial system, can adversely affect economic growth and development.

Based upon a broad perspective, designing appropriate bank regulation should be viewed as part of the process of designing an appropriate overall financial system (Barth and Brumbaugh, 1997; Herring and Litan, 1995; Kaufman and Kroszner, 1996). Since the different components of a financial system are interrelated, one should not focus exclusively on any one entity or subset of entities, such as depository institutions, when designing regulatory structures. Furthermore, one should realize that a financial system can be viewed from either a domestic or global perspective. In any event, by focusing too narrowly on just banks, for example, one might consider certain regulations as appropriate which from a broader perspective would be considered inappropriate. An example might be useful to help make this point clearer.

Prior to 1956, the mixing of commercial banking and commerce was permitted through holding companies. In that year and subsequently in 1970, however, legislation was enacted that permitted commercial banks only to be affiliated with nonbanking firms that were "closely related to banking." The mixing of commercial banking and commerce was effectively terminated. Yet, in 1968 the Congress enacted legislation that permitted a holding company that owns a single savings and loan to engage in any activity, even those activities unrelated to the savings and loan business. As a result of this freedom and other important differences, the value of a savings and loan charter was enhanced relative to a commercial bank charter.[7] Key to this example is that the relative enhancement resulted from legislative and regulatory actions, not market forces. By focusing too narrowly on one particular type of depository institution, in other words, policy makers enacted legislation that unintentionally altered the financial landscape in significant ways.[8]

When one recognizes that there are many different types of financial firms one naturally must ask the question: what is a bank? Legally, a bank is defined as a firm that makes commercial loans, accepts demand deposits and whose deposits are federally insured by the FDIC. Yet, today commercial loans and demand deposits each only amount to about 15 percent of the total assets of commercial banks. What was once a traditional bank no longer exists. Banks have been reinventing themselves to remain viable in a changing financial marketplace. They must compete with a variety of other,

---

[7] Unrestricted nationwide branching and a lower minimum percentage of assets required to be held in home mortgages in 1996 are examples of additional differences that favored savings and loans over commercial banks.

[8] The Gramm-Leach-Bliley Act eliminated any further mixing of banking and commerce, even by savings and loan holding companies.

less regulated financial and nonfinancial firms as well as with the money and capital markets by increasingly offering more services that generate fee income and by relying less on net interest income.

Who would have thought only a few years ago that an automobile firm and an electric company would be direct competitors of banks? In 2002, more than half of Ford Motor Company's net income came from its financial services operations. And General Electric Company earns about 40 percent of its net income from the capital services operations. In view of this situation, one must broaden one's focus beyond the legal definition of a bank to encompass the functions performed by banks when designing bank regulations. As the saying goes, "we need banking services not banks."

Various restrictions on banks undoubtedly contributed to the development and growth of competing nonbank firms and capital markets. For example, the branching restrictions on banks in the 1800s limited their size, and thus their ability to extend loans to increasingly larger corporate entities. This, in turn, provided a greater incentive for these firms to raise funds through the sale of debt and equity in the capital markets. As Appendices 6 and 7 demonstrate, the role of depository institutions has evolved significantly.

A SEPARATE FATE FOR COMMERCIAL BANKS

During the late 1980s and early 1990s commercial banks received far less public attention than savings and loans did, despite the fact that bank failure resolutions cost $37 billion and drove the FDIC into insolvency. Commercial banks suffered from one of the same events that caused the savings and loan crisis: deterioration in asset quality from commercial real estate loans. The main reason savings and loans drew more attention was that their failures were more widespread and costly, and that taxpayer money was required to clean up the mess. Yet, the deterioration in the banking industry was so significant that without the savings and loan debacle, the banks' problems would have been front-page news. Furthermore, if a few large banks had failed, the problems could have been even greater than those of the savings and loans (Barth, Brumbaugh and Litan, 1992).

The financial deterioration in banks was the result of a series of difficulties first involving loans to lesser developed countries in the early 1980s, then loans for highly leveraged transactions in the mid-1980s, and finally commercial real estate loans in the late 1980s. The process that led to this sequence of difficulties had many characteristics similar to the savings and loan debacle. Banks faced geographic banking restrictions that were not removed until the enactment of the Riegle-Neal Interstate Banking and Branching Efficiency Act of 1994. They were also restricted in their ability to engage in securities, insurance, and real estate activities. The enactment of the Gramm-Leach- Bliley Act of 1999 removed the final restrictions to allowing banks to engage in securities and insurance activities. In addition, banks' investments in nonfinancial firms and nonfinancial firms' investments in banks are now strictly prohibited (Barth, Brumbaugh and Wilcox, 2000).[9]

As deterioration in the banks' condition overwhelmed the FDIC's reserves, the banking regulatory authorities adopted some of the same forbearance techniques that had been used for the savings and loans. For instance, banks known to be insolvent were allowed to remain open in the hope that they would be able to recover and spare the deposit-insurance fund further losses. In addition, the traditional accounting techniques used by many banks allowed several very large banks to conceal deep losses.

Unlike the less fortunate savings and loans in the early 1980s, the banks benefited from unexpected interest-rate developments that more than compensated for the existing asset-quality problem. As a result of the 1990-1991 recession and the response of the Federal Reserve to inject more liquidity into the economy, short-term interest rates fell relative to long-term interest rates, allowing banks to restore profitability through greater net interest income. For several years, banks were able to earn substantial profits merely by purchasing Treasury securities with insured deposits rather than making more traditional business loans. Although the Congress granted the depleted bank insurance fund the authority to borrow at government-subsidized rates, taxpayers were spared having to bear losses directly as the overall condition of the banking industry improved.

The consequences of the changes in interest rates provide another great irony of the depository debacle of the 1980s and early 1990s. Whereas the Federal Reserve policy change in the late 1970s precipitated the savings and loan debacle by contributing to raising short-term interest rates relative to long-term rates, its policy during 1990-1991 protected the banks from potentially staggering losses by contributing to lowering short-term rates relative to long-term rates. The former policy change was motivated by a desire to combat inflationary forces, while the latter policy was motivated by a desire to combat a recession.

---

[9] Indeed, of the 19 countries comprising the European Union and G-10, the United States was until recently by far one of the most restrictive in regulating banking activities. It remains so, moreover, with respect to the mixing of banking and commerce.

The implications of these policy changes suggest that insured depositories are more vulnerable than other financial firms to broad government policy changes that may be at cross purposes with narrower regulatory policies. For example, when the Federal Reserve raised interest rates in 1979, savings and loans suffered relatively more than other financial firms because they were hampered by government-imposed interest-rate ceilings and home loan lending restrictions. While these restrictions were beneficial to them when the inflation rate was low and stable, they became disastrous when the yield curve became inverted. Savings and loans could either raise the rates paid on deposits or face massive deposit withdrawals, as depositors would seek higher interest rates elsewhere. Although this was a costly strategy, it was considered far less costly than selling home mortgage loans and simply letting depositors take their funds elsewhere.

Insured depositories also appear more vulnerable than other firms when the government reverses policies. When Congress in 1986 reversed the tax law it had put in place just five years earlier, all financial firms that were engaged in commercial real estate lending and investment suffered. Savings and loans suffered relatively more, however, because of congressional and regulatory encouragement in 1980 and 1982 to diversify into commercial real estate loans and investments. Commercial banks also suffered more heavily in the late second half of the1980s as they had increased their commercial real estate lending following other lending difficulties earlier in the decade.

As described above, in the 1980s and early 1990s, insured depositories failed in greater numbers and imposed greater losses than any other group of financial service firms despite being among the most heavily regulated firms in the nation. Their relatively dismal performance suggests that overly restrictive laws and regulations on insured depositories tend to inhibit their ability to adapt to technological and competitive changes in the global financial marketplace. Given this environment savings and loans are now in the fourth phase of their rapid transformation in the past two decades.

SUMMARY AND CONCLUSIONS

In the 1980s, the U.S. experienced its worst bank problems since the Great Depression. The problems occurred despite an elaborate bank regulatory structure. The obvious conclusion is that the existing structure was not appropriate for fulfilling its assigned responsibilities. Although banking institutions are now in overall good financial condition and bank regulation has been significantly improved, there is still an ongoing debate over the exact way in which to "modernize" the legal definition of a bank. Perhaps the most important lesson from the recent past in the U.S. is that the most appropriate way for all countries to proceed is by viewing banks not in isolation, but instead as an integral part of a much larger financial system. And a financial system that is increasingly global in nature and constantly evolving in response to new developments. Such a broader perspective suggests that relying less on extensive bank regulation and more on market discipline is the best way to proceed.

REFERENCES

Barth, James R. (1991). *The Great Savings and Loan Debacle*, Washington D.C.: The AEI Press.

Barth, James R., Philip Bartholomew and Michael Bradley (1991). Reforming Federal Deposit Insurance: What Can be Learned from Private Insurance Practices?" *Consumer Finance Law Quarterly Report*, Spring. Also issued as Research Paper No. 161, Federal Home Loan Bank Board, June 1989.

Barth, James R. and R. Dan Brumbaugh (1997). "Development and Evolution of National Financial Systems: An International Perspective," *Latin American Studies Association, 1997 Meeting*, Guadalajara, Mexico, April.

Barth, James R., R. Dan Brumbaugh and Robert E. Litan (1992). *The Future of American Banking,* Columbia University Seminar Series, M.E. Sharpe, Inc.

Barth, James R., R. Dan Brumbaugh, and James A. Wilcox (2000). "The Repeal of Glass-Steagall and the Advent of Broad Banking," *Journal of Economic Perspectives* 14(2), Spring, pp. 191-204.

Barth, James R., Gerard Caprio, Jr. and Ross Levine (2003). "Bank Regulation and Supervision: What Works Best?" *Journal of Financial Intermediation*, forthcoming.

Barth, James R., Thomas Hall and Glenn Yago (2000). *Systemic Banking Crises: From Cause to Cure*. Santa Monica, CA: Milken Institute.

Barth, James R. and Robert E. Litan (1998). "Preventing Bank Crises: Lessons From Bank Failures in the United States," in Gerard Caprio, Jr., William C. Hunter, George G. Kaufman and Danny M. Leipziger, editors, *Preventing Bank Crises: Lessons from Recent Global Bank Failures*, EDI Development Studies, World Bank.

Brumbaugh, R. Dan (1988). *Thrifts under Siege: Restoring Order to American Banking*. Cambridge, MA: Ballinger Publishing Company.

Calomiris, Charles W. (1997). "Designing the Post-Modern Bank Safety Net: Lessons from Developed and Developing Economies," Conference

Paper, *The Bankers' Roundtable Program for Reforming Federal Deposit Insurance*, American Enterprise Institute, May 23.

Calomiris, Charles W. (1992). "Getting the Incentives Right in the Current Deposit-Insurance System: Successes from the Pre-FDIC Era," *The Reform of Federal Deposit Insurance: Discipline the Government and Protecting Taxpayers*, edited by James R. Barth and R. Dan Brumbaugh, Jr., New York: HarperBusiness.

Calomiris, Charles W. (1989). "Deposit Insurance: Lessons from the Record," *Economic Perspectives*, Federal Reserve Bank of Chicago, May/June.

Greenspan, Alan (1997). Statement before the Subcommittee on Financial Institutions and Consumer Credit of the Committee on Banking and Financial Services, United States House of Representatives, March 5.

Helfer, Ricki (1997). Oral Statement before the Subcommittee on Capital Markets, Securities and Government Sponsored Enterprises, Committee on Banking and Financial Services, United States House of Representatives, March 5.

Herring, Richard J. and Robert E. Litan (1995). *Financial Regulation in the Global Economy*, Washington, D.C.: The Brookings Institutions.

Hoenig, Thomas M. (1996). "Rethinking Financial Regulation," *Economic Review*, Federal Reserve Bank of Kansas City, 2nd Quarter.

Jordan, Jerry L. (1996). "The Future of Banking Supervision," *Economic Commentary*, Federal Reserve Bank of Cleveland, April 1.

Kane, Edward J. (1992). "The Incentive Incompatibility of Government-Sponsored Deposit Insurance Funds," in *The Reform of Federal Deposit Insurance*, edited by James R. Barth and R. Dan Brumbaugh, Jr., New York: HarperBusiness.

Kane, Edward J. (1989). "Changing Incentive Facing Financial-Services Regulators," *Journal of Financial Services Research*, 2, September.

Kaufman, George G. and Randall S. Kroszner (1996). "How Should Financial Institutions and Markets Be Structured? Analysis and Options for Financial System Design," Working Paper WP-96-20, Federal Reserve Bank of Chicago, December.

Ludwig, Eugene A. (1997). Oral Statement before the Subcommittee on Capital Markets, Securities and Government Sponsored Enterprises, Committee on Banking and Financial Services, United States House of Representatives, March 5.

Shadow Financial Regulatory Committee, Statement No. 137, May 5, 1997.

APPENDICES

Appendix 1: U.S. Federally Insured Savings and Loan Industry, 1980-1989

	1980	1981	1982	1983	1984	1985	1986	1987	1988	1989
Number of Institutions	3,993	3,751	3,287	3,146	3,136	3,246	3,220	3,147	2,949	2,616
Total RAP Assets ($ bls)	604	640	686	814	978	1,070	1,164	1,251	1,352	1,187
GAAP Capital ($ bls)	32	27	20	25	27	34	39	34	46	52
Tangible Capital ($ bls)	32	25	4	4	3	9	15	9	23	NA
Net After Tax Income ($ bls)	781	-4,631	-4,142	1,945	1,022	3,728	131	-7,779	-12,057	-6,783
Net Operating Income ($ mls)	790	-7,114	-8,761	-46	990	3,601	4,562	2,850	907	-8,308
Net Non-Operating Income ($ mls)	398	964	3,041	2,567	796	2,215	-1,290	-7,930	-11,012	2,198
Taxes ($ mls)	407	-1,519	-1,578	576	764	2,087	3,141	2,699	1,952	673
Home Mortgages (% Total Assets)	66.5	65.0	56.3	49.8	44.9	42.4	38.9	37.8	38.6	41.2
Mortgage Backed Bonds (% Total Assets)	4.4	5.0	8.6	10.9	11.1	10.4	13.1	15.6	15.4	14.2
Mortgage Assets (% Total Assets)	70.9	70.0	64.9	60.7	56.0	52.8	52.0	53.4	54.0	55.4
Stock Institutions										
(%Number of Institutions)	20	21	23	23	30	33	37	40	43	43
(%Total Assets)	27	29	30	42	52	56	62	65	68	69
Federally-Chartered										
(%Number of Institutions)	50	51	51	53	54	53	53	56	59	61
(%Total Assets)	56	63	70	69	66	65	66	66	72	76

Appendix 1 (continued): U.S. Federally Insured Savings and Loan Industry, 1980-1989

Capital-to-Asset Categories	1980	1981	1982	1983	1984	1985	1986	1987	1988	1989
> 6.0% Tangible Capital										
Number	1,701	1,171	787	661	643	806	972	1,113	1,136	1,180
Total Assets ($ bls)	181	101	59	84	62	95	156	188	196	206
3.0% to 6.0% Tangible Capital										
Number	1,956	1,766	1,202	1,091	945	1,009	995	891	864	813
Total Assets ($ bls)	379	348	190	222	227	259	316	356	418	480
1.5% to 3.0% Tangible Capital										
Number	230	524	592	569	526	460	354	277	281	245
Total Assets ($ bls)	39	113	136	185	168	212	191	196	244	206
0% to 1.5% Tangible Capital										
Number	63	178	291	310	327	266	227	194	160	120
Total Assets ($ bls)	4	50	81	88	153	135	144	143	182	59
< 0% Tangible Capital										
Number	43	112	415	515	695	705	672	672	508	239
Total Assets ($ bls)	0.4	29	220	234	336	335	324	336	283	192
Resolutions										
Number	11	28	76	54	27	36	51	47	222	327
Total Assets ($ mls)	1,458	13,908	27,748	19,655	5,783	7,066	24,182	10,921	113,965	146,811
Estimated Present-Value Cost ($ mls)	167	1,018	1,213	1,024	833	1,025	3,605	4,509	52,203	51,140
Number of Months Reporting Tangible Insolvent Before Closure	5.4	5.2	12.9	16.4	23.4	25.9	30.6	35.7	42.0	36.0

Appendix 1 (continued): U.S. Federally Insured Savings and Loan Industry, 1990-1996

	1990	1991	1992	1993	1994	1995	1996
Number of Institutions	2,359	2,110	1,871	1,669	1,543	1,437	1,334
Total RAP Assets ($ bls)	1,029	895	807	775	774	771	769
GAAP Capital ($ bls)	52	53	56	58	58	62	61
Tangible Capital ($ bls)	NA	42	52	54	55	57	56
Net After Tax Income ($ mls)	-3,817	1,195	5,103	4,917	4,275	5,360	4,750
Net Operating Income ($ mls)	-4,022	2,265	6,855	7,141	6,597	7,460	NA
Net Non-Operating Income ($ mls)	1,347	1,356	1,047	595	422	835	NA
Taxes ($ mls)	1,142	2,426	2,779	2,819	2,744	2,935	1,748
Home Mortgages (% Total Assets)	43.0	45.6	45.7	45.8	47.0	47.4	49.9
Mortgage Backed Securities (% Total Assets)	14.5	14.2	14.5	15.4	16.5	16.3	14.4
Mortgage Assets (% Total Assets)	59.5	59.8	60.2	61.2	63.5	63.7	64.3
Stock Institutions							
(% Number of Institutions)	44	45	49	54	56	59	60
(% Total Assets)	74	76	80	82	86	86	90
Federally-Chartered							
(% Number of Institutions)	64	65	70	75	78	82	82
(% Total Assets)	83	84	87	90	93	95	96

Appendix 1 (continued): U.S. Federally Insured Savings and Loan Industry, 1990-1996

Capital-to-Asset Categories	1990	1991	1992	1993	1994	1995	1996
> 6.0% Tangible Capital							
Number	1,132	1,148	1,246	1,342	NA	NA	NA
Total Assets ($ bls)	195	227	310	397	NA	NA	NA
3.0% to 6.0% Tangible Capital							
Number	837	763	559	323	NA	NA	NA
Total Assets ($ bls)	484	468	435	372	NA	NA	NA
1.5% to 3.0% Tangible Capital							
Number	163	105	39	2	NA	NA	NA
Total Assets ($ bls)	154	104	33	4	NA	NA	NA
0% to 1.5% Tangible Capital							
Number	101	47	7	2	NA	NA	NA
Total Assets ($ bls)	83	36	13	3	NA	NA	NA
< 0% Tangible Capital							
Number	109	33	3	0	NA	NA	NA
Total Assets ($ bls)	89	41	4	0	NA	NA	NA
Resolutions							
Number	213	144	59	9	2	2	1
Total Assets ($ mls)	134,766	82,626	45,980	6,339	142	456	NA
Estimated Present-Value Cost ($ mls)	21,473	10,823	4,741	532	14	66	NA
Number of Months Reporting Tangible Insolvent Before Closure	43.0	41.0	38.0	NA	NA	NA	NA

Note: NA denotes information not available.
Source: James R. Barth, *The Great Savings and Loan Debacle*, American Enterprise Institute, 1991; James R. Barth and R. Dan Brumbaugh, Jr., *Moral-Hazard and Agency Problems: Understanding Depository Institution Failure Costs in Research in Financial Services*, Volume 6, Edited by George G. Kaufman, Greenwich: JAI Press, 1995; Resolution Trust Corporation, *Statistical Abstract*; Federal Home Loan Board; Office of Thrift Supervision; and Office of the Comptroller of the Currency.

Appendix 2: Federally Insured Commercial Bank Industry, 1980-1989

	1980	1981	1982	1983	1984	1985	1986	1987	1988	1989
Number of Institutions	14,435	14,408	14,446	14,460	14,483	14,407	14,199	13,703	13,123	12,709
Number of Branches	38,738	40,786	39,783	40,853	41,799	43,293	44,392	45,357	46,381	48,005
Number of FTE Employees (thous.)	1,442	1,489	1,499	1,509	1,527	1,562	1,563	1,545	1,527	1,532
Total Assets ($ bls)	1,856	2,029	2,194	2,342	2,509	2,731	2,941	3,000	3,131	3,299
Equity Capital ($ mls)	107,599	118,241	128,698	140,459	154,103	169,118	182,144	180,651	196,545	204,823
Net After Tax Income ($ mls)	14,010	14,722	14,844	14,931	15,502	17,977	17,418	2,803	24,812	15,575
Taxes ($ mls)	4,658	3,904	3,037	4,017	4,721	5,629	5,266	5,404	9,988	9,540
Real Estate Loans (% Total Assets)	14.5	14.4	14.0	14.4	15.4	16.1	17.5	20.0	21.6	23.1
C&I Loans (% Total Assets)	21.1	22.4	23.0	22.4	22.5	21.2	20.4	19.7	19.2	18.8
Agriculture Production Loans (% Total Assets)	1.7	1.7	1.7	1.7	1.6	1.3	1.1	1.0	1.0	0.9
Loans to Individuals (% Total Assets)	10.1	9.5	9.1	9.6	10.6	11.3	11.4	11.7	12.1	12.1
National Commercial Banks										
(% Number of Institutions)	30.7	30.9	31.7	32.8	33.8	34.4	34.3	33.7	35.3	32.9
(% Total Assets)	56.9	57.2	57.4	58.0	59.7	59.8	59.3	59.1	58.9	59.7
State, Fed Commercial Banks										
(% Number of Institutions)	6.9	7.1	7.2	7.3	7.3	7.4	7.7	7.9	8.1	8.1
(% Total Assets)	17.4	17.0	17.6	16.6	18.2	18.1	18.2	17.6	17.1	16.4

Appendix 2 (continued): Federally Insured Commercial Bank Industry, 1980-1989

Capital-to-Assets Categories	1980	1981	1982	1983	1984	1985	1986	1987	1988	1989
> 8% Equity Capital										
Number	7,981	7,941	7,976	7,674	7,423	7,324	6,699	6,790	6,646	6,741
Total Assets ($ bls)	278	300	320	344	353	377	384	438	437	488
6% to 8% Equity Capital										
Number	5,401	5,411	5,292	5,280	5,441	5,339	5,169	4,944	4,703	4,407
Total Assets ($ bls)	434	466	494	560	648	710	755	846	944	1,113
3.0% to 6.0% Equity Capital										
Number	1,038	1,041	1,141	1,426	1,507	1,571	2,028	1,604	1,401	1,295
Total Assets ($ bls)	1,141	1,260	1,375	1,432	1,498	1,633	1,776	1,588	1,680	1,572
1.5% to 3.0% Equity Capital										
Number	12	16	27	53	61	84	124	165	158	109
Total Assets ($ bls)	2	4	3	4	7	6	14	111	39	76
0% to 1.5% Equity Capital										
Number	2	5	12	21	23	36	88	108	96	73
Total Assets ($ bls)	*	*	1	2	1	2	6	5	10	26
< 0% Equity Capital										
Number	1	2	5	14	11	29	71	76	104	82
Total Assets ($ bls)	*	*	*	1	*	1	4	10	21	23

Appendix 2 (continued): Federally Insured Commercial Bank Industry, 1980-1989

	1980	1981	1982	1983	1984	1985	1986	1987	1988	1989
Number of Problem Commercial Banks	NA	196	326	603	800	1,098	1,457	1,559	1,394	1,092
Assets of Problem Commercial Banks ($ bls)	NA	NA	NA	NA	NA	NA	286	329	305	188
Resolutions - Commercial & Savings Banks										
Number	10	10	42	48	80	120	145	203	221	207
Total Assets ($ mls)	236	4,859	11,632	7,027	3,276	8,735	7,638	9,231	52,683	29,402
Estimated Present-Value Cost ($ mls)	31	782	1,169	1,425	1,635	1,044	1,728	2,028	6,866	6,215
Number of Months Rated 4 or 5 Before Closure	15	19	16	19	15	15	20	21	24	28

Appendix 2 (continued): Federally Insured Commercial Bank Industry, 1990-1996

	1990	1991	1992	1993	1994	1995	1996
Number of Institutions	12,343	11,921	11,462	10,958	10,451	9,940	9,528
Number of Branches	50,406	51,969	51,935	52,868	55,145	56,513	57,215
Number of FTE Employees (thous)	1,518	1,487	1,478	1,494	1,488	1,484	1,489
Total Assets ($ bls)	3,389	3,431	3,506	3,706	4,011	4,313	4,578
Equity Capital ($ mls)	218,616	231,699	263,403	296,491	312,088	349,578	375,295
Net After Tax Income ($ bls)	15,991	17,935	31,987	43,036	44,624	48,749	52,390
Taxes ($ mls)	7,704	8,265	14,481	19,838	22,426	26,176	28,227
Real Estate Loans (% Total Assets)	24.5	24.8	24.8	24.9	24.9	25.0	25.9
C&I Loans (% Total Assets)	18.2	16.3	15.3	14.5	14.7	15.3	15.5
Agriculture Production Loans (% Total Assets)	1.0	1.0	1.0	1.0	1.0	0.9	0.9
Loans to Individuals (% Total Assets)	11.9	11.4	11.0	11.3	12.2	12.4	12.4
National Commercial Banks							
(% Number of Institutions)	32.2	31.8	31.5	30.3	29.4	28.8	28.6
(% Total Assets)	58.6	56.5	57.2	56.7	56.3	55.7	55.3
State, Fed Commercial Banks							
(% Number of Institutions)	8.2	8.2	8.4	8.8	9.3	10.5	10.7
(% Total Assets)	16.5	16.9	18.2	19.6	21.1	22.8	24.6

Appendix 2 (continued): Federally Insured Commercial Bank Industry, 1990-1996

Capital-to-Asset Categories	1990	1991	1992	1993	1994	1995	1996
> 8% Equity Capital							
Number	6,377	6,422	6,857	7,542	6,969	7,497	7,104
Total Assets ($ bls)	554	615	994	1,365	1,160	1,719	1,757
6% to 8% Equity Capital							
Number	4,540	4,309	3,924	3,151	3,074	2,281	2,261
Total Assets ($ bls)	1,088	1,377	1,894	2,090	2,185	1,998	2,116
3.0% to 6.0% Equity Capital-to-Asset							
Number	1,234	1,048	624	263	398	159	158
Total Assets ($ bls)	1,684	1,421	626	250	667	598	709
1.5% to 3.0% Equity Capital-to-Asset							
Number	92	66	24	7	8	3	4
Total Assets ($ bls)	41	13	2	1	0.5	*	*
0% to 1.5% Equity Capital-to-Asset							
Number	66	43	14	6	4	2	1
Total Assets ($ bls)	6	3	3	1	*	*	*
< 0% Equity Capital-to-Asset							
Number	35	32	23	2	0	0	0
Total Assets ($ bls)	15	2	8	*	0	0	0

Appendix 2 (continued): Federally Insured Commercial Bank Industry, 1990-1996

	1990	1991	1992	1993	1994	1995	1996
Number of Problem Commercial Banks	1,012	1,016	787	426	247	144	82
Assets of Problem Commercial Banks ($ bls)	342	528	408	242	33	17	5
Resolutions-Commercial & Savings Banks							
Number	169	127	122	41	13	6	5
Total Assets ($ bls)	15,729	62,524	45,485	3,527	1,402	753	190
Estimated Present-Value Cost ($ mls)	2,889	6,037	3,707	655	208	104	NA
Number of Months Rated 4 or 5 Before Closure	34	29	32	NA	NA	NA	NA

Note: * denotes less than $500 million and NA denotes information not available.
Source: Bank Research Division, Office of the Comptroller of the Currency, Federal Deposit Insurance Corporation; and James R. Barth and R. Dan Brumbaugh, Jr., *Moral-Hazard and Agency Problems: Understanding Depository Institution Failure Costs, in Research in Financial Services*, Volume 6, Edited by George G. Kaufman, Greenwich: JAI Press, 1995

Appendix 3: U.S. Federally Insured Credit Union Industry, 1980-1989

	1980	1981	1982	1983	1984	1985	1986	1987	1988	1989
Number of Institutions	17,350	16,960	16,424	15,804	15,180	15,033	14,687	14,335	13,878	13,371
Total Assets ($ bls)	61	65	70	82	93	120	148	162	175	184
Capital ($ bls)	3.7	4.3	4.7	5.3	6.2	7.8	9.2	10.6	12.0	13.5
Net Income ($ mls)	314	677	714	747	1,131	1,303	1,366	1,464	1,659	1,653
Net Operating Income ($ mls)	502	882	922	930	1,316	1,538	1,746	2,074	2,310	2,445
Net Non-Operating Income ($ mls)	0.8	7	1	12	11	66	113	-36	38	21
Provision for Loan Losses ($ mls)	190	212	209	194	195	301	494	574	688	813
Federal Income Taxes ($ mls)	0	0	0	0	0	0	0	0	0	0
1st Mortgages (% Total Assets)	4.7	4.4	3.3	3.7	3.9	4.8	7.4	10.1	11.9	12.6
Mortgage Backed Securities (% Total Assets)	NA	NA	NA	NA	NA	NA	NA	NA	NA	NA
Total Real Estate Assets (% Total Assets)	NA	NA	NA	NA	NA	NA	12.4	16.5	19.6	21.7
Federally-Chartered										
(%Number of Institutions)	71.7	70.8	69.4	69.1	69.4	67.3	66.4	65.6	65.7	66.0
(% Total Assets)	65.8	65.9	65.3	66.5	68.6	65.3	64.6	64.9	65.4	65.7
Federally-Insured State-Chartered										
(% Number of Institutions)	28.3	29.2	30.6	30.9	30.6	32.7	33.6	34.4	34.3	34.0
(% Total Assets)	34.2	34.1	34.7	33.5	31.4	34.7	35.4	35.1	34.6	34.3

Appendix 3 (continued): U.S. Federally Insured Credit Union Industry, 1980-1989

Capital-to-Assets Categories	1980	1981	1982	1983	1984	1985	1986	1987	1988	1989
> 6.0% Capital										
Number	10,286	11,282	11,134	10,460	10,763	10,552	9,719	9,673	9,984	10,496
Total Assets ($ bls)	26.2	30.7	34.2	38.1	46.2	58.3	66.9	81.3	101.7	121.4
3.0% to 6.0% Capital										
Number	4,563	3,811	3,725	3,894	3,490	3,676	4,156	3,875	3,257	2,370
Total Assets ($ bls)	24.3	22.8	27.4	34.4	39.2	52.6	69.9	69.6	64.5	54.2
1.5% to 3.0% Capital										
Number	1,357	1,083	944	960	612	560	575	549	413	294
Total Assets ($ bls)	4.8	5.4	4.9	6.3	5.2	6.7	8.0	8.1	6.0	4.1
0.0% to 1.5% Capital										
Number	872	582	481	347	208	172	175	188	155	130
Total Assets ($ bls)	5.1	4.5	2.7	1.7	1.1	1.0	1.4	2.6	1.9	2.5
<0.0% Capital										
Number	272	202	140	143	107	73	62	50	69	81
Total Assets ($ bls)	0.6	1.1	0.4	1.4	1.3	1.2	1.5	0.6	1.2	1.5

Appendix 3 (continued): U.S. Federally Insured Credit Union Industry, 1980-1989

	1980	1981	1982	1983	1984	1985	1986	1987	1988	1989
Number of Problem Credit Unions	1,180	1,174	1,192	1,124	872	742	794	929	1,022	794
Assets of Problem Credit Unions ($ bls)	2.4	3.0	4.6	4.7	4.1	4.1	6.6	8.1	10.6	8.4
Resolutions										
Number	239	349	327	253	130	94	94	88	85	114
Total Shares ($ mls)	NA	136	156	102	208	47	116	327	297	285
Estimated Present-Value Cost ($ mls)	33	44	79	55	20	12	29	52	33	74
Number of Months Rated 4 or 5 Before Closure	NA	NA	NA	69.6	80.8	64.9	55.4	44.1	30.1	24.0

Appendix 3 (continued): U.S. Federally Insured Credit Union Industry, 1990-1996

	1990	1991	1992	1993	1994	1995	1996
Number of Institutions	12,860	12,960	12,594	12,317	11,991	11,687	11,392
Total Assets ($ bls)	198	227	258	277	290	307	327
Capital ($ bls)	15.0	17.4	20.9	24.9	27.7	31.7	35.2
Net Income ($ mls)	1,691	2,066	3,364	3,743	3,438	3,377	3,530
Net Operating Income ($ mls)	2,609	3,026	4,148	4,419	4,181	4,172	4,620
Net Non-Operating Income ($ mls)	28	36	95	76	(59)	(20)	15
Provision for Loan Losses ($ mls)	946	996	879	752	684	775	1,105
Federal Income Taxes ($ mls)	0	0	0	0	0	0	0
1st Mortgages (% Total Assets)	12.3	11.5	11.3	11.9	12.9	12.8	14.0
Mortgage Backed Securities (% Total Assets)	NA	NA	NA	3.5	3.6	3.1	2.8
Total Real Estate Assets (% Total Assets)	21.9	20.6	19.0	18.7	20.0	20.1	21.6
Federally-Chartered							
(% Number of Institutions)	66.2	63.5	62.8	62.5	62.5	62.7	62.8
(% Total Assets)	65.6	63.4	62.7	62.4	63.1	63.2	63.2
Federally-Insured State-Chartered							
(% Number of Institutions)	33.8	36.5	37.2	37.5	37.5	37.3	37.2
(% Total Assets)	34.4	36.6	37.3	37.6	36.9	36.8	36.8

James R. Barth, Susanne Trimbath and Glenn Yago

Appendix 3 (continued): U.S. Federally Insured Credit Union Industry, 1990-1996

Capital-to-Assets Categories	1990	1991	1992	1993	1994	1995	1996
> 6.0% Capital							
Number	10,367	10,399	10,356	10,901	11,074	11,146	10,990
Total Assets ($ bls)	139.7	168.0	208.5	250.9	268.1	296.6	321.0
3.0% to 6.0% Capital							
Number	2,032	2,141	1,971	1,279	824	465	321
Total Assets ($ bls)	50.3	50.7	46.1	24.3	20.1	9.6	5.6
1.5% to 3.0% Capital							
Number	255	262	178	80	54	37	35
Total Assets ($ bls)	3.7	5.6	1.5	1.4	0.4	0.4	0.1
0.0% to 1.5% Capital							
Number	133	102	59	39	24	16	30
Total Assets ($ bls)	2.5	1.0	1.7	0.5	0.2	0.1	0.1
<0.0% Capital							
Number	74	56	29	17	14	23	15
Total Assets ($ bls)	2.1	1.8	0.6	0.2	0.1	0.1	0.03

Appendix 3 (continued): U.S. Federally Insured Credit Union Industry, 1990-1996

	1990	1991	1992	1993	1994	1995	1996
Number of Problem Credit Unions	678	685	608	474	319	267	NA
Assets of Problem Credit Unions ($ bls)	9.4	10.4	7.4	4.3	2.4	2.0	NA
Resolutions							
Number	164	130	114	71	33	26	19
Total Shares ($ mls)	339	267	223	265	255	545	19
Estimated Present-Value Cost ($ mls)	49	77	107	20	36	13	2
Number of Months Rated 4 or 5 Before Closure	17.5	NA	NA	NA	NA	NA	NA

Note: NA denotes information not available. Capital includes undivided earnings, regular reserves and other reserves but excludes allowances for loan and investment losses. As of 1996, allowances for investment losses no longer exist. Effective January 1, 1995.
Source: James R. Barth and R. Dan Brumbaugh, Jr., (1991) *The Credit Union Industry: Financial Condition and Policy Issues, California Credit Union League*; James R. Barth and R. Dan Brumbaugh, Jr., "A Moral-Hazard and Agency Problems: Understanding Depository Institution Failure Costs," *Research in Financial Services*, Vol. 6. George G. Kaufman, Ed., Greenwich: JAI Press; 1995 National Credit Administration 1995 Annual Report and Tun A. Wai, National Association of Federal Credit Unions.

Appendix 4: Evolution of Federal Savings and Loan Powers, 1933-1975

	Year first Authorized	Home Owner's Loan Act 1933	Housing Act 1959	Housing Act 1961	Public Law 87-779 1962	Public Law 88-560 1964	Admin.'s Fed. Savings Bank Bill 1965[1]	Hunt Commission Study[2] 1972	Admin.'s Financial Institution Act 1973[3]
Home Mortgages	1933	Yes ($20,000 Loan Limit)					Yes (35,000 or 2% of Assets)[8]	Yes	
Non-Residential Mortgages	1933	Yes (15% of assets)			Yes (20% of Assets)		Yes	Yes	Yes
Land Development	1959		Yes (Loans up to 5% of Assets)				Yes (Loans)	Yes	
Direct Investment	1961			Yes (5% of Assets)		Yes (2% of Assets in Urban Renew. Area)	Yes (Up to 50% of Capital)	Yes (3% of Assets)	Yes (For Community Development)
Service Corporation	1964					Yes (1% of Assets)	Yes (No Limit)		
Construction Loans	1978							Yes	Yes

Appendix 4 (continued): Evolution of Federal Savings and Loan Powers, 1933-1975

	Year first Authorized	Home Owner's Loan Act 1933	Housing Act 1959	Housing Act 1961	Public Law 87-779 1962	Public Law 88-560 1964	Admin's Fed. Savings Bank Bill 1965[1]	Hunt Commission Study[2] 1972	Admin's Proposed Financial Institution Act 1973[3]
Corporate Bonds	1980						Yes	Yes	Yes (10% of Assets)
Education Loans	1978						Yes (5% of Assets)	Yes (3% of Assets)	
Consumer Loans	1980						Yes ($ 5000)	Yes (10% of Assets)	Yes (10% of Assets)
Commercial Loans	1982							Yes (3% of Assets)	
Leasing of Personal Property	1982								
Investment in Commercial Paper	1980							Yes (3% of Assets)	Yes (10% of Assets)
Credit Cards	1980							Yes	Yes

James R. Barth, Susanne Trimbath and Glenn Yago

Appendix 4 (continued): Evolution of Federal Savings and Loan Powers, 1975-1982

	Year first Authorized	Fine Study Legislation Passed Senate 1975[4]	House Banking Committee Print 1976[5]	Public Law 95-630 (1978)	Admin. Proposal 1979[6]	Depository Institutions Deregulation Act 1980	Admin. Proposal 1981[7]	Garn-St Germain 1982
Home Mortgages	1933	Yes (Statutory Loan Limit Dele.)	Yes (Statutory Loan Limit Dele.)	Yes ($60,000 Loan Limit)[9]		Yes (90% Loan-to-Value Limit)	Yes (Statutory LTV Limit Dele.)	Yes (Statutory LTV Limit Dele.)
Non-Residential Mortgages	1933	Yes (30% of Assets)	Yes (20% of Assets)	Yes (20% of Assets)		Yes (20% of Assets)	Yes (No Limit)	Yes (40% of Assets)
Land Development	1959	Yes (Loans)		Yes (5% of Assets)				
Direct Investment	1961	Yes (For Community Development)	Yes (For Community Development)	Yes (2% of Assets for Community Dev.)		Yes (2% of Assets for Community Dev.; 5% Bus. Dev.)	Yes (In Small Bus. Invest. Corp.)	Yes (1% Assets In Small Bus. Invest. Corp.)
Service Corporation	1964	Yes (1% of Assets)	Yes (1% of Assets)	Yes (1% of Assets)		Yes (3% of Assets)	Yes (5% of Assets)	
Construction Loans	1978	Yes	Yes (20% of Assets)	Yes (5% of Assets)		Yes (5% of Assets)		

Appendix 4 (continued): Evolution of Federal Savings and Loan Powers, 1975-1982

	Year first Authorized	Fine Study Legislation Passed Senate 1975[4]	House Banking Committee Print 1976[5]	Public Law 95-630 (1978)	Admin. Proposal 1979[6]	Depository Institutions Deregulation Act 1980	Admin. Proposal 1981[7]	Gam-St Germain 1982
Corporate Bonds	1980	Yes	Yes		Yes (10% of Assets)	Yes (20% of Assets[10])	Yes (No Limit)	Yes [11]
Education Loans	1978	Yes (30% of Assets)	Yes (20% of Assets)	Yes (5% of Assets)		Yes (5% of Assets)	Yes (No Limit)	
Consumer Loans	1980	Yes (30% of Assets)	Yes (20% of Assets)		Yes (10% of Assets)	Yes (20% of Assets)	Yes (No Limit)	Yes (30% of Assets)
Commercial Loans	1982						Yes (No Limit)	Yes [12] (10% of Assets)
Leasing of Personal Property	1982						Yes (10% of Assets)	Yes (10% of Assets)
Investment in Commercial Paper	1980	Yes (30% of Assets)	Yes		Yes (10% of Assets)	Yes (20% of Assets)		
Credit Cards	1980	Yes			Yes	Yes		

1. H.R. 14 and H.R. 11508. 89th Congress
2. Report, Pres. Comm. On Fin. Structure and Reg. (1972)
3. S. 2591, 93rd Congress (1973)
4. S. 1267, 94th Congress (1975)
5. Financial Reform Act of 1976, 94th Congress (1976)

6. Depos. Inst. Dereg. Act, 96th Congress (1979)
7. S. 1703, 97th Congress (1981
8. Provided a 80% LTV limit that could be could be waived by regulators
9. The limit was raised to $ 75,000 in 1979, Public Law 96-161

10. By regulation, up to 1% unrated bonds
11. Gam-St Germain continued the placement of corp. rate bond investments in the 20% of assets basket, the Bank Board interpreted the Act to permit up to 100% of assets in corporate bonds, with 1% in unrated bonds.
12. The Bank Board interpreted this authority to allow investment in unrated bonds up to 10% of assets.

Source: James R. Barth, (1991). *The Great Savings and Loan Debacle*, American Enterprise Institute.

James R. Barth, Susanne Trimbath and Glenn Yago

Appendix 5: Major Tax Legislation Directly Affecting the Real Estate Industry and Indirectly Affecting the Savings and Loan Industry, 1980-1992

Legislation	Depreciation	Capital Gains/Passive Losses	Individual Income Tax Rates	Corporate Income Tax Rates
Economic Recovery Tax Act of 1981	(1) Shortened depreciation life for real property placed in service after Dec. 31, 1980 to 15 years, compared to 40-60 years under prior law. (2) Real property placed in service after Dec. 31, 1980 (other than low income housing) could be depreciated under the 175% declining balance method (dbm). Low income housing placed in service after Dec. 31, 1980 could be depreciated using the 200% dbm. Under prior law, non-residential real property was depreciated using a 150% dbm (if new) or the straight line method (slm). New residential real property was depreciated using slm, the sum of years digits, or 200% dbm. Used residential property could be depreciated using 125% dbm or slm.	(1) Reduced the maximum marginal tax rate on long-term capital gains for individuals from 28% (70% of 40% of gain) to 20% (50% of 40% of gain), effective for sales or exchanges occurring after June 9, 1981. (2) Increased from $100,000 to $125,000 the amount of gain excludable from gross income on the sale or exchange of a residence by an individual who has attained age 55, effective for sales or exchanges after July 20, 1981.	(1) Compared to prior law, marginal tax rates were reduced 1.25% in 1991, 10% in 1992, 19% in 1993, and 23% in 1994 and subsequent years. (2) Maximum marginal tax rate reduced from 70% to 50% effective Jan. 1, 1982.	(1) Reduced the marginal tax rate on the first $25,000 of taxable corporate income from 17% to 16% for 1982 and to 15% for 1983 and subsequent years. (2) Reduced the marginal tax rate on the second $25,000 of taxable corporate income from 20% to 19% for 1982 and to 18% for 1983 and subsequent years. (3) The marginal tax rates on the third and fourth $25,000 of taxable corporate income remained unchanged at 30% and 40%, respectively. The maximum marginal tax rate on taxable corporate income greater than $100,000 was unchanged at 46%.

Appendix 5 (continued): Major Tax Legislation Directly Affecting the Real Estate Industry and Indirectly Affecting the Savings and Loan Industry, 1980-1992

Legislation	Depreciation	Capital Gains/Passive Losses	Individual Income Tax Rates	Corporate Income Tax Rates
Deficit Reduction Act of 1984	(1) Depreciation life for real property (other than low income housing) placed in service after Mar. 15, 1984 increased from 15 to 18 years.	Reduction in long-term capital gains holding period from 1 year to 6 months for assets acquired after June 22, 1984.		Effective for tax years beginning after Dec. 31, 1984, the benefits of the graduated rates on the first $100,000 of corporate taxable income was phased out for corporations with taxable income in excess of $1 million. Specifically, an additional 5% tax, up to a maximum of $20,250, was levied on corporate taxable income in excess of $1 million, affecting corporations with taxable income between $1 million and $1,405,001.
Imputed Interest Rules (October 1985)	(1) Depreciation life for real property (other than low income housing) placed in service after May 8, 1985 increased from 18 to 19 years.			

James R. Barth, Susanne Trimbath and Glenn Yago

Appendix 5 (continued): Major Tax Legislation Directly Affecting the Real Estate Industry and Indirectly Affecting the Savings and Loan Industry, 1980-1992

Legislation	Depreciation	Capital Gains/Passive Losses	Individual Income Tax Rates	Corporate Income Tax Rates
Tax Reform Act of 1986	(1) Effective for all real property placed in service after Dec. 31, 1986, the depreciation life was increased from 19 years to 27.5 years for residential property and to 31.5 years for non-residential property. (2) The method of depreciation for all real property placed in service after Dec. 31, 1986 was changed to straight line. (3) A tax credit, to be taken in annual installments over 10 years, was provided to low income housing constructed, rehabilitated or purchased after Dec. 31, 1986 and before Jan. 1, 1990. The credit has a present value of 70% of qualified costs for non-Federally subsidized projects and a present value of 30% of qualified costs for federally subsidized projects.	(1) 60% capital gains exclusion for individuals was repealed effective Jan. 1, 1987. For 1987, the maximum marginal tax rate on capital gains was capped at 28%. For 1988 and subsequent years, the maximum marginal rate rose to 33% for those in the income range where the benefit of the 15% rate was phased out. (2) Limitation on the deductibility of passive losses against ordinary income phased-in beginning Jan. 1, 1987 and becoming fully effective Jan. 1, 1991. (3) Effective July 1, 1987, the maximum tax rate of 28% on corporate long-term capital gains was repealed, increasing the maximum rate to 34%. A 34% rate was also applicable to gains realized between Jan. 1, 1987 and July 1, 1987.	(1) The 15 tax brackets and rates of prior law were replaced by a schedule with 2 brackets and 2 rates – 15% and 28% effective Jan.1, 1988. The benefit of the 15% rate was phased out for taxpayers with income exceeding specified levels, creating specified marginal tax rate of 33% in the affected income range. (2) A transition schedule consisting of 5 brackets and 5 rates — 11% to 38.5% — was in effect for 1987.	(1) The 5 tax brackets with rates ranging from 15% to 46% were replaced with 3 bracket with rates of 15, 25, and 34%, effective July 1, 1987. (2) Effective July 1, 1987, the benefit of the 15% and 25% rates was fully phased out for corporations with taxable income in excess of $335,000. Specifically, an additional 15% tax, up to a maximum of $11,750, was levied on corporate taxable income in excess of $100,000 affecting corporations with taxable income between $100,000 and $335,001.

Appendix 5 (continued): Major Tax Legislation Directly Affecting the Real Estate Industry and Indirectly Affecting the Savings and Loan Industry, 1980-1992

Legislation	Depreciation	Capital Gains/Passive Losses	Individual Income Tax Rates	Corporate Income Tax Rates
Omnibus Budget Reconciliation Act of 1989	(1) Low income housing tax credit was modified and extended for 1 year through Dec. 31, 1990.			
Omnibus Budget Reconciliation Act of 1990	(1) Low income housing tax credit was modified and extended for 1 year through Dec. 31, 1991.	Effective Jan.1, 1991, the maximum marginal tax rate on capital gains for individuals was capped at 28%.	Effective Jan. 1, 1991, the phase-out of the benefit of the 15% bracket is repealed. A third tax bracket of 31% is imposed on taxable income greater than or equal to the level at which the phase-out of the benefit of the 15% rate would have begun under prior law.	
Tax Extension Act of 1991	(1) Low income housing tax credit was extended for 6 months through June 30, 1992.			

Source: James R. Barth

Appendix 6: Percentage Distribution of Total Financial Assets Held by All U.S. Financial Service Firms, 1950-1996

	1950	1960	1970	1980	1990	2000	2001
Depository Institutions[1]							
Commercial Banks	50.7	37.6	34.5	34.1	27.6	21.1	21.9
U.S. Chartered Commercial Banks	50.1	36.9	32.7	29.2	21.9	15.6	16.0
Foreign Banking Offices in U.S.	0.3	0.5	0.6	2.3	3.0	2.6	2.7
Bank Holding Companies	NA	NA	1.0	2.4	2.5	2.8	3.0
Banks in U.S.-Affiliated Areas	0.3	0.1	0.3	0.3	0.2	0.2	0.2
Savings Institutions[2]	13.3	18.4	16.9	18.3	10.9	4.0	4.1
Credit Unions	0.3	1.0	1.2	1.6	1.8	1.4	1.6
Contractual Intermediaries							
Life Insurance Companies	21.2	19.0	13.4	10.7	11.2	10.2	10.5
Other Insurance Companies	4.0	4.3	3.4	4.2	4.4	2.8	2.8
Private Pension Funds[3]	2.4	6.7	8.3	11.6	13.3	14.8	13.3
State and Local Government Retirement funds	1.7	3.2	4.0	4.5	7.3	7.5	6.9

Appendix 6 (continued): Percentage Distribution of Total Financial Assets Held by All U.S. Financial Service Firms, 1950-2001

	1950	1960	1970	1980	1990	2000	2001
Others							
Finance Companies	3.1	4.5	4.3	4.5	4.5	3.7	3.7
Mortgage Companies	0.2	0.3	0.5	0.4	0.4	0.1	0.1
Mutual Funds[4]	1.1	2.8	3.1	1.4	5.0	14.5	13.2
Money Market Mutual Funds	NA	NA	NA	1.8	4.1	5.9	7.1
Closed-End Funds	0.7	1.1	0.4	0.2	0.4	0.5	0.4
Security Brokers and Dealers	1.4	1.1	1.1	1.0	2.2	4.0	4.6
Real Estate Investment Trusts	NA	NA	0.3	0.1	0.2	0.2	0.2
Issuers of Asset-Backed Securities	NA	NA	NA	NA	2.2	6.0	6.7
Bank Personal Trust and Estates[5]	NA	NA	8.8	5.6	4.3	3.2	2.8
Total Assets ($ Billions) End of period; not seasonally adjusted	295	609	1,499	4,342	12,089	30,641	31,410

NOTES:
[1] "Commercial banks" consist of U.S. chartered commercial banks, domestic affiliates, Edge Act corporations, agencies and offices in U.S. Possession. "Foreign banking offices in U.S." include Edge Act corporations and offices of foreign banks. International Banking Facilities are excluded from domestic banking and treated like branches in foreign countries.
[2] Savings and loan associations include all savings and loan associations and federal saving banks insured by the Savings Association Insurance Fund. Savings banks include all federal and mutual savings banks insured by the Bank Insurance Fund. The Flow of Funds Accounts were restructured in the second quarter of 1993, thereby omitting this breakdown.
[3] Private pension funds include Federal Employees' Retirement Thrift Savings Fund.
[4] Mutual funds are open-end investment companies; excludes funding vehicles for variable annuities, which are included in the life insurance sector.
[5] Bank personal trusts are assets of individuals managed by bank trust departments and nondeposit noninsured trust companies.

Source: Flow of Funds Accounts, Board of Governors of the Federal Reserve System (various issues).

Appendix 7: Percent Distribution of U.S. Mortgage Loans by Lender, 1950-1970

	1950			1960			1970		
	Home Mortgages	Multifam. Mortgages	Comm. Mortgages	Home Mortgages	Multifam. Mortgages	Comm. Mortgages	Home Mortgages	Multifam. Mortgages	Comm. Mortgages
Commercial Banks	21.1	10.8	18.4	13.6	5.3	20.4	14.4	5.5	27.2
Savings Institutions	38.0	32.3	12.0	53.1	28.2	15.3	55.6	35.9	22.6
Credit Union	0.2	NA	NA	0.3	NA	NA	0.3	NA	NA
Bank Personal Trusts and Estates	0.0	NA	NA	0.0	NA	NA	0.8	NA	NA
Life Insurance Companies	18.9	28.0	29.6	17.7	18.7	30.0	9.1	26.6	30.3
Other Insurance Companies	NA	NA	0.8	NA	NA	0.3	NA	NA	0.2
Private Pension Funds	0.0	0.0	0.0	0.4	1.9	0.9	0.6	2.0	1.4
State and Local Government Retirement Funds	0.0	0.0	0.0	0.6	2.4	0.6	1.0	3.2	1.1
Finance Companies	0.0	0.0	0.0	0.0	0.0	0.0	0.2	0.0	0.0
Mortgage Companies	0.9	1.1	0.0	1.0	1.0	0.3	1.8	2.0	0.5

NA – Not available

Appendix 7 (continued): Percent Distribution of U.S. Mortgage Loans by Lender, 1950-1970

	1950			1960			1970		
	Home Mortgages	Multifam. Mortgages	Comm. Mortgages	Home Mortgages	Multifam. Mortgages	Comm. Mortgages	Home Mortgages	Multifam. Mortgages	Comm. Mortgages
Real Estate Investment Trusts	0.0	0.0	0.0	0.0	0.0	0.0	0.2	2.2	2.3
Federal Related Mortgage Pools	0.0	0.0	NA	0.0	0.0	NA	1.0	0.2	NA
Government Sponsored Enterprises	0.0	0.0	NA	2.1	0.0	NA	5.3	0.5	NA
Issuers of Asset Backed Securities	0.0	0.0	0.0	0.0	0.0	0.0	0.0	0.0	0.0
Federal Government	3.3	0.0	0.0	3.0	4.8	0.0	2.1	5.2	0.5
State and Local Government	0.4	0.0	0.0	1.0	0.0	0.0	0.6	3.7	0.2
Households	17.1	28.0	39.2	7.3	37.8	32.1	7.1	13.1	12.6
Nonfinancial Corporate Business	0.0	0.0	0.0	0.0	0.0	0.0	-0.1	0.0	0.2
Nonfarm Noncorporate Business	0.0	0.0	0.0	0.0	0.0	0.0	0.0	0.0	0.8
Total Assets ($ Billions)	45.9	9.3	12.5	140.9	20.9	33.3	294.7	60.1	85.7

Appendix 7 (continued): Percent Distribution of U.S. Mortgage Loans by Lender, 1980-2001

	1980			1990			2001		
	Home Mortgages	Multifam. Mortgages	Comm. Mortgages	Home Mortgages	Multifam. Mortgages	Comm. Mortgages	Home Mortgages	Multifam. Mortgages	Comm. Mortgages
Commercial Banks	16.5	9.0	31.9	16.3	12.5	46.0	17.8	18.7	50.2
Savings Institutions	49.6	38.1	23.9	22.7	32.1	13.7	10.8	14.2	5.7
Credit Union	0.5	NA	NA	1.9	NA	NA	2.5	NA	NA
Bank Personal Trusts and Estates	0.5	NA	NA	0.2	NA	NA	0.0	NA	NA
Life Insurance Companies	1.9	13.7	31.3	0.5	10.1	27.0	0.1	7.6	14.6
Other Insurance Companies	NA	NA	0.4	NA	NA	0.9	NA	NA	0.1
Private Pension Funds	0.1	0.2	0.7	0.2	0.4	2.3	0.2	0.2	0.2
State and Local Government Retirements Funds	0.4	2.7	1.4	0.1	1.8	0.9	0.2	1.5	0.7
Finance Companies	1.4	0.0	0.0	2.5	0.0	0.0	2.5	0.6	3.0
Mortgage Companies	1.1	1.5	1.2	1.6	1.0	0.6	0.5	1.2	0.4

Appendix 7 (continued): Percent Distribution of U.S. Mortgage Loans by Lender, 1980-2001

	1980			1990			2001		
	Home Mortgages	Multifam. Mortgages	Comm. Mortgages	Home Mortgages	Multifam. Mortgages	Comm. Mortgages	Home Mortgages	Multifam. Mortgages	Comm. Mortgages
Real Estate Investment Trusts	0.0	0.6	0.6	0.0	0.8	0.6	0.1	0.2	0.5
Federal Related Mortgage Pools	11.1	4.2	NA	37.4	10.0	0.0	47.9	18.0	0.0
Government Sponsored Enterprises	6.0	4.7	NA	4.4	4.6	0.0	3.9	8.3	NA
Issuers of Asset Backed Securities	0.0	0.0	0.0	2.1	0.3	1.5	10.0	12.5	18.4
Federal Government	1.9	7.3	2.2	1.4	8.0	1.7	0.3	3.0	3.2
State and Local Government	2.0	7.5	0.7	2.3	14.2	0.9	1.4	11.1	0.6
Households	5.0	1.3	2.7	4.9	0.3	0.3	1.4	0.3	0.6
Nonfinancial Corporate Business	1.6	7.4	0.7	1.3	0.6	2.2	0.2	0.2	1.1
Nonfarm Noncorporate Business	0.4	1.6	2.4	0.4	3.1	1.5	0.2	2.3	0.6
Total Assets ($ Billions)	964.7	142.1	257.8	2,645.5	285.8	796.7	5,740.1	453.7	1,284.7

Source: Flow of Funds Accounts, Board of Governors of the Federal Reserve System
NA – Not available

Appendix 8: Estimated Savings and Loan Resolution Cost, 1986-1995 (US$ Billion)

		Private Sector	Public Sector	Total
FSLIC/FSLIC Resolution Fund 1986-95	FSLIC year-end equity and reserves, 1985	6.10		6.10
	FSLIC insurance premiums, 1986–89	5.80		5.80
	SAIF assessments diverted to FRF, 1989–92	2.00		2.00
	FICO bond proceeds, 1987–89	8.20		8.20
	FRF appropriations, 1989–95		43.50	43.50
	Less: FRF equity at 12/31/99		-2.50	-2.50
	Estimated Direct FSLIC/FRF Cost	22.00	41.00	63.00
RTC, 1989–95	FHLB payments to defease REFCORP debt	1.30		1.30
	SAIF assessments paid to defease REFCORP debt, 1990	1.10		1.10
	Net present value of FHLB-paid interest on REFCORP bonds	3.50		3.50
	Net present value of REFCORP interest paid by U.S. Treasury		24.20	24.20
	Total REFCORP bond proceeds	5.90	24.20	30.10
	Appropriations from U.S. Treasury		55.90	55.90
	Initial contribution from FHLB system	1.20		1.20
	Less: RTC equity at 12/31/99		(4.50)	(4.50)
	Estimated Direct RTC Cost	7.10	75.60	82.70
Indirect Cost	Estimated cost of tax benefits to acquirers from FSLIC assistance		6.30	6.30
	Increased interest expense from higher interest rates on REFCORP bonds compared with U.S. Treasury borrowings		1.00	1.00
Estimated Total Cost		29.10	123.80	152.90

Source: FDIC

THE SAVINGS AND LOAN CRISIS:

FIVE ILLUSTRATIVE CASE STUDIES

Donald McCarthy
Milken Institute

INTRODUCTION

The savings and loan crisis saw the failure of more than 1,500 institutions and the reduction of the industry's size from nearly 4,000 savings and loans in 1980 to just over 2,000 in 1991. This chapter examines four of these 1,500 failures in detail and one of the 2,000 survivors.

Each of the failed institutions illustrates a specific aspect of the crisis and of the government's response and together they provide specific examples of the regulatory failures that characterized savings and loan regulation in the 1980s. Madison Guaranty was a poorly capitalized and managed institution that grew out of control but was allowed to operate by the overstretched Home Loan Bank of Little Rock in a classic example of "desupervision."[1] Imperial Savings was an example of an unprofitable and poorly capitalized savings and loan that sought to diversify its asset base and fell victim to credit risk and to the Congress's attack on high yield bonds. CenTrust fell victim to the regulatory flip flop over supervisory goodwill while Columbia was a high profile victim of the treatment of high yield bonds under the Financial Institutions Reform Recovery and Enforcement Act (FIRREA).

The single survivor is characteristic of the type of savings and loan that escaped the crisis unscathed. World Savings, the success story, was a large, well-capitalized institution that avoided regulatory interference with its activities by keeping to traditional savings and loan business lines.

DESUPERVISION AND FORBEARANCE

Forbearance was a cornerstone of the Federal Home Loan Bank Board (FHLBB) policy in the 1980s (Barth, 1991; Kane, 1989) and was designed to allow the massively undercapitalized Federal Savings and Loan Insurance Corporation (FSLIC) to delay recognizing the costs of resolving insolvent institutions. Yet, this policy allowed troubled savings and loans to gamble their way to solvency with risky but potentially high yielding investments. This policy of forbearance was compounded by the Home Loan Bank system's severe shortages of qualified supervisors. Although funds for the FSLIC and FHLBB were raised from examination fees, FSLIC investment income, and FSLIC insurance premium assessments from the individual Home Loan Banks, these funds were budget line items and any increases

---

[1] See Edward Kane, "What Lessons might have Crisis Countries in Asia and Latin America have Learned from the S&L Mess" in this volume for a discussion of desupervision.

would translate into an increased deficit. Consequently, requests for more funding for the FSLIC or FHLBB were not well-received by the Reagan administration that had prioritized increased defense expenditures and tax cuts over increased savings and loan supervision. The shortage of funds translated into a strong desire to avoid resolving troubled institutions (and thus keep the FSLIC's growing contingent liabilities "off book") and into a severe shortage of supervisors. Both these results made forbearance an attractive choice for regulators.

The shortage of supervisors was particularly acute in the Ninth District where a regional recession in the oil producing states of Texas and Oklahoma had resulted in a situation where 65 percent of the savings and loans in the Ninth District were reporting losses and 39 percent were insolvent by 1987. Added to this grim picture was the chaotic transition of the district's Home Loan Bank from Little Rock to Dallas. So overstretched were the resources of the Dallas bank that staff from other Home Loan Banks carried out examinations in the Ninth District. It was against this background of widespread savings and loan failures, forbearance and an underfunded Home Loan Bank that Madison Guaranty was allowed to grow out of control.

THE SUPERVISORY GOODWILL FLIP FLOP

Supervisory mergers, the merger of a market value insolvent institution into a solvent institution, were a common practice in the 1980s. To ensure that the resulting institution would be solvent under Regulatory Accounting Principles (RAP), the acquiring savings and loan was allowed to create an intangible asset known as supervisory goodwill. This supervisory goodwill was equal to the difference between the market value of the institution's liabilities and the market value of its assets and could be counted as capital. In effect, supervisory goodwill was designed to make good the gap between an insolvent institution's liabilities and assets and allow it to report an artificially clean bill of health. (Figure 1 shows the divergence of RAP from Tangible Accounting Principles (TAP) due, in no small part, to the creation of supervisory goodwill.) Supervisory goodwill was to be amortized over a period of usually 40 years with the idea being that institutions would grow their way back to solvency, taking advantage of the new investment opportunities offered by the Depository Institutions Deregulation and Monetary Control Act and the Garn-St Germain Depository Institutions Act.

Figure 1: Goodwill and the Divergence of RAP and GAAP Capital-to-Asset Ratios

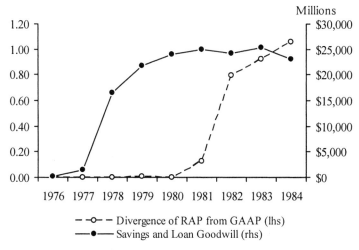

Source: Barth (1991)

FIRREA dramatically changed the treatment of supervisory goodwill. It required the establishment of minimum capital adequacy standards for savings and loans. Specifically, they required institutions to maintain a tangible capital-to-assets ratio of greater than 1.5 percent, a core capital-to-assets ratio of not less than 3 percent and a risk-based capital-to-assets ratio equal to that of banks. Furthermore, FIRREA did not allow savings and loans to include supervisory goodwill in core capital and stipulated that the small amount of supervisory goodwill that could be included was to fall each year until 1995 when it would no longer be allowed to be included at all.

Institutions, such as CenTrust, that had relied on the inclusion of supervisory goodwill found themselves to be in violation of FHLBB standards. A large number of institutions were seized following this regulatory flip flop while many more were forced to scramble to quickly raise more capital to avoid violating the new standards.

FIRREA AND THE ATTACK ON HIGH YIELD SECURITIES

Although high yield bonds never comprised more than 1 percent of all savings and loans' total assets (Table 1) and, in fact, outperformed a number of other alternative investments in the years immediately preceding FIRREA (Figure 2), the asset class was to suffer specific attacks on it due to amendments to FIRREA that were proposed by a long-time opponent of the bonds, North Dakota Rep. Byron Dorgan. These additions to FIRREA were the culmination of several years of negative attention paid the market by lawmakers.

Table 1: High Yield Holdings by Savings and Loans (as of year end)

	Millions	Percent of Assets
1985	$5,587	0.50%
1986	$7,572	0.60%
1987	$12,294	1.00%
1988	$12,810	1.00%
1989	$12,318	1.00%
1990	$10,730	0.90%
1991	$4,018	0.40%

Source: Yago (1994b).

In 1985, Senators Dominici of New Mexico and Proxmire of Wisconsin co-sponsored legislation that would make it illegal for savings and loans to invest in high yield bonds. While these proposed restrictions were not passed into law, plans for compulsory divesture of high yield bonds by savings and loans were eventually incorporated into the Financial Institutions Reform, Recovery and Enforcement Act (FIRREA). High yield bonds had been held in large numbers by a relatively small number of savings and loans but due to legislative concerns, the U.S. General Accounting Office (GAO) undertook in 1988 a lengthy inquiry into the high yield bond market and its potential impact on federally insured depositaries (including savings and loans). Despite the GAO's finding that high yield bonds posed no threat to savings and loans, populist sentiments in the Congress led to FIRREA's inclusion of a number of new rules that had an immediate and negative impact on the market and on the savings and loans that held the bonds.

Figure 2: Average Return on Benchmark Securities – September 1986-June 1989

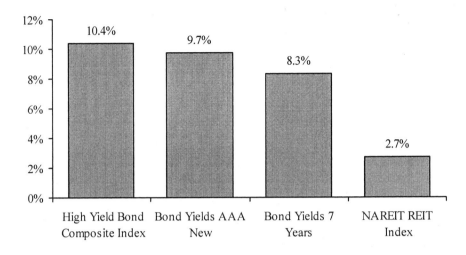

Source: Calculation based on data from Salomon Bros. and Merrill Lynch.

FIRREA included a provision that stated that stock savings and loans would no longer be able to hold debt which was rated below-investment grade at its time of purchase and mutual savings and loans would only be able to participate in the market through separately capitalized subsidiaries (Barth, 1991). In addition to no longer being able to purchase high yield debt, savings and loans were required to sell all high yield bonds they were holding by 1994. As would be expected, FIRREA had a negative impact on the market (Figure 3), driving up yields and depressing values (Yago and Siegel, 1994). The passage of FIRREA established the RTC as a public corporation (managed at first by the FDIC after November 1991 independently operating) with the purpose of resolving failed savings and loans. Between August 9, 1989 and December 31, 1995, the RTC resolved 747 insolvent institutions with assets of $403 billion (FDIC, 2001).

RTC sales failed to minimize losses on the portfolio for a number of reasons. The market for RTC-owned securities was characterized by asymmetric information but it was buyers rather than the RTC who had private information about the value of the high yield bonds the RTC was selling. This problem was compounded by the RTC's "fire sale" approach to asset disposal. The RTC sold large blocks of debt into an increasingly illiquid market further depressing prices and providing sophisticated buyers quality assets at huge discounts. Yago (1994a) provides examples of what he terms "manufactured losses." These include:

- Flying J. Incorporated was sold by the RTC on February 12, 1991 for 0.7801. By September 30, 1991, the price had risen by 14 percent to 0.8900. The RTC could have realized a substantially higher price by holding the bond for just seven more months.

- GACC Holdings was sold for 35.26 by the RTC on November 3, 1992. Less than 2 weeks later on November 16, 1992, the price was 40.00. If the RTC had held the bonds a few more days, it would have realized a 12 percent higher value.

- Pacific Asset Corporation was sold for 85.00 on January 15, 1991. By October 18, 1991, the same bond was trading at par (100.00). The RTC realized a $1.8 million loss that would have been avoided if the bond had been held a few months more.

Figure 3: The Impact of FIRREA on High Yield Bonds

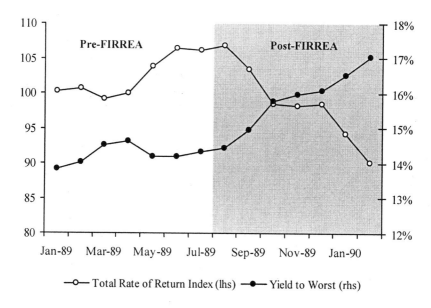

—o— Total Rate of Return Index (lhs)   —•— Yield to Worst (rhs)

Source: Lehman Brothers, Milken Institute.

Perhaps just as damaging to institutions holding high yield bonds as the compulsory divestment was the new requirement for savings and loans to mark their high yield bond holdings to market. The convention that institutions holding high yield bonds for purposes of investment (rather than sale) had followed before FIRREA was to account for them at face value rather than marking them to market. The justification for this was that the bonds were intended to be held until maturity and any sales of bonds were to be carried out only when the fundamentals of such bonds' issuer had deteriorated. Since FIRREA nullified the strategy of holding high yield bonds to maturity and instead obliged savings and loans to sell their holdings, they could no longer be legally accounted for at face value. These two new rules were to lead directly to the rapid decline and failure of a number of savings and loans, including profitable and well-capitalized institutions like columbia.

MADISON GUARANTY

Madison Guaranty was a small Arkansas-based savings and loan that was placed into conservatorship by the FSLIC on March 2, 1989. Although not an economically important savings and loan, the institution attracted national attention because of the business relationship between its management and President Clinton. At its date of failure, Madison Guaranty had assets of nearly $115 million and deposits of $99 million.[2] Its resolution was estimated by the FDIC to cost $33 million.

Background

Madison Guaranty was originally chartered by the State of Arkansas as Woodruff County Savings and Loan Association in 1979. In January 1982, James B. McDougal and Steven Smith purchased a controlling interest in the savings and loan. The following month, McDougal was elected president of Woodruff County Savings and Loan and the name of the institution was changed to Madison Guaranty Savings and Loan.

The Condition of Madison Guaranty in the Early 1980s

Madison Guaranty began in 1979 as a small traditional savings and loan with assets of $2.4 million, 87 percent of which were mortgages. As with nearly all savings and loans, the institution was facing financial difficulties as the inverted yield curve of the late 1970s and the early 1980s had made traditional fixed-rate home loans unprofitable. Madison Guaranty reported losses for 1979, 1980 and 1981 so that the institution's return on assets and return on equity were both negative each year (Table 2).

---

[2] Federal Deposit Insurance Corporation, *Bank and Thrift Failure Reports.*

Table 2: Madison Guaranty's Return on Assets and Return on Equity

	1979	1980	1981
Return on Assets	-1.4%	-0.8%	-3.1%
Return on Equity	-3.0%	-8.1%	-150.1%

Source: Thrift Financial Reports Database, Milken Institute.

Although unprofitable, Madison Guaranty expanded aggressively between 1979 and 1981, increasing its assets by 59 percent while its tangible capital-to-asset ratio fell from 8.9 percent in 1979 to 2 percent in 1981. Despite its thin capitalization and lack of profitability, in 1981 the Federal Home Loan Bank of Little Rock gave the institution a composite examination rating of 2C on a scale of 1 to 5 with 1 being the highest rating (Barth and Brumbaugh, 1996).

Madison Guaranty's Adaptation to the Challenges of the 1980s

This sanguine assessment of the risks posed to the FSLIC by the institution was revised in April 1982 – just three months after McDougal purchased a controlling share of the institution – following a special examination. The examiner noted that rather than posing few risks, the institution was in fact close to insolvency and operating loses had been understated. This examination resulted in a rating of 4D (Barth and Brumbaugh, 1996). A June 1982 infusion of $100,000 improved Madison Guaranty's capitalization and by 1983 its tangible capital-to-asset ratio had risen to 3 percent.

Under the stewardship of Mr. McDougal and his partners, Madison Guaranty followed many other weak institutions in rapid expansion and diversification away from traditional savings and loan business lines. Between 1982 and 1984 Madison Guaranty redoubled its efforts at expansion and grew from an institution with assets of $6.7 million to one of $48.6 million, an increase of 726 percent. At the same time, increased emphasis was placed on nontraditional business lines. Home loans represented 43 percent of Madison Guaranty's assets in 1982. By 1984, they had fallen to below 20 percent while commercial mortgages and commercial loans grew from 0 percent to 13 percent of assets over the same period. In addition to building a commercial lending business, management sought to transform Madison Guaranty into a more active participant in the commercial real estate development market by diversifying into originating acquisition and development (A&D) loans and making direct real estate investments, two markets in which Madison

Table 3: Madison Guaranty's Asset Diversification (percent of Total Assets)

	1982	1983	1984
Retail mortgages	43.2%	37.8%	19.3%
Commercial mortgages	0.0%	2.8%	10.8%
Commercial loans	0.0%	4.1%	2.0%
Acquisition and development loans	0.0%	8.7%	9.8%
Direct investments	1.9%	6.5%	5.8%

Source: Thrift Financial Reports Database, Milken Institute.

Guaranty had no previous experience. The entry into these markets was in part facilitated by Madison Financial Corporation, Madison's service company subsidiary which was later to be linked to the "Whitewater" real estate project. By 1984, acquisition and development loans had grown to 9.8 percent and direct investments to 5.8 percent of total assets, respectively (Table 3).

As Madison Guaranty broadened its line of financial services and expanded aggressively, its capitalization was further weakened as its tangible capital-to-asset ratio fell from 38 percent in 1983 to just 1 percent in 1984.

The Failure of Madison Guaranty: The Unintended Consequences of Regulation

The failure of Madison Guaranty was a consequence of its overheated asset growth, weak capitalization (Figure 4) and risky lending decisions – specifically its real estate development activities. The failure of regulation in this case was the FHLBB and Arkansas authorities' willingness to forbear.

Figure 4: Madison Guaranty's Overheated Growth
Thousands

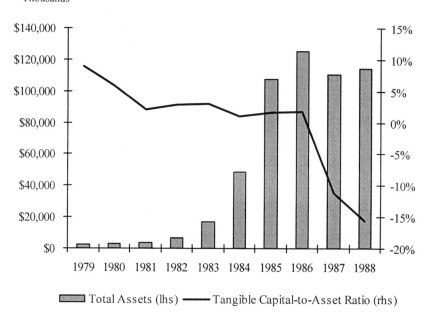

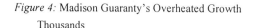 Total Assets (lhs) ——— Tangible Capital-to-Asset Ratio (rhs)

Source: Thrift Financial Reports Database, Milken Institute.

In January 1984, the FHLBB began the first special examination of Madison Guaranty since 1982. The examination found Madison Guaranty to be in a poor state of health and accordingly assigned it a composite rating of 5, the lowest possible rating and one signifying an extremely high probability of imminent failure.[3] The inspection expressed concern about Madison Guaranty's rapid growth and the inexperience of its management. It concluded that the institution was engaged in "unsafe and unsound lending practices" (Barth and Brumbaugh, 1996). Madison Guaranty would have been insolvent in 1984 had its profits been properly accounted for, but the FHLBB decided to allow the institution to remain solvent on paper by requiring it to eliminate only a portion of incorrectly reported profits on the sale of real estate by Madison Financial Corporation. In an act typical of regulatory policy in the 1980s (Barth, 1991), the FHLBB, rather than seize the institution, executed a Supervisory Agreement with Madison Guaranty in July

---

[3] The Office of the Comptroller of the Currency describes a rating of 5 as being "reserved for institutions with an extremely high immediate or near term probability of failure" and notes that "(i)n the absence of urgent and decisive corrective measures, these situations will likely require liquidation" (Office of the Comptroller of the Currency, 1979).

1984. In exchange for Madison Guaranty's agreement to comply with the stipulated minimum capital requirements and correct its regulatory violations, the FHLBB agreed to forbear from enforcement proceedings. Forbearance was a cornerstone of FHLBB policy in the 1980s (Barth, 1991; Kane, 1989) and was designed to allow the massively undercapitalized FSLIC to delay recognizing the costs of resolving insolvent institutions. Yet, this policy allowed troubled savings and loans to gamble their way to solvency with risky but potentially high yielding investments.

The Supervisory Agreement that Madison Guaranty entered into was designed to curtail the savings and loan's unsafe and unsound practices and bolster its financial strength. But it failed to achieve this result. Although Madison Guaranty's tangible assets-to-capital ratio rose slightly between 1984 and 1985 (from 1.0 percent to 1.6 percent) and it increased its holding of retail mortgages (from 19.3 percent to 41.2 percent of total assets), it continued to involve itself in high risk A&D loans and direct real estate investments. A&D loans comprised 9.8 percent of assets in 1984 and 9 percent in 1985 while direct investments *rose* from 5.8 percent of assets in 1984 to 6.2 percent in 1985. At the same time, Madison Guaranty continued its aggressive expansion, increasing its total assets by 122 percent from $48.6 million to $107.7 million in just 12 months.

The institution's growth continued throughout 1985 although at a less feverish pace. Madison Guaranty's involvement in non-traditional business lines also continued. A&D loans fell somewhat as a share of assets (from 9.0 percent to 8.5 percent) but commercial mortgages rose from 15.1 percent to 21.0 percent and direct investments in real estate rose from 6.2 percent to 7.8 percent. During this period, uninsured deposits were steadily replaced by insured deposits (Figure 5). This happens at many troubled banks when the market expects the bank to fail (Kaufman, 2001).

In March 1986, the FHLBB again examined Madison Guaranty and found that instead of adhering to the conditions of the 1984 Supervisory Agreement, management had "blatantly disregarded numerous regulations, including the growth regulation." It noted that Mr. McDougal controlled the activities of the savings and loan and used it to divert funds to himself and other "insiders" (Barth and Brumbaugh, 1996), including relatives and employees. Additionally, it found that if profits associated with real estate sales were properly accounted for, Madison Guaranty would be insolvent. In June 1986, the Federal Home Loan Bank of Dallas requested the FHLBB issue a cease and desist order to Madison Guaranty citing its

Figure 5: Madison Guaranty's Uninsured Deposits as Share of Total Deposits

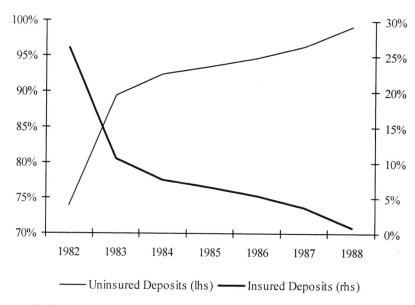

——Uninsured Deposits (lhs) ——Insured Deposits (rhs)

Source: Thrift Financial Reports Database, Milken Institute.

violation of the 1984 Supervisory Agreement and its continued unsafe and unsound practices. One month later, the FHLBB met with the Madison Guaranty Board of Directors and instructed them to immediately remove Mr. McDougal from the institution's management. In August, the FSLIC executed the requested cease and desist order against Madison Guaranty.

Although Madison Guaranty had flaunted the 1984 Supervisory Agreement by continuing in its unsafe and unsound practices and would be insolvent if it accurately accounted for its real estate sales, the institution was not resolved for a further 9 months and was not placed in receivership until February 1989, a full 18 months after the execution of the 1987 cease and desist order. During these 18 months, Madison Guaranty increased its involvement in risky A&D loans (which rose from 7.3 percent of assets to 10.9 percent) and maintained its direct real estate investment business (direct investments remained at 7.8 percent of total assets). The institution's reported net worth collapsed, falling from $2.3 million in 1986 to -$12 million in 1987 and -$17.9 million in 1988. Its tangible capital-to-assets ratio also declined dramatically, decreasing from 1.70 percent in 1986 to -11.12 percent in 1987 and still further to -15.63 percent in 1988.

Despite Madison Guaranty's insolvency and worsening financial condition, the FHLBB continued to forbear. The reasons for this policy are twofold. Firstly, by 1987, 65 percent of the savings and loans in the Ninth District were reporting losses and 39 percent were insolvent. The Federal Home Loan Bank of Dallas was simply overwhelmed by the magnitude of the problem. In 1987, Madison Guaranty was not a priority for the regulators. Secondly, the FSLIC was itself insolvent and its reserves were negative when it executed its cease and desist order in 1987 (Figure 6). Politicians and regulators hoped to delay the realization of the costs of resolving insolvent savings and loans as long as possible in an effort to render their "watch on the bridge less turbulent, to preserve (their) reputations (and) to improve opportunities for reelection or post government employment" (Kane, 2003).

The failure of regulation in the case of Madison Guaranty was thus the failure to swiftly resolve the institution due to a combination of the weakness of the FSLIC, politicians' and regulators' incentives to keep the losses of resolutions off the FSLIC's books for as long as possible and the deterioration of the savings and loan industry in the Ninth District that overstretched the Federal Home Loan Bank of Dallas' resources. The end result was most likely a cost greater than would have been the case without such forbearance.

Figure 6: FSLIC's Reserves 1980-1989

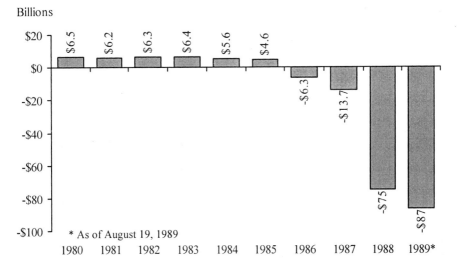

Billions

Source: U.S. League of Savings Institutions Sourcebook, GAO Report to the Congress, Federal Savings & Loan Insurance Corporation's 1989 and 1988 Financial Statements and Cornerstone Research.

IMPERIAL CORPORATION OF AMERICA

Imperial Corporation of America (ICA) was the holding company of Imperial Savings Association (ISA), a San Diego California based savings and loan that was placed into conservatorship by the Office of Thrift Supervision on February 23, 1990. Five days later, ICA filed for bankruptcy. At its date of failure, ISA had assets of nearly $9.4 billion and deposits of $6.6 billion[4]. The resolution of ISA was estimated by the FDIC to cost $422 million.

Background

ICA was formed in 1956 through the merger of three small California savings and loans and by the start of the 1980s was the nation's largest savings and loan holding company[5] with operations in California, Colorado, Kansas and Texas. ICA's savings and loan businesses operated as ISA in California, Silver State Savings in Colorado, American Savings Association in Kansas and Gibraltar Savings Association in Texas.

July 1981, ISA acquired U.S. Life Savings and Loan Association in a tax free move approved by both the IRS and the Federal Home Loan Bank Board. As a multi-state holding company with a number of subsidiaries operating savings and loan franchises, ICA faced restrictions on its ability to expand. Management sought to remedy this situation when in August 1981, the Texas subsidiary, Gibraltar Savings Association, was spun off as a separate entity in a move designed to boost ICA stock and thereby ease restrictions on its subsidiaries' ability to expand through mergers and acquisitions. ICA would eventually also dispose of its Kansas operations in 1987, merging the Colorado and Kansas operations into ISA and thus becoming a unitary holding company, while disposing of the Kansas branches in a sale to Kansas-based Columbia Savings Association, a unit of Western Financial Corporation. In February 1984, ISA converted to a state-chartered savings association.

The Condition of ICA in the Early 1980s

ISA was a relatively large savings and loan at the start of the 1980s with $4.6 billion in assets in 1981. It was, however, not a particularly well-capitalized institution with a tangible capital-to-asset ratio of just 4 percent in

---

[4] Federal Deposit Insurance Corporation, *Bank and Thrift Failure Reports.*
[5] *The American Banker*, August 11, 1981, p. 3.

1981 compared to a 5.4 percent average for the industry as a whole. As with most savings and loans, the inverted yield curve of the late 1970s and the early 1980s had made much of ISA's traditional home loans unprofitable and its return on equity negative (Table 4).

Table 4: Imperial Savings Association's Return on Equity

	1981	1982	1983	1984
Return on Equity	-14.4%	-30.0%	-23.8%	6.5%

Source: Thrift Financial Reports Database, Milken Institute.

As with all savings and loans, ISA's original business model was to lend long in fixed rate 30 year mortgages (its 1981 assets were 84 percent retail mortgages) and fund this lending by borrowing short from depositors. Deregulation of the industry through the 1980 Depository Institutions Deregulation and Monetary Control Act, which phased out Regulation Q over a period of six years, also served to increase deposit costs and this was exacerbated by the secondary market operations of Fannie Mae and Freddie Mac which tended to depress mortgage yields. As mortgage yields rose slower than deposit costs, ISA's net interest income turned negative and was nearly -$42 million in 1982.

The high cost of deposits was a challenge of particular importance as ISA's deposit costs were 50 basis points higher than the industry average, chiefly due to their longer maturities, while its average portfolio yield was 50 basis points lower than average (Imperial Corporation of America, 1986). Despite offering a fairly wide retail product mix and benefiting from a broad and relatively efficient retail distribution system, ISA was no longer profitable and was operating in an increasingly difficult business environment. In addition to a harsh operating environment, ISA faced a serious potential tax liability of $58 million arising from its earlier acquisition of U.S. Life Savings and Loan Association.[6] Clearly, ICA's savings and loan business was in trouble and its management needed to find a new way to make money in the traditional business lines or needed to seek new businesses where money could be made.

---

[6] The Internal Revenue Service had challenged ICA's tax returns for 1980 through 1984 which carried back the operating losses of the ISA portion of the combined U.S. Life-ISA operation into the consolidated tax returns of ICA and claimed refunds for taxes paid by ICA prior to its subsidiary's acquisition of U.S. Life Savings and Loan Association.

ICA's Adaptation to the Challenges of the 1980s

In 1986, ICA and ISA underwent a change in senior management. Kenneth Thygerson, CEO of Freddie Mac, and Kevin Villani, SVP and Chief Economist of Freddie Mac, joined ICA as CEO and CFO, respectively. As with the management of all savings and loans, ICA's new officers faced a period of great change in the industry and were compelled to reassess their institution's business model. While the Depository Institutions Deregulation and Monetary Control Act had brought challenges to the industry, it had offered new opportunities. Savings and loans were allowed to invest up to 20 percent of their assets in a combination of consumer loans, corporate debt and commercial paper (Barth, 1991). This offered savings and loans an opportunity to invest in higher yielding assets than home loans.

Mr. Thygerson sought to take advantage of the new powers granted savings and loans both by the Depository Institutions Deregulation and Monetary Control Act and the Garn-St Germain Act of 1982 by proposing a new business plan designed to cope with the low returns to traditional savings and loan businesses. The plan considered three strategies for the company. The first was to continue investing in increasingly more flexible adjustable rate mortgages. The second and third strategies involved transferring $1 billion of assets from ISA's fixed rate mortgage portfolio into higher yielding investments. The second strategy was to shift $1 billion of assets from low yield fixed rate mortgages into higher yielding mortgage investments, while the third was to transfer these assets into below investment grade and unrated corporate debt.

ICA's management concluded that the first strategy was inappropriate. While noting that well-capitalized competitors with strong branch systems had been able to make the necessary investments to position themselves among the ranks of the most efficient deposit intermediaries and thus guarantee their survival, this was not a feasible path for ICA to choose. Mr. Thygerson and his management team concluded that ISA's savings and loan franchise had little value unless its assets could be shifted into higher yielding investments (Imperial Corporation of America, 1986). The only way its franchise would have economic value would be if ICA moved assets into higher yielding (though less liquid) mortgage investments. These higher yielding mortgage assets were expected by ICA's officers to offer an additional 100 basis points of yield though this would translate into only a 6 percent to 12 percent return on equity. At the same time, this strategy was seen as involving substantial risks associated with the illiquidity of high yielding mortgage investments. ICA's management concluded that shifting assets into high yield mortgages was not the right decision to make and instead chose to enter the high yield bond market. High yield bonds were seen as offering a superior risk-return profile as compared to high yield mortgage investments. Unlike high yield mortgages, high yield bonds combined high yields with sufficient liquidity to avoid the high levels of liquidity risk associated with high yield mortgages.

ISA planned to restructure its fixed rate mortgage portfolio by issuing bonds backed by $1 billion of the total $2 billion of mortgages and using the proceeds of this issuance to purchase high yield corporate debt. On the assumption that these mortgage-backed bonds would be issued at a 75 to 100 basis points spread over Treasury bonds and that the proceeds of the sale would be used to buy bonds yielding a spread of 375 to 400 basis points over Treasury bonds, ICA's management expected to receive a risk arbitrage of around 300 basis points. Of this, 50 basis points of yield were to fund a reserve against defaults and the remaining 250 basis points were to provide income. When the ICA high yield strategy was fully implemented it would generate annually 250 basis points of yield on a portfolio of $1 billion or $25 million in income.

ICA was aware that a high yield bond portfolio would need to be actively managed. So, in February 1986, the ICA board authorized the formation of an asset management subsidiary, Caywood-Christian Capital Management, which would invest ICA assets in the high yield market and manage ICA's high yield investments. ISA was to own 51 percent of the new companies' equity with the remaining 49 percent owned by the three co-founders and managing directors of Caywood-Christian. Upon its formation as a partly-owned ICA subsidiary (later an independent entity), Caywood-Christian had discretion to invest in high yield corporate debt in accordance with pre-approved policies and guidelines. The portfolio limit for Caywood-Christian was $1.5 billion – three quarters of the ISA fixed rate mortgage portfolio – and its traders had a prior approval limit of $25 million per issuer. They were to maintain a well-diversified portfolio of debt. They were never allowed to buy more than 10 percent of a single issue and not more than 5 percent of the portfolio could be comprised of any one credit. Additionally, not more than 15 percent of the overall portfolio could be comprised of any one single issue (with the sole exception of utilities). Overseeing Caywood-Christian was the Executive Loan and Investment Committee (ELIC) which reported directly to the ICA board of directors.

Mr. Thygerson and his management team implemented this strategy aggressively, severing unprofitable business lines, replacing 70 percent of ICA's executives[7] and issuing $750 million of bonds backed by ISA's fixed rate mortgages. ICA also liquidated its small existing high yield bond

---

[7] *National Mortgage News*, January 26, 1987, p. 32a.

portfolio which had been assembled by Mr. Thygerson's predecessor and used the proceeds to amass far larger holdings of below investment grade and unrated bonds. High yield bonds comprised just 1 percent of ISA's total assets in 1985, but as the new business plan was implemented, this grew rapidly to 10 percent of assets in 1986. From 1985 to 1988, ISA's high yield portfolio expanded by over 3,000 percent, rising from $45.5 million to $1,473 million (Table 5) funded by ISA's expanded securitization activity (Table 6).

Table 5: High Yield Bonds Held by Imperial Savings Association

	1985	1986	1987	1988
High Yield Holdings	$45,529	$913,050	$1,425,444	$1,473,021
High Yield as % of Total Assets	1%	10%	13%	12%

Source: Thrift Financial Report Database; Milken Institute.

Table 6: Mortgage Backed Bonds Issued by Imperial Savings Association ($ thousands)

	1985	1986	1987	1988
Mortgage Backed Bonds Outstanding	$ -	$ -	$846,110	$1,510,470
Mortgage Backed Bonds as % of Total Liabilities	0%	0%	8%	14%

Source: Thrift Financial Reports Database, Milken Institute.

The new corporate strategy brought rapid, positive results for the firm. ISA's net interest margin rose from $57 million in 1985 to $99.5 million in 1986 (Table 7). At the same time, ISA returned to profit after posting losses for most of the first half of the 1980s and reported a dramatic reversal in its return on equity (Table 8) in 1986 and 1987.

Table 7: Imperial Savings Association's Net Interest Income ($ thousands)

	1985	1986	1987	1988
Net Interest Income	$57,272	$99,522	$168,918	$174,643

Source: Thrift Financial Reports Database, Milken Institute.

ISA's high yield debt portfolio performed well under the management of ICA's Caywood-Christian subsidiary.

Table 8: Imperial Savings Association's Return on Equity

	1985	1986	1987
Return on Equity	-7%	18%	13%

Source: Thrift Financial Reports Database, Milken Institute.

Between November 1986 and June 1989, ISA's high yield bond portfolio consistently outperformed Treasury bonds and, with the exception of two months, outperformed an index of investment-grade corporate bonds (Figure 7).

In addition to high yield asset management, the innovative use of securitization was another pillar of ICA operations. ISA's securitization activities expanded to include the issuance of bonds backed not just by ISA's legacy fixed rate mortgage portfolio as originally envisioned in ICA's 1986 *Financial Strategy Report,* but also by newly originated loans. In addition to issuing conventional mortgage-backed bonds, ICA was a leading innovator in structured finance. In 1986, ISA issued $192 million of Aaa-rated credit-enhanced notes backed by a letter of credit from the Federal Home Loan Bank of San Francisco, the first time a letter of credit from a Home Loan Bank had been used. In 1987, ISA issued $100 million in Aaa-rated notes backed by high yield debt, the first such Aaa-rated high yield-backed public offering. This innovation was followed in 1988 by the first ever issue of high yield debt-backed mortgage-pass-through-certificates. By concentrating the credit risk of the issue in a tranche of bonds retained by the company, $133.8 million of the issue was rated Aa2.

Figure 7: Relative Performance of Imperial Savings Association's High Yield Portfolio

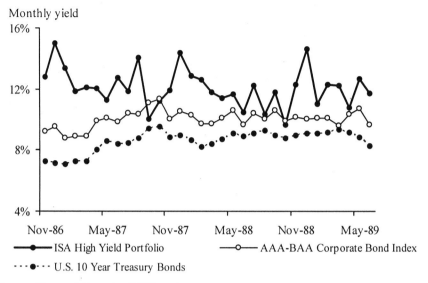

Source: Yago and Bozewicz (1998).

ISA also sought to securitize consumer loans that it had acquired in bulk from other lenders. This business proved costly as ISA suffered substantial losses due to defaults on the portfolio of loans it acquired from other institutions. ISA suffered particularly large losses from defaults on a portfolio of loans purchased from Grand Wilshire Finance Corporation. In the fourth quarter of 1988 and the first quarter of 1989, ISA was compelled to establish a $108 million reserve against losses caused by consumer loan defaults and by the default of Global Motors Incorporated on a large commercial loan.

The Failure of ICA: The Unintended Consequences of Regulation

While the financial damage caused to ICA by losses on its bulk loan purchases and on its commercial lending business was grave, the failure of the institution was largely due to the unintended consequences of government regulation. Upon proposing the new ICA strategy of redeploying assets into high yield bond investments, management noted that the economics of the plan would only be likely to be detrimental to ICA if actual losses on the high yield portfolio exceeded 300 basis points or if it was "forced to sell (its high yield debt) at distressed market prices" (Imperial Corporation of America,

1986). This second scenario would be exactly what ICA would be compelled by government regulation to do.

FIRREA's effect on ISA's high yield portfolio was remarkable (Figure 8). The fair value of the portfolio fell dramatically and the annualized quarterly return on the bonds was strongly negative for more than 4 quarters following the passage of the FIRREA.

Figure 8: The Impact of FIRREA on Imperial Savings Association's High Yield Bond Portfolio

Millions

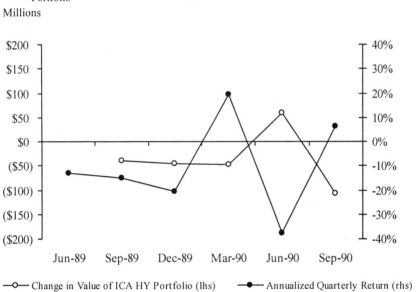

—o— Change in Value of ICA HY Portfolio (lhs)　　—●— Annualized Quarterly Return (rhs)

Source: Yago and Bozewicz (1998).

The need to mark its high yield bonds to market inflicted on ISA a "paper" loss of $209 million for 1989 based on their depreciation – a depreciation caused in large part by the FIRREA itself in addition to other government actions (Yago and Siegel, 1994). ISA was instantly taken from a position where it met the post-FIRREA capital requirements to one where it was technically insolvent (although it continued to meet the regulatory requirements for maintaining 5 percent of assets in liquid form (Table 9)).

Table 9: Imperial Savings Association's Liquid Assets as Percent of Total Assets

	1985	1986	1987	1988	1989
Liquid Assets	6.4%	7.9%	3.6%	4.4%	7.0%

Source: Thrift Financial Reports Database, Milken Institute.

Recognizing that the previous strategy of seeking higher returns in the high yield bond market was no longer feasible given the FIRREA, and that the previously existing incentives to grow assets aggressively were now absent, the board approved a new, much more conservative capital plan following the departure of Mr. Thygerson. ISA's management saw only two paths open for poorly-capitalized savings and loans such as ISA: to shrink dramatically or to liquidate. The board and management chose the first option and approved a plan that involved a return to traditional thrift business lines, the end of ISA's involvement in the high yield market (debt held was to be sold over time to avoid "dumping" the bonds into a depressed market and to take advantage of any future improvements in the market) and a reduction in consumer and commercial lending. Led by a new CEO, Lyman Hamilton, ISA submitted its new capital plan to the newly formed Office of Thrift Supervision (OTS) on January 2, 1990. Two days later, the OTS's 11th District issued an order to ISA to cease immediately all lending and investment activities. This written instruction immediately induced a run on ISA, as depositors saw the cessation of traditional lending as signaling an imminent seizure of the institution. Despite this, management maintained hopes that the OTS would accept its capital plan and allow it to continue operations. These hopes were dashed when the Resolution Trust Corporation (RTC) seized ISA in February 1990.

Postscript: Alternative Resolution Scenarios for ICA

Yago and Bozewicz (1998) provide an analysis of two alternative scenarios as to how the RTS could have liquidated ISA's high yield bond portfolio. The first is representative of the typical RTS "fire sale" approach, where securities are sold in large numbers at steep discounts. The authors assume the liquidation of the entire ISA portfolio on September 30, 1989 and the investment of the proceeds of the sale at market prices in high grade corporate debt. The second scenario assumes that no new purchases of high yield bonds are made, but none are sold, either. Each issue is held to its maturity and all coupons and redeemed principle are invested in high grade corporate debt. The difference in the value for the two strategies in terms of estimated yield is presented below in Figure 10. It is clear that the strategy of holding bonds to maturity is the superior one.

Figure 9: Value of Imperial Savings Association's High Yield Portfolio Under Two Alternative Scenarios

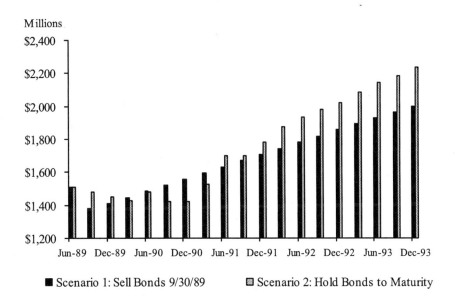

■ Scenario 1: Sell Bonds 9/30/89   ▨ Scenario 2: Hold Bonds to Maturity

Source: Yago and Bozewicz (1998).

It must be noted that, in addition to the price-reducing effects of flooding the bond market, the RTC strategy was subject also to problems of asymmetric information.[8] Insofar as the authors are not fully able to capture either the "dumping" or asymmetric information effect (Yago and Bozewicz, 1998, p. 12) the analysis tends to overstate the revenues that the RTC-type strategy could realize and thus understate the superiority of the strategy of holding debt to maturity.

CENTRUST

CenTrust Savings Bank was a Miami-based state-chartered savings and loan that was placed in conservatorship by the Office of Thrift

---

[8] Paul Horvitz remarked at the 2001 Anderson School-Milken Institute roundtable "What Can an Examination of S&Ls Reveal About Financial Institutions, Markets and Regulation?" that RTC asset sales resembled not so much a "market for lemons" but rather a "market for cherries" with the RTC selling often good quality assets to buyers who knew their real value far better than the RTC's receivers.

Supervision on February 2, 1990. At its date of seizure, CenTrust had assets of $8.2 billion and deposits of nearly $5.9 billion.[9] The resolution of CenTrust was estimated by the FDIC to cost taxpayers over $1 billion.

Background

CenTrust started in 1934 as Dade Savings, a federally chartered mutual institution, and converted in 1979 into a state-chartered mutual savings and loan. By 1980 it was Florida's largest state-chartered savings and loan with assets of $1.9 billion. In addition to a traditional savings and loan business based largely on fixed-rate mortgages, the institution also operated a mortgage company subsidiary based in Los Angeles, California.

The Condition of CenTrust in the Early 1980s

CenTrust entered the 1980s as a large but relatively undercapitalized savings and loan with a tangible-capital-to-assets ratio of 3 percent in 1981 compared to a 5.4 percent average for the industry as a whole. As with most savings institutions, CenTrust's business model had been to lend long and borrow short (in 1981, 68 percent of CenTrust's assets were retail mortgages). High interest rates and the end of Regulation Q severely damaged CenTrust's financial health and rendered much of its traditional business unprofitable and its return on equity negative (Table 10).

Table 10: CenTrust's Return on Equity

	1980	1981	1982	1983
Return on Equity	-5%	-17%	-234%	NA*

* Not meaningful: shareholders' equity and net earnings were negative in 1983.

Source: Thrift Financial Reports Database, Milken Institute.

The growth of competition for deposits from money market mutual funds increased deposit costs faster than mortgage yields. CenTrust's net interest income fell to nearly -$38 million in 1982. The profitability of its thrift business collapsed and by 1983, it was GAAP insolvent (Table 11). Rather than liquidate the institution and immediately impose costs on the poorly funded Federal Savings and Loan Insurance Corporation (FSLIC), the Federal Home Loan Bank Board (FHLBB) sought to find a buyer for CenTrust.

---

[9] Federal Deposit Insurance Corporation, *Bank and Thrift Failure Reports.*

Table 11: CenTrust's GAAP Net Worth

	1980	1981	1982	1983
GAAP Capital as % of Total Assets	3.7%	2.9%	0.9%	0.4%

Source: Thrift Financial Reports Database, Milken Institute.

On September 22, 1982, The Westport Company announced that it had reached an agreement in principle to acquire the institution for approximately $32 million and transform it from a state-chartered mutual to a state-chartered stock institution. Just over a year later, on October 29 1983, Westport received approval for the acquisition, a voluntary Supervisory Conversion.

To ensure that the new stock institution would be solvent (at least on paper) and not violate existing capital requirements, the FSLIC allowed the creation of more than $525 million of "supervisory goodwill" to fill the gap between the market value of CenTrust's liabilities and the market value of its assets to be amortized over a period of 25 years (rather than the normal period of 40). Combined with a capital infusion from Westport, and the sale of mortgages, the regulatory accounting for the merger raised the new institution's regulatory net worth from $2 million (0.1 percent of total assets) to $123 million (3.1 percent of total assets).

CenTrust's Adaptation to the Challenges of the 1980s

In 1984, the name CenTrust was officially adopted and the new management started the process of recasting and expanding the institution in an attempt to create a savings and loan that could survive in the new regulatory and economic environment. The new management sought to transform the institution from an unprofitable traditional savings and loan into a profitable retail/commercial bank with a more diverse mix of assets that would generate a positive interest spread. To effect this change, CenTrust planned to expand assets to rapidly "outgrow" the $525 million supervisory goodwill overhang (which as a non-earning intangible asset damaged the savings and loan's net interest margin). It also sought to diversify the composition of its assets and minimize the maturity mismatch between assets and liabilities and to increase the return on assets. In developing this plan, management sought to take advantage of increased deregulation. At the same time, it sought to lessen the institution's dependence on short term (and increasingly expensive) deposits by borrowing in the corporate debt and mortgage-backed bond markets.

An important part of CenTrust's new strategy was its involvement in the high yield bond market (Table 12). From holding no high yield debt in 1984, CenTrust grew its high yield portfolio to $722 million by 1985 (15 percent of total assets). Over the next three years, CenTrust consistently held more than 10 percent of its total assets in high yield bonds and grew its portfolio to $1,268 million by 1988.

Table 12: CenTrust's High Yield Bond Portfolio

	1985	1986	1987	1988
High Yield Holdings ($ thousands)	$721,607	$742,456	$995,400	$1,268,316
High Yield as % of Total Assets	15%	12%	12%	13%

Source: Thrift Financial Reports Database, Milken Institute.

CenTrust's high yield portfolio performed consistently well. Between September 1986 and June 1989, CenTrust's high-yield bond portfolio outperformed treasury bonds and an index of investment-grade corporate bonds (Figure 11).

Figure 10: Relative Performance of CenTrust's High Yield Portfolio

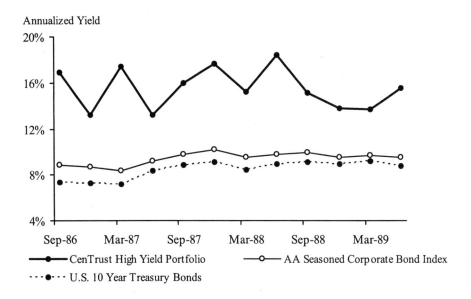

Source: Yago (1994a)

In addition to high yield bonds, CenTrust also invested heavily in mortgage backed bonds, growing its portfolio of these securities by 300 percent between 1983 and 1987. As CenTrust diversified its asset base, it also sought alternative sources of funds in an effort to reduce its reliance on deposits. Between 1984 and 1988, CenTrust issued more than $9,500 million in debt in a total of 11 issues. Of this total issuance, $1,100 million was issued in the form of mortgage-pass-through certificates and mortgage-backed bonds while $8,000 million was issued in the Eurodollar market.

CenTrust's new strategy appeared to offer rapid success in achieving the institution's goals. Its net interest income rose from -$13 million in 1984 to $36 million in 1987 (Table 13).

Table 13: CenTrust's Net Interest Income ($ thousands)

	1985	1986	1987	1988
Net Interest Income	-$13,436	-$48,873	$36,132	$45,928

Source: Thrift Financial Reports Database, Milken Institute.

Over the same period, CenTrust saw a remarkable improvement in its return on equity. In 1983, CenTrust (operating as Dade Savings) returned a dismal -234 percent on equity and in 1984 both net earnings and shareholder equity were negative. From these unpromising origins, the new stock institution reported a return of more than 18 percent on equity in 1985 and 25 percent in 1986 (Table 14).

Table 14: CenTrust's Return on Equity

	1985	1986	1987	1988
Return on Equity	18%	25%	16%	19%

Source: Thrift Financial Reports Database, Milken Institute.

CenTrust's goal to grow its assets to minimize the impact of the $525 million of supervisory goodwill that reflected Dade Savings' negative net worth at its time of acquisition similarly was achieved. Between 1983 and 1988, the institution's assets grew by over 450 percent from $2,236 million to $10,100 million, largely funded by brokered deposits (which grew from 0 in 1983 to $2,969 million in 1988[10]) and heavy issuance of debt and preferred stock. As CenTrust's assets increased and the supervisory goodwill was amortized, the importance of this non-interest earning intangible asset decreased (Table 15).

Table 15: Supervisory Goodwill as a Percent of CenTrust's Assets

	1984	1985	1986	1987	1988
Supervisory Goodwill	13%	10%	8%	6%	4%

Source: Thrift Financial Reports Database, Milken Institute.

Despite the apparent success of management's new strategy, CenTrust began to receive critical scrutiny from the Federal Home Loan Bank of Atlanta (FHLBA) in 1986. Indeed in early 1986, the FHLBA requested a cease-and-desist order against the institution on the grounds that its heavy investment in high yield bonds was "unsafe and unsound." This request was rejected by the FHLBB given the positive assessment of CenTrust's high yield portfolio reported by the FHLBA examiner charged with reviewing its high yield investments. Despite this, in 1987 the FHLBA commissioned a review of the financial condition of CenTrust and its high yield bond investments. The review (Shapiro and Weinstein, 1987) was highly critical of CenTrust's investment practices and suggested that its focus on high yield

---

[10] By 1988, brokered deposits represented nearly half of CenTrust's total deposits and 31 percent of its total liabilities.

investments was unsafe and unsound. The review, which accompanied the FHLBA's release of a critical supplemental report of examination in June, did not lead to a cease-and-desist order partly because CenTrust reported positive earnings that month (a 43 percent increase over the same period in 1986).

The Failure of CenTrust: The Unintended Consequences of Regulation

CenTrust was able to avoid sacrificing its high yield investment strategy to the Atlanta regulators in 1987. Instead, its high yield holdings increased from 12 percent of assets in 1987 to 13 percent in 1988. However, the changing government regulation in the form of FIRREA eventually caused the failure of CenTrust.

The devastating impact of FIRREA on the high yield market in general was mirrored in its effect on CenTrust's high yield portfolio (Figure 12). From June 1986 to June 1989, the average annualized yield on the CenTrust high yield bond portfolio was 15.5 percent. In the 2 years following the passage of FIRREA the return fell to -0.4 percent.

Just as damaging as FIRREA's treatment of what was an important source of return for some savings and loans was its treatment of supervisory goodwill which could no longer be treated as capital. As with many supervisory mergers or acquisitions, the acquisition of CenTrust by Westport relied heavily on the use of supervisory goodwill and without the inclusion of its supervisory goodwill (by 1989 roughly $420 million), CenTrust was in violation of FHLBB capital standards.

Figure 11: The Impact of FIRREA on CenTrust's High Yield Bond Portfolio

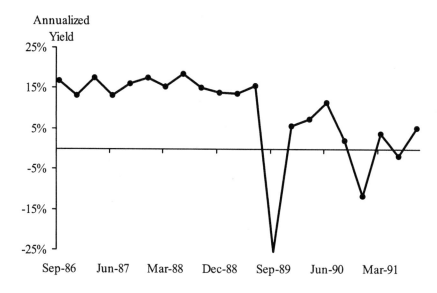

Source: Yago (1994a).

The FHLBB, recognizing this fact, informed CenTrust management that their institution was now operating in an unsafe and unsound manner and instructed them to cease payment of dividends, increase loss reserves and restrict asset growth. CenTrust management sought to save the institution by requesting that the FHLBB "grandfather" the supervisory goodwill or substitute FSLIC credit notes or cash for the $420 million. This request was rejected and the FHLBB concluded in its draft report on CenTrust for the period ending May 31, 1989, that CenTrust was undercapitalized and unable to meet the new capital adequacy requirements. In an attempt to reduce its assets and achieve compliance, CenTrust management sought the sale of three quarters of its branch network to Great Western Financial Corporation. This sale was not approved and on February 2, 1990, the Office of Thrift Supervision (the FHLBB's successor) seized CenTrust.

Postscript: Alternative Resolution Scenarios for CenTrust

The task of liquidating CenTrust's high yield bond portfolio fell to the Resolution Trust Corporation (RTC). The RTC sold the entirety of CenTrust's portfolio, which had a face value of $907 million and a book value of $887 million for just $433 million – a discount of 51 cents on the dollar from book value. The value of high yield bonds in general had declined sharply in the late 1980s and early 1990s and thus it is fair to assume that this generalized decline would have eroded the value of CenTrust's high yield portfolio to some extent. However, this general decline in the market cannot account for all of the losses the RTC realized in the liquidation of CenTrust's high yield bond assets.

The RTC also mispriced bonds using an inappropriate pricing method known as "matrix pricing." Many of CenTrust's bonds were private placements and thus lacked traded prices. In the absence of market prices, the RTC sought to derive prices for these securities based on comparisons with publicly traded bonds with similar features such as coupon, duration, callability, size of issue and so on. Matrix pricing cannot be used, however, when the publicly traded debt that is being used as a benchmark is volatile. Using publicly traded high yield bonds as reference assets was inappropriate given the degree of volatility their prices displayed, especially at that time.

Figure 12: The Performance CenTrust's High Yield Bond Portfolio

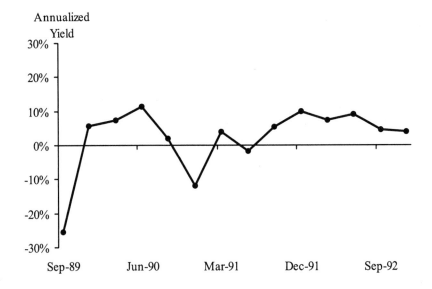

Source: Yago (1994a).

Had the RTC frozen CenTrust's high yield portfolio at the date of the institution's failure, made no new purchases of high yield bonds, but held each issue to maturity investing all coupons and redeemed principle in high grade corporate debt, the outcome for the taxpayer would have been superior (Figure 13) (Yago, 1994a). Rather than selling the bonds at huge discounts, the RTC would have realized positive gains on the portfolio once the high yield market recovered from the impact of heavy-handed government regulation. An even more beneficial strategy would have been for the portfolio's coupons and redeemed principle to be invested in high yield bonds which strongly outperformed other classes of debt in 1991 and 1992 (Figure 14).

Figure 13: High Yield and AA Corporate Bond Indices – Comparative Performance

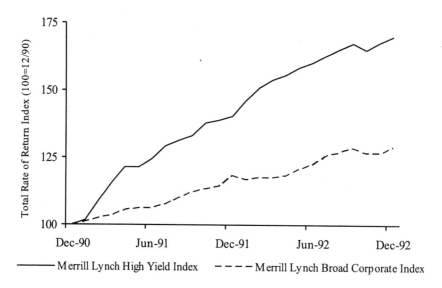

Source: Merrill Lynch.

COLUMBIA

Columbia Savings and Loan was a Beverly Hills, California based savings and loan that was seized by the Office of Thrift Supervision on January 25, 1991. At its date of seizure, Columbia had assets of nearly $5.4 billion and deposits of $5.6 billion.[11] The resolution of Columbia was estimated by the FDIC to cost $275 million.

Background

Columbia had its origins in Eastland Savings and Loan Association, a small savings and loan purchased in 1975 by Abraham Spiegel, a prominent Los Angeles real estate developer. The Czech-born Spiegel invested a

---

[11] Federal Deposit Insurance Corporation, *Bank and Thrift Failure Reports.*

substantial portion of his personal capital in the institution and renamed it Columbia Savings and Loan. In 1977, Abraham Spiegel's son, Thomas Spiegel, joined Columbia in the capacity of Vice President. By 1980, Columbia was a moderately sized savings and loan with assets of $231 million that were mainly concentrated in traditional 1-to-4 family home loans. Residential mortgages comprised more than 75 percent of Columbia's total assets in 1980.

The Condition of Columbia in the Early 1980s

Like many other savings and loans, Columbia's traditional home lending business had been rendered unprofitable by the high interest rates and inverted yield that were the result of Federal Reserve Chairman Paul Volcker's tough monetary policy. Additionally, the end of Regulation Q increased the competition for deposits and further eroded Columbia's financial strength.

By 1980, Columbia was no longer profitable and was losing money at a rate of over $3 million annually by 1981 (Table 16). At the same time, its tangible capital-to-assets ratio plunged from 9 percent in 1977 to 2 percent in 1981 (Table 17). This collapse was mirrored in its GAAP and regulatory capital-to-assets ratios.

Table 16: Columbia's Net Income (thousands)

	1977	1978	1979	1980	1981
Net Income	$703.8	$751.1	$481.9	- $615.1	-$3,049.4

Source: Thrift Financial Reports Database, Milken Institute.

Table 17: Columbia's Tangible Capital-to-Assets Ratio

	1977	1978	1979	1980	1981
Tangible capital	8.8%	8.4%	7.8%	5.5%	2.0%

Source: Thrift Financial Reports Database, Milken Institute.

Abraham Spiegel proposed an increase in acquisition and development lending, a business that in the early 1980s accounted for less than one percent of the institution's assets. Nonetheless, it was a market Spiegel felt confident in entering, given his extensive experience as a developer. Abraham Spiegel's son was strongly opposed to this strategy, arguing that Columbia was too small a savings and loan to deal effectively with developers. Eventually, following his threat to resign, Thomas Spiegel's views prevailed. Father ceded control of the savings and loan son, retaining a position as chairman emeritus of Columbia's board of directors.[12]

---

[12] *National Mortgage News*, January 22, 1990, p.12.

Columbia's Adaptation to the Challenges of the 1980s

Under Thomas Spiegel's leadership, Columbia was transformed from a traditional savings and loan engaged in home mortgage lending to a financial services firm involved in home lending, securities investing, direct real estate investment and, ultimately, corporate finance. This process of transformation was to take a number of years but began in earnest soon after Thomas Spiegel took control of the savings and loan. Beginning in 1981, Columbia's portfolio of residential mortgages was reduced as a share of total, falling from 76 percent of total assets in 1980 to 43 percent in 1981 and just 20 percent in 1982. Although Columbia's holdings of residential mortgages fell as a share of total assets, they continued to grow in absolute terms from 1980 to 1982 (Figure 15).

As Columbia reduced the importance of its home loan portfolio, it rapidly increased its holdings of marketable securities, notably mortgage-backed bonds, both in absolute terms and as a share of total assets. In 1980, Columbia held just $8 million of mortgage securities. By 1981, Columbia had increased its investments by more than 550 percent to $53.3 million and a further 250 percent to $192.4 million in 1982.

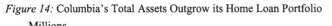

Figure 14: Columbia's Total Assets Outgrow its Home Loan Portfolio

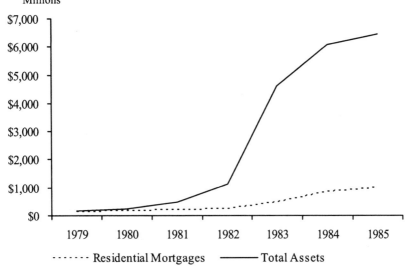

Source: Thrift Financial Repost Database, Milken Institute.

Mortgage-backed bonds were not the only securities Columbia used to diversify its portfolio. In 1981, Columbia began investing in non-mortgage investment securities and in 1982, it started buying corporate bonds. In addition to tradable securities, the institution became involved in direct real estate investments, an asset that grew from 2 percent of total assets in 1982 to 30 percent in 1984.

The year 1983 saw Columbia increase its total assets by 311 percent, with much of the increase due to growth in the institution's holdings of mortgage bonds, especially Ginnie Mae securities (Flynn, 1985). Columbia's total liabilities similarly increased, with growth due to a 5-fold increase in Federal Home Loan Bank of San Francisco advances, growth in savings accounts that were the result of the aggressive marketing of CDs, and increased reliance on brokered deposits. Brokered deposits, deposits obtained by savings and loans through a nonbank deposit broker, were increasingly used by fast growing savings and loans like Columbia that were unable to raise sufficient deposits through traditional marketing. Columbia was to become one of the industry's heaviest users of the product (Figure 16).

Figure 15: Columbia's Brokered Deposits as Share of Total Liabilities

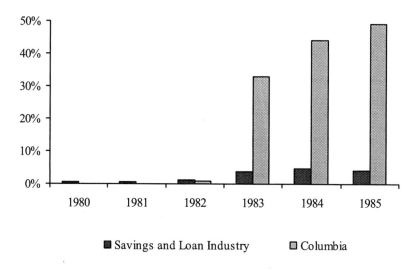

■ Savings and Loan Industry   ▨ Columbia

Source: Thrift Financial Report Database, Milken Institute.

As Columbia diversified away from traditional home lending, its net income rose and the institution returned to profitability in 1982 (Figure 17). Although Columbia sought to maximize the yield on its portfolio and to lower its cost of funds through issuing CDs, the institution's net interest income fell sharply from 1983 and Columbia's impressive earnings were due chiefly to gains on securities sales (Yago, 1994b).

By the mid-1980s, Columbia was a profitable institution but its traditionally strong capitalization had suffered from its rapid asset growth. Columbia's tangible capital-to-assets ratio had fallen to 4 percent in 1984 as its capital failed to keep pace with its asset growth. Recognizing this weakness, Columbia's management strengthened its capitalization by increasing its tangible capital from $145 million in 1984 to $269 million in 1985 and to $492 million by 1986 (Table 18).

Figure 16: Columbia's Income Sources

Millions

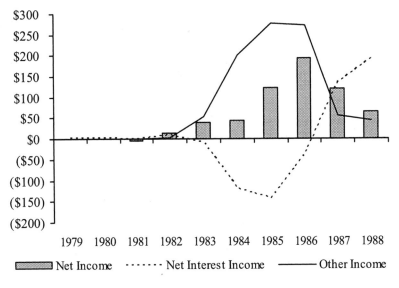

Source: Thrift Financial Report Database, Milken Institute.

Table 18: Columbia's Tangible Capital and Tangible Capital-to-Assets Ratio

	1984	1985	1986	1987	1988
Capital (millions)	$145	$269	$492	$614	$676
Capital-to-Assets	4.2%	4.2%	6.0%	6.1%	5.8%

Source: Thrift Financial Reports Database, Milken Institute.

As management sought to increase the institution's capital, it also sought out new business opportunities that could boost its interest income. The need for increased interest earning assets was strengthened by the fact that, from January 1985, one of Columbia's major business lines, direct real estate investment, was negatively impacted by a new Federal Home Loan Bank Board (FHLBB) regulation. The FHLBB limited savings and loans holdings of direct real estate investments to no more than ten percent of total assets or twice regulatory net worth. At 30 percent of total assets, Columbia's direct investment portfolio was three times larger than permitted by the new FHLBB rules.

Columbia believed it had found an important new source of interest earning assets in high yield bonds. Columbia had no net holding of high yield bonds in 1984, but by the following year, high yield bonds comprised 32 percent of total assets. By 1988, Columbia's high yield portfolio had more than doubled to nearly $4 billion, 34 percent of total assets (Table 19). As Columbia's high yield holdings increased, so did its interest earning assets and its net interest income became positive, eclipsing other income as a source of profitability (see Figure 17 earlier).

Table 19: Columbia's High Yield Bond Portfolio

	1985	1986	1987	1988	1989
High Yield Holdings ($ millions)	$2,051	$2,602	$3,339	$3,994	$4,114*
Share of Total Assets	32%	32%	33%	34%	35%

* As of September 1989

Source: Thrift Financial Reports Database, Milken Institute; American Banker.

The Failure of Columbia: The Unintended Consequences of Regulation

Just after the Financial Institutions Reform and Recovery Act (FIRREA) was passed in 1989, Columbia had a tangible capital-to-assets ratio of 5.82 percent, nearly twice the 3 percent minimum stipulated by FIRREA. However, the treatment of high yield bonds by FIRREA would prove the undoing of the institution. Columbia was required to divest its holdings of high yield bonds and was further required to immediately mark its portfolio to market. The impact of this legislation on Columbia's portfolio was nearly immediate. The market value of the bonds collapsed by $320 million in October and November 1989 resulting in a $130 million write-down on the bonds and a third quarter loss of $226 million.

By year end 1989, Columbia had lost $591 million, $465 million from write-downs on the institution's high yield bonds and from provisions for credit losses on securities and real estate loans. From a position of adequate capitalization, Columbia had been reduced to insolvency in a matter of months. By the first quarter of 1990, Columbia's high yield portfolio had a face value of $3,800 million but a market value of just $2,880, an average discount of almost 25 percent.

At this time, efforts were made to dispose of Columbia's loss-making high yield bond portfolio. In July 1990, Columbia Savings, now led by Merrill

Lynch's Edward Harshfield, announced that a buyer had been found in the form of Gordon America L.P., whose investors included General Electric Capital Corporation. Gordon America agreed to purchase the portfolio which had a market value of $2.9 billion, for $3.1 billion in a complicated transaction that involved $300 million in cash and the issuance of $2.9 billion of debt collateralized by the high yield portfolio. The purchase, that would reduce Columbia's capital deficit by approximately 50 percent, required the approval of the newly formed Office of Thrift Supervision (OTS). The OTS objected to the deal, citing the $300 million cash payment – slightly more than 10 percent of the portfolio's market value – as too low. Negotiations continued between the OTS, Gordon America and Columbia until Gordon America abruptly cut their original offer in half – to $1,500 million. At this point the OTS halted the proceedings and seized the institution, adding Columbia's nearly $3 billion of high yield bonds to the $3.7 billion that the Resolution Trust Corporation (RTC) already owned.

Having precipitated the untimely demise of Columbia Savings the government then launched a costly and, ultimately wholly unsuccessful, prosecution of Thomas Spiegel. Spiegel was indicted on charges ranging improperly obtaining common-stock warrants to knowingly accepting false financial statements from a borrower. Spiegel's trial began in October 1994, more than two years after he was indicted. The proceedings lasted only some two months and the jury took just two hours to acquit Thomas Spiegel on all 45 counts. One of the few savings and loan executives who preferred to defend himself in court rather than accept a settlement, Spiegel's vindication came at a high cost – the loss of the bulk of the family fortune and the destruction of his banking career and his institution.

Postscript: Alternative Resolution Scenarios for Columbia

If Columbia's high yield portfolio had been frozen in August 1989 with no new purchases of high yield bonds but held each issue to maturity investing all coupons and redeemed principle in high grade corporate debt, the outcome for the taxpayer would have been superior (Yago, 1994b). If the proposed sale of Columbia's high yield portfolio to Gordon America had been allowed and the proceeds invested in high grade bonds, a similar result would have occurred. However, allowing Columbia to maintain an actively managed high yield bond portfolio would have produced the best possible results for the taxpayer and Columbia's shareholders (Figure 18, where Case 1 represents the strategy of freezing Columbia's portfolio, Case 2 that of liquidating the portfolio and investing the sale proceeds in investment grade debt and Case 3 allowing an actively managed high yield portfolio). Rather than having the RTC sell the bonds at a steep discount, this strategy would have allowed the institution to remain in an asset class that strongly outperformed other classes of debt in 1991 and 1992 (Figure 14).

Figure 17: Alternative Resolutions for Columbia: Return on Assets

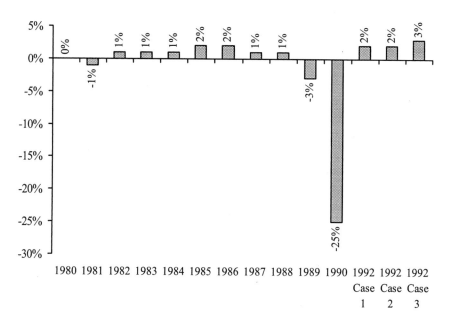

Source: Yago (1994b)

WORLD SAVINGS

World Savings is one of the survivors of the turbulent 1980s. It was one of the few profitable institutions during the first phase of the savings and loan crisis and averaged double-digit earnings growth throughout the decade. World Saving's holding company, Golden West Financial, is currently the second largest savings and loan in the U.S. in terms of assets.[13]

Background

World Savings was formed in 1975 with the merger of World Savings and Golden West Savings. Both were California-based institutions. World

---

[13] Federal Deposit Insurance Corporation, *Twenty-Five Largest Banking Companies,* August 2002.

Savings was established in 1912 in Madera, California and Golden West in 1929 in Oakland, California. In 1959, World Savings expanded beyond the California market by purchasing Colorado-based Guardian Savings and Loan. The combined institution had $90 million in assets and six branches. In 1963, Herbert and Marion Sandler purchased Golden West which then had just two branches and $38 million in assets. The post-merger savings and loan adopted the World Savings brand, and under the Sandlers' leadership grew to more than 130 branches and $4.9 billion in assets by 1980. In 1981, World Savings converted to a state-chartered institution.

The Condition of World Savings in the Early 1980s

World Savings was a fairly large institution with assets of $4.9 billion in 1981. Unlike many other savings and loans, World Savings had remained profitable in the late 1970s and in 1980 by avoiding the trap of lending long and borrowing short. In 1978, World Savings decreased its new home loan originations, and bought short term assets. World Savings substantially increased its holdings of medium-term, fixed-rate advances from the Home Loan Bank of San Francisco and invested the proceeds in cash and short term securities. As interest rates rose from the fourth quarter of 1978 to the first quarter of 1980 and the yield curve inverted, the yield on World Savings' short term assets rose faster than the yields on its long term liabilities and – unlike those savings and loans who had short term liabilities and long term assets – its net interest margin was strongly positive (Table 20) and the institution was highly profitable. However, as interest rates fell sharply in the second quarter of 1980 and the long term rates rose above short term rates, World Savings' previously advantageous asset mix proved a liability as yields on its short term assets fell more quickly than those on its long term liabilities and its margin became negative.

Table 20: World Savings' Net Interest Income (millions)

	1979	1980	1981	1982
Net Interest Income	$62.44	$51.36	-$18.66	-$14.27

Source: Thrift Financial Reports Database, Milken Institute.

In May 1980, World Savings began heavy trading of Ginnie Mae mortgage-backed securities, buying an estimated $750 million in the second quarter of the year and selling $350 million. By year-end 1980, World Savings had bought $2 billion, sold $1.1 billion and had increased its outstanding position in Ginnie Maes from just over $100 million to $1.1 billion. This trading activity allowed the institution to realize almost $40 million in trading gains and boosted World Savings' pretax reported profits

Donald McCarthy

from \$20.2 million to over \$60 million. These gains were made even as Ginnie Mae prices fell throughout the mid- to late 1980 (Figure 19).

Figure 18: Lehman Brothers Ginnie Mae Price Index (monthly)

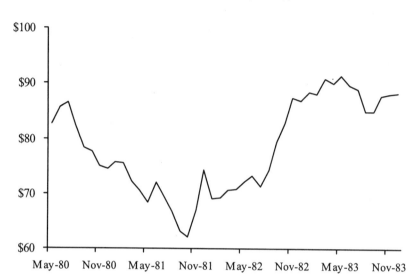

Source: Lehman Brothers

By the second quarter of 1981, World Savings' unbroken 57 quarters of ever higher earnings had come to an end.[14] Losses on its previously profitable short term assets, combined with losses from unprofitable long positions in Ginnie Maes, depressed the institution's earnings and caused it to join the ranks of suffering savings and loans. Herbert Sandler, co-CEO of World Savings, summarized their plight in 1981, remarking that Golden West (had) relied on income from trading mortgage-backed securities to continue its earnings record. The income from those activities in the second quarter fell below the first-quarter level and was insufficient to compensate for an increasingly negative spread between the average yield on earnings assets and the cost of funds.[15]

World Savings' Adaptation to the Challenges of the 1980s

In 1981, regulators allowed savings and loans to offer adjustable rate mortgages (ARM) in an act that effectively superseded the more restrictive

---

[14] *The American Banker*, July 21, 1981 p. 3.
[15] *The American Banker*, July 21, 1981 p. 3.

variable rate mortgages (VRM) and renegotiable rate mortgages (RRM)[16] (Barth, 1991). The ARM was to become the main lending vehicle of World Savings. Unlike other institutions, World Savings chose not to shift significant assets into VRMs or RRMs when they were introduced as they were imperfect in their ability to reduce interest rate risk and could not be readily disposed of on the secondary market. In the ARM, the Sandlers had found an instrument that would allow World Savings to return to the traditional savings and loan business of making home loans while avoiding exposure to interest rate risk. After the introduction of the ARM, World Savings again began to originate large numbers of home loans, the great bulk of them adjustable rate mortgages. World Savings had, by 1981, reduced its portfolio of home loans to such an extent that they accounted for just over 51 percent of the institution's total assets. Following the introduction of the ARM, this percentage would grow every year of the 1980s, reaching nearly 80 percent of total assets by 1989. At the same time, Worlds Savings' portfolio of mortgage backed securities as a share of assets began to recede from its 1982 high (Figure 20). As the institution reduced its holdings of mortgage bonds and certificates it was also able to once again realize trading gains that boosted first quarter earnings in 1983 and sparked a sharp increase in Golden West's share price.

---

[16] Variable rate mortgages had interest rates that could be adjusted by 50 basis points annually. Renegotiable rate mortgages have interest rates that can be adjusted at specified intervals (usually three or five years).

Figure 19: World Savings' Residential Mortgage and Mortgage Securities Portfolios as Share
of Total Assets

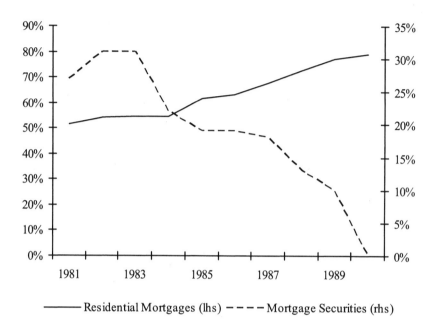

—————— Residential Mortgages (lhs) – – – – Mortgage Securities (rhs)

Source: Thrift Financial Reports Database, Milken Institute.

Herbert and Marion Sandler thus began to recast World Savings as a
traditional savings and loan, collecting savings deposits and originating home
mortgages. This was in marked contrast to much of the rest of the savings and
loan industry, where operators increasingly favored non-traditional business
lines funded by brokered deposits. As other institutions shifted assets into
increasingly complicated and unfamiliar products that required management
to develop new skills to operate safely and profitably, World Savings made
simplicity a hallmark of its business. As other savings and loans grew rapidly
at the expense of their capitalization, World Savings was able to combine a
fairly impressive asset growth rate with the maintenance of a GAAP capital-
to-assets ration that was greater than the industry as a whole. As seen in
Figure 21, which plots a three-year moving average of the total asset growth
rates of World Savings and the savings and loan industry and the GAAP
capital-to-assets ratios for World Savings and for all savings and loans, World
Savings was able to grow faster than the industry while remaining better
capitalized.

Figure 20: World Savings' Asset Growth and GAAP Capital-to-Assets Ratio Compared to All Savings and Loans

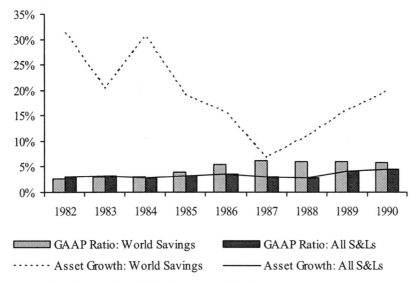

Source: Thrift Financial Reports Database, Milken Institute.

World Savings combined its focus on the traditional savings and loan business of home lending and its prudent growth with a dedication to controlling operating costs. Recognizing that branches could potentially be a drain on revenues, World Savings aggressively sought to control overhead costs by paring down the numbers of branch employees and using part-time employees whenever possible. World Savings' dedication to cost control was famously reflected in its modest Oakland, California headquarters where visitors were surprised to find no receptionist to greet them.

World Savings and FIRREA

World Savings' conservative growth strategy served it well after the Congress passed FIRREA. While those savings and loans that had relied on goodwill to maintain capital compliance or had sought to grow their way to solvency found themselves noncompliant with FIRREA's changes, Golden West substantially exceeded the new capital requirements. Additionally, its focus on traditional savings and loan business lines and its lack of substantial non-traditional assets proved fortuitous as this shielded World Savings from the unintended consequences of regulations governing riskier assets that were introduced as part of FIRREA. Rather than present a challenge to World Savings, FIRREA presented an opportunity.

World Savings was able to expand into other states relatively inexpensively following FIRREA as it was able to purchase the assets or branches of troubled and failed savings and loans. Indeed, as Golden West's 1990 annual report remarked: "we have found ourselves in a buyer's market for savings and loan branch networks, a situation that will undoubtedly exist for the foreseeable future." In May 1990, World Savings purchased 12 branches and $696 million in deposits of the failed Federal Savings of Colorado from the Resolution Trust Corporation (RTC). World Savings subsequently closed eight of the branches and incorporated the remaining four into its existing Colorado operations. The following month, World Savings bought $13 million of deposits from the RTC of the insolvent Missouri-based Blue Valley Savings. These deposits were then consolidated into World Savings' Kansas operations. In September 1990, World Savings acquired the solvent but marginally profitable Community Federal Savings of New Jersey that had assets of $457 million and a network of six branches. The following year, World Savings returned to the market to purchase the Florida institution, Beach Federal, with assets of $1.5 billion and 15 branches from the RTC. World Savings renamed the institution World Savings and Loan Association of Florida when it agreed to take title to the failed savings and loan following the Federal Deposit Insurance Corporation's prepayment of a $1 billion Federal Savings and Loan Insurance Corporation promissory note and World's $100 million capital infusion.[17] Finally, World Savings entered the Arizona mortgage market through its acquisition from the RTC of three branches, $143.5 million of deposits and $1 million of assets of the failed Scottsdale-based Security Savings.

FIRREA provided World Savings with an attractive opportunity to expand its deposit base and its branch network, both at low cost. It did not, however, change the fundamental strategy that Herbert and Marion Sandler had devised for the institution in the early 1980s. Throughout the 1990s and into the next century, World Savings continued to develop as a leading low-cost originator of 1-to-4 family mortgages through its extensive network of branches. By 2002, World Savings was still run by Herbert and Marion Sandler, had expanded its branch network to include 263 offices in all but 11 of the 48 contiguous states, and had grown to $62 billion in assets.

---

[17] *The American Banker*, July 22, 1991, p. 14.

REFERENCES

Barth, James R. (1991). *The Great Savings and Loan Debacle*. Washington, D.C.: AEI.

Barth, James R. and R. Dan Brumbaugh (1996). "The Condition and Regulation of Madison Guaranty Savings and Loan in the 1980s: A Case Study of Regulatory Failure." In Kaufman, G. G. *Research in Financial Services: Private and Public Policy*. Greenwich, CT.: JAI Press.

Federal Deposit Insurance Corporation (2001). Managing the Crisis: The FDIC and RTC Experience. Washington, D.C.: Federal Deposit Insurance Corporation

Flynn, T. J. (1985). *Columbia Savings and Loan Rolls On*. New York: Morgan Stanley.

General Accounting Office (1988). *High Yield Bonds: Nature of the Market and Effect on Federally Insured Institutions.* Washington, D.C.: General Accounting Office.

Imperial Corporation of America (1986). *Financial Strategy Report*. San Diego: Imperial Corporation of America.

Kane, Edward J. (1989). The S&L Insurance Mess: How Did it Happen? Washington, D.C.: The Urban Institute Press.

Kane, Edward J. (2003). *"What Lessons Might Crisis Countries in Asia and Latin America Have Learned From the S&L Mess?"* In Barth, J. R., Trimbath, S. and Yago, G. (eds.). *What Can an Examination of Savings & Loans Reveal about Financial Institutions, Markets and Regulation?* Boston, MA: Kluwer Academic Press.

Kaufman, George G. (2001). *The Failure of Superior Federal Bank, FSB: Implications and Lessons*. Statement before the U.S. Senate Committee on Banking, Housing, and Urban Affairs.

Office of the Comptroller of the Currency (1979). *Uniform Financial Institutions Rating System*. Washington, D.C.: Office of the Comptroller of the Currency.

Shapiro, Alan and M. Weinstein (1987). *The Investment Practices of CenTrust Savings Bank.* Atlanta: Federal Home Loan Bank of Atlanta.

Yago, Glenn (1994a). Analysis of CenTrust's High Yield Portfolio. Expert witness report.

Yago, Glenn (1994b). *Regulating Into Decline: FIRREA and the Unmaking of a Financial Institution.* New York: City University of New York.

Yago, Glenn and Jane Bozewicz (1998). *Analysis of ICA High Yield Investment Strategy.* Expert witness report.

Yago, Glenn and Donald Siegel (1994). "Triggering High Yield Market Decline: Regulatory Barriers in Financial Markets." *Merrill Lynch Extra Credit* 21.

SUMMING UP:

DO SAVINGS AND LOANS PROVIDE A USEFUL PERSPECTIVE?

Kenneth J. Thygerson
Digital University;
Former CEO, Freddie Mac and Imperial
Corporation of America

INTRODUCTION

The Anderson School of Management and Milken Institute Research Roundtable has provided an excellent forum for bringing together many of the nation's experts in financial structure and regulation to review the origins and causes of the savings and loan debacle. After hundreds of studies by professionals from virtually every discipline, it's pretty clear that our research shelves are now full of quality studies about the debacle and its causes.

This leaves the obvious question: "What else is left to say on the subject?" The answer is: "not much." About all that can be done is to try to synthesize this work in such a way as to provide some prospective and suggest some implications for today's policy makers.

Economists, academics, public policy makers, regulators, lawyers, trade executives, politicians and business persons have now all presented their cases. The limitation in this process, if any really exists, is that each of these analysts has a somewhat limited perspective based on the professional training of the author and any bias they have based on where they were and what they were doing at the time the savings and loan debacle unfolded. This is inevitable and appropriate since the reason so many papers were written was to bring to light the many facets of the debacle.

It is the modest goal of this paper to try to pull together the pieces of this multifaceted puzzle in order to provide perspective and completeness to the savings and loan debacle story.

Let's start by identifying the leading causes from an historical perspective.

CREATING AN INFLEXIBLE FINANCIAL SYSTEM

The first set of causes largely summarizes decisions that produced what we now view as the modern history of our financial system. This list describes the most important decisions made by previous Congresses and Administrations that gave us our post-1930s financial structure. As we now know, and as the Commission on Money and Credit and the Hunt Commission concluded in their assessments years before, that structure would prove vulnerable to the competitive and macroeconomic shocks that began to appear in the mid-1960s.

Compartmentalism and Price Controls

Congress creates a highly structured financial system in the 1930s which compartmentalizes different types of financial institutions (i.e., banks, savings and loans, credit unions and investment banks) and attempts to protect them from competition by using price (i.e. interest rate) controls (i.e., Regulation Q and fixed brokerage exchange rates).

Deposit Insurance and Raised Limits

Congress creates the Federal Deposit Insurance Corp. and Federal Savings and Loan Insurance Corp. deposit insurance schemes and over the years expands the maximum deposit insurance amount. This sharply increases moral hazard throughout the various insurance depository systems.

Extends Price Controls to Savings and Loans

Congress extends rate controls to savings and loans when the first signs of macroeconomic stress appear in the mid-1960s. Unregulated savings and loans begin to compete nationwide for deposits with many California savings and loans attracting deposits from the rest of the country.

Prohibits Variable-Rate Mortgages

Congress delays authorization of variable rate mortgages due to pressure from homebuilders and realtors forcing federally chartered savings and loans to continue to originate and hold fixed-rate mortgages.

Denies Use of Due-on-Sale Clauses

In 1981, Congress prohibits mortgage investors from exercising "due on sale clauses" found in most fixed-rate mortgages. This results in savings and loans holding low-rate fixed-rate mortgages for longer periods.

Branching Restrictions Reduce Diversification

The Federal Home Loan Bank Board imposes restrictions on interstate branching of federally chartered savings and loans. This contributes to the undue and unnecessary concentration of risk in several regional real estate markets.

ACTIONS TO REDUCE THE IMPACT OF INSTITUTIONAL RIGIDITIES AND PRICE CONTROLS

The second set of causes was actions taken in the 1970s and 1980s largely to reduce the impact of institutional rigidities and price controls. In order to respond to the painful shocks these caused, various Congresses and Administrations added fuel to the potential savings and loan debacle by attempting to protect consumers from financial risks while simultaneously bringing new capital into the savings and loan industry.

Creates New Mortgage Competitors

Congress moved to correct the rigidity in the financial system which gave rise to periods of "disintermediation" by privatizing the Federal National Mortgage Corporation (Fannie Mae; 1968) and creating the Government National Mortgage Corporation (Ginnie Mae; 1968) and the Federal Home Loan Mortgage Corporation (Freddie Mac; 1970). These firms were justified as a solution to the lack of interregional flows of funds caused by interstate branching restrictions. The government sponsored enterprises (GSEs) had a lower cost of capital for investing in mortgages than savings and loans or banks and were able to out-compete the depositories by bidding up mortgage prices and reducing mortgage rates. The result was that many specialized mortgage portfolio lenders determined that home mortgages were largely unprofitable as portfolio investments. This caused them to consider more risky investments.

Mutual-stock Conversions and Moral Hazard

Congress increased "moral hazard" in the industry by authorizing "mutual-to-stock" conversions of savings and loans in order to shore up the capital of some of the industry. The impact was a sharp increase in risk-taking by management and shareholders of many savings and loans. Many risk-takers, such as developers and others, entered the industry when they realized the potential risk/rewards of a depositor insurance system that could be leveraged to take risk.

The continued relatively low risk of the totally mutual credit union industry is a good juxtaposition to the savings and loan situation after conversion to stock institutions. Credit union management and directors have little incentive to take risks that could result in insolvency of their institutions.

Expanded Asset/Liability Powers

Garn-St Germain and actions by state legislators tried to assist the savings and loan profit problems by authorizing expanded asset and liability powers. This was done without changing capital requirements (e.g., the current risk-based approach) or modifying deposit insurance coverage and/or its cost.

DEREGULATION OF PRICE CONTROLS IN A HOSTILE ECONOMIC SETTING

Economic and political pressures combined in the 1970s to bring down the system of price controls at the time of unprecedented high open-market interest rates and financial turmoil.

Financial Innovation Threatens System

Financial innovations such as commercial paper (1960s), money market mutual funds (1970s) and Negotiable Order of Withdrawal accounts (1970s) all served to weaken the effectiveness of price controls and destroy that system.

Political Pressures to Dismantle Price Controls

By the late 1980s, political lobbying groups such as the Gray Panthers testified in Congress that older Americans were denied market interest rates on savings because of Regulation Q. This put pressure on Congress to dismantle the system.

Monetary Policy Blunders

Monetary-induced inflation in the 1970s and the introduction of Volker's money-growth-rate target policies resulted in record high interest rates that put the savings and loan industry into technical insolvency based on any reasonable mark-to-market valuations of assets and liabilities by early 1982.

Tax Reform Act Reduces Real Estate Values

The Tax Reform Act of 1986 contributed to the problems of some savings and loans by reducing the after-tax cash flows from many income-producing real estate investments and eliminating the incentive for passive investors such as limited-partnerships to purchase real estate. The result was lower collateral values for many savings and loan loans.

Inadequate Interest Rate Risk Financial Management Tools

The state of the art and the use of interest rate risk management tools was wholly inadequate until the early 1980s. Most of the tools that are taken for granted by regulators today were not developed and used until the problem of interest rate risk had done its damage.

REGULATORY FORBEARANCE AND/OR LIQUIDATION: THE DILEMMA

Once the savings and loan industry fell into technical insolvency, the policy choices were few and painful. The Federal Home Loan Bank Board was faced with a combination of two policy options: forbearance and liquidation.

A crude analysis of the extent of the insolvency indicates that as of December 1981, the market value of the savings and loan industry's mortgages with an average note rate of 10.02 percent when marked-to-market at the then current prevailing mortgage rate of 15.58 percent was approximately $103 billion less than their book value. This loss of market value overwhelmed the year-end 1981 savings and loan book value of capital of $28 billion.[1] Clearly, the cost of liquidation would have been huge.

The above analysis, although rough and incomplete, leaves open the question of whether forbearance or liquidation was the best course of action in the early 1980s. With perfect hindsight, it seems clear that a combination of the two approaches was probably the best course of action. Yet, clearly too many bankruptcy-bound savings and loans were allowed to continue to operate after their ongoing-concern value had been totally wiped out, thus increasing the incentive for management to deploy go-for-broke strategies. These were firms with a significant amount of capital represented by

---

[1] Data were taken from the *1981 Savings & Home Financing Sourcebook*, Federal Home Loan Bank Board, July 1982. The industry's total mortgages as of year-end 1981 with an average yield of 10.02 percent were amortized at 10 percent of principal per year for 8 years and then assumed to payoff. The resulting cash flows of interest and principal were discounted at the December 1981 current mortgage rate of 15.58 percent. The future value resulted in an estimated $75 billion liquidation loss, after wiping out savings and loan capital in 1981 dollars, and a loss of $127 billion in 1990 dollars. This turned out to be fairly close to the total cost to the U.S. Treasury of the savings and loan bailout.

substantial assets held in goodwill and other intangibles and considerable net worth held as subordinated debt and regulatory net worth (e.g., appraised equity capital). We can make two important points about the period.

Tax Cuts versus Savings and Loan Bailout

The election of Ronald Reagan in 1980 brought a new group of economic and financial policymakers to Washington, D.C. The Administration ran on a platform of cutting federal income taxes. Clearly, recognition on the budget of some or all of the huge savings and loan losses resulting from a decision to begin liquidation of many insolvent savings and loans in early 1981 would have probably killed the chances of a tax reduction bill. As a result, forbearance, introduced with hopes of lower market interest rates in the years ahead, was the chosen policy until the late 1980s.

Forbearance Policies

Forbearance policies took many forms: (1) reducing net worth requirements; (2) using appraised equity appreciation for office real estate held by savings and loans to count as capital; (3) authorizing subordinated debt as capital; (4) authorizing and encouraging mergers using purchase-asset accounting to create goodwill; and (5) encouraging savings and loan acquisitions by investors seeking access to insured funds for risky investments (e.g., developers). These were all examples of the forbearance tactics that largely succeeded in keeping the industry cosmetically "alive" as interest rates fell in the early 1980s and asset values were being restored.

FRAUD AND CORRUPTION

The most sensational and, therefore, newsworthy aspect of the savings and loan debacle story was related to self dealing, political payoffs and fraud. These stories captured the headlines even though the costs of these problems represented a very small percentage of the total costs imposed on taxpayers.

Many of these problems clearly were the result of lax supervision of owners, managers and business plans and the increased moral hazards created by reduced capital levels, increased asset investment powers and easy fund-raising provided by brokered deposits.

RESOLUTION TRUST CORPORATION'S DISPOSITION POLICES

If an accounting could be made, there was probably as much taxpayer money lost by the Resolution Trust Corporation (RTC) disposing of assets as was lost through fraud and corruption. The RTC was created in 1989 to liquidate and manage the assets of failed savings and loans. Through July 1992, the RTC assumed control of 718 savings and loans with total assets of $382.9 billion.

The primary objective of the RTC was to maximize the net present value of the cash flows generated by the assumed assets through holding or liquidation. The problem with the RTC was that, under pressure to act, it acquired "…a philosophy of sell, sell, sell." (*The Wall Street Journal*, October 3, 1991.) Thomas Horton, the RTC's deputy director of asset sales remarked at the time, "We think the best thing in the world is if somebody makes money off us."

Horton's quote said it all. Among the RTC's less than optimal sales strategies were:

1. Selling risky assets with potentially high returns with put options back to the RTC.
2. Avoiding offering seller financing for risky assets that the Congress outlawed as investments by savings and loans and states outlawed for insurance companies, such as high yield bonds. The potential universe of investors in these assets was adversely affected by the new laws causing the cost of capital of potential investors to rise significantly.
3. Selling assets in large bulk packages which ensured few successful legitimate bids.

These and other hastily developed liquidation strategies caused the RTC to leave billions of dollars on the table. We will never know how much.

SUMMARY AND CONCLUSIONS: DO SAVINGS AND LOANS PROVIDE A USEFUL PERSPECTIVE?

The savings and loan debacle case study provides a useful perspective for many reasons. Just about every public policy mistake that could have been made was made during the 60-year period of modern savings and loan history. Consider the following policy suggestions resulting from our review of the savings and loan experience:

Federal and State Chartering of Institutions with Highly Restrictive Powers Eventually Makes it Impossible for These Firms to Adapt to Changes in Markets

Today's examples are Fannie Mae and Freddie Mac, which have limited authorities and find it necessary to profit by increasing their credit and interest rate risks through large on-balance-sheet portfolio investments, investments in risky security investments, large use of derivatives, and assuming higher credit risks through more liberal underwriting standards. In a few years, we should expect that these firms will outgrow the residential mortgage market they now dominate and that they will be asking for powers to originate mortgages, service mortgages, set up private mortgage insurance company subsidiaries, eliminate loan size limits, package commercial mortgages and much more.

Use of Price Controls Creates Massive Deregulation Problems

The impact of Regulation Q and its successors cannot be underestimated. Price controls have been shown to lead to protected industries that are forced to compete with non-price features and once deregulated are unable to respond quickly to the new environment. For savings and loans and banks, competition under Regulation Q took the form of many branches, free toasters, and free services. Once deregulated the restructuring costs were enormous.

Inevitably price controls lose their effectiveness and must be abandoned. This creates deregulatory transition costs that have been borne by every deregulated industry. The impact on the savings and loans' was similar to the havoc created by price deregulation of telecommunication firms, electricity and natural gas companies, security brokerages, and airlines. Deregulation of a business long subjected to price controls is a risky and potentially dangerous action. Needless-to-say, price controls are a costly policy option and should be avoided.

Creating New Firms to Solve Limitations of the Unregulated Old Firms Creates New Problems

The privatization of Fannie Mae and creation of Freddie Mac are examples of legislating new firms because the old government-created firms with restrictive structures didn't work well. The savings and loans were structured to exacerbate disintermediation due to the price controls. This was not by design; it was just the inevitable consequence.

Fannie Mae and Freddie Mac were free of these controls and therefore, their advocates argued, they were going to reduce the illiquidity problems caused by price controls. These "counter-cyclical" lenders were given very valuable powers which allowed them to dominate the residential mortgage market and all existing competitors. Rather than charter Fannie Mae and Freddie Mac, the policy makers should have fixed the savings and loans.

Investors without an Equity Stake Create Excessive Moral Hazard

Fraud is fueled unnecessarily by allowing risk takers to take risks without having an equity stake. Savings and loan capital requirements in the 1980s were set too low, given the risks inherent in the liberalized asset and liability powers granted them.

Today's equivalent are the managers granted large corporate stock options in companies in which they have little financial stake once they exercise and sell their options. The perverse incentive is to get the stock price up and sell the options.

Social Insurance Creates Moral Hazards and Supervisory Problems

Deposit insurance may be a system that has outlived its useful life. There is little evidence that increases in the insurance limits to $100,000 provided sufficient social benefits when compared to the increased moral hazard represented by the insured depositories. There is no good justification for such a high limit on insurance.

Restricting the Use of Needed Product Reforms Exacerbates the Problem

Congress' effort to avoid imposing additional risks and costs on consumers by restricting the use of variable rate mortgages and voiding the imposition of due-on-sale clauses only served to force the savings and loans to bear a cost they could not afford.

Forbearance May Bring Lower Social and Economic Costs Than Liquidation

Forbearance is a dangerous policy option because it allows comatose institutions to operate and compete against stronger firms, which ultimately weakens them, as well. However, there may be extreme market conditions and circumstances when so many firms in an industry are in a weakened state that liquidating the firms would only serve to further depress market values and create market turmoil. Forbearance can be justified for unexpected losses caused by certain unexpected external events (e.g., record high interest rates in the late 1970s and early 1980s and the impact on the value of mortgages or the September 11th terrorist attack's impact on the airline industry), but it cannot be justified for actions of management and poor loan underwriting or inadequate diversification.

An interesting present-day policy issue concerns the U.S. airlines. A public corporation has been charged with the responsibility to negotiate loan guarantees with those weak airlines facing bankruptcy. The trick will be ensuring that these comatose firms do not weaken the stronger survivors if guarantees are offered and that enough of the excess capacity is removed from the system.

Regulatory Requirements Should Be Transparent and Publicly Disclosed

The use of regulatory capital and creative accounting to increase regulatory capital at savings and loans used by the Federal Home Loan Bank Board made it nearly impossible to determine the true financial condition of these firms. Creditors, stockholders and even regulators couldn't really assess the firms.

The capital requirements and risk tests imposed by the Office of Federal Housing Enterprise Oversight (OFHEO) on Fannie Mae and Freddie Mac appear to be so complicated that even the professionals can't understand how their regulator assesses risk and capital adequacy. This system of capital requirements and risk tests should be reformed so it is more easily understood. It would also be nice to see OFHEO provide a rationale for why capital requirements for the GSEs should be different from the risk-based approach used for banks and savings and loans. Similarly, additional changes should occur for the public reporting requirements of the two government enterprises so they at least conform to Securities and Exchange Commission disclosure requirements.

Housing Subsidies Should Be Transparent

The 1930s to 1970s witnessed the use of a system of specialized savings and loan institutions to help home buyers by forcing specialization primarily into first residential home mortgages. Savings and loans were provided tax benefits and, for a while, were allowed to compete for funds with a favorable edge in the administration of Regulation Q. That system failed.

It is clear that Fannie Mae's and Freddie Mac's primary role today is to deliver a huge subsidy to mortgage borrowers who use residential housing as collateral for loans. It is also clear that this subsidy, while popular, is not efficient in promoting housing for those who need it. Most of the subsidy goes to previous homeowners in the form of refinances, with cash out to be used for other purposes, and loans to upgrade housing. It is also clear that the enormous market power of these public enterprises allows them to protect their profits and managerial benefits by merely increasing the amount of the federal subsidy that they keep for themselves.

The temptation for politicians to capture some of the GSE subsidy to reward various housing constituencies in return for their political support has become more evident in recent years. Increasingly, Fannie Mae and Freddie Mac are being asked to earmark mortgage funds for lower income households and other groups deemed disenfranchised. This *qui pro quo* could serve to weaken the financial status of these GSEs by causing them to take on additional credit risk just as the restraints on the use of variable rate mortgages and due-on-sale clauses weakened the savings and loans' financial position.

The taxpayer would be better served by privatizing these enterprises and creating a targeted transparent subsidy for homebuyers who are deemed to need it.

Charticle 7
Impact of FIRREA Was Temporary on High Yield Bonds

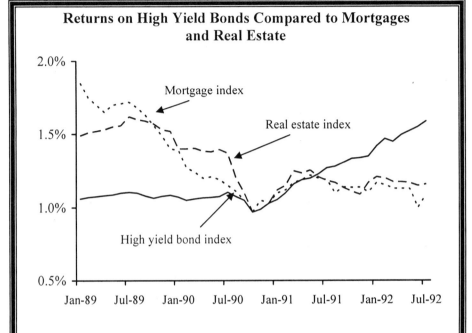

Source: Yago, Glenn (1994).

The decline of high yield was substantially lower than other asset classes held by savings and loans. Once the high yield bond market had recovered from the massive blow caused by FIRREA, its performance was quickly reversed. As mortgages and real estate spent the early 1990s in the doldrums, high yield bonds exhibited high and stable returns.

A ROUNDTABLE ON THE SAVINGS AND LOAN CRISIS

PARTICIPANTS

Bruce Willison, Dean, Anderson School of Management, University of California, Los Angeles

Michael Klowden, President and CEO, Milken Institute

James Barth, Auburn University and Milken Institute; formerly Office of Thrift Supervision and Federal Home Loan Bank Board

Philip Bartholomew, International Monetary Fund; formerly Federal Home Loan Bank Board and U.S. House Banking Committee

Gordon Bjork, Claremont McKenna College

James Bothwell, Federal Housing Finance Board; formerly General Accounting Office

Elijah Brewer, Federal Reserve Bank of Chicago

R. Dan Brumbaugh, Milken Institute; formerly Federal Home Loan Bank Board

Charlotte Chamberlain, Jefferies & Company; formerly Federal Home Loan Bank Board

Michael Darby, Anderson School of Management, University of California, Los Angeles; formerly U.S. Treasury

Mollie Dickenson, Worth Magazine

Stephen Ege, Elias, Matz, Tiernan & Eric; formerly Federal Home Loan Bank Board

Robert Eisenbeis, Federal Reserve Bank of Atlanta

Peter Elmer, Deloitte and Touche; formerly FDIC, RTC and FSLIC

Catherine England, Marymount University; formerly Cato Institute

Daniel Fischel, University of Chicago Law School

Ernest Fleischer, Blackwell Sanders Peper Martin; formerly Franklin Savings

James Freund, Research Institute for Housing America, Mortgage Bankers Association of America

Catherine Galley, Cornerstone Research

Stuart Greenbaum, Olin School of Business, Washington University; formerly Kellogg Graduate School of Management, Northwestern University and Federal Savings and Loan Advisory Council

Peter Haje, Time Warner, Inc.; formerly Paul, Weiss, Rifkind, Wharton & Garrison

William Hamm, Law and Economics Consulting Group; formerly World Savings

George Hanc, Federal Deposit Insurance Corporation

Jean Helwege, Max M. Fisher College of Business Ohio State University; formerly Federal Reserve Bank of New York

Eric Hemel, Merrill Lynch; formerly Federal Home Loan Bank Board

Anne Henry, Farchmin, Ralls Wagoner and Regulatory Watchdog; formerly Overland Park Savings and Loan

Paul Horvitz, University of Houston and Shadow Financial Regulatory Committee; formerly FDIC and Federal Home Loan Bank of Dallas

William Hunter, Federal Reserve Bank of Chicago

Michael Intriligator, University of California, Los Angeles and Milken Institute

Edward Kane, Wallace E. Carroll School of Management, Boston College

George Kaufman, Loyola University and Shadow Financial Regulatory Committee

J. Livingston Kosberg, Remington Partners; formerly Gibraltar Savings and 1st Texas Financial

William Lang, Office of the Comptroller of the Currency

Arthur Leibold, Dechert Price & Rhoads; formerly Federal Home Loan Bank Board

Thomas Lutton, U.S. Office of Federal Housing Enterprise Oversight; formerly Office of the Comptroller of the Currency and Congressional Budget Office

David Malmquist, Office of Thrift Supervision

Angelo Mascaro, Congressional Budget Office; formerly U.S. Treasury

Stephen Neal, Cooley Godward; formerly Kirkland and Ellis

Richard Nelson, Wells Fargo; formerly Federal Home Loan Bank of San Francisco

J.C. Nickens, Clements, O'Neill, Pierce, Nickens & Wilson

Gerald O'Driscoll, Center for International Trade and Economics, Heritage Foundation; formerly Federal Reserve Bank of Dallas

Peter Passell, Milken Institute

James Pearce, Welch Consulting; formerly Federal Home Loan Bank of Atlanta

F. Stevens Redburn, U.S. Office of Management and Budget

Martin Regalia, U.S. Chamber of Commerce; formerly Savings and Community Bankers of America

Jack Reidhill, Federal Deposit Insurance Corporation; formerly Resolution Trust Corporation, Federal Savings and Loan Insurance Corporation

Richard Roll, Anderson School of Management, University of California, Los Angeles; formerly Goldman, Sachs & Co.

Jeffrey Scott, Wells Fargo Bank; formerly Federal Home Loan Bank of San Francisco

William Shear, U.S. General Accounting Office

Lewis Spellman, University of Texas

Kenneth Spong, Federal Reserve Bank of Kansas City

Michael Staten, Credit Research Center, McDonough School of Business, Georgetown University

Timothy Anderson, Former banking consultant and regulatory critic

Kenneth Thygerson, Digital University; formerly Freddie Mac and Imperial Corporation of America

Walker Todd, formerly Federal Reserve Bank of Cleveland

Susanne Trimbath, Milken Institute

Robert Van Order, Freddie Mac

Mark Vaughan, Federal Reserve Bank of St. Louis

Kevin Villani, Economist; formerly Freddie Mac and Imperial Corporation of America

George Wang, Commodity Futures Trading Commission; formerly Federal Home Loan Bank Board

Lawrence White, NYU Stern School of Business; formerly Federal Home Loan Bank Board

James Wilcox, Haas School of Business, University of California at Berkeley; formerly Office of the Comptroller of the Currency

Susan Woodward, Sand Hill Econometrics; formerly Securities Exchange Commission and Council of Economic Advisors and Stanford Law School

Glenn Yago, Milken Institute

Lynne Zucker, University of California, Los Angeles

PROCEEDINGS

On January 25, 2002, the Anderson School of Management and the Milken Institute co-hosted more than seventy current and former regulators, savings and loan officers, and academics at the UCLA Faculty Center for a research roundtable titled "What Can an Examination of Savings and Loans Reveal About Financial Institutions, Markets and Regulation." The following, taken from recorded transcripts, was compiled by Donald McCarthy.

Participants were welcomed by Bruce Willison, Dean of the Anderson School, and Michael Klowden, President and CEO of the Milken Institute.

Dean Willison congratulated the conference organizers for bringing together academics and businesspeople to exchange ideas and went on to outline the program of the day. He concluded by affirming his view that the attendees would no doubt conclude that savings and loans provide a useful perspective for domestic and international financial institutions.

Michael Klowden posed an intriguing question in his opening comments. Why, he asked, was there said to be a savings and loan crisis but no NASDAQ crisis when the cost to shareholders of the fall in high tech stock prices dwarfed the cost of resolving the savings and loan industry's problems. Mr. Klowden then summarized the objective of the conference which was to ask what lessons can be drawn from the industry's experiences and how these lessons can be applied both at home and abroad.

Government Policy: Were There Unintended Consequences?

The first session of the day was introduced by Glenn Yago, Director of Capital Studies at the Milken Institute. He began by establishing an historical context for the development of the savings and loan industry and followed this with an overview of the problems facing savings and loans in the early 1980s, stressing the lack of portfolio diversification. He concluded by inviting some short introductory comments from several participants.

The first of these was from Lawrence White of the Stern School of Business, formerly board member of the Federal Home Loan Bank Board. While praising the deregulation of the asset side of savings and loans' portfolios, he regretted that deregulation had not been accompanied by enhanced safety and soundness regulation. This failure to increase supervision was, Mr. White suggested, a result of the Congress' inability to understand the industry's troubles. He concluded by stressing the need for competent supervisors, market value accounting and adequate capitalization – lessons that he felt had not yet been learned.

Mr. White was followed by R. Dan Brumbaugh of the Milken Institute, formerly with the Federal Home Loan Bank Board, who agreed with Mr. White about the desirability of market value accounting, illustrating the point with a compelling exhibit that showed that the industry as a whole was insolvent by 1981[1]. He went on to provide a characterization of the "savings and loan crisis" as a three stage event; the first caused by interest rate risk, the second by credit risk and the third by the Federal Institutions Reform, Recovery and Enforcement Act (FIRREA) itself which resulted in the still unresolved goodwill cases.

Next to speak was Ernest Fleischer of Blackwell Peper Martin, formerly Chairman of Franklin Savings, who quipped that one should describe the problems of the savings and loan industry not as a savings and loan debacle but as a *government policy* savings and loan debacle. This policy consisted of allowing market value insolvent savings and loans to try to grow their way out of insolvency but was reversed by the Congress which, he said, simply "called in its bet" and undercut the value of savings and loans and their assets. A better path, Mr. Fleischer concluded, would have been for the government to have recapitalized insolvent savings and loans in the early 1980s and then to adopt market value accounting.

Another former savings and loan officer, J. Livingston Kosberg of Remington Partners, formerly CEO of Gibraltar Savings, drew on his twenty years of savings and loan experience to bring an industry view to the discussion. He stressed that the key policy mistake of the deregulation was the failure to strengthen capital requirements. This error, Mr. Kosberg stated, was followed by the failure to implement the Southwest Plan[2] and allow open bank assistance. Instead, the crisis was dealt with in a costly and chaotic manner by the Resolution Trust Corporation (RTC) which, after the Keating Five affair, lacked adequate political oversight.

Arthur Leibold of Dechert Price, formerly General Counsel of the Bank Board, then contended that there was no coherent national savings and loan policy. Short-term goals dominated long-term thinking and fiscal policy concerns disallowed the use of the Federal Savings and Loan Insurance

---

[1] See Figure 1 in Brumbaugh, R. Dan and Catherine Galley *The Savings and Loan Crisis: Unresolved Policy Issues* in this volume.

[2] The Southwest Plan was the FHLBB plan to consolidate insolvent Texas savings and loans for sale. The idea was to allow quick resolutions without expending FSLIC reserves.

Corporation (FSLIC) funds. While the White House favored deregulation, tax cuts and lower deficits, the Congress was interested in avoiding difficult issues and raising campaign contributions from savings and loans. The result was a lack of policy that gave way to blaming third parties.

These opening remarks were then followed by a lively roundtable discussion. Kevin Villani, formerly CFO of Imperial Corporation, related some of his experiences with housing policy in transition economies as an advisor in the formerly communist countries. The lessons policy makers there seem to have taken from the U.S. are that monopoly, budgetary opacity and government price regulation are desirable.

An element of controversy then entered the discussion when Mr. Fleischer suggested that the savings and loan crisis was simply a transfer of resources from taxpayer to homeowner and had no economic cost. Mr. White disagreed pointing out the misallocation of resources caused by excessive savings and loan lending. Mr. Villani noted that the negative user cost of homeowner capital diverted savings away from more productive investments and into housing, contending that the opportunity cost of this misallocation dwarfed the cost to taxpayers of resolving the industry's problems.

Michael Intriligator of the Milken Institute and UCLA returned to the title of the opening session by asking Mr. White what some unintended consequences of government savings and loan policy were. Mr. White answered that the unintended results included the insolvency of a large number of savings and loans due to high interest rates, excessive risk-taking following deregulation, and later, the closure of savings and loans holding high yield debt. Reflecting on the RTC, he remarked that the most surprising outcome of its sale of billions of dollars of savings and loan assets was the lack of a single serious scandal.

Paul Horvitz of the University of Houston then brought an academic note to the discussion of the RTC, calling the room's attention to the small amount of study of the RTC and its asset sales. A key problem for the RTC, he claimed, was that it was not operating in the well-known "market for lemons" but rather in a "market for cherries" where it was the *buyer* that knew more about the real worth of the assets than the seller – the RTC.

This was followed by comments from William Hamm of LECG, formerly World Savings. Reflecting on his experience as California's Legislative Analyst, he observed how the desire to keep budgets down and headcounts low at the Bank Board resulted in a shortage of trained bank examiners.

Mr. Fleischer returned to Mr. White's remarks about the RTC, suggesting that scandals remain undetected as individuals remain unable to question the corporation's conduct.

Richard Nelson of Wells Fargo, formerly the Chief Economist of the San Francisco Home Loan Bank, then added an interesting historical perspective, reminding the roundtable that fixed rate mortgages were not always viewed by savings and loans as the "financial arsenic" of former Bank Board Chairman Ed Gray's famous quote but were seen as the savior of the industry during times of great illiquidity.

Two interesting views of the impact of savings and loans' diversification of the early 1980s were offered by Charlotte Chamberlain of Jeffries and Company and David Malmquist, Chief Economist of the OTS. Ms. Chamberlain noted that by diversifying portfolios savings and loans merely substituted credit risk for interest rate risk. Deregulation and diversification took an interest rate problem, that could have been solved by forbearance, and transformed it into a credit risk problem. Mr. Malmquist elaborated on her point, and recalled the work of Adam Smith to suggest that while portfolio theory teaches the value of diversification, there are also gains from specialization. Many savings and loans in the 1980s got into trouble by diversifying away from lending they understood and into more complex business areas they knew relatively little about.

Anne Henry of Farchmin, Ralls Wagoner, formerly with Overland Park Savings, returned the discussion to the RTC and its handling of the disposal of savings and loan assets. She reflected on the stated focus of RTC officials on accounting rather than economics. Ms. Henry's experiences of RTC priorities were affirmed by Mr. Fleischer, who was followed by Jean Helwege of Ohio State University, formerly of the Federal Reserve Bank of New York, who remarked that by the late 1980s it was clear that it had been a "huge mistake" for regulators to use their discretion to allow insolvent savings and loans to remain open and that this discretion was rightly a casualty of FIRREA. This loss of discretion was in fact an unintended consequence of 1980s policy and a positive one.

Edward Kane of Boston College returned to the discussion of market value accounting opened by Mr. White and suggested that market value accounting would make regulators more accountable and losses more difficult to hide through improper accounting methods. Mr. Kane then questioned the independence of regulators suggesting that regulators were instead the servants of politicians, and those regulators who called for a "clean up" of the industry were coolly received by the Congress.

Stephen Ege of Elias, Matz, Tiernan & Eric, formerly Special Assistant to the Chairman of the Bank Board, questioned conventional wisdom by noting that the right to invest in commercial real estate, the asset class that declined the most, was granted not in the 1980s but almost 50 years earlier in 1933. It was not savings and loans diversification in the 1980s that got them into trouble, Mr. Ege contended, but rather their rapid growth.

Ms. Helwege's remarks on discretion drew a further examination of this issue from the Atlanta Federal Reserve's Director of Research. Discretion was not fully removed but rather the discretion to engage in forbearance, Mr. Eisenbeis stated. Ms. Helwege agreed with this clarification, remarking that one "cannot take enough discretion away from regulators."

Kenneth Thygerson, of Digital University, formerly CEO of Freddie Mac and Imperial Corporation, brought his experience as an officer in both a government-sponsored agency and a leading savings and loan to bear on the discussion next. Mr. Thygerson made two brief comments in deference to the limited time. He focused first on a source of moral hazard not often mentioned – the conversion of savings and loans from mutual to joint stock status. He then returned to the contested topic of the RTC's asset disposals. He noted that, while it was not possible to tell whether the corporation received market value for the assets it was selling, the RTC's approach to asset sales amounted to selling the assets with unpriced embedded puts.

The next speaker was Robert Van Order, Chief International Economist of Freddie Mac. Mr. Van Order returned to the question of the misallocation of resources discussed earlier by Mr. Villani and Mr. White. Low mortgage costs combined with tax advantages resulted in the tendency for American houses to be larger than is socially optimal and a diversion of resources to homebuilding from other investments. Mr. Van Order contended that this misallocation of capital was linked to slow economic growth.

An RTC insider's view of the controversial corporation was provided by Peter Elmer, now of Deloitte and Touche. Mr. Elmer recalled the numerous sources of information about the RTC that were available to those who sought to investigate its performance. Indeed, he candidly noted that the RTC was the most intensely examined and scrutinized agency for which he had ever worked. He then went on to ask whether a policy of action that closed insolvent savings and loans in 1980 rather than in 1990 would really have been less costly.

Finally, Mr. White drew the first session to a close with another intriguing counterfactual suggestion that had savings and loans been regulated by an organization located within the executive branch of government in the

Treasury the problems of the industry would have been recognized and dealt with sooner.

The Public Record: Was There Fair and Accurate Coverage?

After a short break during which the first session's discussions were continued informally, participants regrouped for the second session introduced by Peter Passell, Editor in Chief of the *Milken Institute Review*, formerly of the *New York Times*. Mr. Passell offered what he deemed "a tepid defense" of the press coverage of the savings and loan industry in the 1980s. He noted that the incentive structures at newspapers do not encourage accurate coverage of complex issues. Editors, who make content decisions, are by their nature generalists. He observed that ironically there were in fact two positive consequences of the poor media coverage of the "savings and loan crisis." The media's failure to understand and report the insolvency of the industry prevented a widespread loss of confidence in the financial system while its focus on "fraud and malfeasance" prevented calls for increased regulation of the U.S. economy. Mr. Passell then asked Mollie Dickenson of *Worth Magazine* to make some introductory remarks.

Ms. Dickenson decried the inaccurate reporting of savings and loan issues by the Washington D.C. press corps. Her own experiences led her to believe that journalists were overly trusting in their dealings with savings and loan regulators. Indeed, she contended that regulators were able to directly influence writers and guide their reporting. At the same time, "there is an anti-business bias among newspaper people." Drawing links with the scandals of the second Clinton administration, Ms. Dickenson remarked that the same reporters who failed to cover the savings and loan story accurately also misreported Whitewater.

Mr. Van Order, Chief International Economist of Freddie Mac, presented an overview of a rather different type of writing on savings and loans. He reflected on academic writings on the issues and how they diverged from popular accounts. While the mass media focused on issues of equity, economists were interested in efficiency. At the same time, the mass media was interested in dividing out "crooks" from honest individuals while economists tended to view everyone involved as simply responding to incentives and emphasized issues of moral hazard and the option value of different behavior.

The next introductory speaker was Stephen Neal of Cooley Godward, who brought to the roundtable his experience as a litigator involved in a number of high profile savings and loan cases including defending Lincoln

Savings' Charles Keating. Mr. Neal drew attention to the irony of the press attitude towards the Bill of Rights. While newsmen relied upon the First Amendment to guarantee the existence of a free press, they had little respect for the rest of that document. The press had failed and continues to fail to provide "fair, accurate, complete information about critically important issues of the day" he argued. From savings and loans to the collapse of Enron, the press has failed in its duties for two main reasons. The first is the complexity of the issues and the second is the overriding desire to sell newspapers.

This poor quality reporting results in an uninformed population. Indeed one would be fortunate, contended Mr. Neal, to be able to find "one in 10,000 people who could relate, to the satisfaction of anybody in this room, with any degree of accuracy, what the savings and loan crisis was really about." A practical result of this misinformation reporting by the press was that many savings and loan officers were unable to get a fair trial due to the bias of juries. Mr. Neal himself found this as Charles Keating's lead lawyer. When litigating over Lincoln Savings, he found that "the press had so permeated the air... that neither the judges nor the jurors had any objectivity whatsoever."

Mr. Neal's presentation was followed by Peter Haje's remarks. Formerly Chief Counsel of Time Warner, Mr. Haje had served as Centrust' CEO David Paul's lawyer and brought a great deal of personal experience both as a litigator and more recently a media executive to the discussion. Mr. Haje suggested that the media coverage afforded the savings and loan industry was about as good as one could expect given the complexity of the issues as well as the often colorful characters involved. The audience of the mass media simply is not, he contended, interested in depth. The media therefore seeks to "entertain, amuse and titillate" rather than inform and believes its audience is interested chiefly in "sex, violence and villainy." These assumptions made about viewers' and readers' tastes leads newsmen and other media figures to focus on the human factor of stories and to seek villains to blame for problems. The savings and loan industry was filled, Mr. Haje remarked, with individuals who could be made into villains by the press.

Another barrier to accurate reporting was touched on by Ms. Dickinson, Mr. Haje remarked. "Business and financial reporters have little business experience," he noted. Working to tight deadlines they also are characterized by both a great deal of "cynicism about business and business ethics" and an inappropriately high level of empathy with government employees.

Mr. Haje was followed in his comments by Marymount University's Catherine England. Ms. England, who wrote on the savings and loan industry and the crisis for the Cato Institute, noted that there were a few "bright spots" in the dismal coverage of the crisis. However, these bright spots were not widely circulated and the bulk of the coverage of her work at Cato required that she distill it into "five minute sound bites." Before the conference, she reported, she had carried out a search of articles related to the savings and loan crisis. Many of the articles compared the problems of Japan and Asia to the U.S. problems of the late 1980s and just one dealt with issues of moral hazard. Echoing the remarks of Mr. Neal, Ms. England noted that a number of recent articles drew sensationalist comparisons between Enron and the savings and loan industry of the 1980s.

These opening comments were the preface to a roundtable discussion involving all attendees. Mr. Thygerson began the discussion noting that there was a good deal of asymmetry in the reporting. It was far easier for regulators or politicians involved in the crisis to get favorable press coverage than operators of savings and loans. Savings and loan executives facing lawsuits typically were advised to make no comments to the media and their silence was often taken as an admission of guilt by the media.

Villainy, Mr. Thygerson noted, was still recalled by some of his students as the chief cause of the crisis. Indeed, he related the amusing anecdote of a student who remained convinced that the failure of Lincoln was due to Charles Keating stealing deposits and secreting them in a subterranean trove. Mr. Thygerson's former colleague at Imperial Corporation, Mr. Villani, also emphasized the selling power of villains. Indeed, early problems at mutual savings and loans were not publicized, he noted, due to the fact that there were "no good villains at the time." Mr. Spellman also agreed, remarking that "if there are losses, we must find a villain and play the blame game."

Edward Kane of Boston College suggested that the incentive structures for journalists did not encourage accurate reporting and further that editors and advertisers did not favor thoughtful reporting of financial issues. Remarking that his institution had recently implemented a masters degree program in financial journalism, Mr. Kane stated that "The financial world is getting so complicated … that reporters need to have this kind of training… unless (editors) prefer to have ignorant people they can tell to report the story wrongly in the end."

George Kaufman of Loyola University quipped that reporters on the business pages were promoted to sports or fashion as soon as they were fully trained. On a less lighthearted note, he agreed with Ms. England that there had been some accurate reporting of the issues facing the savings and loan industry. Particularly, *The American Banker* had reported well on the crisis and had sought to maintain accuracy in its reporting. It is important, he stressed, not to "short change" the media too much. Catherine Galley of

Cornerstone Research agreed, remarking that "there is good reporting out there, and you may have to be selective in what you look at."

The problem of an uninformed public was returned to by Richard Nelson of Wells Fargo, formerly chief economist of the Federal Home Loan Bank of San Francisco. The public is expected to hold the government to account but this is quite impossible if it is wholly uninformed. While there were a few reporters who did a good job of informing the public, there was a great amount of information on the savings and loan industry and the crisis that went unreported. Another cost of an uninformed public was mentioned by Mr. Horwitz. Press emphasis on fraud and criminal wrongdoing caused, he argued, mistakes by lenders whose attention was not brought to similarities between their own lending practices and those of savings and loans whose problems were falsely represented by the press as due to fraud. Media coverage of the industry influenced not just lenders but the government as well, maintained banking consultant Timothy Anderson. In his experience with the problems of the Illinois savings and loan industry, "Congress only reacts to the public's perception which is gained from media coverage."

Mr. Kosberg remarked that the media's reporting on the so-called "Keating Five" had the effect of "freezing the legislative branch" and allowing organizations like the OTS and the RTC to carry out their work free of any congressional oversight. Mr. Kosberg then asked Mr. White what impact the "Keating Five" publicity had on policy and whether those at the Bank Board were relieved or frustrated by this withdrawal of congressional oversight. Mr. White responded that the whole "Keating Five" affair had the effect of making everyone at the Bank Board rather nervous and Danny Wall, when he arrived at the Bank Board to replace Ed Grey, viewed it as "a radioactive type of situation." However, Mr. White disagreed with Mr. Kosberg regarding the impact of the negative publicity on congressional activism. Rather than freezing legislative oversight, he felt that it merely slowed it.

U.S. Savings And Loan Experience: Are There Parallels in Other Countries?

After lunch, the participants reconvened to address the third session's question. James Barth of the Milken Institute and Auburn University, formerly Chief Economist of the OTS and the Federal Home Loan Bank Board, served as moderator for the panel and opened the session with a brief overview of the costs and frequency of international banking crises.

Banking problems are not, Mr. Barth noted, concentrated in one part of the world, nor do they occur more frequently in countries at a certain level of economic development. He then went on to discuss the estimated costs of crises. Resolving the banking crisis in Indonesia, for example, cost between 60 and 70 percent of GDP, a figure that does not take into account other costs such as the social cost of the crisis or the value of lost output growth. The costs of resolving banking crises seem, he suggested, to be higher in countries with financial systems dominated by banking and lower in countries with well developed bond markets. Citing recent research from U.C. Berkeley and the Wharton School, Mr. Barth argued that countries with deep and liquid bond markets are also less likely to experience a banking crisis than countries with bank-based rather than market-based financial systems.

Crises can, however, present countries with the opportunity to reform their economic systems and to adopt policies more conducive to growth. A crisis, he argued, can "actually lead to the sorts of changes that over a long period of time are indeed quite beneficial." Reflecting on some remarks made by Mr. O'Driscoll, Mr. Barth pointed out that crises were turning points, opportunities to do things differently and perhaps better.

To conclude, he drew on his recent research to discuss the question of which regulatory/supervisory structure is most appropriate for financial institutions. Is it better, he asked, to have a single banking regulator, as has been adopted in the United Kingdom where the supervisory capacities of the Bank of England have now been transferred to the Financial Services Authority, or is it better to have multiple supervisors? Mr. Barth closed his remarks by inviting the participants to consider some of these questions.

Edward Kane of Boston College followed Mr. Barth's introduction. He noted that three of the unsatisfactory policies that contributed to the savings and loan crisis – or "mess" as he preferred to call it – are still part of banking policy throughout the rest of the world today. Publicly subsidized risk taking, politically directed lending and budgetary opaqueness – all three of which were characteristics of the savings and loan industry and government savings and loan policy – are all common today throughout the world of banking.

Mr. Kane emphasized the microeconomic incentives that regulators and bankers face that can lead to highly distorted lending decisions. Indeed, political pressures can lead to "banks and regulators gambling on long-shot projects with negative present value in the long run but which look good in the short run." In the savings and loan industry, incentives existed for lenders and regulators to act in a myopic fashion, and these incentives reinforced each other. Banking policy encouraged excessive risk taking and allowed lenders to keep losses off their books through the use of regulatory accounting. Regulators allow lenders, Mr. Kane suggested, to build up large unbooked government guarantees, that are in fact unbooked deficits. "What we call a crisis is merely the refinancing of that implicit debt," a change in the ownership of the affected institutions' losses. Leading up to such crises, he argued, were "silent runs," the withdrawal of large amounts of funds by small numbers of sophisticated depositors. These "silent runs" are financed by foreign banks, often with the help of domestic government or IMF guarantees.

Next to speak was Jerry O'Driscoll of the Heritage Foundation. Mr. O'Driscoll drew parallels between the savings and loan crisis and crises in Mexico, Argentina and Turkey where, as in the U.S. savings and loan industry, politically directed lending was commonplace. During the privatization of Mexican banks, policymakers studied the lessons of the Texas savings and loan and banking problems but failed to implement them. Although they were aware of the costs, the "political system in Mexico did not know how to wean itself from the ... use of financial institutions to provide funds to politically favored classes."

As with Mexico, the Turkish political elites have been unable to treat the banking system as anything other than a tool for the "financing of politically favored constituencies." Unlike Turkey or Mexico, Argentina had a strong banking system; however, the strength of its banking system wasn't matched by the quality of its other institutions. The reforms of the 1990s were the "story of trying to put in market reforms without market institutions," he argued. Argentina was able to weather the Tequila Crisis due to the strength of its banking system – a banking system that was largely foreign owned. However, during the last crisis in Argentina, "the De La Rua government managed to undermine the one institution or set of institutions – the monetary system and the banking system – that worked."

Mr. O'Driscoll was followed by Philip Bartholomew of the International Monetary Fund. Prior to the 1990s, Mr. Bartholomew noted, researchers did not pay much attention to banking failures and banking crises outside the U.S. Indeed many U.S. observers spent the 1980s believing that banks do not fail anywhere else in the world. While other countries have had banking crises, no other country but Canada has had a crisis that closely resembles the savings and loan crisis. Unlike some of the other participants who saw close parallels between the causes of the savings and loan industry's problems and the causes of banking crises abroad, Mr. Bartholomew stressed that only the Canadian near-banking industry suffered the same problems of asset-liability mismatches and interest rate risks that damaged the U.S. savings and loan industry.

In addition to some of the causes highlighted by Mr. O'Driscoll and Mr. Kane, Mr. Bartholomew mentioned the role that real estate lending has had in a number of banking crises as well as the role of exogenous events such as civil and military disturbances. Another cause of crises – especially in the former communist countries – is the misinterpretation of lessons learned from the 1980s. For instance in Poland, free-market enthusiasm led policy makers to completely deregulate the chartering of financial institutions and to allow them to operate unsupervised, creating a highly fragile system rife with failures.

Mr. Bartholomew's observations were followed by some comments from the UCLA Anderson School's Michael Darby. Mr. Darby focused on the macroeconomic fundamentals underlying crises. Typically, crises in advanced market economies are caused by a sharp increase in interest rates that negatively impacts lenders who borrow short and lend long or by a downturn in credit quality due to a recession. The system of politically directed lending that was the U.S. savings and loan industry broke down as inflation and then interest rates rose rapidly, making it "impossible to keep savings in banks and savings and loans," Mr. Darby suggested. The cause of the inflation was the refusal of the pre-Volcker Federal Reserve to accept that money matters.

He then touched on the topic of forbearance, a subject that would later excite some controversy in the discussion. "Forbearance," he remarked, "was the great hope of those who wanted to cover up the disaster." Contrary to the hopes of its advocates, forbearance merely allowed honest savings and loan operators to make one way bets and created opportunities for fraud for dishonest ones. The final introductory speaker was Robert Eisenbeis of the Atlanta Federal Reserve. In a light hearted fashion, he proposed to follow late night television host David Letterman in presenting a list of the "top ten" lessons from the savings and loan and other U.S. financial crises.

Lesson number ten in Mr. Eisenbeis's list – is that it is not a question of whether problems in financial institutions will occur, it is rather a question of when they will occur. Since 1980, he noted, there have been some 149 banking and financial crises in over 130 countries around the world.

Lesson number nine, Mr. Eisenbeis noted, is that bailouts only work in the short-term. While they are expedient in the short run, he stated, they create moral hazard and damage managerial and regulatory incentives.

Number eight, contrary to what regulators and others who wish to protect depositors' savings may think, is that even small depositors are not naive. Mr. Eisenbeis referred at this point to the failure of Superior Bank where uninsured deposits were withdrawn by savers concerned by the institution's viability and replaced by federally insured money. The public, Mr. Eisenbeis contended, can distinguish healthy institutions from unhealthy institutions.

Lesson number seven is the point elaborated upon by Mr. Darby. Crises are closely related to irresponsible monetary policy. As Mr. Darby pointed out, when inflation is high, crises are more likely. Indeed, inflation is typically followed, Mr. Eisenbeis noted, by low growth, by fiscal imbalances and by debt financed deficits. These fiscal problems are then transmitted to the financial sector. Thus, the monetary authority is "an important propagator of financial crises," much as Mr. Darby stressed.

Skipping the sixth lesson – that the more important a troubled sector is the more likely it is that its regulators will forbear – Mr. Eisenbeis went on to reveal his fifth and perhaps most controversial lesson: that is, that explicit or implicit deposit insurance guarantees do not decrease the likelihood of crises, but rather seem to increase the frequency of crises.

The number four lesson, Mr. Eisenbeis remarked, was that the larger and more important a financial system is, the more severe its crisis is likely to be. Partially, this correlation is a result, he suggested, of the fact that large and critically important financial systems present regulators with great temptations to forbear on troubled institutions rather than resolve the crisis promptly. The eventual successful resolution of the savings and loan crisis, Mr. Eisnebeis contended, was partially due to the fact that savings and loans were not the only source of housing finance in the U.S. The existence of the Government Sponsored Enterprises (GSEs) such as Fannie Mae, Freddie Mac and Ginnie Mae, allowed the government to "face up to the fact that there was a problem (without) destroy(ing) the source of funding to housing." The experience in other countries has been less positive, Mr. Eisenbeis remarked. Indeed, in countries dependent on troubled banks such as Japan, it is too costly to deal with their problems and there are "incentives to engage in broader kinds of forbearance activities."

Lesson three is a timely one given recent concerns over corporate transparency. Reliable accounting and accurate information are critical to limiting the costs of financial crises.

Lesson number two is that crises are very expensive. The savings and loan crisis cost around $150 billion, Mr. Eisenbeis noted, yet this was trivial "compared to the costs that other countries have incurred ... (where) the average cleanup cost is around 12 to 97 percent of GDP." Indeed, these estimates may be somewhat too conservative as they do not include the opportunity cost of foregone GDP growth.

The number one lesson and one which had been noted by other speakers including Mr. Darby, is that "forbearance is the enemy of the taxpayer." While this was lesson number one, Mr. Eisenbeis deviated slightly from the

Letterman protocol by presenting a "lesson number zero" – the most important lesson that crises teach. This lesson is that there are no innocent victims of a crisis. Whether one is a savings and loan operator, a regulator or a politician, there are no innocent parties and the savings and loan debacle was not something imposed upon any of the participants. With this sobering thought, Mr. Eisenbeis finished his remarks and the moderator opened the discussion up to the rest of the participants.

The first to speak was Mr. Brumbaugh. He offered an alternative view of forbearance that diverged sharply from some of the opinions offered thus far in the discussion. Mr. Brumbaugh contended that negative net worth of the savings and loan industry in 1981 was roughly the same as the amount that resolving the crisis cost in 1990. In light of this, he questioned why forbearance was seen as so damaging. Mr. Eisenbeis, an avowed opponent of forbearance, responded by suggesting that if the U.S. had had a functioning closure system in place in 1981, the problems of the savings and loan industry would have been less severe.

Mr. Malmquist of the Office of Thrift Supervision then posed a two part question. He asked Mr. Darby whether he felt that a gradualist approach to reducing inflation in the early 1980s would have caused less pain than the October 1979 "big bang" strategy that the Federal Reserve under Volcker choose to pursue. He then asked whether, in light of the moral hazard problems Mr. Eisenbeis had outlined in his remarks, the government should offer any deposit insurance at all.

Mr. Darby responded by suggesting that a more gradualist approach would have been worse for savings and loans, not better. The main problem for institutions was, he claimed, the inflation premium in interest rates. It was in their interests to get this premium down as low as possible as quickly as possible. Mr. Kane, a leading authority on deposit insurance, was then asked by Mr. Barth to respond to Mr. Malmquist's question. Mr. Kane made the important point that although insurance may not be openly guaranteed, "everybody has implicit deposit insurance." Furthermore, in countries that have adopted explicit insurance in the last ten years the value of the guarantees have increased and there has been less risk-shifting.

Mr. Villani raised an issue on which he has great expertise as former Chief Economist of Freddie Mac, the role of GSEs and the subsidization of housing. Was it better, he asked, to have a U.S. style system with too-big-to-fail GSEs or perhaps to follow the Malaysian example of having only a "glorified central bank discount facility" that discounts privately originated home loans at a steep haircut. Mr. Villani thought that, if politicians insisted on doing something, following the Malaysian example would be the course that would do the least harm. Mr. Eisenbeis highlighted a different side of the GSE debate, referring to Alan Meltzer's study of housing subsidies. Meltzer concluded, and Mr. Eisenbeis agreed, that rather than rely on cumbersome indirect subsidies that were impossible to target, it would be rather better to simply give money to the people whom one wanted to benefit and to do so in the most transparent way possible.

The debate over forbearance was returned to by Jeffries and Company's Ms. Chamberlain. Ms. Chamberlain noted that forbearance remains in the regulators' play book. Indeed forbearance is being carried out at Providian, at Bank Plus and at Next Card. Forbearance, rather than being the taxpayers' enemy, is valuable as a way of dealing with institutions like Providian and many savings and loans that regulators have allowed to grow out of control, contended Ms. Chamberlain. If one looks at a financial history of the U.S., "since the Second World War (it) has shown that values come back" and forbearance can work if there is a liquid banking system.

A respite from the discussion of forbearance was brought by a return to the deposit insurance issue. Richard Roll, of UCLA's Anderson School of Management, questioned whether deposit insurance really increased the risk of crisis. Mr. Eisenbeis, referring to the work of Demirgüç-Kunt and others, highlighted the empirical evidence that links explicit insurance to the likelihood of crises. Mr. Eisenbeis was supported by Mr. Kane who added the caveat that if "the insurance system is well-designed, in the sense of having some risk controls built in that enlist depositor participation and discipline, you do not see (the) problems" of increased crisis probability. Mr. Kane then remarked that to forbear without taking some claim to the potential upside of the gamble that forbearance entails is a poor policy. Forbearance at a bank is essentially "the government ... putting in risk capital and ... not charging for it" and clearly is inferior to a policy where the government makes a formal claim to the possible appreciation in the bank's assets and equity. This raised problems in the view of Mr. Villani, who noted that such a policy could be abused by a government simply causing problems for institutions, taking warrants on them and then forbearing long enough for the artificial problems to dissipate and the warrants to appreciate – a kind of nationalization.

Another opinion on GSEs was offered by Mr. Van Order who recently filled Mr. Villani's former position as chief economist of Freddie Mac. Mr. Villani's Malaysian bank board suggestion might, Mr. Van Order believed, be superior to the current second-best GSE model employed by the U.S. Mr. Van Order then turned back to the question of forbearance on which he offered a slightly different perspective. Forbearance on loans provides incentives to insolvent institutions to invest in projects with low net present values and is inferior often to a policy of writing off part of the debt so the debtor still has some of his own capital at stake. Another aspect of forbearance was raised by Mr. Bartholomew of the IMF. Forbearance could, he stressed, be valuable in resolving national crises when it allows the reallocation of losses to solvent institutions.

The session was brought to an end with the remarks of the University of Texas's Mr. Spellman. He noted that investors have rational expectations of forbearance and price securities to include these expectations. What occurs, then, is that these expectations of forbearance encourage further forbearance and it should be the goal of the government to convince investors that forbearance will not occur.

Do Savings And Loans Provide a Useful Perspective?

Mr. Klowden welcomed panelists back to the final session of the day. He opened the panel with the striking display of the "tombstones" of failed savings and loans. Remarking on the many hundreds of lost institutions, he noted that the savings and loan crisis was not unique in terms of its size or its scope.

Indeed, Mr. Klowden noted that the "dot.com crisis" was its rival in terms of the number of firms that failed. The savings and loan debacle was also not unique terms of the size of losses realized, he observed. In 2001, more than 45 companies with assets of more than $ 1 billion filed for Chapter 11 protection and the assets of all public companies filing for bankruptcy was greater than $258 billion – nearly 170 percent of the FDIC's latest estimate of the cost of resolving the savings and loan crisis.

While not unique in term of its size or scope, the savings and loan crisis was unusual in the fact that it involved taxpayer insured and heavily regulated firms. This involvement of the public and the government ensured that the crisis would become politicized resulting in "far more finger-pointing and far more of an attempt to lay blame on individuals and to find villains." It was the task of this final session to seek to draw together and summarize the observations and conclusions of the preceding panels. To start this process, Mr. Klowden asked Mr. Kaufman of Loyola University to make some opening remarks about what lessons have been learned from the great savings and loan debacle.

Academics, Mr. Kaufman contended, have learned a great deal while it is less clear just how much regulators have learned. Since the end of the clean up of the savings and loan mess, fewer than ten banks a year have failed. Fewer still of any great size have failed. Indeed from 1995 to the present day, a mere three banks with assets of more than $1 billion have failed and no institutions with assets of greater than $2.5 billion have been lost. While the number of failures and their size paints a positive picture, the image is less attractive when one considers the costs of cleaning up the failures relative to the size of the banks.

Keystone Bank failed at a cost of 75 percent of total assets while Best Bank and Superior (the largest bank failure since the savings and loan crisis) cost between 40 percent and 50 percent of total assets to resolve. Clearly, Mr. Kaufman argued, regulators are not engaging in prompt corrective action as they are failing to catch banks operating with negative capital and thus allowing costly resolutions.

There is, however, a case that can be made that the large post-crisis bank failures are outliers. Indeed both Superior and Keystone specialized in securitizing risky subprime loans and both held the junior most tranche of the resulting obligation. Furthermore, each institution was characterized by "massive fraud ... legal maneuvers by the bank to delay responding to enforcement actions (and) in some cases, physical interference with the supervisors and the examiners."

While these were atypical banks, they still exhibited many of the same warning signs that troubled savings and loans showed in the 1980s. These "red flags" included rapid asset growth, a run on uninsured deposits (and the replacement of uninsured with FDIC insured deposits) and a focus on complex transactions and risky assets. Regulators were not, however, "caught with their pants down," argued Mr. Kaufman. Rather, they were aware of the problems at the institutions but failed to take the tough actions needed. Rather than the "regulatory bullying," which occurred on occasion in the 1980s, the regulators of Superior, Keystone and other troubled banks engaged in what Kaufman colorfully described as "regulatory chickening-out." Regulators have learned the lessons of the savings and loan crisis but have failed to apply them. The problem, Mr. Kaufman concluded, is not one of the quality of regulators but rather one of the incentives that exist for regulators. Regulators are not properly incentivized to engage in prompt corrective action as they pay no penalty for high-cost failures.

Next to speak was Martin Regalia, Chief Economist of the U.S. Chamber of Commerce. Mr. Regalia offered a somewhat different perspective as he reflected on his tenure as a bank regulator at the FDIC in the late 1970s. Faced with ailing savings banks in New York State, the FDIC chose to forbear rather than resolve them simply because they did not know how to best resolve the problem.

The cause of the savings and loan crisis was, Mr. Regalia suggested, an unfortunate combination of micro- and macroeconomic events and of poor incentives and that this combination could recur "as we really have not done a whole lot in the way of changing the fundamental structure" of financial services and its regulation. Although a crisis of equivalent scale and scope to the savings and loan mess *could* recur, Mr. Regalia suggested the likelihood of the confluence of events that sparked the savings and loan debacle was small. Indeed, even if another large scale crisis were to occur again, the U.S. economy could weather the shock. Concluding on a sanguine note, Mr. Regalia remarked that the savings and loan debacle "which might have brought lesser economies to their knees, really, in the greater scheme of things, will be shown to be not much more than a blip."

Mr. Regalia was followed in his remarks by Susanne Trimbath, Research Economist at the Milken Institute. Ms. Trimbath opened her remarks by observing that much of what had been discussed in the preceding panels could be said about all regulated financial service firms and was not unique to savings and loans. Indeed, she noted that as Mr. Brumbaugh and Mr. White had earlier pointed out, more commercial banks failed than savings and loans during the 1980s. Savings and loans also were not unique in having large unrealized losses and in being insolvent economically. At various times throughout the same period as the savings and loan crisis, insurance companies and commercial banks would have been bankrupt had they been compelled to follow market value accounting and mark their portfolios to market. Savings and loans were not unique in their problems but were unique in their being compelled to realize their losses.

Reflecting on the previous panel discussion, Ms. Trimbath noted that the question of regulating cross-border financial institutions remains unanswered as does that of what system of financial regulation is appropriate. She pointed out that "when it comes to developing financial institutions that provide the infrastructure for robust capital markets, there is no one size fits all set of regulations." Rather than a set of standard rules, what is needed, she asserted, is a more flexible supervisory system that allows regulated firms to adapt to changing market conditions. Lacking this, she warned, the threat of a repeat of the savings and loan crisis remains real.

Mr. Ege of Elias Matz, Tiernan & Herrick, formerly Special Assistant to the Chairman of the Federal Home Loan Bank Board, was next to speak. Mr. Ege remarked that although the entire day had been spent in discussion of banks, no-one had yet offered a definition of what a bank actually is and how regulation in part defines what banks are. Indeed, in the U.S. at least, without supervision one cannot have a bank. Banks have, historically, Mr. Ege observed, been created by regulation as much as by market forces. Central to the definition of a bank is the role of supervision and the impact of the savings and loan crisis on supervision has been a negative one. As a result of the savings and loan mess, institutions are subject not to a single regulator but to four separate regulatory entities: the Federal Reserve, the Comptroller of the Currency, the Federal Deposit Insurance Corporation and the Office of Thrift Supervision. This system of multiple regulators has, moreover, tended to be self supporting as it has resulted in "an excessively complex regulatory structure designed to preserve these entities." In addition to the unnecessary complexity of current regulation, bank supervision remains subject to tension between "the desire of the government to control the behavior of the bank while absolving itself of all responsibilities for the results of the actions taken in response to the directions given to it."

The perspective of both a former regulator and a former savings and loan officer was brought to the discussion by Mr. Thygerson of Digital University. Mr. Thygerson, formerly the CEO of Imperial Corporation of America and of Freddie Mac, opened his remarks with some history of the savings and loan industry. The savings and loan industry that fell prey to the problems of the 1980s was created in 1933 with a "social contract" between savings and loan institutions, home builders, realtors and home owners. As time passed, Mr. Thygerson explained, the costs of maintaining this agreement grew ever higher. By the 1970s, several members of the coalition created in 1933 began growing dissatisfied with the social contract. Aging Americans no longer were interested in subsidizing low cost mortgages as they already owned homes, while realtors and builders saw in Fannie Mae, Ginnie Mae and Freddie Mac an alternative to savings and loans. By the 1970s there was no longer a need for the savings and loan industry and no desire to maintain the 1933 social contract. This was the real basis of the savings and loan crisis. While moral hazard in the conversion of mutuals to stock institutions was of importance, as was the 1986 Tax Reform Act, at the root of the crisis was "a social contract that, for a variety of reasons, no longer needed to be served."

The main lesson to be learned from the crisis, Mr. Thygerson suggested, is to keep government subsidies transparent. If the government wishes to subsidize home ownership, let it do so directly rather than through the financial system. Direct subsidies can then, he noted, be accounted for clearly as part of the government deficit. The alternative is to have the sort of complex system we have today, Thygerson argued, a system "that we do not understand, (and) cannot measure the risk of."

Mr. Thygerson's comments brought the preliminary remarks to a close and Mr. Klowden then invited the other panelists to join the discussion.

William Lang of the Office of the Comptroller of the Currency opened the debate by contending that even in a rule-based regulatory structure such as Prompt Corrective Action, regulators still have at least some discretion. What the savings and loan crisis has done is to make it more difficult and more costly for regulators to engage in the kind of forbearance that went on in the 1980s. James Wilcox of the University of California at Berkley's Haas School of Business followed Mr. Lang and presented what he saw as a more optimistic view of the lessons of the savings and loan crisis. The crisis has, he insisted, taught a great deal about the value of diversification and of risk management. Also, the importance of market value accounting was made clear as much of the industry's problems were due to "driving in the rear-view mirror, both on the part of the institutions themselves and on the part of their regulators."

Mr. Kaufman's comments on Prompt Corrective Action were, to some extent, contested by Mr. Elmer of Deloitte and Touche. Keystone was not, Mr. Elmer argued, a failure of regulation or regulators, but was rather a "flat-out fraud situation … where holes were dug in people's front yards to bury documents." Mr. Kaufman returned to the question of Keystone to agree, in part, with Mr. Elmer. Fraud was, he admitted, of importance, but the Inspector General's report on the failed institution did provide evidence that the OCC failed to apply Prompt Corrective Action.

Gordon Bjork of Claremont McKenna College returned to a point made by Mr. Regalia about the resiliency of the American economy, and suggested that the misallocation of capital in the U.S. towards housing and real estate and away from more productive uses, of which others including Mr. Villani had spoken earlier in the day, was less important to the U.S. economy as a whole relative to other countries where similar misallocation resulted in financial instability.

A similarly optimistic note was sounded by Mr. Spellman who suggested that deposit insurance was a relatively low cost way of providing a liquid riskless asset. Mr. Spellman argued that since deposit insurance has been in place for more than 50 years and the savings and loan crisis cost the U.S. a little more than three percent of GDP, the cost of this subsidy was really quite low. Mr. Spellman's point was disputed, however, by Mr. Van Order who argued that public guarantees of private liabilities such as deposit insurance schemes are a most inefficient way of providing a risk free asset. A much better, and simpler, way he contended was through maintaining a Treasury bill market.

Elijah Brewer of the Federal Reserve Bank of Chicago returned to the issue of insurance companies raised by Ms. Trimbath in her comments, noting that they provide better disclosure of their assets and liabilities than banks or savings and loans and that the insurance industry is characterized by a significant amount of self regulation as "surviving institutions are on the hook for bailing out failed institutions." Perhaps, he suggested, the practices of insurance companies can provide some potential lessons for savings and loans. The issue of appropriate regulation was also addressed by James Freund of the Mortgage Bankers Association of America who suggested that Mr. Kaufman's criticisms of current regulation do not go far enough. What is needed, Mr. Freund argued, is a body of supervisors organized along the same lines as the Federal Reserve. Featuring a strong and stable staff and a degree of insulation from political pressure, such a supervisory organization, would be more effective than current institutions even if they employ Prompt Corrective Action.

William Shear of the General Accounting Office agreed with Mr. Brewer and observed that with an increasingly integrated financial services industry, one needs to rethink what kind of regulatory structures and practices are most appropriate. Mr. Shear also suggested optimistically that the savings and loan crisis had a positive impact on regulators by acting as a catalyst or "triggering event in the policy community" that led to a greater understanding of the industry and its issues. A more skeptical view was presented by Mr. Nelson. He noted that a similar practice to Prompt Corrective Action was in use in the 1930s and "regulators were actually doing things such as closing institutions before they became insolvent." However, this knowledge seemed to slip from memory and Mr. Nelson suggested that "we seem to go in cycles ... and if we have learned some lessons, they somehow have to be passed on to future generations."

Dr. Yago of the Milken Institute brought the session, and the roundtable, to an end by thanking the attendees and stressing that conferences such as these do a great deal to prevent an important type of failure – not a business or regulatory failure – but a failure of knowledge.

Charticle 8
Impact of Goodwill Reversal

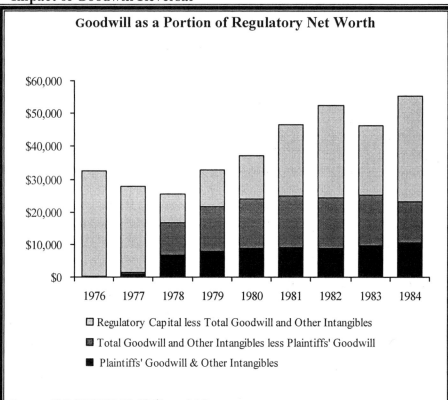

Goodwill as a Portion of Regulatory Net Worth

☐ Regulatory Capital less Total Goodwill and Other Intangibles

▩ Total Goodwill and Other Intangibles less Plaintiffs' Goodwill

■ Plaintiffs' Goodwill & Other Intangibles

Source: FHLBB/OTS Thrift Financial Reports

In an effort to encourage healthy savings and loans to take over ailing institutions, regulators allowed buyers to report their targets as solvent by bridging the gap between liabilities and assets with a newly invented asset class: supervisory goodwill. When it was eliminated as a component of capital, institutions sued for damages.

REVIEW OF THE SAVINGS AND LOAN LITERATURE

Bibliography

CAUSES OF THE SAVINGS AND LOAN CRISIS

The causes of savings and loan failures and the extent of institutional and governmental costs are well documented. Regulatory failure at the state and federal level led to flawed examination and supervision measures, leading in turn to delays by the mid-1980s in declaring insolvencies. For the entire decade, Carron (1987) found that abuses at the operational level increased amid increasing competition between financial institutions for access to funds and ever-higher interest rates. The abuses and mistakes included fraud, reliance on access to federally insured deposits to overcome risky capitalizations, and regulatory expectations that Regulation Q, however revised, would hold liability costs at below market rates.

The most overwhelming conclusion from the literature is that the overall regulatory framework—particularly the charging of a flat premium for deposit insurance, calculated as a percentage of deposits—created distorted incentives for savings and loans to increase risks as their net worth shrank. True, the savings and loans' troubles make for a long list—the inflation of the 1960s and 1970s, interest rate volatility in the 1970s and 1980s, the collapse of regional real estate markets, the overheated market for brokered deposits, and lax regulatory efforts. The underlying problem, however, continued to be the deposit insurance pricing system, which failed to establish market incentives for savings and loans to limit government losses. Quite the opposite occurred. An incentive to increase risks developed. Once the rash of insolvencies and failures began in the mid-1980s, troubled savings and loans were able to continue operating by covering losses with new deposits without having to bear the cost of potential default, which was displaced to the government.

Kormendi, Bornero, Pirrong and Snyder (1989) found that FSLIC actions increased resolution costs of problem savings and loans. In organizing the sale of troubled savings and loans, a $1 increase in tax benefits to acquirers was offset by only a 40-cent reduction in other FSLIC costs. In fact, if one excludes a single outlier from the regression, the FSLIC received no compensation for granted tax benefits. Moreover, from a consolidated government estimation of costs, FSLIC resolution activity had a negative effect. As Kormendi and his coauthors concluded:

> The evidence is not consistent with the FSLIC having adopted a consolidated government perspective ... The result reveals that for each $1 of tax benefits to be retained, the FSLIC gave up $0.63 of its (government) resources to achieve an intra-government transfer of $1 from the U.S. Treasury to itself. That trade leaves the FSLIC

better off by 37 cents on the dollar, but leaves the consolidated government worse off by 63 cents.[1]

In summary, the economic evidence regarding the impacts of shifting patterns of regulation associated with the requirements and distortive market effects of deposit insurance suggest that the unintended consequences of federal action were a financial entrapment of the savings and loan industry. (See Table 1 for a summary of the findings of selected studies on the determinants of savings and loan profitability.) The government mandated a course of investment action – through deregulation and portfolio diversification – and then regulated a different policy through legislation and prosecution. In doing so, the government simultaneously confounded investment strategies with changes in yet other policy areas (such as tax and banking reform) which undermined existing long-term investments (e.g., real estate). This was not unlike a traffic cop waving cars through a red light – and then slapping the drivers with tickets. In this case, they even seized the cars.

REGULATIONS AFFECTING INDUSTRY STRUCTURE

Historically, competition was constrained in the savings and loan industry, given geographic restrictions and resulting market concentration. Along with market concentration came stable earnings, as well as higher average loan rates, lower deposit rates, and relatively smaller allocations of total loan portfolios (Davis and Verbrugge, 1980). Data on 800 savings and loans subject to geographic limitations prior to deregulation confirm that those regulations inhibited price and non-price performance to the detriment of the communities they were chartered to serve. Additionally, an analysis of regulatory limits on advertising (as measured by passbook savings deposits in different market areas) indicated that market intensity was constrained by such regulations (Lapp, 1976). Other research examining savings and loan performance showed that the regulated entry to the market and resulting market structure, rather that aggregate economic demand, was the primary factor affecting savings and loan performance. Market entry was a determinant of price competition, affecting total profits and margins.[2] A later study by Marlow[3] of 2,143 savings and loans further demonstrated the

---

[1] Kormendi, *et.al.* (1989) p. 95
[2] Spellman (1978), Kalish and McKenzie (1979).
[3] Marlow (1983).

secondary factor of market demand affecting savings and loan performance as constrained by regulated market structure restricting entrants.

Evidence on ownership change and structure regarding savings and loans reveals relatively weak results. A comparison of merging and non-merging savings and loans indicates that, on the basis of risk characteristics, profitability, and performance benefits, weak evidence exists of economies of scale resulting from consolidations. Bradford's[4] study, which compared two groups of savings and loans (merging and non-merging) covering 646 mergers during the 1969 to 1975 period, shows no operating efficiencies or associated synergy's from mergers. Similarly, Neely and Rochester[5] found no scale benefits from mergers. These studies were relatively early and did not examine the impact of mergers and acquisitions in the heightened competitive environment for financial services that characterized the 1980s. Balderston[6] examines the structural consolidation of savings and loans in post-regulatory mergers for the period 1980 to 1982 and found positive results on savings and loan balance sheet and income performance. In examining the problem of savings and loan industry structure for this later period, Brumbaugh and Carron[7] argue convincingly that over the past decade, balance sheets, issues of interest rate risk, net worth requirements and the roles of savings and loans and banks in general were converging. As the differences between savings and loans and banks became less apparent, the logic of separate regulatory and deposit insurance systems lessened.

EFFECTS OF GOVERNMENT INTERVENTION ON SAVINGS AND LOANS

If a cacophony of excessive, and sometimes contradictory, regulation was the initial cause of the savings and loan crisis, deposit insurance introduced market distortions that contributed to the high cost of the savings and loan bailout, costs that were increased by further government efforts to restructure the industry. This pattern of regulatory failure began early and is documented in a number of studies. The Glass-Steagall Act of 1933 (The National Banking Act) prohibited banks from issuing, underwriting, selling or distributing stocks and bonds, debentures, or other securities in an effort to stave off bank panics. Under modeling analysis of this regulatory process,

---

[4] Bradford (1978).
[5] Neely and Rochester (1982).
[6] Balderston (1985).
[7] Brumbaugh and Carron (1987).

Gorton and Haubrich[8] found the Act to cause the precise problems it was initially enacted to solve. In short, Glass-Steagall increased the probability of bank and savings and loan failure. Their ancillary finding that prohibitions on interstate banking limited bank and savings and loan diversifications exacerbating regional and industrial specific cyclical risks, was corroborated by Romer.[9]

Early assessments of measures of deregulation yielded positive results. Daly (1972) argued that proposals to institute variable interest rate mortgages ignored the important risk-bearing services of savings and loans. Variable rate instruments are shown as important elements of portfolio risk management for savings and loans.

A great deal of literature has emerged dealing with the impacts of government intervention in the savings and loan crisis. When state and federal governments stepped in to ameliorate the savings and loan operating condition problems in the 1970s and 1980s with deregulation, a spate of reregulation measures rapidly ensued. Romer's study of the Resolution Trust Corp. operations[10] indicates that new legislation combined with traditional Federal Deposit Insurance Corp. insolvency procedures transformed and intensified the principal agent problems of the Federal Savings and Loan Insurance Corp. This finding is amplified in important research by Brewer and Garcia[11] which examined the characteristics for the strongest and weakest savings and loans nationwide based on a set of theoretically diverse financial ratios which were contrasted at three points in the recent interest rate cycle – 1976, 1979 and 1981. They also sought evidence of inappropriate regulations which may have hurt the industry during those periods. They found that many, but not all of the same factors that determined profitability in 1976 were also relevant throughout the second half of the 1970s and early 1980s. Yet, interest rate risks were exacerbated, if not caused, by government regulations of the industry. Profitability was associated with loan and mortgage-backed securities income (positive in 1976, negative in 1981) and relatively higher advertising ratios in both periods. Unprofitable expense ratios included high expenses for borrowing and office occupancy rates in both periods. Large expenses for deposit interest were found among profitable savings and loans in 1976, but also for unprofitable ones in 1981.

---

[8] Gorton and Haubrich (1987).
[9] Romer (1987).
[10] Romer (1991).
[11] Brewer and Garcia (1987).

Deliberately slow and inefficient, the FDIC and RTC, according to Kane,[12] were themselves increasing the cost of the savings and loan bailout, at a time when the government was inadequately allocating funds to mask the size and scope of the savings and loan disaster. Kane suggests that by stalling the recognition process, politicians, FDIC officials, and the RTC Oversight Board were monitoring insolvency resolutions for loose and corrupt dealing. Brumbaugh and Litan[13] further confirm how Financial Institution Reform, Recovery and Enforcement Act legislation failed to address the fact that the negative net worth of a large and growing segment of market value insolvent banks and savings and loans could exceed the reserves of the bank insurer. Regulatory forbearance evidence through the "Too Big to Fail" issue resulted in weak banks bidding up the cost of capital for healthy institutions, thereby further weakening both.

Evidence from earlier deregulation measures shows initial positive results that were mitigated over time because of the distortive effect of deposit insurance. Kane[14] argues that the Depository Institutions Deregulation and Monetary Control Act (DIDMCA, 1980) had some effect on savings and loan profitability since the FSLIC insurance coverage – not deposit rate ceilings – buoyed the industry through inflation-induced declines in the value of savings and loan mortgage holding. A later analysis of DIDMCA[15] showed that the return risk of both money center and regional banks on a short-term basis increased while that for savings and loans decreased as measured by shareholder wealth. The return risk gained on the longer run, but was mitigated by Federal Reserve activity in pursuing interest rate targets which ultimately offset those gain by creating a more volatile interest rate environment.

In the case of the Garn-St Germain Depository Institutions Act of 1982, evidence indicates that positive and significant returns ensued because of the terms of new money market deposit accounts. Prior and after provision announcements, and consistent with legislative intent, equity investment was perceived positively. (See Table 2 for a summary of the findings of selected studies on the impact of savings and loan regulation.)

---

[12] Kane (1989).
[13] Brumbaugh and Litan (1991).
[14] Kane (1990).
[15] Aharony, Saunders and Swary (1987).

THE IMPACT OF ASSET DIVERSIFICATION

Asset diversification was a critical strategy of savings and loans in adapting to interest and asset risks. Asset diversification provisions of the Depository Institutions Act did not inhibit availability of mortgages and housing as some critics had argued. Instead, in diversifying their asset base to include corporate bonds, profitable savings and loans actually increased available funds for homes. There was no zero-sum trade-off between bond instruments and home mortgages.[16] Further evidence on diversification by Gart[17] and Fabozzi and Konishi[18] examining investment strategies, liquidity requirements, and risk control indicated that diversification into corporate securities provided improved asset/liability management strategies for savings and loans.

Previous research (Yago, 1994b) sought to review the overall performance of the portfolios of each savings and loan, taking into account the major factors that influence both profit and loss over a long period of time. A Freedom of Information Act request for routine trading information and public filings was turned down by the RTC in a way that raised questions about the care with which that agency evaluated savings and loans' financial health in carrying out its work. "We are not in the business of doing research or finding out what happened to savings and loans, we are in the business of shutting down financial institutions," an RTC official told the reseacher.[19]

Raising an equal set of concerns was the response given by Sen. Howard Metzenbaum's office when contacted for help. The office refused to get involved, added that it was naive to think the government would develop data at such a detailed level on which to base policy, and made clear what that policy was. "The role of the government," said an aide, who was also counsel to the Senate Anti-Trust Committee, "is to do nothing."[20]

---

[16] Hendershott and Villani (1984).
[17] Gart (1985).
[18] Fabozzi and Konishi (1990).
[19]Interview by Glenn Yago with Brian McTigue, July 14, 1992.
[20]Interview by Glenn Yago with Brian McTigue, July 14, 1992.

SAVINGS AND LOAN INTERNAL MANAGEMENT

A good deal of the empirical literature on savings and loans reviews internal management. These studies on internal financial management and models of savings and loan risk premiums indicate that capital ratios, asset size, geographical location and asset diversification favorably impact savings and loan profitability. Sandor and Sosin[21] developed a comprehensive model of mortgage risk premiums based on borrower property and neighborhood characteristics. Wang and Saurhaft[22] examined major financial characteristics of problem versus non-problem FSLIC-insured savings and loans to find a subset of financial ratios that would capture an examiner's perception of risk. They used estimated statistical models to predict examination ratings. Simonson and Stock[23] mapped savings and loan institution value paths with both single and multiple duration models of exposure to interest rate risk based on Federal Home Loan Board Section H schedules in the quarterly reporting of 74 savings and loans. They based economic values on term structure, savings and loan prepayment data, and prepayment assumptions. Once they determined the institution's real portfolio net worth, they measured the interest rate elasticity of savings and loans' equity values. Simonson and Stock concluded that simple duration gap modeling captured more than 50 percent of the ordinal changes in value. Kaplan[24] examined eight distinct operating strategies for 2,087 FSLIC-insured institutions as of June 30, 1988. Besides mortgage lending, savings and loan activities included mortgage banking and wholesale, consumer, multifamily and real estate oriented loans. For the majority of savings and loans, Kaplan found that single family residential mortgage lending was the primary product line for smaller (asset size) institutions. At savings and loans with sizable assets, however, diversified strategies were more common than single family mortgages. Single family lending was highly profitable. Capital ratio, asset size and diversification, plus geographical location were all found to have an impact on profitability.

Much of the attention on the savings and loan crisis relates to the issue of fraud. Though cases of fraud certainly existed, the empirical literature goes beyond the headlines to document the specific, limited extent of the problem. The studies capture the extent to which fraud was a material cause of savings

---

[21] Sandor and Sosin (1975).
[22] Wang and Saurhaft (1989).
[23] Simonson and Stock (1991).
[24] Kaplan (1988).

and loan closure, what component of cost to the federal government fraud represented, and the number of cases in which fraud actually occurred. Barth, Bartholomew and Labich[25] tested econometrically for fraud in the 205 closures of 1988. FHLBB enforcement section found that fraud was a material problem in 30 percent to 40 percent of the cases, while the study documents the problem at 10 percent of the losses. Barth and Brumbaugh[26] estimate the overall cost of fraud at $20 billion. The cost estimates and nearly all systematic studies of the savings and loan debacle suggest that the major policy issues did not involve extensive fraud, but the distorted incentives of depository insurance and regulatory requirements. There is evidence that the focus on fraud was based on political objectives, as opposed to economic purposes. As Brumbaugh and Litan (1991, p.52) conclude:

> One irony of the emphasis on fraud is that the resources allocated to combat it seem extremely small. This suggests that the official emphasis on fraud is not connected to a strong program to confront fraud but rather may be designed to divert attention away from the need to deal with the larger issues of deposit insurance and regulation.[27]

---

[25] Barth, Bartholomew and Labich (1990).
[26] Barth, Bartholomew (1992).
[27] Brumbaugh and Litan (1991, p.52).

BIBLIOGRAPHY

Acharya, Sankarshan (1996). "Charter Value, Minimum Bank Capital Requirement and Deposit Insurance Pricing in Equilibrium," *Journal of Banking and Finance,* 20: 361-375.

Acharya, Sankarshan and Jean-Francois Dreyfus (1989). "Optimal Bank Reorganization Policies and the Pricing of Federal Deposit Insurance," *Journal of Finance*, 44: 1313-1333.

Adams, Dirk S. and Rodney R. Peck (1988). "The Federal Home Loan Banks and the Home Finance System," *Business Lawyer*, 43: 833-864.

Altman, Edward I. (1977). "Predicting Performance in the Savings and Loan Association Industry," *Journal of Monetary Economics*, 3(4) pp. 443-466.

American Bankers Association (1987). *Savings and Loan Association Regulatory Reform: Action Recommendations and Historical Perspective,* FSLIC Oversight Committee Report. Washington, D.C.: American Bankers Association.

American Bankers Association (1988). *The FSLIC Crisis: Principles and Issues, a Call to Action.* Washington, D.C.: American Bankers Association.

Austin, Richard, Christina L. Cebula, and Richard J. Cebula (1996). "Savings and Loan Failure Rate Impact of the FDICIA of 1991," *Atlantic Economic Journal,* 24.

Avery, Robert B. (1991). "Risk Based Capital and Deposit Insurance Reform," *Journal of Banking and Finance*, 847-874.

Bagdikian, Ben (1990). *The Media Monopoly*. Boston: Beacon Press.

Balderston, Frederick E. (1982). "Analysis of the Viability of S&L Firms," Working Paper Series No. 82-54, Center for Real Estate and Urban Economics, University of California.

Balderston, Frederick E. (1983). "New Entry Into the S&L Industry, 1980-82 and Beyond," Working Paper Series No. 83-71, Center for Real Estate and Urban Economics, University of California.

Balderston, Frederick E. (1985a). "Deterioration Processes in Troubled Financial Institutions and Their Implications for Public Policy," Working Paper Series No. 85-104, Center for Real Estate and Urban Economics, University of California.

Balderston, Frederick E. (1985b). *Thrifts in Crisis: Structural Transformation of the Savings and Loan Industry*. New York: John Wiley & Sons, Inc.

Balderston, Frederick E. (1989). "The S&L Bailout: A Policy Review," Institute of Business and Economic Research, University of California.

Barak, G., ed. (1995). *Media, Process and the Social Construction of Crime*. New York: Garland.

Barth, James R. (1984). "Financial Crises and the Role of the Lender of Last Resort," *Economic Review*, Federal Reserve Bank of Atlanta, January: 58-67.

Barth, James R. (1990). "Post FIRREA: The Need to Reform the Federal Deposit Insurance System," Game Plans for the '90s, Federal Reserve Bank of Chicago: 333-351.

Barth, James R. (1990). Statement before the House Committee on Banking, Finance, and Urban Affairs. 101st Congress, 2nd Session, April 1990.

Barth, James R. (1991). *The Great Savings and Loan Debacle*. Washington, D.C.: AEI Press.

Barth, James R. (1994). "Financial Economics - High Rollers: Inside the Savings and Loan Debacle by Martin Lowy," *Journal of Economic Literature*, 32(144) March.

Barth, James R. and Philip F. Bartholomew (1992). "The Thrift Industry Crisis: Revealed Weaknesses in the Federal Deposit Insurance System," in Barth, James R. and R. Dan Brumbaugh, Jr., eds. *The Reform of Federal Deposit Insurance*. New York: Harper Business.

Barth, James R., Philip F. Bartholomew, and Peter J. Elmer (1989). *The Cost of Liquidating versus Selling Failed Thrift Institutions*. Research Paper No. 89-02, Office of the Chief Economist, Office of Thrift Supervision.

Barth, James R., Philip F. Bartholomew, and Michael G. Bradley (1990a). "Reforming Federal Deposit Insurance: What Can Be Learned from Private Insurance Practices?" *Consumer Finance Law Quarterly Report.*

Barth, James R., Philip F. Bartholomew, and Michael G. Bradley (1990b). "The Determinants of Thrift Institution Resolution Costs," *Journal of Finance*, 45(3) pp.731-54.

Barth, James R., Philip Bartholomew and Michael Bradley (1991). Reforming Federal Deposit Insurance: What Can be Learned from Private Insurance Practices?" *Consumer Finance Law Quarterly Report*, Spring.

Barth, James R., Philip F. Bartholomew, Michael G. Bradley, and Carol J. Labich (1989). "Moral Hazard and the Thrift Crisis: An Analysis of 1988 Resolutions," in *Banking System Risk: Charting a New Course.* Federal Reserve Bank of Chicago.

Barth, James R., Philip F. Bartholomew, and Carol Labich (1989). "Moral Hazard and the Thrift Crisis: An Analysis of 1988 Resolutions," in *Proceedings of the Conference on Bank Structure and Competition.* Federal Reserve Bank of Chicago, May.

Barth, James R., Philip F. Bartholomew, and Carol J. Labich (1990). "Moral Hazard and the Thrift Crisis: An Empirical Analysis," *Consumer Finance Law Quarterly Report*, Winter.

Barth, James R., Gregory J. Benston, and Philip R. Wiest (1990). "The Financial Institutions Reform, Recovery, and Enforcement Act of 1989: Description, Effects, and Implications," *Issues in Bank Regulation*, 13: 3-11.

Barth, James R., and Michael G. Bradley (1989). "Thrift Deregulation and Federal Deposit Insurance," *Journal of Financial Services Research*, 2: 231-59.

Barth, James R., and R. Dan Brumbaugh, Jr. (1990). "The Continuing Bungling of the Savings and Loan Crisis: The Rough Road Ahead from FIRREA to the Reform of Deposit Insurance," *Stanford Law and Policy Review*, 2:58-67.

Barth, James R., R. Dan Brumbaugh, Jr. (1992). *The Reform of Federal Deposit Insurance: Disciplining the Government and Protecting Taxpayers*, New York: Harper Business Publishers.

Barth, James R. and R. Dan Brumbaugh, Jr. (1994a) "Moral-Hazard and Agency Problems: Understanding Depository Institution Failure Costs," *Research in Financial Services*, January.

Barth, James R. and R. Dan Brumbaugh, Jr. (1994b). "Risk Based Capital: Information and Political Issues," *Global Risk Based Capital Regulations*. 1.

Barth, James R. and R. Dan Brumbaugh (1996). "The Condition and Regulation of Madison Guaranty Savings and Loan in the 1980s: A Case Study of Regulatory Failure," In Kaufman, George G., ed. *Research in Financial Services: Private and Public Policy*. Greenwich, CT.: JAI Press.

Barth, James R. and R. Dan Brumbaugh (1997). "Development and Evolution of National Financial Systems: An International Perspective," Latin American Studies Association, 1997 Meeting, Guadalajara, Mexico, April.

Barth, James R., R. Dan Brumbaugh and Robert E. Litan (1992). *The Future of American Banking*. Columbia University Seminar Series, M.E. Sharpe, Inc.

Barth, James R., R. Dan Brumbaugh, and Daniel E. Page (1992). "Pitfalls in Using Market Prices to Assess the Financial Condition of Depository Institutions," *Journal of Real Estate Finance and Economics*, June:231-259.

Barth, James R., R. Dan Brumbaugh, Jr., and Daniel Sauerhaft (1986). "Failure Costs of Government-Regulated Financial Firms: The Case of Thrift Institutions," Research Working Paper No. 132, Office of Policy and Economic Research, Federal Home Loan Bank Board.

Barth, James R., R. Dan Brumbaugh, and Daniel Sauerhaft (1996). "Failure Costs of Government-Regulated Financial Firms: The Case of Thrift Institutions," Research Working Paper No. 123, Federal Home Loan Bank Board.

Barth, James R., R. Dan Brumbaugh, Jr., Daniel Sauerhaft, and George H.K. Wang (1985a). "Insolvency and Risk-taking in the Thrift Industry: Implications for the Future," *Contemporary Policy Issues*, 3(1) pp.32.

Barth, James R., R. Dan Brumbaugh, Jr., Daniel Sauerhaft, and George H.K. Wang (1985b). "Thrift Institution Failures: Causes and Policy Issues," in *Proceedings of the Conference on Bank Structure and Competition*, Federal Reserve Bank of Chicago. May, 184-216.

Barth, James R., R. Dan Brumbaugh, Jr., Daniel Sauerhaft, and George H.K. Wang (1989). "Thrift-Institution Failures Estimating the Regulator's Closure Rule," *Research in Financial Services*, 1.

Barth, James R., R. Dan Brumbaugh, and James A. Wilcox (2000). "The Repeal of Glass-Steagall and the Advent of Broad Banking." *Journal of Economic Perspectives,* 14(2), Spring, 191-204.

Barth, James R., Gerard Caprio, Jr. and Ross Levine (2002). "Bank Regulation and Supervision: What Works Best?" National Bureau of Economic Research (NBER) Working Paper No.9323.

Barth, James R., and James L. Freund (1984). "Financial Crises' and the Role of the Lender of Last Resort" *Economic Review*, Federal Reserve Bank of Atlanta, January: 58-67.

Barth, James R., James L. Freund (1989). "The Evolving Financial Services Sector, 1970-1988," Office of Thrift Supervision. Mimeo.

Barth, James R., Thomas Hall and Glenn Yago (2000). *Systemic Banking Crises: From Cause to Cure.* Santa Monica, CA: Milken Institute.

Barth, James R., Carl D. Hudson and John S. Jahera, Jr. (1995). "Risk-Taking in the Texas S&L Industry: Charter and Ownership Effects," *Financial Review*, 30.

Barth, James R. and Robert E. Litan (1998). "Preventing Bank Crises: Lessons From Bank Failures in the United States," in Caprio, Gerard Jr., William C. Hunter, George G. Kaufman and Danny M. Leipziger, eds. *Preventing Bank Crises: Lessons from Recent Global Bank Failures.* Washington, D.C.: World Bank.

Barth, James R., Daniel E. Page, and R. Dan Brumbaugh, Jr. (1990) *What Do Stock Prices Tell Us about the Financial Conditions of Federally Insured Thrift Institutions?* Mimeo.

Barth, James R., and Martin A. Regalia (1988). "The Evolving Role of Regulation in the Savings and Loan Industry," in England, Catherine and Thomas Huertas, eds. *The Financial Services Revolution: Policy Directions for the Future.* Norwell, Mass.:Kluwer Academic Publishers.

Barth, James R. and Philip R. Wiest (1989). Consolidation and Restructuring of the U.S. Thrift Industry Under the Financial Institutions Reform, Recovery, and Enforcement Act, Office of the Thrift Supervision.

Bartholomew, Philip F. (1989a). "Foreign Deposit Insurance Systems," Special Report, Federal Home Loan Bank Board, March.

Bartholomew, Philip F. (1989b). "How Some Nations Regulate Depository Institutions," Office of Thrift Supervision Journal, 19: 20-23.

Bartholomew, Philip F. (1991). *The Cost of Forbearance During the Thrift Crisis*, Congressional Budget Office Memorandum, June.

Bartholomew, Philip F. (1993). *Resolving the Thrift Crisis.* Washington, D.C.: Congressional Budget Office.

Belton, Jr., Willie J., and Richard J. Cebula (1995). "A Brief Note on Thrift Failures: A More Rigorous Analysis of Casual Factors," *Southern Economic Journal,* 62(247).

Bennet, James. (1990). "How the Cleaver Family Destroyed Our S&Ls," *Washington Monthly*, pp. 38-46.

Benston, George J. (1983). "The Regulation of Financial Services," in Benston, George J. (ed.) *Financial Services: The Changing Institutions and Government Policy.* Englewood Cliffs, N.J.:Prentice-Hall.

Benston, George J. (1984a). "Brokered Deposits and Deposit Insurance Reform," *Issues in Bank Regulation*, Spring: 17-24.

Benston, George J. (1984b). "Financial Disclosure and Bank Failure," *Economic Review*, Federal Reserve Bank of Atlanta, March: 5-12.

Benston, George J. (1985). *An Analysis of the Causes of Savings and Loan Failures.* Salomon Brothers Center for the Study of Financial Institutions, New York: New York University.

Benston, George J. (1986). Perspectives on Safe & Sound Banking: Past, Present, and Future. Series on the Regulation of Economic Activity. MIT Press, Commissioned by the American Bankers Association.

Benston, George J. (1987). "Direct Investment and Losses to the FSLIC," Testimony before the Federal Home Loan Bank Board. February.

Benston, George J. (1989). "Direct Investment and FSLIC Losses," *Research in Financial Services: Private and Public Policy,* JAI Press.

Benston, George J., and Mike Carhill (1992a). "FSLIC Forbearance and the Thrift Debacle: Credit Markets in Transition," Proceedings of the Conference on Bank Structure and Competition, Federal Reserve Bank of Chicago, May. 121-133.

Benston, George J., and Mike Carhill (1992b). "The Thrift Disaster: Test of the Moral-Hazard, Deregulation, and Other Hypotheses," prepared for the Annual Conference on Bank Structure, Federal Reserve Bank of Chicago.

Benston, George J. and George G. Kaufman (1988a). "Regulating Bank Safety and Performance," in Haraf, W. F. and Kushmeider, R. M. eds., *Restructuring Banking and Financial Services in America.* Washington, D.C.: American Enterprise Institute. pp. 63-99.

Benston, George J. and George G. Kaufman (1988b). *Risk and Solvency Regulation of Depository Institutions: Past Policies and Current Options.* Monograph Series in Finance and Economics No. 1988-1, Salomon Brothers Center for the Study of Financial Institutions, New York: New York University.

Benston, George, and John Tepper Marlin (1974). "Bank Examiners' Evaluation of Credit: An Analysis of the Usefulness of Substandard Loan Data," *Journal of Money, Credit and Banking,* 6: 23-44.

Benston, George and John Tepper Marlin (1989). "Market Value Accounting: Benefits, Costs, and Incentives," *In Banking System Risk: Charting a New Course.* Federal Reserve Bank of Chicago.

Berger, Allen N., Anil K. Kashyap, and Joseph M. Scalise (1995). "The Transformation of the U.S. Banking Industry: What a Long, Strange Trip It's Been," *Brookings Papers on Economic Activity*, 2.

Bierman, Leonard, Donald R. Fraser, and Asghar Zardkoohi (1999). "On the Wealth Effects of the Supervisory Goodwill Controversy," *Journal of Financial Research*, 22 no. 69.

Bierwag, G.O. and George G. Kaufman (1983). "A Proposal for Federal Deposit Insurance with Risk Sensitive Premiums," *Bank Structure and Competition*, Federal Reserve Bank of Chicago, 223-242.

Bisenius, Donald J. (1989). *Dividend Payments by Thrifts,* Federal Home Loan Bank Board, Special Report. Washington, D.C.: Federal Home Loan Bank Board.

Bisignano, Joseph, William C. Hunter and George G. Kaufman (2000). *Global Financial Crises: Lessons from Recent Events*. Boston: Kluwer Academic Publishers.

Blacconiere, Walter G. (1997). "An Investigation of Independent Audit Opinions and Subsequent Independent Auditor Litigation of Publicly-Traded Failed Savings and Loans," *Journal of Accounting and Public Policy*, 16: 415-454.

Blacconiere, Walter G. and Robert M. Brown (1993). "Intra-industry Market Reactions to Failures of Publicly Held Savings and Loans," *Journal of Accounting, Auditing & Finance*, 8, pp. 369.

Black, William K. (1990). "Ending Our Forbearers' Forbearances: FIRREA and Supervisory Goodwill," *Stanford Law and Policy Review*, 2:102-16.

Black, William K. (1993a). "Examination/Supervision/Enforcement of S&Ls, 1979-1992," Staff report no 4, National Commission on Financial Institution Reform, Recovery and Enforcement.

Black, William K. (1993b). Southwest Plan and Resolution. Staff report no 3, National Commission on Financial Institution Reform, Recovery and Enforcement.

Black, William K. (1993c). Thrift Accounting Principles. Staff report no 20, National Commission on Financial Institution Reform, Recovery and Enforcement.

Blalock, Joseph B., Timothy J. Curry, and Peter J. Elmer (1991). "Resolution Costs of Thrift Failures," *FDIC Banking Review*. 4, 1: 15-25.

Bodfish, Morton (1935). "The Depression Experience of Savings and Loan Associations in the United States," Address delivered in Salzberg, Austria.

Bodfish, Morton, and A.D. Theobald (1940). *Savings and Loan Principles,* New York: Prentice-Hall.

Bogen, David and Michael Lynch (1989). "Taking Account of the Hostile Native: Plausible Deniability and the Production of Conventional History in the Iran-Contra Hearings," *Social Problems* 36(2).

Born, Waldo L., and John A. Valenta (1986) "A Synopsis of Texas Savings-and-Loan Associations' Operations," Texas Real Estate Research Center Technical Report 286-1M-519 College Station, Texas: Texas A&M University.

Borowski, David M., and Peter J. Elmer (1988). "An Expert System Approach to Financial Analysis: The Case of S&L Bankruptcy," Research Paper No. 144, Federal Home Loan Bank Board.

Bosworth, Barry P., Andrew S. Carron, and Elisabeth H. Rhyne (1987). *The Economics of Federal Credit Programs*, Washington, DC: The Brookings Institution.

Bovenzi, John F., James A. Marino, and Frank E. McFadden (1983). "Commercial Bank Failure Prediction Models," *Economic Review*, Federal Reserve Bank of Atlanta, 68:27-34.

Brewer III, Elijah (1980). "The Depository Institutions Deregulation and Monetary Control Act of 1980," *Economic Perspectives*, Federal Reserve Bank of Chicago, September/October.

Brewer III, Elijah (1985a). "A Logit Analysis of Insolvent S&L Recovery or Merger," Presented at the American Economic Association meeting.

Brewer III, Elijah (1985b). "The Impact of Deregulation on the True Cost of Savings Deposits: Evidence from Illinois and Wisconsin Savings and Loan Associations," *Federal Reserve Bank of Chicago Staff Memoranda,* 85-4.

Brewer III, Elijah (1989). "The Impact of Deposit Insurance on S&L Shareholders' Risk/Return Trade-Offs," Working Paper 89-24. Federal Reserve Bank of Chicago. December.

Brewer III, Elijah (1992). "Ex Ante Risk and Ex Post Collapse of S&Ls in the 1980s," *Economic Perspectives,* 16(2) Federal Reserve Bank of Chicago.

Brewer III, Elijah and Gillian Garcia (1987). "A Discriminant Analysis of Savings and Loan Accounting Profits, 1976-1981," *Advances in Financial Planning and Forecasting,* 2:204-244.

Brewer III, Elijah, William E. Jackson and James T. Moser (1996). "Alligators in the Swamp: The Impact of Derivatives on the Financial Performance of Depository Institutions," *Journal of Money, Credit, and Banking,* 28, no.3.

Brickley, James A., and Christopher M. James (1986). "Access to Deposit Insurance, Insolvency Rules and the Stock Returns of Financial Institutions," *Journal of Financial Economics,* 345-371.

Brinkman, Emile J., Paul M. Horvitz, and Ying-Lin Huang (1996). "Forbearance: An Empirical Analysis," *Journal of Financial Services Research,* 10.

Brown, Richard (1990). "Going Beyond Traditional Mortgages: The Portfolio Performance of Thrifts," Financial Industry Studies Working Paper No. 1-90, Federal Reserve Bank of Dallas.

Brumbaugh, R. Dan Jr. (1987). "Thrift-Institution Failures: Estimating the Regulator's Closure Rule," Working Paper No. 125, Federal Home Loan Bank Board. February.

Brumbaugh, R. Dan, Jr. (1988). *Thrifts under Siege: Restoring Order to American Banking,* Ballinger Publishing Co.

Brumbaugh, R. Dan Jr. (1989). *On the Condition of the Thrift Industry.* Testimony Before the House Committee on the Budget. January 1989.

Brumbaugh, R Dan Jr. (1993). *The Collapse of Federally Insured Depositories: The Savings and Loans as Precursor*, Garland Publishing.

Brumbaugh, Jr., R. Dan and Andrew S. Carron (1987). "Thrift Industry Crisis: Causes and Solutions," *Brookings Papers on Economic Activity.* 2: 349-388.

Brumbaugh, Jr., R. Dan, Andrew S. Carron, and Robert E. Litan (1989). "Cleaning Up the Depository Institution Mess," *Brookings Papers on Economic Activity*, 1: 243-283.

Brumbaugh, Jr., R. Dan and Eric Hemel (1983). "Federal Deposit Insurance as a Call Option: Implications for Depository Institutions and Insurer Behavior and Resulting Levels of Risk," *Federal Home Loan Bank Board Journal* 243-283.

Brumbaugh, Jr., R. Dan and Robert E. Litan (1988). "Facing up to the Crisis in American Banking," *The Brookings Review*, 7, no. 1 231:59.

Brumbaugh, R. D and Robert E. Litan (1989a). Joint testimony before the Subcommittee on Financial Institutions Supervision, Regulation and Insurance of the House Committee on Banking, Finance and Urban Affairs on the Condition of the Federal Deposit Insurance Corporation. September.

Brumbaugh, Jr., R. Dan and Robert E. Litan (1989b). "The S&L Crisis: How to Get Out and Stay Out," *Brookings Papers on Economic Activity*, 7(2).

Brumbaugh Jr. R. Dan and Robert E. Litan (1991). "Ignoring Economics in Dealing with the Savings and Loan and Commercial Banking Crisis," *Contemporary Policy Issues* 9, 1: 36-53.

Cairns, John B. (1981). "Understanding Obligations of the FSLIC," *Journal of Accountancy*, 171(59).

Calomiris, Charles W. (1989). "Deposit Insurance: Lessons from the Record," Economic Perspectives, Federal Reserve Bank of Chicago. May/June.

Calomiris, Charles W. (1992). "Getting the Incentives Right in the Current Deposit Insurance System: Successes from the Pre-FDIC Era," In Barth, James, R. and R. Dan Brumbaugh eds. *The Reform of Federal Deposit Insurance: Disciplining the Government and Protecting Taxpayer*. New York: HarperBusiness.

Calomiris, Charles W. (1997). "Designing the Post-Modern Bank Safety Net: Lessons from Developed and Developing Economies," Conference Paper, The Bankers' Roundtable Program for Reforming Federal Deposit Insurance, American Enterprise Institute, May 23.

Caprio, Gerald, William C. Hunter, George G. Kaufman (1998). *Preventing Banking Crises: Lessons from Global Banking Failures*. Washington, D.C.: The World Bank.

Caprio, Gerard and Daniela Klingebiel (1999). "Episodes of Systemic and Borderline Financial Crisis," Washington, D.C.: The World Bank, Financial sector Strategy and Policy Development.

Cargill, Thomas F., and Gillian G. Garcia (1982). *Financial Deregulation and Monetary Control: Historical Perspective and Impact of the 1980 Act*. Washington, D.C.: Brookings Institution Press.

Carron, Andrew S. (1982). *The Plight of the Thrift Institutions. Studies in the Regulation of Economic Activity Series*, Brookings Institution.

Carron, Andrew S. (1983). *The Rescue of the Thrift Industry*, Washington, D.C.: The Brookings Institution.

Cebenoyan, A. Sinan, and Elizabeth S. Cooperman (1993). "Firm Efficiency and the Regulatory Closure of S&Ls: An Empirical Investigation," *Review of Economics & Statistics*, 75(540).

Cebenoyan, Fatima, A. Sinan Cebenoyan and Elizabeth S. Cooperman (2002a) "Banking Market Structure and Financial Stability: Evidence from the Texas Real Estate Crisis in the 1980s," Working paper.

Cebenoyan, Fatima, A. Sinan Cebenoyan and Elizabeth S. Cooperman (2002b). "The Determinants of Takeovers: Recent Evidence from U.S. Thrifts," Working paper.

Cebula, Richard J. (1993). "The Impact of Federal Deposit Insurance on Savings and Loan Failures," *Southern Economic Journal*, 59, no. 620.

Cebula, Richard J. (1995). "The Impact of Federal Deposit Insurance on Savings and Loan Failures; Reply," *Southern Economic Journal*, 62(256).

Cebula, Richard J. (1997a). "The Rate of Return on Savings and Loan Assets," *Studies in Economics and Finance*, 17, pp. 3-24.

Cebula, Richard J. (1997b). *The Savings and Loan Crisis.* Dubuque, IW: Kendall/Hunt Publishing.

Cebula, Richard J. and Chao-shun Hung (1992). "Barth's Analysis of the Savings and Loan Debacle: An Empirical Test," *Southern Economic Journal*, 59, no. 305.

Chamberlain, Charlotte A., Thomas King, Mark Meador, and Larry Ozanne (1982). "Structure of the Savings and Loan Industry," Federal Home Loan Bank Board, Technical paper No. 1.

Chan, Yuk-Shee, Stuart I. Greenbaum, and Anjan Thakor (1988). "Is Fairly Priced Deposit Insurance Possible?" Working Paper No. 152, Banking Reserve Center, Kellogg Graduate School of Management, North Western University.

Chang, Roberto and Andres Velasco (1998). "The Asian Liquidity Crisis," Cambridge, MA: National Bureau of Economic Research, Working Paper No. 6796.

Christiansen, Hans (2001). "Moral Hazard and International Financial Crises in the 1990s," *Financial Market Trends*. No. 78, March, pp. 115-139.

Cohen, William S. and George J. Mitchell (1989). *Men of Zeal*. New York: Penguin.

Cole, Rebel A. (1990a). "Thrift Resolution Activity: Historical Overview and Implications," Financial Industry Studies Working paper. Federal Reserve Bank of Dallas.

Cole, Rebel A. (1990b). "Agency Conflicts and Thrift Resolution Costs," Financial Industry Studies Working paper No. 3-90, Federal Reserve Bank of Dallas.

Cole, Rebel A. (1990c). "Insolvency Versus Closures: Why the Regulatory Delay in Closing Thrifts?" Financial Industry Studies Working paper No. 2-90, Federal Reserve Bank of Dallas.

Cole, Rebel A., Robert A. Eisenbeis, and Joseph A. McKenzie (1989). "Excess Returns and Sources of Value in FSLIC-Assisted Acquisitions of Troubled Thrifts," Federal Reserve Bank of Dallas, FIS no. 1-89, Financial Industry Studies.

Cole, Rebel A., Robert A. Eisenbeis, and Joseph A. McKenzie (1994). "Asymmetric-Information and Principal-Agent Problems as Sources of Value in FSLIC-Assisted Acquisitions of Insolvent Thrifts," *Journal of Financial Services Research*, 8:5.

Cole, Rebel A., Joseph A. McKenzie, and Lawrence J. White (1990). "The Causes and Costs of Thrift Institution Failures: A Structure-Behavior-Outcomes Approach," Financial Industry Studies Working paper No. 5-90, Federal Reserve Bank of Dallas.

Cook, Douglas O. and Lewis J. Spellman (1989). "Federal Financial Guarantees and the Occasional market Pricing of Default Risk," Mimeo.

Cook, Douglas O. and Lewis J. Spellman (1990). "Market Cynicism of Government Guarantees: The Warning Days of the FSLIC," Mimeo, University of Texas.

Curry, Timothy, Lawrence Goldberg, and Sylvia Hudgins (1997). Characteristics of Failure and the Cost of Resolution in the Thrift Industry. Unpublished paper, FDIC.

Darby, Michael R. (1975). "The Financial and Tax Effects of Monetary Policy on Interest Rates," *Economic Inquiry*, 13: 266-76.

Dash, Samuel (1976). *Chief Counsel: Inside the Ervin Committee*. New York: Random House.

Davison, Lee (1997). "Chapter 2: Banking Legislation and Regulation," in *History of the Eighties—Lessons for the Future*, Washington, DC: Federal Deposit Insurance Corporation.

DeGennaro, Ramon P., and James B. Thompson (1993). "Capital Forbearance and Thrifts: An Ex Post Examination of Regulatory Gambling," in

Proceedings of the Conference on Bank Structure and Competition. Federal Reserve Bank of Chicago.

DeGennaro, Ramon P. and James B. Thompson (1996). "Capital Forbearance and Thrifts: Examining the Costs of Regulatory Gambling," *Journal of Financial Services Research*, 10:199-211.

Demirguc-Kunt, A. (1991). "Deposit-Institution Failures: A Review of the Empirical Literature," *Federal Reserve Bank of Cleveland Economic Review*, 27.

Demirgüç-Kunt, Asli and Enrica Detragiache (forthcoming). "Does Deposit Insurance Increase Banking System Stability? An Empirical Investigation," *Journal of Monetary Economics*.

Dowie, Mark (1977). "Pinto Madness," *Mother Jones* 2 (September/October).

Ely, Bert (1985). "Yes – Private Sector Depositor Protection is a Viable Alternative to Federal Deposit Insurance!" *Proceedings*, 338-353.

England, Catherine (1989). "A Market Approach to the Savings and Loan Crisis," In Carne, Edward H. ed. *An American Vision: Policies for the '90s.* Washington, D.C.: Cato Institute.

England, Catherine (1992). "Lessons from the Savings and Loan Debacle: The Case for Further Financial Deregulation," *Regulation: The Cato Review of Business and Government*, Summer: 36-43.

Fabritius, M. Manfred and William Borges (1989). *Saving the Savings and Loan: The U.S. Thrift Industry and the Texas Experience, 1950-1988.* New York: Praeger.

Federal Deposit Insurance Corporation. *Annual Report.* Washington, D.C.: Federal Deposit Insurance Corporation. Various years.

Federal Deposit Insurance Corporation. *News Release.* Washington, D.C.: Federal Deposit Insurance Corporation. Various dates.

Federal Deposit Insurance Corporation (1997) *History of the Eighties: Lessons for the Future.* Washington, D.C.: Federal Deposit Insurance Corporation.

Federal Deposit Insurance Corporation (2001). *Managing the Crisis: The FDIC and RTC Experience.* Washington, D.C.: Federal Deposit Insurance Corporation.

Fischel, Daniel R. (1995). *Payback: The Conspiracy to Destroy Michael Milken and His Financial Revolution.* Harper Business.

Fischel, Daniel R. and Alan O.Sykes (1999). "Governmental Liability for Breach of Contract," *American Law and Economics Review.* 1:313-385.

Fischel, Daniel R., Andrew M. Rosenfeld and Robert S. Stillman (1987). "The Regulation of Banks and Bank Holding Companies," *Virginia Law Review.* March. 301-338.

Fischer, Stanley (2001). "Financial Sector Crisis Management," Seminar on Policy Challenges for the Financial Sector in the Context of Globalization, Sponsored by the World Bank, IMF, and Board of Governors of the Federal Reserve System. Washington D.C., June 14.

Flynn, T. J. (1985). *Columbia Savings and Loan Rolls On.* New York: Morgan Stanley.

Freund, James L., and Seelig, Steven A. (1993). "Commercial Real-Estate Problems: A Note on Changes in Collateral Values Backing Real-Estate Loans Being Managed by the Federal Deposit Insurance Corporation," *FDIC Banking Review*, 6(1) pp. 26-30.

Friedman, Milton and Anna J. Schwartz (1971). *A Monetary History of the United States, 1867 – 1960.* Princeton: Princeton University Press.

Gans, Herbert (1980). *Deciding What's News.* New York: Vintage.

Gao, Lin (1999). "When and Why did FSLIC Resolve Insolvent Thrifts?" *Journal of Banking and Finance*, 23: 955-990.

Garcia, Gillian (1998). "The East Asian Financial Crisis," in Kaufman, George G. ed. *Bank Crises: Causes, Analysis and Prevention, Research in Financial Services: Private and Public Policy.* Stamford, CT: JAI Press.

Gardner, Cyrus J., Roger C. Kormendi and Gregg M. Breen. (1996). "Retained Interest Transactions vs. Bulk Sales: Evidence from the RTC AMDA," *Journal of Financial Engineering*, 5(2).

Garrison, Roger W., Eugene D. Short, and Gerald P. O'Driscoll, Jr. (1984). "Financial Stability and FDIC Insurance," Research Working Paper No. 8410.

General Accounting Office (1988). *High Yield Bonds: Nature of the Market and Effect on Federally Insured Institutions.* Washington, D.C.: General Accounting Office.

Gilbert, R. Alton. (1991). "Supervision of Undercapitalized Banks: Is There a Case for Change?" *Federal Reserve Bank of St. Louis Review*, 73, pp. 16-30.

Gilbert, R. Alton (1992). "The Effects of Legislating Prompt Corrective Action on the Bank Insurance Fund," *Federal Reserve Bank of St. Louis Review*, 74: 3-22.

Gioia, Dennis A. (1996), "Why I Didn't Recognize Pinto Fire Hazards: How Organizational Scripts Channel Managers' Thoughts and Actions," in M. David Ermann and Richard J. Lundman, eds. *Corporate and Governmental Deviance.* 5th ed., New York: Oxford University Press.

Goldberg, Lawrence G. and Sylvia C. Hudgins (1996). "Response of Uninsured Depositors to Impending S&L Failures: Evidence of Depositor Discipline," *Quarterly Review of Economics and Finance*, 36, no. 3.

Gorton, Gary and Anthony M. Santomero (1990). "Market Discipline and Bank Subordinated Debt," *Journal of Money, Credit and Banking*, 22: 118-128.

Greenbaum Stuart I. and C.F. Haywood (1971). "Secular Change in Financial Services Industry," *Journal of Money, Credit and Banking*, 571-589.

Greenspan, Alan (1997). Statement before the Subcommittee on Financial Institutions and Consumer Credit of the Committee on Banking and Financial Services, United States House of Representatives, March 5.

Gunther, Jeffery W. (1990). "Financial Strategies and Performance of Newly Established Texas Banks," Federal Reserve Bank of Dallas, *Financial Industry Studies*. 9-14.

Gup, Benton E., J. Thomas Lindley, James E. McNulty and James A. Verbrugge (1989). "The Performance of De Novo Thrift Institutions: Risk, Return," *Journal of Retail Banking Services*, 11.

Haraf, William S. (1988). "Bank and Thrift Regulation," *Regulation: The Cato Review of Business and Government*, 12(3).

Hazlitt, Henry (1996). *Economics in One Lesson*. San Francisco: Laissez Faire Books.

Helfer, Ricki (1997). Oral Statement before the Subcommittee on Capital Markets, Securities and Government Sponsored Enterprises, Committee on Banking and Financial Services, United States House of Representatives, March 5.

Hemel, Eric (1985). "Deregulation and Supervision Go Together," *Outlook of the Federal Home Loan Bank System*, November/December: 10-11.

Hendershott, Patrick H., and Edward J. Kane (1992). "Causes and Consequences of the 1980s Commercial Construction Boom," *Journal of Applied Corporate Finance*, 61-70.

Hendershott, Patrick H. and Kevin Villani (1980). "Savings and Loan Usage of the Authority to Invest in Corporate Bonds," Federal Home Loan Bank Board of San Francisco Annual Conference. December 8-9.

Herman, Edward S., and Noam Chomsky 1988. *Manufacturing Consent: The Political Economy of Mass Media*. New York: Pantheon Books.

Herring, Richard J. and Robert E. Litan (1995). *Financial Regulation in the Global Economy*. Washington, D.C.: The Brookings Institutions.

Hill, John W. (1993). "The Association Between S&Ls' Deviation from GAAP and Their Survival," *Journal of Accounting and Public Policy*, 12.

Hill, John W., Robert W. Ingram (1989). "Selection of GAAP or RAP in the Savings and Loan Industry," *Accounting Review*. 64: 667-79.

Hoenig, Thomas M. (1996). "Rethinking Financial Regulation," *Economic Review,* Federal Reserve Bank of Kansas City, 2nd Quarter.

Horvitz, Paul M. (1980). "A Reconsideration of the Role of Bank Examination," *Journal of Money, Credit, and Banking*, 654-659.

Horvitz, Paul M. (1989). "The FSLIC Crisis and the Southwest Plan," American Economic Review, 146-150.

Hunter, William C., and Aruna Srinivasan (1990). "Determinants of De Novo Bank Performance," *Economic Review,* Federal Reserve Bank of Atlanta, 14-25.

Hunter, William C., James A. Verbrugge and David A. Whidbee (1993). "Risk Taking and Failure in de Novo Savings & Loans in the 1980s," Working paper 93-2, Federal Reserve Bank of Atlanta.

Imperial Corporation of America (1986). *Financial Strategy Report.* San Diego: Imperial Corporation of America.

Jensen, Michael and William Meckling (1976). "Theory of the Firm: Managerial Behavior, Agency Costs, and Ownership Structure," *Journal of Financial Economics*, 3: 305-360.

Jordan, Jerry L. (1996). "The Future of Banking Supervision," *Economic Commentary, Federal Reserve Bank of Cleveland*, April 1.

Kane, Edward J. (1970). "Short-Changing the Small Saver: Federal Discrimination against the Small Saver during the Vietnam War," *Journal of Money, Credit and Banking*. 2:513-522.

Kane, Edward J. (1977). "Good Intentions and Unintended Evil: The Case Against Selective Credit Allocation," *Journal of Money, Credit, and Banking*, 55-69.

Kane, Edward J. (1980). "Reregulation, Savings and Loan Diversification, and the Flow of Housing Finance," *Federal Home Loan Bank Board of San Francisco Annual Conference.* Dec. 8-9.

Kane, Edward J. (1982). "Savings & Loans and Interest Rate Regulation: The FSLIC as an In-Place Bailout Program," *Housing Finance Review*, 219-243.

Kane, Edward J. (1985). *The Gathering Crisis in Federal Deposit Insurance.* Cambridge: MIT Press.

Kane, Edward J. (1986). "Appearance and Reality in Deposit Insurance: The Case for Reform," *Journal of Banking and Finance*, 10:175-88.

Kane, Edward J. (1987a). "Dangers of Capital Forbearance: The Case of the FSLIC and Zombie S&Ls," *Contemporary Policy Issues*, 5:77-83.

Kane, Edward J. (1987b). "No Room for Weak Links in the Chain of Deposit Insurance Reform," *Journal of Financial Services Research*, 1:77-111.

Kane, Edward J. (1989). "Changing Incentive Facing Financial-Services Regulators," *Journal of Financial Services Research.* 2:207-229.

Kane, Edward J. (1989). *The S&L Insurance Mess: How Did It Happen?* Washington, D.C.: Urban Institute Press.

Kane, Edward J. (1990a). *Defective Regulatory Incentives and Bush Initiative; Restructuring the American Financial System.* Norwell, MA:Kluwer Academic Publishers.

Kane, Edward J. (1990b). "Principal Agent Problems in S&L Salvage," *Journal of Finance*, 45(3) pp.755-764.

Kane, Edward J. (1992). "The Incentive Incompatibility of Government-Sponsored Deposit Insurance Funds," in Barth, James R. and R. Dan Brumbaugh, Jr. eds. *The Reform of Federal Deposit Insurance.* New York: HarperBusiness.

Kane, Edward J. (1993). "What Lessons Should Japan Learn from the U.S. Deposit Insurance Mess?" *Journal of the Japanese and International Economies.* 7, pp. 329-355.

Kane, Edward J. (1995). "Three Paradigms for the Role of Capitalization Requirements in Insured Financial Institutions," *Journal of Banking and Finance*, 19: 431-59.

Kane, Edward J. (2000a). "Capital Movements, Banking Insolvency, and Silent Runs in the Asian Financial Crisis," *Pacific-Basin Finance Journal.* 8:153-175.

Kane, Edward J. (2000b). "The Dialectical Role of Information and Disinformation in Regulation-Induced Banking Crises," *Pacific-Basin Finance Journal.* 8: 285-308.

Kane, Edward J. (forthcoming). "Using Deferred Compensation to Strengthen the Ethics of Financial Regulation," *Journal of Banking and Finance.*

Kane, Edward J. and Robert J. Hendershott (1994). *The Federal Deposit Insurance Fund That Didn't Put a Bite on U.S. Taxpayers.* Working Paper No. W4648, NBER.

Kane, Edward J. and Min-The Yu (1996a). "How Much Did Capital Forbearance Add to the Tab for the FSLIC Mess," *Quarterly Journal of Economics and Finance*, 36: 271-290.

Kane, Edward J., and Min-Teh Yu (1996b). The Opportunity Cost of Capital Forbearance during the Final Years of the FSLIC Mess," *Quarterly Review of Economics and Finance*, 36: 271-90.

Kaufman, George G. (1972). "A Proposal for Eliminating Interest-Rate Ceilings on Thrift Institutions," *Journal of Money, Credit and Banking,* 735-743.

Kaufman, George G. (1985). "Implications of Large Bank Problems and Insolvencies for the Banking System and Economic Policy," *Issues in Bank Regulation*, pp. 735-742.

Kaufman, George G. (1995). "The U.S. Banking Debacle of the 1980s: An Overview and Lessons," *The Financier.* May, pp. 9-26.

Kaufman, George G. (2001a). "Reforming Deposit Insurance - Once Again," *Chicago Fed Letter*, No. 171, November.

Kaufman, George G. (2001b). *The Failure of Superior Federal Bank, FSB: Implications and Lessons.* Statement before the U.S. Senate Committee on Banking, Housing, and Urban Affairs.

Kaufman, George G. (2002). "FDIC Reform: Don't Put Taxpayers Back at Risk," *Policy Analysis.* No. 432 (Cato Institute), April 16.

Kaufman, George G. and Roger C. Kormendi (eds.) (1986). *Deregulating Financial Services: Public Policy in Flux.* Cambridge, Mass.: Ballinger Publishing.

Kaufman, George G. and Randall S. Kroszner (1996). "How Should Financial Institutions and Markets Be Structured? Analysis and Options for Financial System Design," Working Paper WP-96-20, Federal Reserve Bank of Chicago, December.

Kendall, Leon T. (1962). *The Savings and Loan Business*. Englewood Cliffs.: Prentice-Hall.

Kindleberger, Charles P. (1978). *Manias, Panics, and Crashes: A History of Financial Crisis*. New York: John Wiley & Sons.

Kormendi, Rogert C., Victor L. Bernard, S. Craig Pirrong, and Edward A. Snyder (1989). *Crisis Resolution in the Thrift Industry: A Mid America Institute Report*. Boston, MA: Kluwer Academic Publishers.

Kroszner, Randall S., and Philip E. Strahan (1996). "Regulatory Incentives and the Thrift Crisis: Dividends, Mutual-to-Stock Conversions and financial Distress," *Journal of Finance*, 51:1285-1319.

Lane, Mark (1966). Rush to Judgment, A Critique of the Warren Commission's Inquiry, New York: Holt, Rinehart, Winston.

Lane, William R. (1987). "An Examination of Bank Failure Misclassifications Using the Cox Model," in *Proceedings of the Conference on Bank Structure and Competition*. Chicago:Federal Reserve Bank of Chicago.

Lane, William R., Stephen W. Looney, and James W. Wansley (1986). "An Application of the Cox Proportional Hazards Model to Bank Failure," *Journal of Banking and Finance*, 10, pp. 511-31.

Lee, Matthew T., and M. David Ermann (2002). Pinto Madness: Flaws in the Generally Accepted Landmark Narrative," in M. David Ermann and Richard J. Lundman, eds.: *Corporate and Governmental Deviance*, 6th ed., New York: Oxford University Press.

Lexecon Incorporated (1988). *Analysis of CenTrust's Operations and Financial Performance*. Chicago: Lexecon Incorporated.

Lintner, John (1948). *Mutual Savings Banks in the Savings and Mortgage Markets*. Andover, Mass.: Andover Press, Ltd.

Litan, Robert E. (1991). "The End of the Savings and Loan Industry," *Domestic Affairs.*

Ludwig, Eugene A. (1997). Oral Statement before the Subcommittee on Capital Markets, Securities and Government Sponsored Enterprises, Committee on Banking and Financial Services, United States House of Representatives, March 5.

Maas, Peter (1973). *Serpico.* New York: Harper.

Mahoney, Patrick I., and Alice P. White (1985). "The Thrift Industry in Transition," *Federal Reserve Bulletin.*

Manchester, Joyce, and Warwick J. McKibbin (1994). "The Macroeconomic Consequences of the Savings and Loan Debacle," *The Review of Economics and Statistics,* 76, p. 579.

Markus, Alan J., and Israel Shaked (1984). "The Valuation of FDIC Deposit Insurance Using Option Pricing Estimates," *Journal of Money, Credit and Banking.* 20: 446-460.

Marlow, Michael L. (1983). "A Canonical Correlation Analysis of Savings and Loan Association Performance," *Applied Economics.* 15(6), pp. 815-820.

McCord, Thomas (1980). "The Depository Institutions Deregulation and Monetary Control Act of 1980," *Issues in Bank Regulation,* 3, pp. 3-7.

Merton, Robert C. (1977). "An Analytic Derivation of the Cost of Deposit Insurance and Loan Guarantees: An Application of Modern Option Pricing Theory," *Journal of Banking and Finance,* 1, pp. 3-11.

Merton, Robert C. (1978). "On the Cost of Deposit Insurance When There are Surveillance Costs," *Journal of Business,* 51(3) pp.439-452.

Molotch, Harvey, and Marilyn Lester (1974). "News as Purposive Behavior: On the Strategic Use of Routine Events, Accidents and Scandals," *American Sociological Review,* 39(1).

Nanda, Sudhir, James E. Owers and Ronald C. Rogers (1997). "An Analysis of Resolution Trust Corporation Transactions: Auction Market Process and Pricing," *Real Estate Economics,* 25(5) pp.271-294.

Nichols, Lawrence T. (1990). "Discovering Hutton: Expression Gaming and Congressional Definitions of Deviance," in Denzin, Norman K. ed.: *Studies in Symbolic Interaction,* 11. Stamford, Conn: JAI Press.

Nichols, Lawrence T. (1991). "'Whistleblower' or 'Renegade': Definitional Contests in an Official Inquiry," *Symbolic Interaction,* 14(4).

Nichols, Lawrence T. (1997). "Social Problems as Landmark Narratives: Bank of Boston, Mass Media and 'Money Laundering,'" *Social Problems,* 44(3).

Nichols, Lawrence T. (1999). "White-Collar Cinema: Changing Representations of Upper-World Deviance in Popular Films," in Holstein, James and Gale Miller, eds.: *Perspectives on Social Problems,* 11.

Office of the Comptroller of the Currency (1979). *Uniform Financial Institutions Rating System.* Washington, D.C.: Office of the Comptroller of the Currency.

Office of Inspector General (2000). *Material Loss Review of the First National Bank of Keystone (01G—00—067).* Washington, D.C.: U.S. Department of the Treasury.

Office of Inspector General (2002a). *Issues Related to the Failure of Superior Bank, FSB, Hinsdale, Illinois* (Audit Report No. 02-005). Washington, D.C.: Federal Deposit Insurance Corporation.

Office of Inspector General (2002b). *Material Loss Review of Superior Bank, FSB (01G-02-040).* Washington, D.C.: Department of the Treasury.

O'Shea, James and Jane Roseman (1990). *The Daisy Chain: How Borrowed Billions Sank a Texas S&L.* New York: Crown.

Passmore, Wayne (1992). "The Influence of Risk-Adjusted Capital Regulations on Asset Allocation by Savings and Loans," Board of Governors of the Federal Reserve System, Finance and Economics Discussion Series 213.

Peltzman, Sam (1965). "Entry in Commercial Banking," *Journal of Law & Economics,* 8, pp.11-50.

Peltzman, Sam (1976). "Toward a More General Theory of Regulation," *Journal of Law & Economics*, 19(2) pp. 211-240.

Pilzer, Paul Z. with Robert Deitz (1989). *Other People's Money: The Inside Story of the S&L Mess*. New York: Simon and Schuster.

Pizzo, Stephen (1989). *Inside Job: The Looting of America's Savings and Loans*. New York: McGraw-Hill.

Potter, G. W., and V. E. Kappelev (1998). *Constructing Crime: Perspectives on Making News and Social Problems*. Prospect Heights, Ill: Waveland Press.

Pyle, David H. (1974). "The Losses on Savings Deposits from Interest Rate Regulation," *Bell Journal of Economics*, 14, p. 622.

Rashke, Richard, and Kate Bronfenbrenner (2000). *The Killing of Karen Silkwood*. Ithaca, NY: Cornell University Press.

Ray, Robert W. (2001). *Final Report of the Independent Counsel In Re: Madison Guaranty Savings & Loan Association*. Washington D.C.: U.S. Government Printing Office.

Rose, Peter and Donald Fraser (1988). *Financial Institutions*. New York: Basic Publications.

Rossi, Clifford V. (1994). "Implications of FIRREA for Thrift Industry Cost Structure," *Journal of Financial Services Research*, 8: 29.

Rule, Ann (1981). *The Stranger Beside Me*. New York: Signet.

Rush, Jeffrey Jr. (2002). "Testimony before the Senate Committee on Banking, Housing and Urban Affairs," Washington, D.C. February 7, 2002.

Saunders, Anthony, Elizabeth Strock, and Nicholas G. Travlos (1990). "Ownership Structure, Deregulation, and Bank Risk Taking," *Journal of Finance*, 45: 643-54.

Schudson, Michael (1993). *Watergate in American Memory*. New York: Basic Books.

Schumer, Charles E., J. Brian Graham (1989). "Deposit Insurance and Bank Regulation: The Policy Choices," *Business Lawyer*, 44:907-933.

Scott, Kenneth E. (1977). "The Dual Banking System: A Model of Competition in Regulation," *Stanford Law Review*, 30, pp. 1-49.

Scott, Kenneth E. (1989). "Deposit Insurance and Bank Regulation: The Policy Choices," *Business Lawyer*, 907-933.

Scott, Kenneth E. (1995). *Never Again: The Savings and Loan Bailout Bill*. Stanford, CA: Hoover Institution, Stanford University.

Scott, Kenneth E., and Thomas Mayer (1971). "Risk and Regulation in Banking: Some Proposals for Deposit Insurance," *Stanford Law Review*, 23, pp. 537-82.

Shadow Financial Regulatory Committee (1997). *Statement No. 137*, May 5, 1997.

Shaffer, Sherrill, and Catherine Pich (1984). "Brokered Deposits and Bank Soundness: Evidence and Regulatory Implications," Federal Reserve Bank of New York, Research Paper no 8405.

Shapiro, Alan and M. Weinstein (1987). *The Investment Practices of CenTrust Savings Bank*, Atlanta: Federal Home Loan Bank of Atlanta.

Short, Eugenie D. (1985). "FDIC Settlement Practices and the Size of Failed Banks," Economic Review, Federal Reserve Bank of Dallas.

Short, Eugenie D., and Jeffrey W. Gunther (1988). "The Texas Thrift Situation: Implications for the Texas Financial Industry," Occasional Paper, Financial Industry Studies Department, Federal Reserve Bank of Dallas.

Short, Eugenie D., and Gerald P. O'Driscoll, Jr. (1983). "Deregulation and Deposit Insurance," Economic Review, Federal Reserve Bank of Dallas.

Short, Eugenie D., and Kenneth J. Robinson (1990). "Deposit Insurance Reform in the Post-FIRREA Environment: Lessons from the Texas Deposit Market," Federal Reserve Bank of Dallas, Financial Industry Studies Working paper.

Shull, Bernard and Lawrence J. White (1998). "The Right Corporate Structure for Expanded Bank Activities," *Banking Law Journal*, 115, pp. 446-476.

Silverberg, Stanley C. (2000). *The Savings and Loan Problems in the United States.* Washington, D.C.: World Bank - Country Economics Dept.

Spellman, Lewis J. (1978). "Entry and Profitability in a Rate-Free Savings and Loan Market," *Quarterly Review of Economics and Business*, 18(2) pp. 87-95.

Spellman, Lewis J. (1982). The *Depository Firm and Industry: Theory, History, and Regulation.* New York: Academic Press.

Strunk, Norman, and Fred Case (1989). *Where Deregulation Went Wrong: A Look at the Causes behind Savings and Loan Failures in the 1980s.* Washington, D.C.: United States League of Savings Institutions.

Surrette, Ray (1992). *Media, Crime and Criminal Justice.* Pacific Grove: Brooks/Cole.

Taggart, J.H., and L.D. Jennings (1934). "The Insurance of Bank Deposits," *Journal of Political Economy*, 42, pp. 508-516.

Thomson, James B. (1987). "FSLIC Forbearances to Stockholders and the Value of Savings and Loan Shares," *Economic Review,Federal Reserve Bank of Cleveland*, 26.

Thomson, James B. (1992). "Modeling the Bank Regulator's Closure Option: A Two-Step Logit Regression Approach," *Journal of Financial Services Research*, 6, pp. 5-25.

Tuchman, Gaye (1978). *Making News: A Study in the Construction of Reality*, New York: Free Press.

U.S. Census Bureau, Historical Census of Housing Tables: Homeownership. www.census.gov/hhes/ www/ housing/census/historic/owner.html.

U.S. Census Bureau (2002). Table 5: Homeownership Rates for the United States: 1965 to 2002, Housing Vacancy Survey, First Quarter 2002. www.census.gov/hhes/www/housing/ hvs/q102tab5.htm. April 25.

U.S. General Accounting Office (1986a). "Thrift Industry: Cost to FSLIC of Delaying Action on Insolvent Savings Institutions." GAO/GGD-86-122BR.

U.S. General Accounting Office (1986b). "Thrift Industry: Forbearance for Troubled Institutions, 1982-1986." GAO/GGD-87-78BR.

U.S. General Accounting Office (1986c). "Thrift Industry Problems: Potential Demands on the FSLIC Insurance Fund." GAO/GGD-86-48BR.

U.S. General Accounting Office (1988). "The Federal Savings and Loan Insurance Corporation - Current Financial Condition and Outlook." GAO/T-AFMD-88-12.

U.S. General Accounting Office (1989). "High Yield Bonds: Issues Concerning Thrift Investments in High Yield Bonds." GAO/AFMD-89-48.

U.S. General Accounting Office (1990). "Failed Thrifts: Resolution Trust Corporation and 1988 Bank Board Resolution Actions," GAO/T-GGD-90-29.

U.S. General Accounting Office (1990). "Resolving Failed Savings and Loan Institutions: Estimated Cost of Additional Funding Needs," GAO/T-AFMD-90-32.

U.S. General Accounting Office (1992). "Bank and Thrift Criminal Fraud: Information on Justice's Investigations and Prosecutions," GAO/GGD-93-10FS.

U.S. House of Representatives (1989-1990). *Investigation of Lincoln Savings and Loan Association*, Washington, DC: Government Printing Office.

U.S. House of Representatives (1990). *Lincoln Savings and Loan Association*. Washington, DC: Government Printing Office.

U.S. League of Savings Institutions. *Savings and Loan Sourcebook. 1981-1983.* U.S. League of Savings Institutions.

U.S. League of Savings Institutions. *Savings Institutions Sourcebook. 1984-1988.* U.S. League of Savings Institutions.

Upham, Cyril B., Edwin Lamke (1934). *Closed and Distressed Banks.* Washington, D.C.: Brookings Institution.

Vartanian, Thomas P. (1983). "Regulatory Restructuring of Financial Institutions and the Rebirth of the Thrift Industry," *Legal Bulletin*, 99: 1-22.

Vaughan, Diane (1996). *The Challenger Launch Decision.* Chicago: University of Chicago Press.

Vaughan, Diane (2002). "The Challenger Space Shuttle Disaster: Conventional Wisdom and a Revisionist Account," in M. David Ermann and Richard J. Lundman, eds.: *Corporate and Governmental Deviance.* New York: Oxford University Press.

Wall, Larry D. (1993). "Too-Big-to-Fail after FDICIA," *Economic Review*, 78(1) Federal Reserve Bank of Atlanta.

Walsh, Lawrence E. (1998). *Firewall: The Iran-Contra Conspiracy and Cover-Up*, New York: Norton.

Wang, George H.K. and Daniel Sauerhaft (1989). "Examination Ratings and the Identification of Problem/Non-Problem Thrift Institutions," *Journal of Financial Services Research*, 2(4) pp. 319-342.

White, Lawrence J. (1991). *The S&L Debacle: Public Policy Lessons for Bank and Thrift Regulation.* New York: Oxford University Press.

White, Lawrence J. (1993). "A Cautionary Tale of Deregulation Gone Awry: The Savings and Loan Debacle," *Southern Economic Journal.* 59:496-514.

White, Lawrence J. (2002). "Bank Regulation in the United States: Understanding the Lessons of the 1980s and 1990s," *Japan and the World Economy.* 14, pp.137-154.

White, Lawrence J., and Edward L. Golding (1989). "Collateralized Borrowing at Thrifts Poses Risk to FSLIC," *American Banker*, February 24.

Woodward, Bob, and Bernstein, Carl (1974). *All The President's Men.* New York: Simon and Schuster.

Yago, Glenn (1991). *Junk Bonds – How High Yield Securities Restructured Corporate America*. New York: Oxford University Press.

Yago, Glenn (1992). "Scapegoat Litigation: The Economic Costs of Criminalizing Business," prepared for Policy Forum on the Crisis in Professional Liability, Manhattan Institute, Harvard Club, New York City, June 11.

Yago, Glenn (1993) "Ownership Change, Capital Access, and Economic Growth," *Critical Review*, 7(2).

Yago, Glenn (1994a). *Analysis of CenTrust's High Yield Portfolio*. Expert witness report.

Yago, Glenn (1994b). *Regulating Into Decline: FIRREA and the Unmaking of a Financial Institution*. New York: City University of New York.

Yago, Glenn and Jane Bozewicz (1998). Analysis of ICA High Yield Investment Strategy. Expert witness report

Yago, Glenn and Donald Siegel (1994). "Triggering High Yield Market Decline: Regulatory Barriers in Financial Markets," *Merrill Lynch Extra Credit*, 21.

Yago, Glenn and Susanne Trimbath (2003). *Beyond Junk Bonds: Expanding High Yield Markets*. New York: Oxford University Press.

Table 1: Determinants of Savings and Loan Profitability

	FHLB Bonds	Branching	Mergers	Entry	Mutual to Stock Conversions	Market Structure
Van Horne (1973)	Correlation between FHLB bonds and savings deposits as substitutes is not observed					Determined exogenously
Lapp (1976)		Branching has a positive effect on advertising				
Bradford (1978)			No synergy from mergers			
Kalish and McKenzie (1978)				Negative correlation between number of firms and profitability		
Kowalewski (1978)					Could not be proved that mutual ownership was superior to stock ownership	
Spellman (1978)				Increased entry decreases profitability		

Table 1: Determinants of Savings and Loan Profitability (Continued)

	FHLB Bonds	Branching	Mergers	Entry	Mutual to Stock Conversions	Market Structure
Davis and Verbrugge (1980)						High concentration leads to high loan rates and low deposit rates
Neely and Rochester (1982)			Synergy could not be proved			
Marlow (1983)				Has significant impact on performance		

Source: City University of New York, Center for Capital Studies.

Table 2: Impact of Regulation on Savings and Loans

	Variable interest rate regulation	Deposit rate regulation	DIDMCA	Glass - Steagall	Prohibition of Interstate Banking	Garn-St Germain	FIRREA	RTC
Daly (1972)	Policies are short sighted							
Spellman (1978)		Leads to misallocation of resources						
Kane (1980)			Should enhance profitability					
Brumbaugh and Carron (1987)			Positive					
Gorton and Haubrich (1987)				Act is binding	Limits diversification			
Romer (1987)				Unclear	Negative			

Table 2: Impact of Regulation on Savings and Loans (Continued)

	Variable interest rate regulation	Deposit rate regulation	DIDMCA	Glass - Steagall	Prohibition of Interstate Banking	Garn - St Germain	FIRREA	RTC
Aharony, Sanders and Swary (1988)			Positive					
Fraser and Kolari (1990)						Introduction increased common stock values		
Kane (1990)							Negative	
Brumbaugh and Litan (1991)							Negative	Negative

INDEX